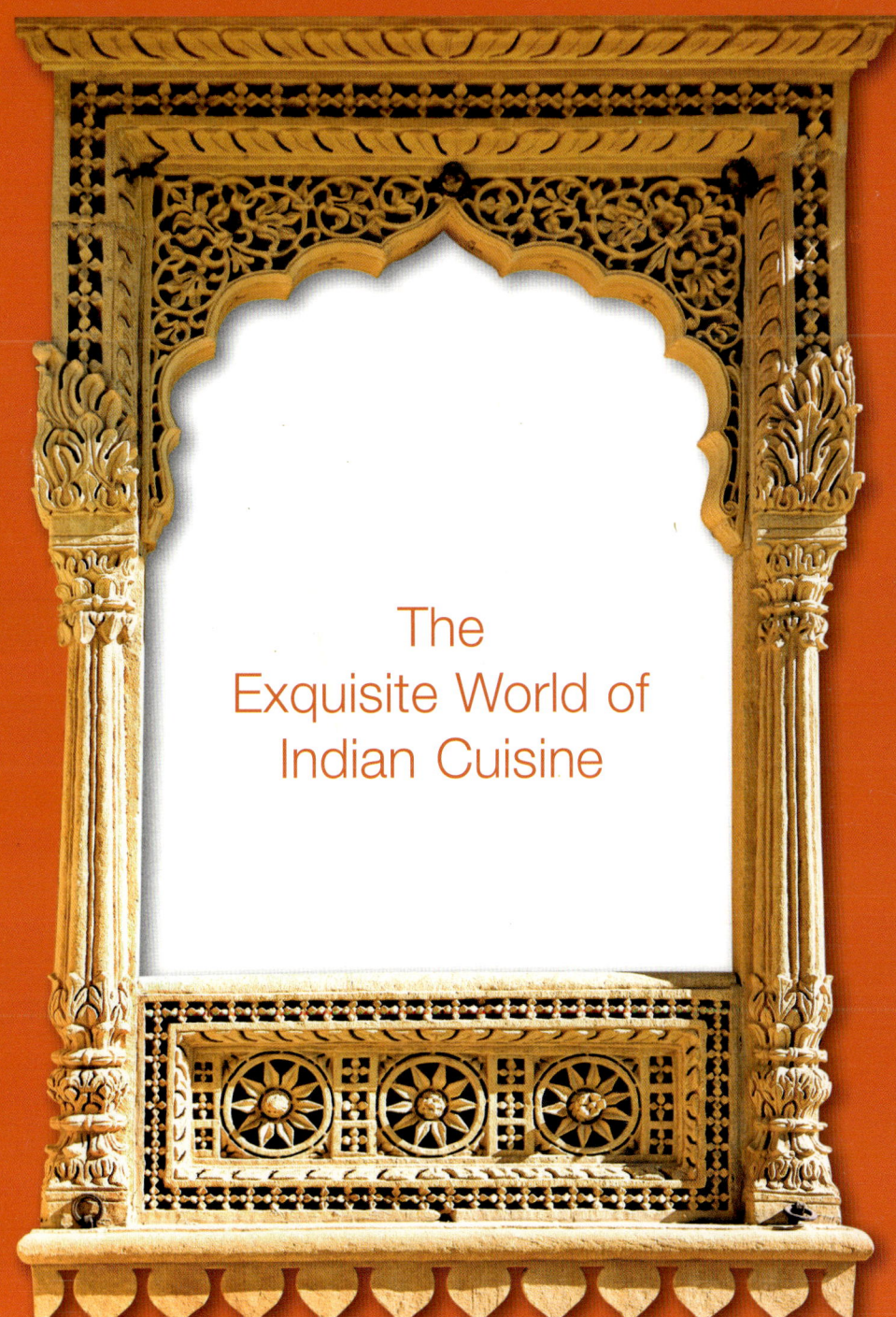

The
Exquisite World of
Indian Cuisine

the exquisite world of
indian cuisine

Uma Aggarwal

ALLIED PUBLISHERS PRIVATE LIMITED
NEW DELHI MUMBAI KOLKATA CHENNAI NAGPUR AHMEDABAD BANGALORE HYDERABAD LUCKNOW

The Exquisite World of Indian Cuisine
English
First published September 2009

ISBN: 978-81-8424-474-8

©Uma Aggarwal 2010

No part of the material protected by this Copyright notice may be reproduced or utilized in any form or by any means, electronic or mechanical including photocopying, recording or by any information storage and retrieval system, without prior written permission from the copyright owners.

Allied Publishers Private Limited
Regd. Off. : 15 J.N. Heredia Marg, Ballard Estate, Mumbai–400001
Ph: 022-22626476 E-mail: mumbai.books@alliedpublishers.com

12 Prem Nagar, Ashok Marg, Opp. Indira Bhawan, Lucknow–226001
Ph: 0522-2614253 E-mail: appltdlko@sify.com

Prarthna Flats (2nd Floor), Navrangpura, Ahmedabad–380009
Ph: 079-26465916 E-mail: ahmbd.books@alliedpublishers.com

3-2-844/6 & 7 Kachiguda Station Road, Hyderabad–500027
Ph: 040-24619079 E-mail: hyd.books@alliedpublishers.com

5th Main Road, Gandhinagar, Bangalore–560009
Ph: 080-22262081 E-mail: bngl.books@alliedpublishers.com

1/13-14 Asaf Ali Road, New Delhi–110002
Ph: 011-23239001 E-mail: delhi.books@alliedpublishers.com

17 Chittaranjan Avenue, Kolkata–700072,
Ph: 033-22129618 E-mail: cal.books@alliedpublishers.com

81 Hill Road, Ramnagar, Nagpur–440033
Ph: 0712-2521122 E-mail: ngp.books@alliedpublishers.com

751 Anna Salai, Chennai–600002
Ph.: 044-28523938 E-mail: chennai.books@alliedpublishers.com

Website: www.alliedpublishers.com

Cover design: Ishtihaar
Cover picture: Dr. Surinder Aggarwal

Pictures ©
- All dishes and uncredited pictures: Dr. Surinder Aggarwal
- Other pictures: respective credits given

Designed and printed by
ISHTIHAAR
New Delhi, India
91-11-2373-3100
info@ishtihaar.com

Published by Sunil Sachdev and printed by Ravi Sachdev at Allied Publishers Private Limited (Printing Division), A-104, Mayapuri Phase II, New Delhi 110 064, India.

To my beloved mother
late Mrs. Shakuntala Agarwal
whose love for good food
and
her belief in its health benefits
kept inspiring me to write this book

ACKNOWLEDGEMENTS

I would like to thank Mr. Rajinder Arora and his entire team at Ishtihaar, New Delhi for designing this book and the editor Mr. Surojit Banerjee who constantly and patiently worked on the manuscript as it grew from its small beginnings to its present scope and size.

My mother has always believed in serving and preparing delicious food, no matter how long it might take, and I thank her for all the inspiration that she has given me over time.

My husband Dr. Surinder K. Aggarwal has not only provided the photographs of most of my recipes, but as one who has published extensively as a research scientist in international journals, provided me with very valuable editorial suggestions. He has a great taste for good food and thus motivated me to cook better.

My brothers, my sister and my daughters Dr. Aanshu and her husband Dr. Tapan Shah and Dr. Tushina and her husband Dr. Ravi Reddy constantly encouraged me with their admiration for my cooking. My son Arun and his wife Ruthe were a major source of inspiration and assistance as I struggled to put this book into shape.

My special thanks to my Las Vegas friends who always admired my cooking and supported me in my quest to write this book. I would be failing in my duty if I did not extend my special appreciation to our dearest friends Mr & Mrs Surrinder Nath for their helpful comments and suggestions during the proof reading of this book.

PREFACE

I have lived in the United States of America for more than 40 years. I grew up in a very traditional household in the company of my parents and grandparents with strong family values. The kitchen was a center of most activity and from my elders I gradually imbibed much knowledge about Indian cuisine and the importance of herbs and spices used in it. I also learned from them that a dish was made perfect not only by following the recipe but by the care and love that went into its preparation. The last minute touch of seasoning and the way we present and serve the food also plays a substantial role in cooking. Since there is a great emphasis on the freshness of the raw material used in Indian cuisine, we also learnt how to modify our cuisines from time to time depending upon the availability of local produce in a country with changing seasons. My knowledge of regional cooking is based on the experience I gained by socializing with friends in the U.S. and it may differ in some respects from traditional regional recipes of India. I realize that in spite of regional variations, Indians by and large, share a basic philosophy which clearly emphasises the healthful benefits of ingredients used in Indian cooking. I have tried to capture the essence of this philosophy in my book. During my stay in America I belonged to a Faculty Folk international gourmet club of Michigan State University and also did extensive western cooking. I also won some cooking contests held at the pharmaceutical company I worked for. However, Indian cuisine – its aroma, its history, its Vedic origin and the use of spices – always fascinated me. My belief in India's great history and its culture sustained me during my stay in America and I have always believed that India's glorious past, its spiritual achievements and its magnificent cuisine have to be shared with the rest of the world.

Uma Aggarwal

Rangoli, *a popular art form for decoration of floors and walls that uses finely ground white powder and colours, and is usually done outside homes in India.*

Nataraj, The Lord of Dance, is a depiction of the Hindu god Shiva as the cosmic dancer

contents
the exquisite world of indian cuisine

CHAPTER 1
Exotic Indian Cuisine
17 – 51

Introduction	18	Recipe for making the Curry Masala	38
History and origin of Indian cuisine	20	Ingredients giving color to the curries	38
The 'Open' markets of India	24	Thickening agents used in Indian curries	39
Spices that are used in Indian cooking – their origin and health benefits	26	Souring agents for the curries and other stir-fries	42
The significance of spices	31	Special spice mixes	43
Fresh herbs and seasonings	32	Special flours, lentils, cereals and other ingredients used in Indian cooking	46
Cooking made easy	35	Dal / Legumes used in Indian cooking	48
Clarified butter / ghee	36		
Special ingredients to highlight the flavor and aroma of curries	37	Utensils and appliances needed in an Indian kitchen	50

CHAPTER 2
Appetizers and Snacks
52 – 107

Grilled Chicken	55	Tapioca Potato Puffs	83	Crunchy Rice Puffs with Salad	97
Ground Meat Kebabs	56	Yams in Peanut Sauce	84	Yogurt dipped Lentil Fritters	98
Meat Cutlets	57	Stuffed Mushrooms	85	Crunchy Lentils Wafers	99
Salmon Cutlets	58	Cream of Wheat with Vegetables	88	Rolled and Stuffed Wafers	100
Indian Cheese Cutlets	59	Spiced Rice Flakes	89	Rice Noodles Stir-Fried	101
Potato Cutlets	60	Rice Flake Cutlets	90	Lemon Rice Noodles	102
Lotus Root Cutlets	62	Steamed Lentil Cake	91	Spicy Fruit Salad	103
Stuffed Potatoes or Meat Pastries	63	Steamed Cream of Wheat Cakes	92	Spiced Sweet Potatoes	104
Meatballs in Tamarind Sauce	64	Steamed Lentil Rolls	93	Fruity Yogurt Poha	105
Cocktail Cashew Nuts	65	Tortilla chips with Tamarind Sauce	95	Tapioca Stir-Fried	106
Fried Cheese Cubes	68	Flour Puffs with Tamarind Water	96	Spicy Saltine Sticks	107
Cocktail Shrimp	69				
Vegetable Fritters	70				
Spinach Fritters	71				
Plantain Fritters	73				
Green Pepper Fritters	74				
Mushroom Fritters	76				
Baked Spinach and Fenugreek Fritters	77				
Lentil Patties	78				
Lentil Fritters	79				
Potato Croquettes	80				
Cheese Puffs	81				
Corn Fritters	82				

CHAPTER 3

Chicken

108 – 131

Chicken cooked with Lentils and Vegetables	111
Chicken Curry	112
Chicken in Coconut Gravy	113
Goan Chicken Curry	114
Chicken in Creamy Sauce	115
Chicken Stew	116
Clay Oven Grilled Chicken	118
Grilled Chicken in Gravy	119
Chicken with Cashew Nuts	120
Onion Chicken	121
Cardamom Chicken Curry	124
Butter Chicken	125
Chicken in Fenugreek Sauce	126
Chicken Pickle Style	127
Fried Chicken	128
Twice Cooked Chicken	129
Hot Chicken Curry with Almonds	130
Madras Chicken Curry	131

CHAPTER 4

Sea Food and Fish

132 – 155

Fish baked in Coconut Sauce	135
Fish Curry	136
Fish Curry with Vegetables	137
Fish in Fenugreek Sauce	138
Fish Curry with Yogurt	139
Fish Curry with Nuts	140
Fried Fish	141
Clay Oven Grilled Fish	142
Madras Fish Curry	143
Fish in Tamarind Sauce	144
Fish in Mustard Sauce	145
Lobster Delight	146
Shrimp Curry	147
Shrimp Stir-Fried	148
Fried Shrimp	149
Scallops & Squid Curry	152
Crab Stir-Fried	153
Crab Croquettes Curry	154
Shrimp in Mango Sauce	155

CHAPTER 5

Exotic Vegetables

156 – 233

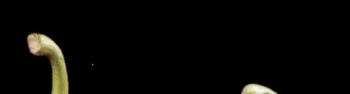

Stuffed Mushrooms in Pomegranate Sauce	159
Eggplant Stir-Fried	160
Roasted Eggplant Curried	161
Egg Curry	162
Scrambled Eggs with Vegetables /Italian Frittata	163
Eggplant in Tamarind Sauce	164
Eggplant in Sweet & Sour Sauce	165
Mixed Vegetable Curry	166
Potatoes and Onions Stir-Fried	167
Bottle Gourd Croquettes Curry	168
Potato Curry	170
Mustard Greens Curried	171
Okra Stir-Fried	174
Flavored Zucchini	175
Tofu Curry	176
Turnip Stir-Fried	177
Cheese and Mushroom Curry	178
Peas & Cheese Curry	179
Baked Cauliflower	180
Fried Potato Curry	181
Fenugreek Leaves and Potatoes	182
Kerala Vegetable Curry	183
Paneer & Potatoes in Coconut Sauce	184
Spinach with Fried Cheese	185
Creamy Cheese Croquettes in Curry Sauce	186
Cabbage and Peas Stir-Fried	188
Eggplant, Potatoes and Tomatoes Stir-Fried	189
Mixed Vegetable Curry Baked	190
Bread Croquettes in Curry	191
Mixed Vegetable Croquettes Curry	192
Beans with Coconut	194
Bitter Gourd Stir-Fried	195
Bitter Gourd Stuffed	196
Carrots and Potatoes Stir-Fried	197
Whole Stuffed Okra	198
Okra and Peanuts	199
Bell Pepper, Potatoes and Tomatoes Stir-Fried	200
Stuffed Bell Peppers	201
Stuffed Whole Tomatoes	202
Stuffed Eggplants	203
Yam Curry	206
Dry Yam Curry	207
Plantain Curry	208
Beans and Potatoes Stir-Fried	209
Cauliflower and Potatoes Stir-Fried	210
Cauliflower with Figs	211
Pumpkin Stir-Fried	212
Assam Vegetable Curry	213
Sinhalese Vegetable Curry	214
Sweet Potato and Spinach Curry	215
Sweet Corn and Beans	216
Carrots and Peas Stir-Fried	217
Round Gourd Stuffed	218
Pointed Gourd Curry	219
Soyabean and Carrots Curry	220
Corn Curry with Spinach	221
Baby Vegetables Curry	222
Spinach and Potatoes Stir-Fried	224
Bean Sprouts Stir-Fried	225
Lotus Root and Mushroom Curry	226
Asparagus Stir-Fried	227
Beetroot Curry	230
Okra Curry	231
Mushrooms in Spinach Sauce	232
Jackfruit Stir-Fried	233

CHAPTER 6
Legumes

234 – 259

Chick–peas Curry	237	Dal Vadodara	250
Chick–peas in Tamarind Sauce	238	Oriya Dal	251
Andhra Dal	240	Gram Dal	252
Lentils and Vegetables in Tamarind Sauce	241	Matar Dal with Meat	253
		Spinach Dal	254
Whole Black Beans with Cream	242	Curried Kidney Beans	255
Black Split Beans Curried	243	Gram Flour Curry	256
Legume Stir–Fried	246	Whole Mung Dal	258
Royal Mix Legume	248	Dal with Coconut Milk	259

CHAPTER 7
Rice and Pulav

260 – 279

Plain Cumin Rice	263
Peas and Cheese Pulav	264
Royal Pulav	265
Peas Pulav	266
Mushroom Pulav	267
Multicolored Pulav	268
Biryani	270
Cauliflower Pulav	272
Yogurt Rice	273
Coconut Rice	274
Tamarind Rice	275
Lemon Rice	276
Vegetable Masala Rice	277
Shrimp Masala Rice	278
Rice & Lentils with Vegetables	279

CHAPTER 8
Breads

280 – 319

Griddle Flat Bread	283	Griddle Fried Rice Flour & Coconut Crepes	302
Milk Kneaded Griddle Bread	284	Cream of Wheat Crepes	303
Clay Oven Bread	285	Ground Rice Crepes	304
Mint Bread	286	Griddle Fried Cheese and Legume Stuffed Bread	306
Onion Bread	287		
Unfermented Deep–Fried Bread	288	Steamed Ground–Rice Cakes	307
Fermented Deep–Fried Bread	289	Rice and Lentils Crepes	308
Whole Wheat Fried Puffs	290	Crisp Fried Pastries	309
Griddle Fried Bread	292	Crisp Potato Pastries	311
Grilled Fried and Stuffed Onion Bread	293	Griddle Millet Flour Bread	312
Griddle Fried Stuffed Potato Bread	294	Griddle Sorghum Flour Bread	313
Griddle Fried Fenugreek Bread	296	Griddle Gram Flour Bread	316
Griddle Fried Daikon Stuffed Bread	298	Persian Bread	317
Griddle Fried Stuffed Cauliflower Bread	299	Griddle Fried Corn Flour Bread	318
Griddle Fried Tricolor Bread	300	Griddle Fried Gram Flour Pancakes	319
Griddle Fried Stuffed Meat Bread	301		

320 – 343

CHAPTER 9
Lamb, Beef and Pork

Beef Curry with Nuts	323
Lamb or Beef with Turnips	324
Bombay Lamb Curry	325
Ground Meat Curried	326
Kashmiri Beef Curry	327
Goa Beef Stir-Fried	330
Kerala Beef Curry	331
Lamb Cooked with Spinach	332
Mughlai Lamb Curry	333
Lamb Tikka Masala	334
Lamb Curry	335
Marinated Leg of Lamb	336
Meat Croquettes Curry	337
Pork Curry	338
Mediterranean Pork & Peas	339
Pork Stir-Fried	340
Pork Curry in Vinegar Sauce	342
Pork with Potatoes & Peppers	343

344 – 383

CHAPTER 10
Desserts

Cream of Wheat Pudding	347
Rice Pudding	348
Dried Carrot Pudding or Fudge	350
Golden Cream Cheese Balls in Syrup	351
Cheese Balls in Sweet Syrup	352
Sweet Cheese Patties in Cream	353
Sweet Cheese Cakes	354
Sweet Cheese Balls	355
Sweet pieces of Cheese	356
Gram Flour Sweet Balls/Lentil Balls	357
Sweet Balls of Cream of Wheat	358
Sugar Coated Doughnuts	360
Cookies without Eggs	361
Apple or Zucchini Pudding	362
Sweet Vermicelli Pudding	363
Ground Rice Pudding	364
Sweet Rice	365
Mango Pie	366
Mango Mousse	367
Fried Spiral Sweet Rings	368
Crunchy Lentil Sweet Rings	369
Cashew Fudge	370
Milk Fudge	371
Pistachio Fudge	372
Almond Fudge	373
Coconut Fudge	376
Cheese Fudge	378
Indian Ice Cream	379
Crisp Stuffed Pastry	381
Gram Flour Fudge	382
Sweet Pancakes	383

CHAPTER 11
Condiments, Pickles and Dips

384 – 421

Bananas & Raisins Condiment	387
Mint Condiment	388
Spinach Condiment	389
Cucumber Condiment	390
Gram Flour Balls Condiment	391
Fresh Vegetable Condiment	392
Baked Eggplant Condiment	393
Mango Condiment	394
Mint Dip	395
Coconut Dip	396
Tomato Dip	398
Tamarind Dip	399
Eggplant Dip	401
Coriander Dip	402
Apple Dip	403
Cranberry Dip	404
Ripe Mango Dip	405
Red Pepper Dip	406
Zucchini Dip	407
Peanut Dip	408
Pineapple Dip	409
Gram Legume Dip	410
Sweet Mango Dip	411
Onion & Coconut Dip with Fish Flavor	412
Carrots Pickle	413
Radish Pickle	414
Sweet & Sour Lemon Pickle	415
Green Chilies, Onions and Ginger in Vinegar	415
Green Chilies Pickle	416
Papaya and Mango Pickle	417
Lemon Pickle	418
Mango Pickle	419
Avakai Mango Pickle	420
Classic Sweet & Sour Pickle	421

CHAPTER 12
Salads

422 – 433

Mixed Vegetable Salad	425
Cooked Beans Salad	426
Mango Salad	427
Radish Salad	430
Kosambri Salad	431
Onion, Beetroot and Tomato Salad	432
Green Mango Salsa	433

CHAPTER 13
Soups

434 – 451

Tomato Soup	437
Mixed Vegetable Soup	438
Cauliflower Soup	439
Chicken Vegetable Soup	440
Mulligatawny Soup	441
Mung Beans Soup	442
Indian Hot and Sour Soup	443
Bottle Gourd Soup	446
Potato Soup	447
Spinach Soup	448
Cream of Pumpkin Soup	449
Cream of Corn Soup	450
Coconut Milk Soup	451

CHAPTER 14
Drinks

452 – 465

Yogurt Shake	455
South Indian Coffee	456
Cumin flavored Drink	458
Fermented Carrot Drink	459
Kokum Water	459
Lemonade	460
Mango Drink	462
Spiced Tea	463
Kashmiri Tea	463
Milk & Almond Drink	465
Paan and Mouth Fresheners	466

Annexure

Map of India	469
Suggested Menus	472
Measurement Equivalent	474
Glossary of English and Hindi names for cooking raw material	475
Alphabetical Index of Recipes	478

Index of dishes by their popular Indian names

	Page No.
APPETIZERS & SNACKS	
Chicken Tikka	55
Seekh Kebab	56
Shaami Kebab (Shikampuri Kebab)	57
Machhli ke Kebab	58
Paneer Cutlets	59
Aalu ki Tikki	60
Kamal Kakdi ki Tikki	62
Samosa	63
Meat Balls in Tamarind Sauce	64
Namkeen Kaju	65
Cocktail Paneer	68
Cocktail Shrimp	69
Pakora	70
Palak Pakora	71
Kela Pakora	73
Shimla Mirch Pakora	74
Khumb Pakora	76
Muthia	77
Urad Dal Vada	78
Channa Dal Vada	79
Bonda	80
Paneer Vada	81
Makki ke Vade	82
Sabudana Vada	83
Arbi Tikka Masala	84
Bharvan Khumb	85
Uppama	88
Poha / Aval	89
Poha Patties	90
Dhokla	91
Khaman Dhokla	92
Khandvi	93
Papri	95
Golgappa	96
Bhelpoori	97
Dahi Vada and Pakori	98
Papadum	99
Papad Rolls	100
Rice Noodles Stir–Fried	101
lemony Rice Noodles	102

Fruit Chaat	103
Shakarkandi ki Chaat	104
Payesh / Poha Kheer	105
Sabudana ki Khichdi	106
Mathri / Nimki	107

CHICKEN

Dhansak	111
Murg Curry	112
Murg Nariyal Masala	113
Murg Vindaloo	114
Murg Korma	115
Kolhapuri Murg	116
Murg Tikka	118
Murg Tikka Masala	119
Bombay Murg Korma	120
Murg Do Pyazaa	121
Kukul Mas Curry	124
Murg Makhani	125
Methi Murg	126
Achaari Murg	127
Tala hua Murg	128
Bhune hue Murg ki Curry	129
Bangladeshi Murg Curry	130
Murg Chettinad	131

SEA FOOD & FISH

Bhuni hui Machhli	135
Fish Curry	136
Fish Curry with Vegetables	137
Methi Machhi	138
Doi Machh	139
Fish Korma	140
Tali hui Machhli	141
Tandoori Machhli	142
Madras Fish Curry	143
Fish in Tamarind Sauce	144
Fish in Mustard Sauce	145
Lobster Delight	146
Jhinga Curry	147
Shrimp Stir-Fried	148
Fried Shrimp	149
Scallops & Squid Curry	152
Crab Stir-Fried	153
Kekra Curry	154
Shrimp in Mango Sauce	155

EXOTIC VEGETABLES

Kandhari Khumb Curry	159
Baingan Dum	160
Bharta	161
Anda Curry	162
Anda Bhurjee	163
Bhagara Baingan	164
Khatte-Mithe Baingan	165
Navratan Korma	166
Aalu Pyaz ki Sabzi	167
Ghia Kofta Curry	168
Aalu ki Sabzi	170
Sarson ka Saag	171
Bhuni hui Bhindi	174
Tori ki Sabzi	175
Soya Meat Curry	176
Shalgam ki Sabzi	177
Cheese & Mushroom Curry	178
Matar Paneer	179
Bhuni Gobhi	180
Dum Aalu	181
Methi Aalu	182
Aviyal	183
Paneer-Aalu Nariyalwale	184
Palak Paneer	185
Malai Kofta	186
Patta Gobhi aur Matar ki Sabzi	188
Baingan, Aalu aur Tamatar ki Sabzi	189
Gujarati Undiya	190
Bread Kofta	191
Kofta ki Curry	192
Nariyalwali Sem ki Phali	194
Karele ki Sabzi	195
Bharwan Karela	196
Gaajar-Aalu ki Sabzi	197
Bharwan Bhindi	198
Bhindi aur Moongphali ki Sabzi	199
Shimla Mirch, Aalu aur Tamatar ki Sabzi	200
Bharwan Shimla Mirch	201
Bharwan Tamatar	202
Bharwan Baingan	203
Raswali Arbi	206
Dum Arbi	207
Kele ki Sabzi	208
Beans Aalu	209
Aalu Gobhi	210
Phool Gobhi aur Anjeer ki Sabzi	211
Kaddu ki Sabzi/Dry Petha Curry	212
Assam Vegetable Curry	213
Sinhalese Vegetable Curry	214
Shakarkandi Curry	215
Sweet Corn and Beans	216
Carrots & Peas Stir-Fried	217
Bharwan Tindey	218
Parwal aur Aalu ki Sabzi	219
Soyabean aur Gaajar ki Sabzi	220
Makki aur Palak ki Sabzi	221
Baby Vegetables Curry	222
Aalu Palak ki Sabzi	224
Ankur Dal ki Sabzi	225
Kamal Kakadi aur Khumb ki Sabzi	226
Shatwar ki Sabzi	227
Chukandar ki Sabzi	230
Bhindi ki Sabzi	231
Palak aur Khumb Curry	232
Kathael ki Sabzi	233

LEGUMES

Kabuli Channa	237
Khattey Kabuli Channe	238
Palakura Pappu	240
Sambhar	241
Dal Makhni	242
Urad aur Channe ki Dal	243
Dal Sookhi	246
Dal Baati/Dal Panchratan	248
Gujarati Dal/Dal Dhokli	250
Dalma	251
Dal Channa	252
Matar Dal with Meat	253
Dal Palak	254
Rajmah	255
Besan ki Karhi	256
Mung Sabut	258
Dal with Coconut Milk	259

RICE & PULAV

Zeera Chawal	263
Matar–Paneer Pulav	264
Shahi Pulav	265
Matar Pulav	266
Khumb Pulav	267
Navratan Pulav	268
Biryani	270
Gobhi Pulav	272
Dahi Chawal	273
Nariyal Chawal	274
Imli Chawal	275
Nimbu Chawal	276
Masala Chawal (Vaangi Bhaat)	277
Konkani Rice	278
Khichdi/Bisi Bele Bhaat	279

BREADS

Chappati	283
Rogini Roti	284
Tandoori Nan	285
Pudina Nan	286

Tandoori Onion Nan	287
Luchhi	288
Bhatura	289
Poori	290
Plain Parantha	292
Lachhedar Parantha	293
Aalu ke Paranthe	294
Methi ke Paranthe	296
Muli ke Paranthe	298
Gobhi ke Paranthe	299
Tiranga Parantha	300
Shaphale (Meat Parantha)	301
Appam	302
Rava Dosa	303
Plain Dosa	304
Paneer aur Dal ke Paranthe	306
Idli	307
Aadai	308
Khasta Kachauri	309
Aalu ki Kachauri	311
Thepla	312
Jowar ki Roti	313
Missi Roti	316
Taftan	317
Makki ki Roti	318
Besan ke Pudey (Cheela)	319

LAMB, BEEF & PORK

Beef Korma	323
Shabdeg	324
Bombay Lamb Curry	325
Keema	326
Kashmiri Beef Curry	327
Goa Beef Stir-Fried	330
Kerala Beef Curry	331
Saag Gosht	332
Roghan Josh	333
Kebab Curry	334
Gosht Curry	335
Raan	336
Shahi Kofta Curry	337
Pork Curry	338
Mediterranean Pork & Peas	339
Pork Stir-Fried	340
Pork Vindaloo	342
Pork with Potatoes & Peppers	343

DESSERTS

Suji Halwa	347
Kheer	348
Gaajar Halwa or Burfi	350
Gulabjaman	351
Rasgulla	352
Rasmalai	353
Chumchum	354
Kamal Bhog	355
Sandesh	356
Besan Laddoo / Dal Pinni	357
Rava Laddoo / Modak	358
Balushahi	360
Khatai	361
Seb Kheer / Ghia Kheer	362
Sevian Kheer	363
Phirni	364
Meethey Chawal	365
Mango Pie	366
Aam ki Phirni	367
Jalebi	368
Imerti	369
Kaju Burfi	370
Burfi	371
Pista Burfi	372
Badam Burfi	373
Nariyal Burfi	376
Kalakand	378
Kulfi Faluda	379
Gujjia	381
Besan ki Burfi / Mohan Thaal	382
Maalpua	383

CONDIMENTS, PICKLES & DIPS

Kele aur Kishmish ka Raita	387
Pudina Raita	388
Palak Raita	389
Kheere ka Raita	390
Boondi Raita	391
Vegetable Raita	392
Baingan ka Raita	393
Aam ka Raita	394
Pudina Chutney	395
Nariyal Chutney	396
Tamatar ki Chutney	398
Imli ki Chutney	399
Baingan ki Chutney	401
Dhaniye ki Chutney	402
Seb ki Chutney	403
Karonde ki Chutney	404
Aam ki Chutney	405
Lal Mirch ki Chutney	406
Tori ki Chutney	407
Mungphali ki Chutney	408
Ananaas ki Chutney	409
Channa Dal Chutney	410
Aam ki Meethi Chutney	411
Seeni Sambol	412
Gaajar ka Achaar	413
Mooli ka Achaar	414
Khatta-Meetha Nimbu ka Achaar	415
Sirkey-wali Hari Mirch, Pyaz aur Adrak	415
Hari Mirch ka Achaar	416
Papeetey aur Aam ka Achaar	417
Nimbu ka Achaar	418
Aam ka Achaar	419
South Indian Mango Achaar	420
Khatta-Meetha Achaar	421

SALADS

Mixed Vegetable Salad	425
Channe aur Rajmah ka Salad	426
Aam ka Salad	427
Gaajar ya Mooli ka Salad	430
Mung ki Dal ka Salad	431
Pyaz, Chukandar aur Tamatar ka Salad	432
Aam ka Salsa	433

SOUPS

Tamatar ka Shorba	437
Sabzion ka Shorba	438
Gobhi ka Shorba	439
Murg aur Sabzion ka Shorba	440
Mulligatawny Soup	441
Mung Dal ka Shorba	442
Rasam	443
Ghia ka Shorba	446
Aalu ka Shorba	447
Palak ka Shorba	448
Kaddu ka Shorba	449
Makki ka Shorba	450
Nariyal ka Shorba	451

DRINKS

Dahi ki Lassi	455
South Indian Coffee	456
Zeera Paani	458
Kanji	459
Kokum Water	459
Shikanjvi	460
Panna	462
Masala Chai	463
Kashmiri Kahva	463
Thandai	465

Paan & Mouth Fresheners   466

CHAPTER 1

The Qutub Minar, a tower in Delhi, is the world's tallest brick minaret. The Qutub Minar is notable for being one of the earliest and most prominent examples of Indo-Islamic architecture.

Introduction

Indian cuisine is famous around the world and enjoys the enviable reputation of being very unique and healthy. With a charm of its own, it has such a great variety of tastes, colors and aroma that those who experience it once, sometimes find other foods somewhat tasteless.

India is an ancient country and was once called the 'golden sparrow'. Several invaders like Alexander the Great, the mighty Gengis Khan and Taimur the Lame came here to seek its riches, jewels and spices. In fact, the lure of the spices that are used in Indian cuisine is what brought the British, the French, the Dutch and the Portuguese to the Indian coast. India has seen the rise and fall of many empires and dynasties. Subsequently, it has absorbed some of their cultures and cuisines. Because of the assimilation of these cultures and their influence, there has emerged a cuisine of unparalleled variety and taste.

For thousands of years Indians have used spices to decorate and enhance the enticing aroma of their cuisine. They use them like an artist trying to paint a beautiful picture. This painting of color and flavor in Indian food is not somebody's imagination but originates from the basic philosophy and thought enshrined in the ancient *Vedas*. It clearly emphasizes that in order to stay healthy and happy one should eat food which has a mix of herbs and spices. When this is followed, the results can be beyond our imagination — a colorful, fragrant, exotic and romantic fare that is not only exquisite and delicious but by far the most healthy cuisine in the world. The art of Indian cooking lies not in heavy spicing, but how delicately one uses these herbs and spices. It is an art to use the selected spices, and if you use them correctly and precisely, it brings about the dormant flavors of a dish or it can drown the undesirable taste of another. Besides, these spices have innumerable health benefits which I have tried to emphasize wherever possible.

Sampling of Indian food is an unforgettable experience. The delicious meat curries and beautiful *pulavs* (often spelt *pilafs*) will haunt one's memory forever and the mere mention of *gulabjamans, samosas,* and *kebabs* will make the mouth water. Along with the pleasures comes the hidden dividend of health benefits. Its *dals* (lentil preparations) are full of digestible proteins. Its various delicious vegetable curries contain many

> **For thousands of years Indians have used spices to decorate and enhance the enticing aroma of their cuisine. They use them like an artist trying to paint a beautiful picture**

vitamins and have lots of fiber. Indian breads are commonly made with whole-wheat flour rich in essential nutrients and minerals. The food is ideally prepared with all fresh ingredients. Yogurt, very good for our digestive system, is also an essential part of an Indian meal.

This book also offers innumerable number of proteinaceous vegetarian dishes keeping the vegetarian reader in mind. My love of Indian cooking, its artful, deliberate use of spices, the health benefits, and the joy I have seen in sharing this cuisine, are some of the reasons which have inspired me to write this book. To help you understand the origin and foundations of Indian cooking, I have also included bits of information on the history of the Indian subcontinent and its influence on Indian cooking. The recipes are written with a global appeal in mind and most of them include its Indian name and an English description as well as step-by-step instructions on how to create a quick, easy, delicious and healthy Indian dish. I have also described the health benefits of each spice used and its Indian name. The recipes are authentically Indian but often I have fused locally available ingredients so as to appeal to the western palate. Helpful *'Hints'* and *'Notes'* are given in some recipes to help you in preparation of that recipe.

India is one of the most diverse countries with many religions and races living together for centuries. It has 28 States and 7 Union Territories each with their own official languages and cuisines. I have tried to give you a glimpse into most of these cuisines. The book has recipes for every occasion – from an easy and simple quick preparation to a classic weekend dinner you might have had at an upmarket restaurant. You will also find step-by-step preparation methods to make yogurt, *ghee*, and fresh home made breads, *paneer* and your favorite appetizers. Photographs of recipes, Indian landscape and historical monuments intersperse the text and provide much visual relief.

I welcome you now into my Indian subcontinent kitchen and would like to take you on a journey to explore the *Exquisite World of Indian Cuisine* in all its glory.

History and origin of Indian cuisine

The strongest influence on Indian cuisine, or at least among 80 percent of Indians – the *Hindus* – is of *Ayurveda*, a treatise on health. Its origins are in the *Atharva Veda*, the contents of which date back to around 1,000 BC. It is not only the science of health but covers the whole subject of life in its various ramifications. According to *Ayurveda* a person can stay healthy only if one regulates one's diet, exercises, recreates and controls sensual pleasures, and is generous, just, truthful, forgiving, and has a happy family life. In other words if you are unhappy and have bottled up emotions, diseases emanate. Besides, there are three primary forces in your body called *vatta, pitta,* and *kapha*, translated as air, fire and water. Air means that which moves, like breathing and beating of the heart. Fire is bile which digests things including mental digestion or the ability to comprehend, *Kapha* is phlegm which holds things together. *Ayurveda* believes that when these three are thrown out of balance and aggravated, they manifest themselves in the body and one contracts all sorts of diseases. According to *Ayurveda* diseases should first be treated with food, and medication should only be given later, if needed. Hippocrates also said, "Let your food be your medicine... and let your medicine be your food." Treatments using foods are based on the six tastes of foods which are sweet, salty, sour, pungent, bitter and astringent. Each taste has its specific therapeutic value. The tastes increase or decrease the three forces of our body as the case may be. Everyone needs a certain amount of each of these six tastes depending on the individual's physique. Too much of any one taste can be harmful.

The sweet taste gives strength to the tissue elements and harmonizes the mind. The sour taste stimulates the digestive fire and sour foods like lime and tamarind are easy on digestion and good for the heart. The salty taste stimulates digestion and clears the channels in the body by causing sweating. Pungent tastes as in onion, pepper and garlic help digestion, improve metabolism and dilate channels of the body. Bitter foods like bitter gourd, fenugreek seeds and lemon rind eliminate

An idol of Nandi, the bull which Lord Shiva rides, in Mysore, Karnataka.

bacterial and viral elements, purify the blood and enhance metabolism. Potatoes, apples, betel nut leaves, and most green vegetables and drinks like tea have an astringent taste and heal ulcers and wounds. They also act as water absorbent in the body and help in the assimilation of moisture and fat. A lack of any of these tastes in the food will aggravate the body forces and cause all sorts of health problems. There are several great schools of *Ayurvedic* medicine in India, the US, and Europe, based on these very ideas and theories.

In a traditional Indian meal you will be able to observe and appreciate the distribution of various dishes according to the above–mentioned six different tastes. A typical meal has a dash of hot and bitter sweet pickle, has plenty of rice and bread rich in sugar, spicy-salty and sour tasting vegetable, and meat curries rich in astringent and pungent taste because of the ingredients used in these dishes. A yogurt based item is added to coat the stomach of excessive burning due to spices and replenishing the essential stomach bacteria which are naturally found in the yogurt. Lentils provide the much needed proteins for the majority of the vegetarian population. Vegetable curries give the fiber as well as the astringent taste with vitamins. *Ayurveda* strongly believes that 'you are what you eat'. It does specify the preparation of different meats but it also specifies that consumption of flesh induce the factor of violence and give rise to emotions like fear and hatred. So in order for you to get spiritually enlightened and to keep your mental well-being meats are not recommended.

Influences from the 'Outsiders'
Indian cuisine truly offers a mind–boggling variety of foods today because of the influences from the past cultures of the Mughals, the Persians, the Zoroastrians and the Greeks that came and merged into the local culture. The most significant influence in the north including Punjab, Haryana, Kashmir, Uttar Pradesh and Delhi is from the Mughals who were the Central Asian invaders and ruled India for about 400 years. They were connoisseurs of food and brought with them the taste for lamb, chicken, nuts and dried fruits, and thus came about the wonderful *tandoori* chicken, *kormas*, *kebabs*, *biryani*, *pulavs* and desserts like Baklava. Prior to their arrival, the foods in the north and south were prepared with the belief that eating meat is not good for mental and spiritual well-being and was consumed only by a select group of people.

In the south there was a major influence on local foods left by the great spice traders who were Phoenicians, Romans, Portuguese and the Arabs. Marco Polo came to India in 1294, and Vasco da Gama in 1498; the Dutch and the British came in the 17th century – these seafarers brought with them new foods that worked their way into south Indian cuisine. Saffron from the Arabs, fenugreek from the Mediterranean, chili peppers, the new world tomatoes, potatoes and the cashew came with the Portuguese.

Regional and climatic influences
Each state evolved its very own cuisine influenced by the climate of the region and the availability of certain raw foods. The people of Rajasthan, the desert state, make up for the lack of color in their landscape by flaunting vivid colors in their dresses as well as in their cuisine. They use plenty of red chili and turmeric in all the dishes. Similarly in Kashmir since saffron and dry fruits grow in abundance, they lend a lot of color,

distinction and delicacy to the foods of this region. Cinnamon, mace, nutmeg, cardamom and black pepper are used here in food to ward off the long winter chill and the cold weather. In contrast, in the naturally warm and humid southern climates, tamarind, coconut and curds take over to impart a cooling effect to the cuisine while the fragrant curry leaves and mustard seeds provide a peppy counterpoint. The food in the south is generally light and digestible but chili-hot to induce perspiration which is what is needed in a hot climate to cool you off and also help clean the body channels. Karnataka produces perhaps the best coffee, cardamoms and cashew nuts. The seacoast of Kerala is abundant in fish, shellfish and coconut especially in the summer and monsoon months. Mustard seeds and fragrant curry leaves grow in abundance here. Along their extensive waterways, you can see green rice paddy which is the staple food of Kerala. Talking of seafood also takes you to another region of India – Bengal. The Bengalis boast that no one can cook or savor fish like they can. They are quite convinced that no oil has a better flavor as the mustard oil has and no blend of spices is as flavorful as *panchphoran* and certainly no dessert as delectable as the *rasgulla* or *rasmalai*. The Bay of Bengal offers a rich haul of fish, shellfish and its hot and humid climate is perfect for growing rice, mustard and coconut.

If you still have not had your fill of hot and spicy food you could move on to Goa. Here, you can look forward to more seafood and other fiery specialties flavored with coconut and the locally grown cashew. If you decide to cook Goan food, keep a bottle of vinegar or preferably cashew vinegar called Feni, because it creeps into many preparations giving them a distinctive flavor.

Still talking of exquisite blending, one comes to Hyderabad, in Andhra Pradesh – where Muslim and Hindu influences blend so very harmoniously – in the exotic, aromatic way. In the cuisine of this famous state dishes like *Bagara Baingan*, *Shikampuri Kebab*, Lamb Curry, fragrant *Pulavs* and desserts give you a good example of this harmonious blend.

The jewel of Muslim art in India and one of the universally admired masterpieces of the world's heritage. A mausoleum located in Agra, built by Mughal Emperor Shah Jahan in memory of his favorite wife, Mumtaz Mahal

The Exquisite World of Indian Cuisine

Indian cuisine truly offers a mind-boggling variety of food. The Mughal, the Persian, the Zoroastrian and the Greek influence strongly reflecting in numerous dishes popular even today. It can be seen significantly in Punjab, Haryana, Kashmir, Uttar Pradesh and Delhi which bears the hallmark of the Mughals who were the Central Asian invaders and ruled India for about 400 years.

The north Indian state of Punjab is an agricultural state with a very dry and hot summer, perfect weather for growing wheat and corn. It is referred to as the bread basket of India – its people have a good appetite and like to fix quick hearty meals. Their mustard greens preparation called *Sarson ka Saag* which is quite hot and delicious for the palate, is usually topped with lots of home made butter and suitable for the climate of this state. A Punjabi will consider the meal of *Sarson ka Saag* and *Makki ki Roti* (mustard greens and cornmeal bread) quite wholesome and delicious enough to be irreplaceable.

The foods of Gujarat are hot, spicy and sweet because Gujaratis like to add a dash of sugar to all their dishes. Their *papads* (paper thin tortillas made with the lentil flours) are the glory of each of their meals. They make this very delicious snack called *dhokla* (steamed rice cakes) with amazing finesse. Their sweet and sour *chidva* is being relished all over India and is a famous teatime snack.

From the state of Maharashtra comes the delectable pomfret fish. The food here has a perfect blend of sweet, sour and fiery tastes which will make your tongue tingle for days. To satiate your sweet tooth do not forget that from this state also comes the king of mangoes, *Alphanso*.

Each spice has dozens of different flavors depending on whether they are cooked in oil or dry roasted or ground. When they are cooked in oil it is called *tadka* (tempering). This technique is quite unique to Indian cooking. Spices when cooked in hot oil, transfer their flavor to that oil and anything cooked in it carry the flavor of these spices. Some spices used in a ground form are for taste and those used whole are for aroma. The spices used as whole are discarded during eating. Once in a while some spices are roasted and ground to enhance the taste and to decorate the main course dish. The genius of Indian cooking lies in mixing and matching different spices for each dish. The spices should be used as fresh as possible – they stay fresh if they are whole and can be ground as needed. There are regional variations on use of these spices and in this book my focus will be more on the regional specialties. The choice of spices makes the sum total of the taste and flavor of a dish. Thickening agents used for the curries are mainly onions, coconut milk, groundnuts or seeds, heavy cream and sometimes yogurt.

Beneficial uses of all the spices are recorded in the ancient treatises and I have mentioned in the next few pages their uses and health benefits. For example cinnamon helps lower high cholesterol levels and regulates blood-sugar whereas cumin, fennel and cardamom help in the digestion of the food. Ginger is called the universal healer and turmeric acts as antiinflammatory, an anti cancer agent, and helps in the prevention of Alzheimer's disease. It has in fact been called the 'solid gold' of India.

As I rave enthusiastically over the exquisite Indian cuisine, let me assure you that there is nothing complicated about preparing these dishes. What is essential is a thorough knowledge of all the fresh herbs and spices, their unique flavoring and combinations. Some basic experimentation can prepare you for this unique journey.

The 'Open' markets of India

Almost all cities in India have roadside markets (called *haat*) which sell vegetables, fruits, sweets, groceries, spices, lentils, household and clothing items. Here, you can also find fresh homemade products like *chutneys*, pickles and breads.

There may be vendors selling mutton, fresh fish, chicken and cooking pots too. These places vibrate with a life of their own. It is quite an experience to buy stuff here because you know that it is authentic and fresh. Moreover, it is great place to catch up with your neighbours and also do your weekly shopping. Visiting a market like this makes you feel as if time has stood still here. The kerb side markets and shops have been an integral part of Asian communities for a very long time.

Fresh herb and vegetable sellers in India

The Exquisite World of Indian Cuisine

A vegetables and fruits store in the US

INTRODUCTION

Spices that are used in Indian cooking – their origin and health benefits

The Spice Box: Traditionally, in earlier times, when a girl got married she used to get a spice box as a part of her dowry which had spices that the bride would take with her to start her new household. These boxes could be beautifully, ornamented or simple wooden boxes. Nowadays, they may not be an item of dowry but the spice box is still an essential item of a Indian lady's kitchen. Listed below are some of the gems from my Spice Box.

Parsley / *Ajwain* : Carom seed or Bishop's weed or Lovage (*Ajwain*) / (*Carum Capticum*) – resembles parsley seeds. They are used in lemon pickles and in batter for frying fritters (*pakoras*). They are also used in the flavoring of vegetable dishes like carrots, cabbage and some breads. They are also used to relieve stomach pain due to gas or indigestion. *Ajwain* contains thymol which is germicidal and antiseptic, and is valued in *Ayurvedic* medicine for diarrhoea, colic, flatulence, asthma and indigestion. It helps expel gas and mucus.

Asafoetida / *Heeng* : A gum derived from the root of a plant (*Ferulla alliacea*). Used in the preparation of pickles, *sambhar, rasam*, and some lentil preparations. Native to Iran. It is also called the devil's dung. It should be stored in an air tight container because of its smell. This smell goes away once it is cooked. It even eliminates offending smell of any food it is used for like meats and fish. It is mainly antiflatulent and digestive, is helpful in cases of asthma, and bronchitis. It is a folk tale remedy to treat cold in children. It has been reported that in humans it acts both as a contraceptive as well as abortifacient. Therefore, it is used in very minute quantities.

Bay leaves / *Tej patta* : Bay leaves come from the Bay laurel tree (*Laurus nobilis*) native to the Mediterranean and Asia Minor. They are admired for their beauty, smell and medicinal uses. In Indian cooking bay leaves are used mainly for flavoring curries and *pulavs*. This tree is considered sacred in Greece and Rome and is popular for its healing power. Untimely withering of a laurel tree manifested disaster for the ancient Romans and Greeks. Oil of bay leaves is used as a rub to relieve joint pains and it also prevents tooth decay. Its use in food promotes appetite and helps in secretion of upper digestive track juices. It has a strong aroma and makes an effective anti dandruff rinse. Greeks welcomed their Olympic champions with wreathes of bay leaves.

Black pepper / *Kali mirch* : It is called the king of spices and is used as a condiment and also for its medicinal values. A native of Malabar Hills of western India it is a fruit of the *Piper Nigum L*. It has been a highly prized spice as far back as 2nd century A.D. Christopher Columbus set out to discover India in search of cloves and black pepper. A culinary spice, which is used all over the world by almost every race and in all cuisines. It is bitter, carminative, diuretic, digestive and a stimulant. It is useful to treat arthritis, fever, cough, dysentery, dyspepsia and flatulence. It is a marvel of nature and is used in *Ayurvedic*, *Unani* and Persian medicine. In India it grows mainly in Kerala. Boiled in tea with basil leaves, it is used to cure common colds and asthma and is used extensively in Indian cooking – ground as well as whole to flavor dishes.

Brown Cardamoms / *Illaichi* : Large Brown Cardamoms (*Amomum sublatum*) are valued as the queen of spices in the annals of herbs and spices. There are two varieties of cardamoms, large brown and smaller green. Large brown is mostly used in Indian entrée dishes and is used as a whole spice to flavor the curries and *pulavs*. It is grown only in north-east India and Sikkim and is extensively used in Chinese and Vietnamese cooking. It has a strong aroma and when its seeds are ground it forms a part of *garam masala* recipe. Green cardamoms (*Amomum elettaria*), besides flavoring some meat curries and other main dishes, are used in powder form to flavor most Indian desserts. It is native to India, Guatemala and Sri Lanka. The sugared and silver coated pods are offered as a mouth freshener after a feast in weddings and other celebrations in India. Tea made with cardamoms cures any digestive disorders and cures depressions. Daily gargles of cardamom tea prevents flu, relieves cough and throat problems. It is a calcium supplier to the body if taken regularly, and also prevents dizziness.

Spices used in Indian cooking

Cayenne pepper / *Lal mirch* : It is also called dried fruit of capsicum (*Capsicum fourtescens*). The small variety is very hot. Chilies are a great source of Vitamin C and help in digestion. The correct use of red chili is of great importance, if you want to make a gourmet style curry with a perfect red color. India is the largest producer of chili. It is grown throughout India but chilies from Kashmir are best to give the red color to curries and at the same time it is mild in taste. It is very effective when added to liniments for arthritis, muscle aches and benefits the heart, blood circulation and wheezing.

Cinnamon / *Dalchini* : It has been known since remote antiquity. Native to the hills of south India (*Cinnamon verum*) it is the dried inner bark of a type of laurel tree. It is mostly used whole to give flavor to the dishes and is also used as a powder to make *garam masala*. In the west it is mostly used to garnish and to add flavor to desserts. Recent research has indicated it to have great effect in making insulin more sensitive. It was highly prized among ancient nations and was regarded as a gift for monarchs and nobles.

Clove / *Laung* : (*Eugenia caryophyllates*) It is the dried unopened flower bud of an evergreen tree native to India. It has a sweet penetrating smell. In powder form it is part of the recipe of *garam masala*. As a whole-spice it is used to flavor rice and curries. Its health benefits are numerous. Clove oil will stop a toothache and is useful for the common cold. It promotes sweating in patients with fevers, colds and flu. Its hot and sweet taste has made it a breath freshener since antiquity. It is a powerful phyto chemical that numbs pain and kills bacteria and fungi.

Coconut / *Nariyal* : It is also known as *Cocos nucifera*. In south India the abundant coconut palm is called the '**the tree of life**'. The fruit yields a rich meat, milk and oil. It requires a lot of skill to extract meat and milk from a fresh coconut. Dried grated unsweetened coconut is available in Indian grocery stores and health food stores and it works very well as a substitute. Imagine how boring the beaches would be without tall, elegant swaying palm trees and how boring would the world be without its flavor in tropical drinks.

Coriander seeds / *Dhania* seeds : It is one of the oldest known spices and is also known as *Coriandrum satiram*. It is one of the most widely used seasoning in India it has a lemony aroma. It is used in all vegetable, meat and lentil preparations in its unroasted ground form. It should be cooked in hot oil over low heat for a minute for its full flavor to be released. To enhance the flavor of some dishes the seeds are roasted on a hot griddle (*tawa*) without oil for 3 minutes or so and ground just before use. Coriander has diuretic properties and is used for the treatments of upper abdominal problems like flatulence or mild cramp like gastrointestinal upsets. Coriander is grown all over India. The state of Rajasthan and parts of central India produce most of the coriander needed in India but the variety from Rajasthan has the best flavor and aroma.

Cumin seeds / *Zeera* powder : Cumin seeds (*Cuminum cyminuml*) are also one of the most widely used spices with a pleasant, unassertive flavor. The seeds are pale green in color and resemble fennel seeds. Cumin seeds are used to flavor almost all meats, vegetable, and lentil preparations. They are cooked very briefly in hot oil over low heat until they start popping to release their full flavor and are used for tempering (*tadka*) invariably. They can be dry roasted on a hot griddle and ground into a powder to flavor dishes like *raita* (a yogurt preparation), *pulav* (a rice dish) and *chaat*.

Cumin has many health benefits. In south India it is used in its unroasted ground form. Cumin is available in supermarkets, at Indian grocers and in health stores all over the US. It is used as a remedy for colic, dyspepsia and headache and is also antispasmodic and carminative. It is sometimes compounded with other drugs to form a stimulating liniment.

Stone flower / *Dagadphool* : It is a combination of fungus and algae and is a lichen. It is used in the *Goda masala* mix. Its health benefits and medicinal values are not known.

Fennel seeds / *Saunf* : These seeds (*Foeniculum vulgare*) look a bit like cumin seeds but are much plumper and greener. Fennel powder is a part of *Kashmiri* cuisine and is used extensively in meat preparations. Fennel seeds are also a part of *panchphoran,* a five-spice mixture from Bengal, and is used in almost all Bengali cooking. In north India, Fennel seeds are seldom used in cooking but they form a major part of pickles, *chutneys* and several snack preparations. Fennel seeds are also used all over the country as an after meal mouth freshener — sometimes dry roasted or sweetened — they are presented as a mint when you are leaving the restaurant after a hearty

The Exquisite World of Indian Cuisine

Indian meal. They are known for their digestive quality and are very therapeutic when boiled in the tea for the cure of common cough and cold. Fennel seeds also help cancer patients in providing them a good mouth freshner after radiation and chemotherapy treatments.

Fenugreek seeds / *Methi seeds* : These angular yellowish seeds (*Trigonella foneum*) are a very healthy spice to use. In north India, these are first fried in hot oil for a few seconds before the other ingredients are added. They are used in pickles, *chutneys* and several vegetable dishes. In western, eastern and southern India these seeds are used in meat and fish dishes. In Bengal these are a part of *panchphora*n. In south India, fenugreek seeds are used in *dosa, sambhar* and *idli* preparations. These seeds have antiseptic properties and are very digestive in nature. In India, traditionally, it is given to new mothers to relax their uterus post delivery. Use of Fenugreek seeds also regulates blood sugar and is very helpful for diabetic patients. They are also effective as an antioxidant.

Mixture of Spices / *Garam masala* : This Spice Mixture has the most exotic aroma and flavor and is used towards the end of cooking to garnish the dish and to retain its full flavor. *Garam* literally means hot in Hindi and *Masala* means spices. So *garam masala* is a mixture of those spices, which according to the ancient *Ayurveda,* produce heat in the body. Typical *garam masala* would be a mixture of powdered large cardamoms, black pepper, cinnamon, cloves, cumin, nutmeg and mace. Almost all Indian grocery stores sell it. It is used to garnish meat, poultry, fish and vegetable curries before serving. It is also used to garnish yogurt preparations like *raita, dahi vada* and *chaat* among the north Indian dishes.

Nigella / *Kalonji* : This tear shaped tiny black seed (*Nigella saliva*) is mostly used in oven breads but in Bengali food it is part of *panchphoran* five spice mixture. Some vegetable dishes like eggplants, cabbage etc. team very well with Nigella. It is also used in sweet mango *chutney*, mango pickles and other pickles. This black seed has unique medicinal properties, containing eight of the essential amino acids found in the body proteins. Nigella seeds have anticancer, antibacterial, anti inflammatory and non allergenic properties and strengthen the body's immune system besides helping in bronchial asthma and arthritis.

Black Mustard seeds / *Rai* : Ancient *Vedic* writings dating back 5,000 years mention mustard seeds (*Brassica atba nigra*). Mustard seeds have been used for thousands of years in Greece and Egypt for flavor and as medicine. The *New Testament* compares our faith in God with mustard seeds. When we keep using our faith like mustard seeds it grows into a large plant with leaves and flowers. Both mustard seeds and greens are edible. Mustard seed acts as a laxative when taken whole. It has Omega 3 fatty acid, is diuretic and reduces migraine attacks. It also helps to cure rheumatoid arthritis, helps reduce blood pressure and inhibits growth of cancer cells. Its leaves are rich in minerals like selenium, phosphorus, manganese, iron, calcium, and zinc; Vitamin B and C, dietary fiber, proteins and phytonutrients. There are three varieties of Mustard seeds. The round little balls are either yellowish, reddish brown (*sarson*) or black (*rai*). The reddish brown variety is mostly grown and used all over India. In south India most dishes are flavored by these seeds. They are first heated in oil and once they start popping the rest of the ingredients are added. Whether it is a meat dish, rice, *sambhar, idli* or the famous *dosa* or any of their *chutney*s. Even in Bengal, Gujarat and Maharashtra, mustard seeds are used in almost every dish. In Punjab, mustard greens are a favorite winter vegetable and mustard oil is also used as a preservative in pickles and for cooking. I think it is the most used spice in the whole of India. It is also used as a powder in a marinade to coat the fish or to make a sauce in Bengal giving a rather pungent spicy taste. When the seeds are used whole they give a sort of sour nutty flavor as well as a nice speckled look to the dish and they are supposed to be antiseptic in nature.

Cobra's Saffron / *Naagkeshar* : The dry flowers of *Naagkeshar* (*Mesua ferrea*) tree are used in the *goda masala* mix. The *Naagkeshar* tree is one of the highly regarded and sacred trees. Native to India, its other name is *Naagchampa*. This is a tree of healing, pleasing and attractive qualities. The flowers of this tree are offered to Lord Buddha in temples. These flowers are fragrant and their oil has significant anti fungal, antibacterial, antiinflammatory, antihemorrhagic as well as antihelminitic properties. Extract from its leaves is used in *Ayurvedic* medicine and is useful for alleviating asthma and bronchial spasms.

Nutmeg and Mace / *Jaiphal* and *Javitri* : Nutmeg (*Myristica fragrans*) is the seed of a pear shaped fruit and its outer covering, when dried, is called mace. These two spices are used very delicately to flavor meats and few vegetable dishes. In India, it is used as a medicinal herb by women who have just delivered babies. It is said that these herbs helps clean the blood and give strength to the body. In the north of India nutmeg and mace are a part of the spice mixture, *garam masala*. India is the most eminent supplier of nutmeg and mace to the world.

Five spice mixture / *Panchphoran* : *Panch* means five and *phoran* means seeds. It originated in Bengal. The mixture has fennel seeds, brown mustard seeds, nigella seeds, fenugreek and cumin seeds in equal amounts. It is used as tempering (*tadka*) to flavor vegetables or lentils, as whole seeds mixture or as a ground powder. Grind them all well in a coffee grinder and store in an airtight container in a cool place. The flavor will be retained longer in the seeds (2 months) but powder should not be stored for more than 3 or 4 weeks.

South Indian spice mixture / *Podi powder* : Roast and grind coarsely a mixture of ½ cup *urad dal*, ½ cup *channa dal*, 2 Tbs red hot chili powder, 1 Tbs sesame seeds and add to it ½ tsp salt with ¼ tsp asafoetida. Store it in an airtight container and season your vegetables, lentils and meat curries as you please.

Turmeric / *Haldi* : Called the solid gold of India or the saffron of India. This root of a plant (*Curcuma Longal*) is boiled, dried and powdered before use. This is the spice which gives yellow color to the curries. Fresh turmeric is available in the spring months in India and it actually gives a better yellow color to the dish. It is found in almost every Indian household. It has antiinflammatory properties and prevents certain cancers and even Alzheimer's disease. It also acts as an antiseptic. Its paste applied over a wound or a swelling greatly reduces pain and swelling. It takes a little frying in hot oil to release its flavor and then it gives a beautiful yellow color to every dish you prepare. It is also used as a dye and also in the preparation of cosmetics and medicines for skin problems. It is grown mainly in the southern states of India. It is important that Turmeric is of good quality and therefore should be bought from a good Indian grocery store.

Star anise / *Badalphool* : Native to China and Vietnam, Star anise (*Pimpinella anisum*) has been taken by Indians from the Chinese cuisine. Mandarin people in China used to chew star anise as a mouth freshener thousands of years ago and even to this day it is a major ingredient of Chinese five spice mix. Peking duck and steamed pork belly would not be possible without this aromatic spice. Shanghai style of Chinese cuisine makes the most of this spice. However, Beijing, Cantonese and Sichuan styles also make wide use of this spice in their spice powder. It is an ingredient of *podi powder* of south of India and is used in *goda masala* mix of Maharashtra and is called *Badalphool*. It was also used in the summer palace kitchens of the Mughals in Kashmir to flavor different kinds of meats. Japanese plant star anise trees in their temple gardens and use the bark of its tree as incense. Extract of star anise called shikimic acid is a key ingredient in bird flu medicine. In the west the extract is used to flavor wines and baked goods, fruit compotes and jams. It was introduced in the Indian continent by Chinese travellers.

The Exquisite World of Indian Cuisine

THE SIGNIFICANCE OF SPICES

It has been proven that herbs and spices act as potent antibiotics, blood thinners, anticancer agents, antiinflammatory, insulin regulators and antioxidants. When taken in small doses in regular foods they act as unique health boosters. Inflammation is a suspect in heart disease, stroke, cancer, Alzheimer's disease and arthritis.

The use of **Ginger** compounds reduce pain and acts as a Cox-2 inhibitor, similar to the anti-arthritic drug celebrex. There is strong evidence that ginger is antiinflammatory. When patients with osteoarthritis of the knee were treated with 255 mg of ginger extract twice a day they showed far less pain than those with placebo. It is also a potent antitumor agent.

A whiff of **Cinnamon** can enhance motivation, alertness, blood flow, which in turn would stimulate the brain. It is proven that cinnamon's most active ingredient MHCP increased the processing of blood sugar 2000% in test-tube studies. So for diabetic patients, cinnamon when sprinkled in tiny amounts in desserts or by flavoring their tea, will make their insulin intake more efficient.

Turmeric contains high concentrations of the potent antioxidant curcumin. In test tubes, 80% of malignant prostrate cells self-destructed when exposed to curcumin. Its antiinflammatory activity reduces arthritic swelling and progressive brain damage in animals. It also fights heart burn, indigestion and Alzheimer's disease. Mice that were fed ½ tsp of curcumin daily developed 50% less brain plaques (main cause of Alzheimer's disease) than those that did not and it is a far safe antiinflammatory agent with the minimum side effects than any other found at the drug store.

Red pepper or Cayenne pepper can fight congestion faster than drugstore decongestants. It makes your nose run, so you can breathe easier. Mice injected with cancer cells and red pepper extract had smaller tumors than the mice without any. It helps combat wheezing.

The most effective killers of bacterial species in current research are in order, onion, garlic, allspice, oregano, thyme, tarragon, cumin, cloves, bay leaf, and cayenne pepper. According to modern research the strongest antioxidants are oregano, thyme, sage, cumin, rosemary, saffron, turmeric, nutmeg, ginger, cardamom, coriander, basil, and tarragon. Oregano oil has been found as effective as the common antibiotic drug vanomycin in treating staph infections in mice.

So the use of spices not only contributes to flavor, aroma, color, taste and pungency to the food but has unparalleled pharmaceutical and medicinal benefits as well.

Fresh herbs and seasonings

Almost all curries have these green herbs in one form or another. They give a refreshing look to the dish and are also very healthy. In India some vendors only sell these green herbs and spices.

Onions / *Pyaz*: One of the oldest vegetables known to mankind. They are eaten chopped, sliced, used in cooking food, fresh salads and as a spicy garnish. It is one of the most widely used vegetable in cuisines all over the world. Onions are fundamental to Indian cooking. Almost all main course dishes first get a garnish of onions. The Egyptians worshipped them and buried their pharaohs with slices of onions. Greek athletes ate them in large quantity to get muscle strength and the Roman gladiators rubbed their bodies to get muscle strength. In the Middle Ages they were used as money. They were introduced to North America in 1492 by Columbus during his expeditions. Onions are a powerhouse of health benefits ranging from being antiinflammatory, anticholesterol, anticancer and a powerful antioxidant.

Ginger / *Adrak*: Originated in India, this plant has been traditionally used in *Ayurvedic* medicine for its health benefits for nearly 5,000 years. It is one of the wet trios used in the beginning of each curry. Along with black pepper, it was one of the main trading spices as far back as 2,000 years in the Roman Empire and mid-eastern countries. Its health benefits are innumerable. It breaks down fatty foods for easy digestion and is excellent for reducing gas. It is a natural antihistamine and antiinflammatory. Relieves nausea and morning sickness and lowers cholesterol. It is more effective when used with garlic. Ginger tea is my favorite on a wintry day to relieve minor cold and flu symptoms.

Garlic / *Lahsan*: Garlic is also an essential part of the Indian curry *masala*. Since time immemorial garlic has been used to ward off evil spirits, build stamina, enhance immunity and ward off infections. It has been proven by research that garlic used on a regular basis reduces blood pressure and plays a role preventing cancer. It lowers cholesterol and relieves asthmatic conditions.

Green chilies / *Hari mirch*: Green chili pepper is also one of the wet trio used in the *curry masala*. Its benefits are numerous. It is rich in Vitamin A and C. They enhance and stimulate digestion. Capsicum stimulates the mucous membranes of the nose, therefore increasing blood flow to these membranes and help us clear the nose. Chilies lower blood sugar as they stimulate the pancreas to produce more insulin. They also kill cancer cells and are highly effective in killing bacteria and viruses in the body.

Cilantro or coriander leaves / *Dhania*: Besides acting as a beautiful garnish for all the curries, this herb has numerous health benefits. It protects you against Salmonella, aids in digestion and helps alleviate the symptoms of arthritis. It is antiflatulent, antiinflammatory and lowers blood sugar. It protects against the urinary tract infection. It is a good source of iron, magnesium, rich source of phytonutrients and flavonoids. So next time you are shopping for vegetables pick up this aromatic herb because it may be the best vegetable purchase you made that day. Cilantro is mostly used for garnishing and you may think that you can do without it but it is probably the most important of all the ingredients.

Curry leaves / *Kadi patta*: Used in *Ayurvedic* medicines because of their many health benefits. Curry leaves have a special place in Indian cuisine. They are native to India and Sri Lanka and are rich in Vitamin C, Calcium, Phosphate, Iron and Nicotinic acid. They have been used in south India for thousand of years to flavor curries and *sambhar* and are now used extensively all

The Exquisite World of Indian Cuisine

over India. Curry leaves paste is used to cure minor cuts and abrasions. The extract of curry leaves prevents diarrhoea and vomiting and it strengthens the stomach functions.

Dill / *Sooa*: It was used in ancient Rome. In Greece, Hippocrates used it on the burn wounds of his soldiers. They are stomach soothers and help overcome insomnia and have very high calcium content. Except among the Persian community, it is not used much in Indian cooking.

Fenugreek leaves / *Methi*: Native to India and southern Europe, the Mediterranean and North Africa Fenugreek is used in the herbal medicinal tradition of the Middle East, India, Egypt, and later in China and Europe. Known as *methi* in India. It was used by ancient Egyptians to combat fever and chronic cough. It is very easy to grow from seeds and has a very unique flavor but a slightly bitter taste. It is used in practically all cuisines in every part of India and has great therapeutic benefits. It lowers blood sugar and acts as a great digestive aid. It relieves congestion, reduces inflammation and fights infection. Stimulates the production of mucosal fluids to remove allergens and oxidants from the respiratory tract. When it is used in meat preparations it enhances the flavor of any meat like chicken, lamb, fish, pork or beef. It is mixed in the flour to make breads like *parantha* and *poori*. When chopped fine it can be mixed in fritter batter to make appetizers like *pakoras*. It is used to make vegetable stir-fries. It is sold dried in stores also and can be used after soaking in the water for a while. Its seeds give the same type of benefits as its leaves. Fenugreek is available fresh as well as dry at your local Indian grocery store.

Holy Basil / *Tulsi*: Queen of herbs, Tulsi is the most revered plant in India for more than 5,000 years. It adorns the courtyard of Indian households. It has its great medicinal significance and is called the '*elixir of life*' as it promotes longevity. *Tulsi* leaves, when boiled with tea leaves, make a perfect cup of tea, that has tremendous calming effect on the human mind and body. The extract prevents and cures common colds, headaches, stomach disorders, heart diseases and is a universal healer of malarial fever. It is known to regulate blood sugar and blood pressure.

Neem (*Azadirachta indica*): In India, the Neem tree is known as a '*divine tree*', '*heal all*', '*nature's drug store*', '*village pharmacy*' and a '*wonder tree*'. Its tender shoots and flowers are used as a vegetable. Neem is used to make a soup-like dish in south India called *Ugadi pachdi* on *Ugadi* day and is also used to make a soup *Veerampoo Rasam*. In Maharashtra, on *Gudi Padva*, the new year festival, there is an ancient practice of drinking Neem juice before starting the festivities. It is used in *Ayurvedic* medicine as an antiseptic to fight viruses and bacteria. It is also used for urinary disorders, diarrhoea, fever, skin disorders, burns and inflammatory diseases. Its leaves are sprinkled fresh near the beds of patients of flu and fever to disinfect the air of viruses and bacteria.

Mint / *Pudina*: Originating in India and the Mediterranean regions, Mint symbolized hospitality and welcome in ancient Rome and Greece. In earlier times Mint was used as an air freshener and as a perfume in bathing soaps. It has always been an aid to digestion, heartburn and acts as a powdered antioxidant and relieves the symptoms of cold and flu. Mint is used as base for an ancient drink *zeerapaani*. It contains Vitamin A, C and B2, and a wide range of minerals like manganese, copper, iron, potassium and calcium. A cup of Mint tea soothes and calms the body and mind. Besides cooking, it is used universally in toothpastes, gums, soaps and medicines. It is used to adorn drinks, desserts, curries, meats and almost any dish.

Henna / *Mehndi*: (*Lawsonia Inermis*): It is a very active disinfectant and the extract of *mehndi* leaves helps when taken in jaundice. It also acts as an antiseptic, bactericide,

fungicide and as an insect repellent. Its paste when applied reduces body temperature, fever, burning feet and even hysteria. The paste made of ground seeds of henna and anise with water or vinegar is used as a remedy for headache.

Henna has been in use in India for over 5000 years. This herb has tremendous importance as a dye with numerous healing properties. Its cosmetic use in an Indian wedding is of great importance as no wedding is complete without it. The night before the wedding is called *Mehndi Raat* (night). The bride and all the women of the family adorn and deck their hands and feet with fine designs using *mehndi* paste. It gives a beautiful reddish brown color to the skin and the patterns stay on the skin for at least 7-10 days. *Mehndi* is also widely used in Egypt, Iran, Pakistan, Yemen and African countries. Cleopatra used to dye her hair with henna. Henna promotes hair growth and gives the hair beautiful dark brown color with a shiny luster. The uses are numerous and in western countries men and women are using it for tattoos and as a hair dye.

Decorative pattern of Henna (mehndi) on the hands of a bride to be

Cooking Made Easy

As you go through this cookbook please do not get overwhelmed by all the ingredients and the time it takes to make Indian food. Living in America for 43 years and working full time I had to find ways to fix a decent meal for my family. Rest assured that there are shortcuts to make a fancy Indian meal in 30 minutes and that means making 4–5 dishes to your taste every day. I usually fix a simple meal comprising a vegetable curry and *chappati* or a meat curry with pea pulav in practically 5-10 minutes. These are the few things that I did on the weekends that helped me prepare a good balanced meal for my family during the workweek.

1. Pressure-cook the lentils and any meat you want to cook during the week and freeze them.
2. Prepare the *curry masala* enough to last at least 2 weeks. Freeze it in small bags to be used as needed each day.
3. Chop all the vegetables and onions, ginger, green chilies (the Wet Trio) and garlic needed for the week and refrigerate them.
4. Make dough to make fresh *chappatis* every day and refrigerate the dough.
5. Make any *koftas* or desserts you need for the week or for entertaining any friends and freeze them.
6. You can also make the *masala* powders in advance and freeze them in your freezer.
7. You can also make clarified butter ahead of time for your cooking. For tempering salads, *chutneys* and vegetable stir-fries use olive oil, but for meat curries and vegetables curries etc. I do not recommend olive oil because at high temperatures it completely loses its flavor.

All you need to fix the meal on a workday is your spice box that should have the four essential spices needed for Indian cooking — cumin seeds, turmeric, coriander powder, red pepper and *garam masala* to garnish a dish. Hope you will find these few hints helpful to make Indian food on more regular basis and even on a working day.

Clarified butter / *ghee*

Clarified butter / Ghee : Also called *desi ghee,* has been used in Indian cooking to cook almost every dish since the early times. I personally think it gives the food a wonderful flavor though some chefs and cooks prefer oil for their own reasons. *Ghee* can be purchased at the local Indian grocery store. It can also be prepared at home by boiling and simmering the butter, preferably unsalted butter, on a moderate heat (see picture below).

Step-by-step method to make clarified butter / *ghee*

1. Melt 1 lb pound unsalted butter in a 1 quart pan.
2. Turn the heat to medium low and let it simmer for 15–20 minutes. While simmering, the butter will make popping sounds and a layer of foam will form on the top.
3. Keep simmering until just a thin layer of scum remains. Remove it with a large spoon and let it simmer. Soon it will be a clear golden liquid and all the solids would have settled at the bottom.
4. Pour off the clear liquid into a stainless steel container and when the sediments start to mix while pouring, strain the sediment from the *ghee* by pouring it through a cotton cloth placed over a stainless steel container. The *ghee* will stay fresh on the kitchen shelf for a couple of weeks but it can be stored in the refrigerator for many weeks.

The Exquisite World of Indian Cuisine

Special ingredients to highlight the flavor and aroma of curries and other main courses

Nuts and seeds: Almonds, cashew nuts, pistachios are used to decorate and flavor rice *pulav* to give it a rich and nutritious look and a ground mixture of seeds of watermelon, cantaloupe, pumpkin and squash called *Char magaz* are also used as a thickening agent in the curries. The same mixture of these nuts when mixed with milk, water and sugar is made into a cooling drink called *Thandai (see the recipe in the drinks section)*. This drink is very popular in the hot summer months in the state of Punjab. Sesame seeds are widely used to make *ladoos* or sweet round balls when mixed with sugar and dry milk powder. Poppy seeds are used to flavor breads like *Nan* and when ground they are used in various meat curries. Almonds, pistachio and cashews also ground and mixed with dry milk powder and sugar to make a very popular Indian dessert called *Burfi*. Sure enough, nuts do highlight the flavor and aroma of various dishes.

Screw pine flower essence / *Kewra*: *Kewra* water is used to flavor *kormas, kebabs, and biryanis*. The flower is grown in Orissa and Kerala and belongs to the screw pine family of plants. It has a very strong aroma. The extract of the male flowers is made into *kewra* essence and a drop of this when mixed with water, is sold as *kewra* water. It is used mainly in the cuisine from Hyderabad and Lucknow influenced by Mughal cuisine. *Kewra* essence is also used in flavoring several desserts.

Powdered rose flower petals and its essence / *Gulab patti - Gulab jal*: Rose petals are sun-dried and ground for use in cooking. These are used to marinate meats in Mughlai cuisine in India. They have very astringent and antiinflammatory properties. These are used to flavor *sherbets* and to sprinkle over *biryani, pulav* and some sweets. Rose water is available in Indian grocery stores.

Saffron / *Kesar*: It is widely used in Indian cooking and was a favorite of the Mughlai courts. It is the stigma of the flower of the crocus family and grows mainly in the Kashmir valley in India. It is also imported from Spain and Mediterranean countries. It is used to flavor *biryani, pulavs, kormas, kebabs* and many desserts. The strands are soaked first in a little warm water or milk and then transferred to the dish. It should be stored in a refrigerator, otherwise it loses its flavor very quickly.

Raisins / *Kishmish*: Raisins are used to flavor desserts like *halwa* (a cream of wheat pudding) and *kheer* (the rice pudding). These are very popular desserts of north India. Raisins are also used to flavor *pulavs, raita* (a yogurt dish) as well as *tamarind chutney.*

Lentils / *dal*: In dishes like the Persian *dhansak* lentils are used as a thickening agent. Sometimes meats are also cooked with lentils. In south India some vegetables and almost all rice dishes get flavored with not only the wet trio but also a teaspoonful of *urad dal* and sometimes *channa dal*. They are fried in hot oil and then rest of the ingredients are added. Some lentils are ground roasted and then mixed with *khoa* (dried milk) sugar and *ghee* to make *pinni* – a popular dessert also flavored with almonds, pistachio and raisins.

Ground raw papaya: It is used as a meat tenderizer. Sometimes *tandoori* chicken or *seekh kebabs* are rubbed well with this powder and then grilled or cooked. It makes the meat very tender and juicy.

Very thin silver and gold leaves to decorate desserts / *Varq*: These are prepared by beating real gold and silver metal into ultra thin leaves to decorate Indian desserts and are sold at the Indian confectioners. A trace of these is no health hazard.

Recipe for making the *Curry Masala*

Ingredients

Onion	2 lbs	Coriander powder	2 Tbs
Garlic chopped	2 Tbs	Cumin powder	1 tsp
Green chilies chopped	1 Tbs	Turmeric powder	1 tsp
Ginger chopped	2 Tbs	Red pepper	1 tsp
Tomatoes chopped	2 cups	*Garam masala*	1 tsp
Oil (Olive oil or *ghee*)	¼ cup	Salt	1 Tbs
Coriander leaves chopped	¼ cup	Cumin seeds	1 tsp
Tomato sauce	1 cup	Heavy cream (optional)	½ cup

METHOD:

Chop the onions, ginger, garlic, green chilies and tomatoes fine. Heat the oil on low heat in a pan and fry the onions, ginger, garlic and chilies till light brown. Add the cumin seeds and wait till they start popping and then add the coriander powder, cumin powder, red pepper, turmeric and salt and continue frying for 2 more minutes. Add the tomatoes, stir well. Keep stirring and cook over low heat until the tomatoes become completely soft and paste like and the oil separates from the *masala*. Add the tomato sauce and stir well and simmer for 5 more minutes. Cool and store in the freezer in small zip lock bags and use as needed to make the curries. If you want richer curry, add ½ cup of yogurt or sour cream to the curry *masala*, at the time of preparation of the main dish and cook the curry *masala* on low heat before adding the main ingredient to make the curry. Heavy cream, *garam masala* and the chopped coriander leaves are added 2–3 minutes prior to the end of cooking of the dish. Heat the added ingredients through and serve.

Note: It is very sensible to use olive oil as it is low in saturated fats but it totally loses its flavor when it is heated to high temperature.

Ingredients giving color to the curries

Turmeric : Bright yellow **Red pepper** : Reddish brown **Tomatoes** : Bright red
Onions : Light to dark brown **Green chilies** : Bright green *Garam masala* : Dark brown
Fresh coriander leaves : Fresh green color

Caution : Over cooking or burning will ruin these colors.

The Exquisite World of Indian Cuisine

Thickening agents used in Indian curries

Onions / *Pyaz* : Onions are invariably used in most Indian dishes for gravy. They are finely chopped or puréed and first fried in hot oil in a thick bottom pan so they do not stick to the bottom. Regular stirring is required during this process of frying. They are cooked until they start turning brown. Sometimes a little water can be added to prevent sticking to the pan. Onions are usually fried with chopped ginger, garlic and green pepper to give bulk to the gravy and also make it healthy and flavorful. All the other ingredients are then added to this gravy. Garlic tends to cook faster and therefore it is added at the end.

Heavy cream : It was imbibed into Indian cooking from the Mughlai cuisine. The cream gives nice rich taste to a dish. It is used mainly in meat curries and some vegetable curries like *palak paneer*, *kofta* curry or a mixed vegetable curry. It is mostly added at the end of the cooking. As soon as the curry is done lower the heat, add the cream and simmer for few minutes and serve.

Nuts and seeds / *Mewa* or *beej* : Groundnuts, poppy seeds and sesame seeds are used widely as thickening agents in curries around the country. They were introduced by the Mughals. When groundnuts are used in *curry masala* as a thickening agent, it is important that you keep stirring to prevent it from sticking to the bottom of the pan, otherwise the curry will lose its entire flavor. Nuts not only give texture to the curry but also provide a very good flavor if cooked with care.

Mustard seeds / *Rai* : Mustard seeds are used for gravy only in some parts of India like Bengal and Goa. Ground seeds are used as a paste to coat the fish or chicken before cooking. This paste gives them flavor as well as some gravy. In Bengal, mustard seeds are used as thickening agent in meats and vegetable dishes too.

Peanuts / *Moongphali* : Peanuts are native to Gujarat, many parts of southern India, and are widely used as a thickening agent in curries of these regions.

Lentils : Lentils are used as thickening agents in dishes like *Dhansak* and *Khichdi*. They are either ground first or cooked and then ground and mixed with the basic onion, ginger and garlic mixture and fried in hot oil before being added to the rest of the ingredients.

Yogurt / *Dahi* : It can be used at the end of cooking of the curry *masala*. It adds little sourness and a creamy texture to the curry. Lower the heat and then add the well-beaten and smooth yogurt. Gently stir it in and simmer the curry until done and serve. Plain yogurt can be purchased at your local grocery store but nothing beats homemade yogurt which can be made at home as follows:

Ingredients:

Milk   1 quart   Culture or plain yogurt   1–2 Tbs

Step-by-step method to make fresh yogurt

Boil the milk on medium-low heat in a heavy bottom saucepan. Cool it and bring it to about 110°±5°F and it should feel warm to your finger. Stir in one heaping Tbs of the culture and stir the milk vigorously either by pouring from one pan to another or by stirring with serving spoon for 2 minutes. Cover it and place the bowl with milk in your cooking oven. Turn the oven light on to maintain the warmth especially if it is winter time. Yogurt will set in 5–6 hours. If the milk temperature drops and the milk is not warm to touch yogurt will not set. In which case warm the oven a little for 2 minutes and turn it off and let the cultured milk sit in the oven for another 2 hrs. As soon as the yogurt is set remove from the oven and transfer it to the refrigerator. Stays fresh for 2–3 days in the refrigerator.

Coconut and Coconut milk: Coconut flesh can either be grated fresh or as a dry powder or soaked in water to extract its milk. Sometimes it is ground to paste with other spices and onions in a curry *masala*. When the milk is used then it is added to the curry at the end while the curry is cooking. When it is freshly grated or is a dry powder it is added at the end of preparation in the tempering or *tadka* because coconut cooks very quickly and can burn easily. You can also use canned (unsweetened) cream of coconut, or coconut milk, for thickening a curry. Fresh grated coconut has to be used immediately as it spoils very quickly. Coconut is used in almost all south Indian dishes, in one form or another, be it vegetable or meat curry, *sambhar*, *dosa* or *chutney*. Even in Bengal, Maharashtra and Gujarat it is used quite extensively especially in snacks and various other dishes. Ready to use coconut milk is available at your local grocery store in cans but here is a method to make fresh coconut milk at home.

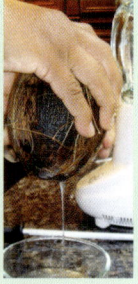

Step-by-step method to make fresh coconut milk

1. Pierce the three eyes of the fresh whole coconut with a corkscrew and drain the coconut water. This is not coconut milk but it is very healthy nutrient water. Pierced coconuts filled with coconut water are sold by the vendors all over India wherever coconut grows. It has digestive properties and, if used regularly, can cure many stomach ailments. (Pix 1-2)

2. Tap around the middle line of the coconut with a hammer and crack it open. Remove the white meat from inside the coconut with a knife and cut the meat in ½ inch pieces. Taste the meat. If it tastes bad – throw it away. (Pix 3-6)

3. Try to remove the outer brown covering with a paring knife and transfer the pieces into a blender. Pour 2 cups of hot water (add 1 cup more water for thinner milk) and grind the meat for about a minute. (Pix 7)

4. Place a cheese cloth over a medium size bowl and transfer the puréed coconut flesh into the cheese cloth and strain the milk. Squeeze the cloth to take out all the milk from the coconut flesh. (Pix 8-11)

You can get about two cups of thick milk from one coconut. If you want thinner milk transfer the residue coconut into the blender and add another 2 cups of hot water. Process the meat again in the blender for a minute and filter it in the same way as before to get some more thinner milk. It is as fresh as the first extract.

Souring agents for the curries and other stir-fries

Tomatoes : Tomatoes are grown throughout the country and are an essential part of a curry for giving it a beautiful red color, and a little sourness. They are usually cooked with onions, ginger, garlic and green chilies in the beginning in hot oil, with the *curry masala*.

Yogurt / *Dahi* : It is often used as souring agent in some meat dishes and sometimes as a fermenting agent to make some breads like *nan* and *bhatura*. Meats are often marinated, prior to cooking, in spiced smoothly beaten yogurt. Sometimes, it is added to the gravy of the curry of dishes like lamb, chicken and fish and in some vegetable curries too. Yogurt gives a creamy as well as a slightly sour taste to the curry. It is also used as a base to make a typical *besan* (gram flour) curry that is one of the very well liked and popular curries of India.

Vinegar / *Sirka* : Vinegar is used to make *paneer* from milk. As a souring agent it is used in areas where there is Portuguese influence like Kerala, Mangalore and Goa. It is used in Parsi cooking also.

Tamarind / *Imli* : The most popular souring agent used in south India. Tamarind grows all over India but it is native to south India. The flesh of its ripe fruit is first soaked in water and then the pulp is extracted by filtering and squeezing the pulp through cheesecloth. The pulp is sold in Indian grocery stores in a bottle and this pulp is what is used in recipes like *sambhar*, *chutneys* and other meat and vegetable dishes. Keep the pulp refrigerated after opening the bottle.

Lemon or Lime / *Nimbu* : Lime is used as a souring agent in the preparation of mint *chutney* and in marinades for chicken and other meats. It is rarely used as a souring agent while cooking. It is always used at the end of cooking. It is a main salad dressing of the tossed green Indian salad and is used in lots of snacks like *chaat* and *hhelpuri*. It is used to make fresh lemonade drink which is also very popular all over India in the summer months. Bottled lemon juice can be bought in a regular grocery store.

Cocum (*Garcinia indica*) : It grows mostly in coastal regions of southern India. The fruit has deep purplish flesh and that is what is used in cooking. It is used in *Sindhi Besan Curry* and in Goan fish curries as a souring agent. It has anti-allergic properties and is also used to make a refreshing drink like lemonade called Kokum water. It gives a very pale purplish color to a dish. It is used in Gujarat, Maharashtra and in Konkani cooking as a souring agent.

Raw mango powder / *Amchoor* : Raw mango slices are dried and then powdered to make *amchoor*. It is used as souring agent in *samosas* filling and some vegetables like okra, bitter gourd, and yams in north Indian cooking. It is also used in marinating fish in some parts of the country. It is also used as a souring agent in snacks and *chaat* (a favorite party snack) and grilled meats.

Dry pomegranate seeds crushed / *Anaardana* : Dried seeds of pomegranate are roasted and powdered to be used as souring agent in chick-peas curry and *samosas*. It is mostly used only in north Indian cooking and its use is limited to the dishes specified.

Special spice mixes
to enhance the flavor of various lentils, rice, meats and vegetable preparations

North Indian spice powder mix / Garam masala
It is used to garnish and flavor numerous dishes and is one of the most used spice mixes in Indian cooking.

Cinnamon powder	1 Tbs	Cloves powder	1 tsp
Cumin seeds powder	1 tsp	Black pepper powder	1 Tbs
Cardamom powder	1½ tsp	Coriander powder	1 Tbs
Nutmeg powder	½ tsp	Mace powder	½ tsp

Mix all the spice powders in a bowl and store in an airtight container. The shelf life is about 2 weeks. You can use it longer but it will not be as fresh and fragrant. No roasting of spices is required prior to making the *masala*.

Five spice mix from Bengal / Panchphoran
The spices mix is used whole for *tadka* or tempering in Bengal to flavor vegetables, lentils and other main course dishes. It is used in powder form also in some recipes.

Fennel seeds	1 Tbs	Nigella seeds	1 Tbs
Fenugreek seeds	1 Tbs	Cumin seeds	1 Tbs
Brown mustard seeds	1 Tbs		

Mix them in equal amounts. Use them whole or grind them as needed. No roasting of spices is needed.

Sambhar spice powder from south India
Used to flavor *sambhar* (a lentil curry from south India). It is a delicious, very fragrant lentil curry prepared with almost every meal in south India. It is served with *dosas*, *Idlis*, plain rice and all appetizers like *vadas*, corn fritters and *uttapam* etc.

Coriander seeds	1½ cup	Red chili peppers broken	1 cup
Fenugreek seeds	2 Tbs	Black mustard seeds	1½ tsp
Cumin seeds	1 Tbs	Cinnamon stick	½ inch
Coconut powder	½ cup	Asafoetida powder	1½ tsp
Turmeric	1 tsp	Bay leaves firmly packed	¼ cup

Roast together chili peppers, fenugreek seeds, mustard seeds, coriander seeds and cumin seeds until fragrant. Set them aside. In the same pan roast coconut powder until light brown. Transfer the roasted coconut powder into the rest of the spices. Dry roast the curry leaves until fragrant and add them also to the rest of the spices. Cool and add the asafoetida powder and turmeric. Store in an airtight container. It will stay fresh for at least 3–4 months in a refrigerator. Grind to use when needed.

South and east Indian spice mixture / Podi powder
The spice mix is used to flavor vegetable dishes and some lentils primarily in south India.

Mung dal	4 Tbs	*Channa dal*	2 Tbs
Urad dal	2 Tbs	Coriander seeds	2 Tbs
Cumin seeds	1 Tbs	Sesame seeds	4 Tbs
Curry leaves	8–10	Coconut powder	2 Tbs
Garlic pods	8–10	Salt	to taste
Turmeric powder	1 tsp	Asafoetida powder	½ tsp
Red chili dry crushed (use according to taste)			2 Tbs

Roast and grind together the *urad dal, channa dal, mung dal*, red dry chilies, sesame seeds, coriander seeds, cumin seeds and curry leaves. Cool the spices and grind them in a coffee grinder. Add the salt, turmeric powder and asafoetida powder and store in an airtight container.

North Indian pickled spice powder / Achari masala
Used for flavoring certain meat and vegetables dishes like okra, eggplant and potatoes.

Chili peppers	2 tsp	Cumin seeds	2 tsp
Mustard seeds	2 tsp	Nigella seeds	2 tsp
Fenugreek seeds	2 tsp	Fennel seeds	2 tsp
Turmeric	1 tsp	Coriander powder	1 Tbs
Salt	to taste	Paprika	1 tsp

Pan-fry the chili peppers, cumin seeds, mustard seeds, nigella seeds, fenugreek seeds and fennel seeds in 3 Tbs of oil. Cool the spices and grind them in a coffee grinder. Add salt, turmeric, coriander powder and paprika to the ground mixture. The *masala* is ready to be used for stuffing okra or eggplants or to marinate or for adding it to the curry of any meat you desire. It is used in *Achari Chicken* in this book. It can be stored for a couple of weeks in an airtight container.

Ceylonese spice powder mix

Spice powder from Sri Lanka, it is used mostly in Ceylonese cooking to flavor vegetable dishes and lentil curries. The spice mix has great similarity with the *podi powder* of south India.

Raw rice	2 Tbs	Cinnamon 2 pieces	2 inch
Cloves	½ tsp	Coriander seeds	4 Tbs
Curry leaves	8–10	Black peppers	1 Tbs
Green cardamom seeds	1 tsp	Cumin seeds	2 Tbs
Mustard seeds	1 Tbs	Coconut powder (grated unsweetened)	2 Tbs

Roast the rice on a hot iron griddle on medium low heat until light red in color and set it aside in a bowl. Roast the coconut powder separately and set it aside. Transfer the rest of the spices into the hot skillet and roast them until just fragrant. Remove them from heat and add the roasted rice and roasted coconut. Cool the roasted spices and store them in an airtight container. Grind them before use as needed to flavor.

Tandoori (Grilling) masala

It is used mostly in grilling *Seekh Kebabs,* Chicken *Tikka*, fish and other meats and vegetables cooked on the grill.

Paprika	1 tsp	Coriander powder	1 Tbs
Cumin powder	1 tsp	Red pepper	1 tsp
Amchoor	1 Tbs	Garam masala	1 tsp
Salt	1 tsp	Mustard seeds or ground (crushed)	1 tsp

Mix the powders and add to the marinade or as directed in the recipe. No roasting of spices is needed.

Chaat masala

It is used to flavor the fruit snacks and other snacks as directed in the recipes.

Red pepper	1 tsp	Garam masala	1 tsp
Salt	1 tsp	Amchoor	1 Tbs
Kala namak (Black salt)	1 tsp	Cumin powder (roasted ground)	1 Tbs

Mix together the powders and use the mixture for flavoring your favorite snacks.

Baffad masala (from Hyderabad)

This *masala* is used for flavoring pork chops, chicken legs, thighs and breast pieces of chicken, fish fillets and lamb chops.

Brown cardamom seeds	1 tsp	Cumin seeds	1 Tbs
Cloves	2 Tbs	Pepper corns	1½ Tbs
Cinnamon sticks crushed	1 Tbs	Coriander seeds	½ cup
Red chilies dry crushed	1 ½ cup		

Dry roast the spices in an iron skillet on medium heat until fragrant. Cool and transfer the spices into a container and add the turmeric, store till ready to use. Just before use, grind them as needed in a spice grinder or a coffee grinder.

Rasam masala mix

Rasam masala is used in a soup known in south India as *Rasam*. It is usually served before the dinner. It is a *toor dal* soup flavored with tamarind pulp, tomatoes, coriander leaves, lemon, crushed garlic, ginger, a dash of *garam masala*, and *rasam masala* mix.

Dry red chilies crushed	¼ cup	Coriander seeds	½ cup
Cumin seeds	1 Tbs	Curry leaves	8–10
Black pepper corns	1 tsp	Mustard seeds	¾ tsp

Dry roast the spices on a hot iron griddle on medium-low heat until they become fragrant and lightly roasted. Cool them and store them in an airtight container. Keep the container at a cool place. If refrigerated the mix can stay fresh for months. Grind the spices before use.

Bharuchi (Mughlai) masala

It is a *masala* mix that originated in the Mughlai kitchens and has a Persian and Chinese touch especially in its use of nutmeg, star anise and mace. It is similar to the five-spice mix that is used extensively in the Cantonese cooking and consists of cinnamon, Sichuan red hot peppers, cloves, fennel seeds and star anise.

Cinnamon pieces	2 Tbs	Whole cloves	2 Tbs
Star anise	2 Tbs	Black pepper corns	2 Tbs
Cardamom seeds	2 Tbs	Mace crushed	2 Tbs

Mix all the spices in a bowl (no roasting of spices is required) and store them as a mixture. Grind them as needed to flavor any chicken, lamb, beef or pork curry. You will love the fragrance of the curry.

Reiachado masala mix (from Goa)

This marinating *masala* is hot and tangy with a Portuguese influence in the use of vinegar, abundant use of jalapeño peppers, dry red and black peppers corns. It is used to marinate prawns, fish, and meatballs.

Black peppers	2 Tbs	Crushed garlic	2 Tbs
Curry leaves	4–6	Tamarind pulp	1 Tbs

The Exquisite World of Indian Cuisine

Vinegar	4 Tbs	Turmeric powder	1 tsp
Cumin seeds	1 tsp	Dry red chilies crushed	2
Ginger chopped	1 tsp	Salt	to taste
Jalapeño peppers (chopped)	1 tsp		

Mix together tamarind pulp, fine chopped jalapeño peppers, crushed garlic, chopped ginger, chopped curry leaves and lemon juice in a bowl and set it aside. Grind together peppercorns, red pepper and cumin seeds in a coffee grinder and mix in with mixture of spices in the bowl. Add the turmeric powder and salt as directed in the recipe.

Tea *masala*
This *masala* is used to flavor the Indian tea or *chai*.

Cardamom powder	½ tsp	Cinnamon powder	½ tsp
Cloves powder	½ tsp	Ginger powder	½ tsp
Black pepper powder	¼ tsp		

Mix the powders together and use when needed to flavor your tea. It can stay fresh for 6–8 weeks on the kitchen shelf.

Goda masala
Mix from Maharashtra. It is used in many vegetarian and meat dishes and lentils. The cuisine of Maharashtra includes hot and aromatic dishes which are flavored with hot and tangy *Goda masala*. It can be added before or after to vary the taste from mild to strong.

Cloves	1 tsp	Cinnamon	2 tsp
Black cardamom seeds	2 tsp	Bay leaves	5–6
Dagadphool	1 tsp	*Naagkeshar*	1 tsp
Badalphool	1 tsp	Red chilies	2½ Tbs
Sesame seeds	2½ Tbs	Coconut powder	1 cup
Asafoetida	2 tsp	Turmeric powder	1 tsp
Oil	½ cup	Salt	1 Tbs

Heat ¼ cup of oil and fry the cloves, cinnamon, cardamom, *Dagadphool* (a lichen), *Naagkeshar* (*Nagchampa* flower), *Badalphool* (star anise), bay leaves and lastly cumin seeds. Remove the fried spices onto a plate lined with paper towel and drain the oil. Fry the red chilies and coriander seeds one after another and transfer them to the same plate. Roast the coconut powder over low heat and set it aside. Fry the sesame seeds and mix them with coconut powder. Grind the spices very fine in a coffee grinder and set them aside. Grind the coconut and sesame seeds together and mix them with rest of the *masala*. Add salt, turmeric powder and asafoetida to the mixture. Stir and mix the spices well. Store in an air tight container. It will stay fresh for a long time. It is hard to find *naagkeshar* and *dagadphool* outside India but some Indian grocery stores may carry them. If not available this *masala* can be made without these two ingredients also and it will still be as good.

Huliyana masala
(Famously known in Hyderabad and Karnataka). This *masala* is used to make *Masala Bhaat* (rice) chicken curry or other meat dishes.

Channa dal	½ cup	Urad dal	2 tsp
Fenugreek seeds	½ tsp	Red chilies whole	2 Tbs

Dry roast the spices on an iron griddle and cool. Grind them into powder in a coffee grinder and store in a cool place. It will stay fresh in the refrigerator for a long time. Grind it before using.

Malwani masala
(From the Malabar coastal region of Karnataka and Kerala): Is used in gravies for chicken, meats, vegetables and rice dishes.

Dry red chilies	5 cups	Coriander seeds	2 cups
Cloves	¾ tsp	Peppercorns	1 Tbs
Fennel seeds	2 Tbs	Cumin seeds	1 tsp
Shahi zeera	1 tsp	Cinnamon (two)	1 inch
Stone flower	1 Tbs	*Naagkeshar*	1 tsp
Mustard seeds	1 tsp	Turmeric powder	1 tsp
Asafoetida	1 tsp	Nutmeg	2
Badalphool	½ tsp	Black cardamom seeds	½ tsp

Dry roast the ingredients, cool and grind them to use.

Bombay *masala* mix / *Pathare Prabhu masala*
It is used by the *Pathare Prabhu* community of Bombay. This community has a great history of nobility and integrity. They have preserved their traditions and culture. They use it to flavor their vegetable curries, meat curries and rice dishes.

Coriander seeds	1 cup	Cumin seeds	3 Tbs
Mustard seeds	3 Tbs	Whole wheat	¼ cup
Channa dal	¼ cup	Dry red chilies	1 cup
Turmeric powder	1 Tbs	Fenugreek seeds	1 tsp
Asafoetida	⅛ tsp	Peppercorns	1 Tbs

Dry roast all on an iron griddle (except turmeric powder and asafoetida) individually and cool. Grind them for use.

Special flours, lentils, cereals and other ingredients used in Indian cooking

Whole wheat flour / *Aatta* flour or *chappati* flour : For making the typical Indian *chappati* or *roti* (staple diet of north Indians) nothing is better than the whole-wheat flour. It is available in Indian grocery stores and sold as *chappati* flour. It can be substituted by fine ground whole-wheat flour for tortillas available in regular markets.

Gram flour / *Besan ka Aatta* : It is prepared by grinding black grams and is very high in protein content. It is used extensively in Indian cooking to make vegetable fritters or *pakoras* and it is also mixed, Half-and-half, with wheat flour to make breads for diabetics. It is also used to make some desserts like *burfi* and *laddoos*. It also acts as a binding agent.

Rice flour / *Chawal ka Aatta* : It is used to make dessert called *phirni* in north India, but in south India, rice flour is used as a staple food. It is used most extensively in making many main course dishes like *dosas, idlis* and *appam*. It is available in Indian grocery stores.

Cream of wheat / *Suji* : Semolina or farina is the granular cereal derived from the proteinaceous germ of wheat. It is used in India for making desserts like *halwa, gulabjaman* and *ladoo* etc. It is a highly prized cereal of India and is used in several savory dishes like *rava dosa, idli, uppama* etc. It is available at your local Indian grocery store. Partially cooked cream of wheat is used as a breakfast cereal and is commonly available at any local grocery store in the western countries.

All purpose flour / *Maida* : Fine ground wheat flour is used in making only few breads like *nans* and some desserts in India but in western countries it is more or less a staple flour in making all breads, cakes and some sauces and has many more uses. It can be purchased at grocery stores anywhere in the world.

Millet flour / *Bajre ka Aatta* : Obtained from the plant called *Panicum Milaceum*. Millet flour is used the most in Gujarat, Rajasthan and Punjab states of India in making griddle breads. You can buy it at your local Indian grocery store. It is the oldest and highly nutritive grain of India.

Sorgham flour / *Jawar ka Aatta* : Related to millet, Sorgham is used to make breads in India. It is highly proteinaceous and has no gluten. Therefore, It is mostly mixed with wheat flour to make breads. Some of its varieties produce sugar. It is the third most produced grain in America but is not used for human consumption.

Corn flour / *Makki ka Aatta* : The flour is made into delicious breads in all parts of India especially in Punjab but it is not a staple food as it is in Mexico and western countries. Corn is consumed fresh as a whole stalk grilled and smeared with lemon juice, salt and pepper called *bhutta* and it is sold by vendors at street corners all over India. It is not used as extensively as a cooked vegetable as in the western countries. It can be purchased from Indian as well as Western grocery stores.

Cream of rice: Used in making *rava idli or dosa* in south Indian cooking and making the *kheer* or pudding in north India. Only available in Indian grocery stores.

Fine vermicelli / *Sevian* : It is a type of vermicelli. Cooked especially on *Eid* (a Muslim festival) by the Muslim community as *sevian* which is a very well liked dessert all over India. These are also cooked as spicy noodles and used for snacks. Available in Indian and Pakistani grocery stores.

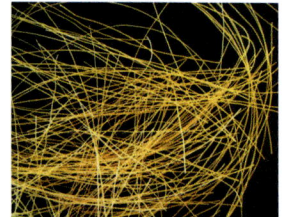

***Basmati* Rice**: It is long grain very fragrant rice grown in the foothills of the Himalayas. This rice is also now grown in America and is available in local supermarkets but does not match the fine quality and fragrance of Indian grown *basmati* rice.

The Exquisite World of Indian Cuisine

Spiced and roasted wafers / *Papads or Papadums* : These delightful thin wafers made from lentil flour are sold in Indian grocery stores and are always made commercially as their preparation needs special skill and experience. They are made of *urad* or *mung dal* flour, oil and spices kneaded well with water into a very smooth and tight dough. Then they are rolled very thin like tortilla and air-dried. These are served with a regular meal toasted or deep fried in hot oil. These can be served as a snack and can be bought as mild or highly spiced, from your local Indian grocery store. Papadums are the ornaments of a Gujarati meal.

Indian dehydrated milk / *Khoa* : This is another preparation from homogenized milk. The milk is cooked on low heat until it dries up to a stiff dough. Continuous stirring is important because milk tends to stick to the bottom of the pan and burns very easily. This is a key ingredient which is used to make desserts like *burfi, gulabjaman, pinnis,* carrot *halwa* etc. Nowadays *khoa* is substituted by using 'Half and Half' dry milk powder or heavy cream and cooked on low heat stirring continuously, until it is dry. Now it is ready to be used as needed.

Indian style Ricotta cheese / *Paneer* : It can be purchased as a slab from an Indian grocery store. Refrigerate until ready to use. Ricotta cheese (available with your local grocer) is very wet, and when it is used as *paneer*, the water has to be squeezed out by putting a lot of weight over it for at least 4–6 hours. Remove Ricotta from the plastic container onto a double layer of paper towel and cover it with more paper towel. Wrap it in a small cloth towel and put some heavy object over it to squeeze out all the moisture (3–4 hours). When it is a firm slab, cut into cubes and use as directed. You can prepare *paneer* at home too. Follow the given preparation method.

Ingredients

Whole milk	1 gallon	Half-and-half	1–2 cups
Vinegar	½–⅔ cup	Or cream of tartar	2 Tbs
Or Lemon juice	¼ cup		

METHOD

Heat the milk in a heavy bottom two quart saucepan on medium low heat and add the 'Half and Half'. Bring it to a full boil. Remove from heat and add the vinegar. Stir it well. The milk will curdle. Set it aside. Line a colander with cheese cloth and let the cloth hang around at least 6 inches and place the colander over a large pan to hold the whey. Pour the curdled milk into the cheese cloth lined colander. Lift the sides of the cheese cloth up from around the colander and squeeze out the whey with your hands as much as you can. Wash it with running cold water, squeeze and wrap it up in a towel and place on a flat chopping board. Place a heavy weight over it for 2–4 hours.

Once it is firm and forms a slab, take it out of the cheese cloth transfer it into a pan to hold it flat and pour some whey over it to store it in the refrigerator until ready to use. Cut it into cubes or use as it is needed. Cheese cubes are usually deep fried to make curries and added into *pulav* and when fresh and soft it is used to make desserts like *rasgulla, burfi, sandesh* and *chum chum* etc. Its spiced roasted cubes are served as an appetizer.

INTRODUCTION

Dal / Legumes used in Indian cooking

Black beans / *Urad* : It is used extensively in Indian cooking. These are black beans just like *mung* beans but lot more proteinaceous. They are cooked whole, split or washed. In south India its flour is used in making *dosa* and *idli* (staple food of southern India besides rice). Sometimes it is browned in oil and is used to flavor rice and other vegetable dishes to give them a little crunchy taste.

Split hulled black grams / *Channa dal* : Used in making *dal* in north and south and are also used in tempering to garnish rice and vegetable dishes. In ground form its uses are mentioned under 'gram flour'.

Yellow beans /*Toor* : These small pale yellow beans cook rather quickly and are used mostly in south India to make *sambhar* and also cooked sometimes as *dal* all over India. They also make a very good base for some soups in Indian cooking.

Very small red beans / *Masoor* : The whole beans are beige in color and when hulled and washed, they have pale reddish color. They do not take very long to cook.

Green beans / *Mung* : *Mung* beans are extensively used for bean sprouts as salads in various parts of the world. In Indian cooking they are used as whole, split or washed for making *dals*. They are dark green on the outside and light yellow on the inside. They are easily digestible and therefore given to very young children when they start their solids. They cook pretty fast and are also used for making *khichdi*.

Chick-peas (*Garbanzos*) / *Kabuli channa* : Chick-peas (highly proteinaceous among all the beans) are commonly used in cuisines all over the world. They are never sold split or hulled and are cooked always as whole beans. In mid-eastern cooking these are a source of many main dishes like Humus and some of their sauces and soups. In Indian cooking they are usually curried (Chick-pea Curry or *Khatta Channa*) or added to salads or *chaats* (snack). They used to take a long time to cook but pressure cooking has made it very easy to cook them. They are always preferred over other beans as a good meal for their rich protein content.

Red kidney beans / *Rajmah* : They are also quite proteinaceous and used all over the world. In western countries they are served as re-fried beans and also used in soups. In Mexican cooking, these beans play a major role in preparation of almost every dish. Kidney beans are always sold whole – and cooked as whole beans. In India they are very popular in Punjab and are called *Rajmah*. Here, they are served curried as well as in salads and some snacks. These beans can be bought in any grocery store anywhere in the world.

Whole black grams / *Channa* : Whole grams are cooked in their dry as well as green form and their curry is very popular in North of india. Dry roasted grams are sold by the vendors as "Channa Jor Garam" a delicious spicy proteinaceous snack every body likes.

Peas / *Matar dal* : Dry peas are often used to make dal and the beans are either green or yellow. Both make a very delicious preparation. In the western countries pea-soup with Ham is very popular.

Black eye beans / *Lobia* : These dry beans are cooked all over India. Sometimes tender green black beans or *lobia* is also available with the vegetable vendors and their curry is more delicious than the dry beans. Its flour is used to make fritters in some parts of India.

Lima beans and soya beans : are usually cooked as a vegetable while they are still green and fresh.

Pictures: ©Chandni Arora

Urad split

Black gram split / *Channa dal*

Urad washed

Red Kidney Beans / *Rajmah*

Chick-peas / *Kabuli Channa* Mung washed Black eye Beans / *Lobia* Black gram / *Channa*

Utensils and appliances needed in an Indian kitchen

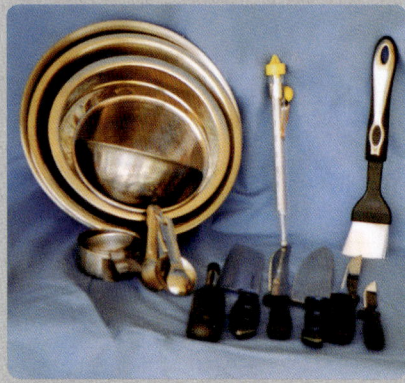

A set of measuring cups, mixing bowls and measuring spoons; a set of knives, a basting brush and a candy thermometer for deep-frying and making sweets.

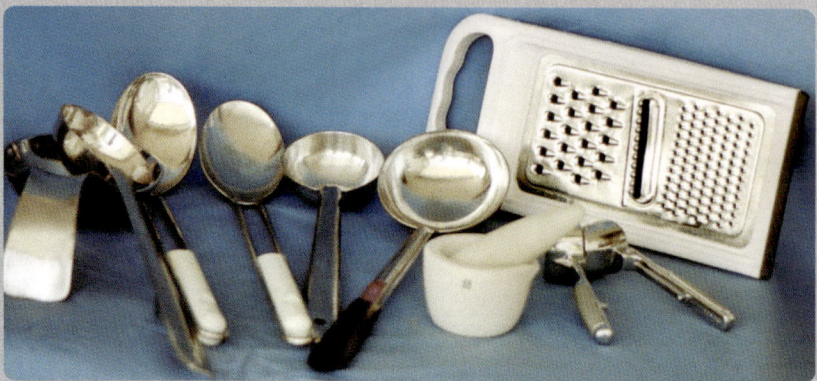

Serving spoons, a grater and a mortar with pestle.

A deep, heavy 10–12 inch non-stick frying pan with a lid, a wok (*karahi*).

Colanders for washing vegetables.

A container with spatulas, serving spoons and turners with salt & pepper shaker.

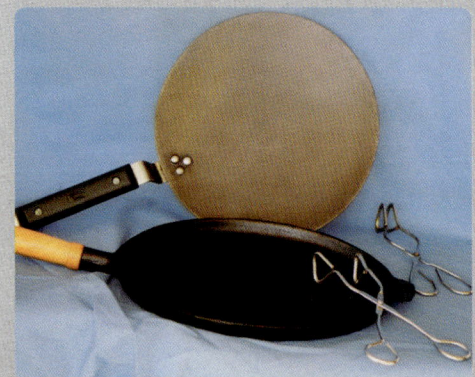

A *tawa* or a iron skillet for making flat breads and *paranthas*.

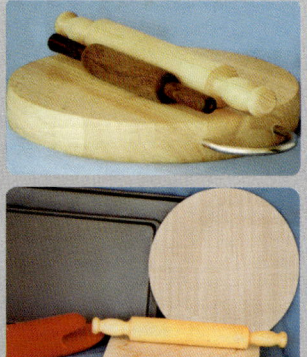

A rolling pin and a thick wooden board for rolling *chappatis* and *pooris*. Some baking trays.

An *idli* stand for making *idlis* and grilling pan used for grilling in the oven.

The Exquisite World of Indian Cuisine

These are some of the items that are used most frequently in an Indian kitchen

A pressure cooker and a steamer.

Couple of heavy bottom 4–6 quart Dutch ovens for making *dals* and *pulav*.

A wok for stir-frying dry curries and mesh basket for deep-frying.

Large non-stick spatulas for turning griddle breads and *paranthas*.

A food processor, blender to grind lentils and rice for *dosas* and *idlis* and spice grinder to grind roasted spices.

Oil or *ghee* dispensing bottles and jar.

Tea pots and strainers.

CHAPTER 2

Appetizers and Snacks

There are many appetizers in Indian food, as Indians love to snack and munch. Afternoons are tea times and Indians love to socialize. There is always time for a small sweet and spicy snack for the guests. As is the custom, it is common practice to serve the guest with a cup of tea and some snack. The smell of spices and *chutneys* served with various appetizers activate your taste buds.

Popular snacks like *pakoras*, *samosas*, *corn puffs*, *cheese puffs*, *tapioca potato puffs*, *cutlets* are fritters and finger foods. You can make them by dipping the raw or cooked vegetables into spicy gram flour batter. They are then deep fried. Each of these snacks are served with a certain *chutney* like coconut, mint, tamarind or red pepper *chutney*. From the north of India comes various fruit *chaats*, *golgappas* (thin wafers filled with boiled chopped potatoes, chick-peas, *Tamarind Chutney*, and *Zeera paani*), *dahi-*

vadas, and the regular *chaat*. From Maharashtra and Gujarat come the *bhelpuri*, *poha* or *aval*, *dhokla*, *khandvi*, and *muthia*. Appetizers like *vadas*, *bondas*, *uppama*, come from the south and are proteinaceous and rich in carbohydrates as lentils and grains play a major part in their preparation. Though south Indian yet they are popular all over the country. They are served with *sambhar* and *chutney*. There are several baked and grilled snacks and in this category come the *kebabs*, *chicken tikka masala*, various *cutlets*, *cocktail meatballs*, *cocktail shrimp* and *cocktail paneer*. These snacks have their origin during the Mughal times. *Shaami kebabs* and *chicken tikka masala* are a perfect cocktail choice. All these snacks are served as appetizers or hors d'oeuvres and they go beautifully as a first course with any dinner of your choice.

Some Indian spices, legumes and vegetables are not available at your regular local grocery stores and they have been used in this book. Fresh herbs and spices like fenugreek leaves and its seeds, dry unsweetened coconut powder, pomegranate seed powder, *garam masala*, curry leaves, tamarind and special flours like gram flour, *urad* flour and rice flour (needed to make the various kinds of fritters) are only available at your local Indian grocery stores. All spices are sold in bulk there and a trip to your local Indian grocery store will be very appropriate and economical before you venture into making some authentic Indian food. I welcome you into the world of Indian cuisine and hope you will find your journey as interesting as I have. *Bon appetit*.

Grilled Chicken
Chicken Tikka

UTTAR PRADESH

An excellent appetizer from north India for all festive occasions. Baked in the oven or grilled on an electric grill until light brown and tender. Tastes best when served with mint *chutney*.

METHOD

1. Dry roast the cumin seeds, grams, poppy seeds on a iron griddle until aromatic and grind them. Set them aside.
2. Prepare the marinade by mixing ground roasted grams, poppy seeds, cumin seeds into the yogurt. Add chopped spices like ginger, garlic, green chilies, and onions, tomato paste and paprika. Mix in the lemon juice, red pepper, coriander powder, salt and 1Tbs of *ghee*. Stir well to make a smooth paste.
3. Put chicken pieces into this marinade for 2–3 hours, if possible, but they can be cooked after an hour of marinating.
4. Broil them in an oven on skewers or grill outdoors until light brown. Turn them and brush them with the remaining *ghee* during cooking.
5. Serve them sprinkled with sliced onions and slices of lemon, roasted ground cumin seeds, *amchoor* and *garam masala* and sprinkle with chopped coriander leaves.
6. They make an excellent appetizer before dinner or can be served as hors d'oeuvres with drinks.

SERVES 6 – 8

Ingredients

Breast of chicken cut into 1 inch pieces	2 lbs
Yogurt	½ cup
Tomato paste	1 Tbs
Paprika	1 tsp
Ginger chopped	1 Tbs
Garlic chopped	1 Tbs
Green chilies chopped (optional)	4
Onions chopped	1 cup
Raw papaya or raw mango chopped	¼ cup
Or	
Amchoor or dry mango powder	2 Tbs
Lemon juice or vinegar	2 Tbs
Poppy seeds ground	1 Tbs
Grams roasted & ground (optional)	1 Tbs
Red pepper	to taste
Coriander powder	1 Tbs
Cumin seeds roasted and ground	1 Tbs
Garam masala	½ tsp
Coriander leaves chopped	2 Tbs
Salt	1 tsp
Clarified butter or *ghee* or Vegetable oil	2 Tbs

Ground Meat Kebabs
Seekh Kebab

UTTAR PRADESH

Seekh kebabs are minced meat balls roasted on skewers on grills or broiled in the oven. They are one of the most popular appetizers of north India. Well-cooked kebabs are soft, juicy and very flavorful. They go very well with a drink and make an excellent hors d'oeuvre.

SERVES 8 – 10

Ingredients

Beef or lamb ground lean	1½ lbs
Pork or Turkey ground	½ lb
Onions	½ cup
Ginger	1 Tbs
Garlic	1 Tbs
Raw mango chopped	1 Tbs
Or	
Raw papaya chopped	1 Tbs
Red pepper (optional)	1 tsp
Coriander seeds	1 Tbs
Black pepper	1 tsp
Bread crumbs	½–1 cup
Or	
Gram flour	¼ cup
Poppy seeds (ground)	1 tsp
Cumin seeds	1 tsp
Almonds (ground)	1 Tbs
Yogurt	2 Tbs
Garam masala	1 tsp
Salt	1½ tsp
Coriander leaves	1½ Tbs
Green chilies chopped	1 Tbs
Lemon juice	2 Tbs
Roasted cumin powder	2 Tbs
Mint leaves	a few

METHOD

1. Roast cumin seeds, coriander seeds, almonds, poppy seeds on a hot skillet and grind the mixture. Put it aside.

2. Mix the ground beef with ground turkey, lime juice and salt and let it sit in this marinade for a couple of hours.

3. Add to the meat chopped onion (squeezed of any water), ginger, garlic, green pepper, raw mango or raw papaya chopped, gram flour, yogurt, red pepper, black pepper, ground spices mixture, *garam masala* and the chopped coriander leaves. Add water to make the mixture a little sticky, if needed.

4. Divide the mixture into 30 equal parts and pass a skewer through each of them and fold the meat around the skewer. Leave them on the skewer for 10–15 minutes before grilling on a charcoal or gas grill. Broil them in an electric oven until light brown. Place the skewers on a lined baking dish with a grill so the fat can drain to the bottom of the dish. Keep turning them around the skewer until they are brown and done. Brush them with little oil or *ghee* during cooking.

5. Serve them with mint *chutney* topped and sprinkled with ground roasted cumin powder, *garam masala* and slices of onions, mint leaves and lemon juice.

Meat Cutlets
Shaami Kebab (Shikampuri Kebab)

UTTAR PRADESH

Ground meat patties with a spicy filling of nuts and raisins, pan-fried in a little oil make an appealing appetizer. They are usually served with mint or tamarind *chutney*, tomato ketchup or salad.

METHOD

1. Cook meat in a skillet in 1 Tbs of oil or *ghee*. Add the onions, green chilies and ginger and cook until the water dries up.
2. Add the chopped garlic, red pepper, salt, dry fenugreek leaves and *amchoor*.
3. Mix the spices into the meat mixture and remove from heat.
4. Add 1 cup of bread crumbs, eggs, tomato sauce and *garam masala*, and knead the mixture well with hands. Add more bread crumbs, if needed.
5. Divide the mixture into 20 equal parts and shape them into balls. Set them aside and prepare the filling as follows.

Filling

1. Heat the remaining 2 Tbs of oil in the same skillet and fry the onions until light brown. Add the chopped slivered almonds, raisins, salt, red pepper, and *garam masala* and mix the ingredients well.
2. Stir-fry for 2 minutes or until the almond are a shade of brown and remove from heat.
3. Add the chopped coriander leaves, *amchoor* and mix well.

Stuffing the meatballs to make flat patties:

1. Make a hole in the meat ball and fill it with 1 tsp of filling. Push the filling down and close the hole.
2. Flatten the meatballs gently into a patty making sure that the stuffing does not come out.
3. Pan-fry them in oil in a heavy-bottom skillet until light brown or broil them in an oven, brush them with *ghee* during cooking.
4. Take them out with slotted spoon onto a plate lined with a paper towel and serve them with a *chutney* of choice or mint *chutney*. Sprinkle some roasted cumin powder and *amchoor*.

Note: 2 cups of mashed potatoes can be used instead of bread crumbs to make softer patties.

SERVES 10 – 12

Ingredients

Ground lamb, beef or turkey	2 lb
Onions finely chopped	½ cup
Ginger finely chopped	1 Tbs
Garlic finely chopped	1 Tbs
Salt	1 tsp
Red pepper	1 tsp
Green chilies finely chopped (optional)	1 tsp
Vegetable oil or Ghee	3 Tbs
Eggs	2
Tomato sauce	2 Tbs
Amchoor	1 Tbs
Garam masala	1 tsp
Vegetable oil (for frying the patties)	¼ cup
Bread crumbs	2 cups

Ingredients for stuffing

Vegetable oil or *ghee*	1 Tbs
Onions chopped	½ cup
Almonds blanched finely chopped	2 Tbs
Raisins	2 Tbs
Red pepper	½ tsp
Salt	½ tsp
Coriander leaves	½ cup
Amchoor	1 Tbs
Garam masala	1 tsp

Salmon Cutlets
Machhli ke Kebab

Tantalizing fish *kebabs* are a sure favorite of everyone. Low fat, proteinaceous and delicious. Mix the fish pieces with mashed potatoes, ginger, garlic, green chilies, gram flour and marinade them in spiced yogurt and grill them.

METHOD

1. Marinade the fish fillets in lemon juice and salt. Set them aside for at least ½ hour.
2. Remove the fish from the marinade leaving the lemon juice behind and dice them into small pieces. Set them aside.
3. Mix the mashed potatoes, ginger, garlic, green chilies, salt, pepper and gram flour.
4. Add the diced fish to the potato mixture and make patties.
5. Beat the yogurt smooth and add red pepper, salt, ground roasted cumin powder, dry fenugreek leaves, crushed fennel seeds, lemon juice and oil or *ghee*.
6. Coat the fish patties in the yogurt mixture and broil them in a grilling pan in the oven for 10–12 minutes until light brown. Brush them with oil or *ghee* in between and turn once or twice. Remove from oven and garnish with lemon slices and slices of onions and chopped coriander leaves. Serve them with mint *chutney*.

SERVES 4 – 6

Ingredients

Fillet of any large fish Halibut, Pomfret, or Salmon	1 lb
Lemon juice	2 Tbs
Mashed potatoes	1 cup
Ginger chopped	1 Tbs
Garlic chopped	1 tsp
Green chilies hot	1 Tbs
Gram flour	2 Tbs
Salt	1 tsp
Pepper	½ tsp
Lemon slices	a few

Marinade:

Yogurt	½ cup
Lemon juice	2 Tbs
Crushed fennel seeds	1 tsp
Fenugreek leaves dry	2 Tbs
Vegetable oil or *ghee*	1 Tbs
Ground roasted cumin powder	1 tsp
Salt	½–1 tsp
Red pepper	1 tsp
Coriander leaves chopped	1 Tbs
Vegetable oil or *ghee*	1 Tbs

Indian Cheese Cutlets
Paneer Cutlets

These cheese cutlets are made with a mixture of mashed boiled potatoes, homemade cheese or Ricotta cheese, bread crumbs, spices, onions, green chilies, red pepper, chopped coriander leaves, lemon juice, salt, *garam masala* and finely chopped peanuts or cashew nuts. They make a great appetizer and snack particularly for a formal occasion.

METHOD

1. Mix the mashed potatoes with well blended cheese, arrow-root flour and 1 cup of bread crumbs. Add to this mixture chopped onions, ginger, garlic, green chilies, green coriander leaves, fenugreek leaves and mix them well.

2. Add also the ground roasted cumin powder, red pepper, black pepper, *garam masala*, salt, lemon juice, nuts and one Tbs of *ghee*. Knead everything until well blended and make 10 patties about 2½–3 inch in diameter. Roll them in beaten eggs and then coat them completely in fine bread crumbs, and set them aside.

3. Heat 4 cups of oil in a wok. Fry until they are golden brown on both sides on medium low heat. Keep turning them when needed. It takes about 5–7 minutes. Serve them with tomato sauce or tamarind *chutney*. They can be pan fried in ¼ cup oil too!

Note: Ready to use *paneer* is available at your local Indian grocery. Ricotta cheese in western stores is comparable to Indian cheese called *paneer*. Ricotta usually is very wet when you buy it. In order to use it as *paneer*, drain out its water by putting some weight on it for a couple of hours.

SERVES 6 – 8

Ingredients

Boiled potatoes mashed	1½ cups
Paneer or Ricotta cheese (completely drained and firm) creamed	1 cup
Bread crumbs	3 cups
Arrow-root flour	2 Tbs
Eggs	2
Salt	1 tsp
Black pepper	1 tsp
Garlic chopped	1 tsp
Ginger chopped	1 tsp
Green onions chopped	½ cup
Green chilies chopped (optional)	1 Tbs
Ground roasted cumin seeds	1 Tbs
Green coriander leaves chopped	2 Tbs
Fresh fenugreek or dry fenugreek leaves	1 Tbs
Red pepper	1 tsp
Lemon juice	1 Tbs
Vegetable oil for frying	4 cups
Cashew or peanuts chopped (roasted)	¼ cup
Garam masala	½ tsp
Vegetable oil or *ghee*	1 Tbs

Potato Cutlets
Aalu ki Tikki

Potato patties stuffed with curried lentils, peas, onions and spices are very delicious. This north Indian snack is mostly favored as a light teatime snack. They also serve as an appetizer and are served with mint or tamarind *chutney*.

SERVES 6 – 8

Ingredients

Potatoes	2 lbs
Arrow-root flour	2 Tbs
Bread crumbs	1 cup
Salt	1 tsp
Green chilies (optional) chopped	2
Ginger	1 Tbs
Garlic	1 Tbs
Cumin seeds	1 tsp
Dry fenugreek leaves	1 Tbs
Green peas	½ cup
Onions chopped	1 cup
Channa dal soaked overnight	½ cup
Red pepper	½–1 tsp
Vegetable oil	4 Tbs
Water as needed	
Garam masala	½ tsp
Coriander powder	1 Tbs
Green coriander leaves chopped	1 Tbs

METHOD

1. Boil the potatoes and peal them. Mix 2 Tbs of arrow-root flour, salt and 1 cup of bread crumbs into it. Stir and mash smooth.

2. Cook the chopped onion, ginger, garlic and green chilies in a skillet in 2 Tbs of oil until light brown and add the cumin seeds. Wait till they pop. Now add the soaked and washed *channa dal* and stir-fry until light brown. Add the peas, dry fenugreek leaves, red pepper, coriander powder, salt, *garam masala* and water, and cook until the *channa dal* is tender. Add the chopped coriander leaves and set aside.

3. Shape the mashed potatoes into balls and stuff them with 1 tsp full of peas and spiced *dal* mixture and flatten them into round or oval patties. Making sure that none of the stuffing is showing outside the mashed potatoes covering. Set aside.

4. Heat a large iron skillet or a pancake maker and cover the surface with a layer of oil. Heat for a minute. Place the patties on the hot oiled skillet and pan-fry them until dark golden brown. Serve them with mint or tamarind *chutney*.

Note: Arrow-root plant has been in use since times unknown. It is called the obedience plant (*Maranta arundinacea*). It is found in America and some of its species are found in India as well. The plants have tuberous roots containing large amounts of starch. The main use of the arrow-root is as a thickening agent. The rhizomes are peeled, grated and soaked in water. The water turns milky-white and the residue of this milky water is dried and used as an arrow-root starch. It is a white powder similar in texture as corn starch but has lot more potential as a thickening agent. It thickens at a lower temperature and it is clear without any flavor. It also grows in the West Indies. The natives use the paste from its powder to remove poison from the wounded with poisoned arrows, hence the name arrow-root. Its starch is easily digestible and is used to make cookies for infants. It is made into noodles by the Korean people and they also use it in puddings, cakes, hot sauces and jellies. Arrow-root flour is also a great replacement for people who are allergic to gluten found in wheat flour. This starchy powder besides being used in cooking is also used as a baby powder and has been used for making paper.

The Exquisite World of Indian Cuisine

Jain Temple, Ranakpur, Rajasthan

Lotus Root Cutlets
Kamal Kakdi ki Tikki

Lotus flower is exotic to look at and it is revered in India. Hindu gods Vishnu (Lord of well being and prosperity) and Lakshmi (goddess of wealth) have their abode in a blooming lotus flower. Its roots are very much sought after for making curries, croquettes and pickles. This cutlet or croquette recipe gives you a pretty good idea of its crunchy and rich taste. The roots are boiled first and then mixed with mashed potatoes and spices. The patties thus made can be curried or they can be served as an appetizer with a *chutney*.

METHOD

1. Dice and boil the lotus roots until soft and chop them into small cubes and transfer them into a mixing bowl. Add the mashed potatoes, arrow-root flour, ginger, green chilies, garlic, onions, chopped coriander leaves, lemon juice, salt, pepper, coriander powder, dry roasted cumin powder, dry fenugreek leaves, bread crumbs and *garam masala*. Mix them all and make into patties 2 inches in diameter and ¼ inch thick.

2. Heat ¼ cup oil in a heavy-bottom 12 inch frying pan or skillet. Transfer the patties, few at a time, and brown them both sides by turning them occasionally. When they are done, transfer them to a paper towel lined dish or a bowl and let the oil drain. Serve as an appetizer with mint or tomato *chutney* sprinkled with coriander leaves.

> SERVES 4 – 6
>
> **Ingredients**
>
> | | |
> |---|---|
> | Lotus roots cleaned, washed | 1 lb |
> | Arrow-root flour | 1–2 Tbs |
> | Potatoes boiled and mashed | 1 cup |
> | Onions chopped | 2 Tbs |
> | Ginger chopped | 1 tsp |
> | Garlic and green chilies chopped each | 1 tsp |
> | Fenugreek leaves dry (methi leaves) | 1 Tbs |
> | Cumin powder (dry) roasted | 1 tsp |
> | Lemon juice | 1 Tbs |
> | Coriander powder | 1 Tbs |
> | Salt | 1 tsp |
> | Red pepper | ½ tsp |
> | Bread crumbs | 1 cup |
> | *Garam masala* more as needed | ½ tsp or |
> | Vegetable oil | ¼ cup |
> | Coriander leaves chopped | 2 Tbs |

The Exquisite World of Indian Cuisine

Stuffed Potatoes or Meat Pastries
Samosa

Deep fried pastries filled with spiced potatoes or meat are among the most famous snacks in Indian cuisine. These are served in restaurants all over the world.

METHOD:

1. Rub the oil into the flour, add salt and water and knead into smooth dough (uncooked tortilla dough) and leave it covered with a wet cloth.

   (Step 1 can be avoided if uncooked tortillas are used.)

2. Heat the oil and add the chopped ginger, garlic, chilies, and chopped onions and fry for few minutes until the onions turn slightly brown and add the peas. Stir for a while and add the cumin seeds and when they stop popping add the salt, red pepper and coriander powder and stir well.

3. Mix 4 Tbs of water and cook on slow heat and then add the chopped cooked potatoes or cooked cubed chicken, or lean ground lamb or beef and add the coriander leaves, *garam masala*, *amchoor* or the lemon juice, stir 4–5 min and cool.

4. Divide the dough (prepared as in Step 1) into 24 equal pieces. Shape them into balls, dredge them with the dry flour and roll them into rounds 4–6 inch in diameter as thin as possible. Cut each into 2 halves. Moisten the edges of each half. Hold one of these from its two extremes, keeping the arc of the circle downward and fold it over, so that they meet each other and form a cone opposite the center of the arc. Coat the edges with the little paste made from flour and water.

5. Fill the cone thus formed with a tablespoon of the stuffing. Seal by pinching the edges all around and decorate with very small scallops. Set them aside in a large deep dish lined with wax paper to be fried. Cover them with a slightly wet paper towel.

6. Heat the oil to 150°C or 300°F in a deep frying pan and fry the *samosas* till crisp and golden in color. If the *samosas* are turning brown too fast, lower the heat and cook them till they brown slowly. Serve with mint *chutney*, tamarind *chutney* or ketchup. They make a superb appetizer.

MAKES 24 *SAMOSAS*

Ingredients

Pastry shells:

All purpose flour	4 cups
Water	1¼ cup
Vegetable oil	1 cup

Stuffing:

Vegetable oil	¼ cup
Cumin seeds	1 tsp
Ginger	1 Tbs
Garlic	1 Tbs
Green chilies chopped (optional)	1 tsp
Potatoes chopped	3 cups
Or	
Finely ground pieces of lamb or chicken	
Salt	1½ tsp
Garam masala	½ tsp
Coriander leaves chopped	2 Tbs
Onion chopped	1 cup
Coriander powder	2 Tbs
Peas frozen	1½ cup
Red pepper	1 tsp
Mango powder or *amchoor*	1 Tbs
Or	
Lemon juice	2 Tbs
Vegetable oil (for frying)	4 cups

HINT

Instead of the potatoes these pastries can be stuffed with cooked cubed breast of chicken or ground beef.
*Use uncooked flour tortillas instead of making them from the dough. Uncooked tortillas are available at some major supermarkets or Mexican grocery stores.

APPETIZERS AND SNACKS

Meatballs in Tamarind Sauce

KERALA

Cashew nuts and coconut grow abundantly in south India. These meatballs made with ground lamb, cashew nuts, coconut and simmered in tamarind sauce tell you everything about their taste and origin.

SERVES 4 – 6

Ingredients

For the meatballs:

Ground turkey or beef or lean lamb meat	1 lb
Cashew nuts crushed	½ cup
Coconut freshly grated	½ cup
Raisins	2 Tbs
Onions chopped	2 Tbs
Garlic and ginger finely chopped	1 tsp each
Green chilies finely chopped	1 tsp
Salt	1 tsp
Red pepper	½–1 tsp
Egg beaten	1

Tamarind Sauce:

Tomato sauce	2 cups
Vegetable oil	2 Tbs
Salt	1 tsp
Sugar	1 Tbs
Turmeric powder	½ tsp
Fenugreek leaves dry (*Kasuri methi*)	2 Tbs
Fennel seeds (optional)	1 tsp
Cumin powder	1 tsp
Coriander powder ground	1 tsp
Tamarind pulp dissolved in ¼ cup water	2 Tbs
Curry leaves chopped	2 Tbs

METHOD

1. Mix together the ingredients for the meatballs and make balls of the size of a walnut. Transfer them to a small grilling pan and broil them in an oven until the meatballs are slightly brown, turning them once.
2. Heat the oil on low flame in a heavy-bottom saucepan.
3. Add the fenugreek leaves and curry leaves. Add the fennel seeds, coriander powder, cumin powder. Stir them in. Add the tomato sauce, salt, sugar and mix them well.
4. Add the tamarind dissolved in water. Stir it well and lower the heat. Let the sauce simmer for a few minutes. Add the meatballs. Stir it gently and let them simmer in the sauce for another 5 minutes. Serve them hot as an appetizer.

Cocktail Cashew Nuts
Namkeen Kaju

Cashew nuts deep fried and freshly flavored with ground roasted cumin powder, black salt, red pepper, black pepper and regular salt are unbelievably tasty. They make a very tempting snack at the bar.

METHOD

1. Heat the oil in a medium size thick-bottom skillet for a minute. Add cashew and fry them stirring continuously on low flame to prevent burning until they are golden brown.
2. Take a large sieve, set it up on a large bowl and transfer the cashews along with oil on to this sieve.
3. Save the oil. Transfer the cashew on to a plate lined with a paper towel. Sprinkle them with ground roasted cumin powder, black salt, regular salt, red pepper and black pepper. Toss them around well to coat them with spices and cool.
4. Serve them with drinks or soda.
5. They make an excellent appetizer.

SERVES 6 – 8

Ingredients

Fresh cashew nuts	2 cups
Oil	½ cup
Cumin powder ground, roasted	1 Tbs
Black salt	½ tsp
Regular salt	½ tsp
Red pepper	1 tsp
Black pepper	½ tsp

Note:
Steps 1 and 2 can be avoided by using canned roasted cashew nuts. Do not use table salt and black salt.
Step 3: The fried cashew nuts can be coated with the spices in the following manner also:
Melt a packet of unflavored gelatin in ¼ cup of water on low heat. Add all spices and stir well. Pour this mixture over the drained cashew and coat them well with this mixture. Heat the oven and set it on warm. Transfer the cashew onto a baking tray and let them dry in the warm oven. Once dry, remove them from the oven and serve when cool.

Ashvamedh Ghat on Ganga river, Varanasi, Uttar Pradesh

Fried Cheese Cubes
Cocktail Paneer

Deep fried *paneer* pieces or ricotta cheese cubes when cooked with chopped green bell pepper strips, ginger, garlic, lemon juice and spices are delicious and healthy. These are quite easy to fix too. Serve them with any wet curry and bread or best as an appetizer.

METHOD

1. Roast the cumin seeds and sesame seeds on a hot skillet (*tawa*) and grind them with a mortar and pestle. Set them aside. Heat the oil for frying in a deep saucepan or a fryer. Cut the cheese (*paneer*) slab into one inch cubes. Deep fry the cubes until slightly brown and take them out of the oil onto a platter lined with a paper towel. Drain the oil and set them aside.
2. Heat the oil for cooking in a deep large thick-bottom saucepan. Add the cumin and mustard seeds, and when they start popping, add the ginger and green chilies. Fry for 2 minutes and then add the garlic. Stir and fry for 2 more minutes.
3. Lower the heat and add the turmeric, coriander powder, salt and red pepper. Mix well. Add the deep fried cheese (*paneer*) cubes, onions and bell pepper. Stir to mix and coat the cubes well.
4. Add the water and cover the pan with a lid. Let it simmer for at least 5 minutes or until the cheese (*paneer*) cubes become soft but still holding their shape.
5. Add the *garam masala*, ground roasted cumin, sesame seeds, cilantro leaves, *amchoor*, chopped green onions and the lemon juice.
6. Stir gently to coat the cubes with spices and serve as an appetizer.

SERVES 8 – 10

Ingredients

Ricotta cheese drained of all water or *paneer* slab from an Indian grocer or home made	2 lb
Green onions chopped	2 Tbs
White onion sliced vertically in strings	1 cup
Bell pepper sliced in thin strips	½ cup
Ginger chopped	1 Tbs
Garlic chopped	1 Tbs
Turmeric powder	¾ tsp
Coriander powder ground	1 Tbs
Red pepper	1 tsp
Salt	1 tsp
Garam masala	½ tsp
Amchoor (use if serving as an appetizer)	1 Tbs
Ground roasted cumin powder	1 tsp
Lemon juice	1 Tbs
Vegetable oil or *ghee* (for cooking)	2–3 Tbs
Water	1 cup
Cilantro leaves finely chopped	2 Tbs
Cumin seeds	1 tsp
Mustard seeds	½ tsp
Sesame seeds ground, roasted	1 Tbs
Oil for frying	3 cups

Note: Drain the water from the Ricotta cheese by wrapping it in a clean fine cloth and leave it under a heavy weight for a couple of hours.

The Exquisite World of Indian Cuisine

Cocktail Shrimp

GOA

In this recipe from Goa, the shrimp is marinated in the spicy ground paste of garlic, ginger, red pepper, black pepper, ground cumin, *garam masala*, turmeric powder, *feni* or gin (cashew gin), brown sugar or palm sugar. Shrimp is then grilled and served on top of the greens. Serve it with bread rolls and a drink of your choice or as a side dish to complete a meal.

SERVES 6 – 8

Ingredients

Shrimp peeled and deveined	1 lb
Lemon juice	1 Tbs
Garlic minced	1 Tbs
Ginger minced	1 Tbs
Onions chopped	2 Tbs
Cayenne pepper (optional)	1 Tbs
Ground roasted cumin	1 Tbs
Garam masala	1 tsp
Salt	1 tsp
Black pepper	1 tsp
Palm sugar	1 Tbs
Gin (Goan cashew gin)	2–3 Tbs
Mustard oil for frying	2 Tbs
Or	
If grilling add to the marinade	1 Tbs
Salad leaves	

METHOD

1. Mix ground onions, ginger, garlic, cayenne pepper, black pepper, *garam masala*, salt, sugar, lemon juice and gin in deep bowl and add the shrimp. Coat the shrimp with the spice mixture and leave the shrimp in this marinade for at least 20–30 minutes.
2. Grill on electric grill on skewers or outdoors on a gas grill by spreading a foil on the grill and spread them evenly on the surface. Cook them by turning them until they turn pinkish brown.
3. If pan-frying the shrimp, then heat the oil in a large skillet. When heated add the shrimp and gently turn and fry them until they shrivel and turn pink. Takes about 5–7 minutes.
4. Serve on a platter-lined with salad leaves and sprinkle a little lemon juice and *garam masala* on top.
5. Serve them with a toothpick and a drink of your choice as an appetizer or as one of the main courses in a meal.

Note: Reiachado *masala* can be substituted for the above marinade.

Vegetable Fritters
Pakora

These spicy vegetable fritters made in a gram flour batter are among the most favorite and common appetizers of Indian cuisine. They are crispy, crunchy and are traditionally served with tamarind or mint *chutney*. Ketchup can be substituted for the *chutney*. It is a delightful appetizer for every occasion.

METHOD

1. Transfer gram flour to a medium size bowl and stir in enough water to make a thick batter. Beat hard with a fork or an eggbeater to make it smooth, of the consistency of a cake batter.
2. Add salt, red pepper, coriander powder, cumin powder, *garam masala*, and ½ cup of chopped onions, ginger, garlic and green chilies. Beat a little and add *ajwain* (carom seeds), ground pomegranate seeds powder, or lemon juice, green coriander leaves and baking powder.
3. Stir the mixture well. Heat the oil to about 300°F in a deep frying pan or a fryer. Do not overheat the oil. Coat the cauliflower florets, eggplant slices, zucchini slices and the potato slices with the batter by dipping them in the batter one by one and deep-fry them in the heated oil until light brown. Similarly coat the cheese slices with batter and fry them. Take them out with a slotted cooking spoon onto a platter lined with paper towels.
4. As soon as the slices of vegetables and cheese slices are all fried add the remaining onions and chopped spinach into the remaining batter and stir the mixture. Drop tablespoons full of this mixture into the hot oil. A number of them can be cooked at the same time. Fry them on medium heat until golden brown. Take the *pakoras* out of the oil with a slotted spoon onto a platter lined with a few layers of paper towel.
5. Serve them hot with mint *chutney*, tamarind *chutney* or ketchup.

Note: Gram flour, *paneer*, pomegranate seeds powder, fenugreek leaves fresh or dry and carom seeds are available at your Indian grocery store. Slow frying of the *pakoras* makes them crisp.

SERVES 8 – 10

Ingredients

Gram or split-pea flour	4 cups
Water	3¾ cups
Onions chopped	1 cup
Ginger chopped	2 Tbs
Garlic chopped	2 Tbs
Green chillies chopped	2 Tbs
Salt	1½ tsp
Red pepper	1½ tsp
Coriander powder	1½ Tbs
Cumin powder	1 tsp
Garam masala	1 tsp
Coriander leaves chopped	2 Tbs
Pomegranate seeds powder	2 Tbs
Or	
Lemon Juice	2–3 Tbs
Oil for frying	4 cups
Baking powder	¼ tsp
Carom seed or *Ajwain*	1½ tsp
Spinach chopped	1 cup
Cauliflower florets 2" long	1 cup
Sliced Zucchini 2" long and ⅛" thick	1 cup
Slices of peeled potatoes	1 cup
Slices of eggplant	1 cup
Ricotta cheese slices (well drained and firm cut into slices) or *paneer* rubbed with salt, red pepper, *garam masala* and *amchoor*	20

The Exquisite World of Indian Cuisine

Spinach Fritters
Palak Pakora

These fritters are made by mixing chopped cabbage, spinach and fenugreek leaves into spicy gram flour batter and deep-fried. They are so crunchy and delicious that they are often favored over even the vegetable fritters.

SERVES 8 – 10

Ingredients

Gram flour	2 cups
Water	1½–1¾ cups
Spinach chopped	2 cups
Fenugreek leaves chopped	1 cup
Cabbage chopped	1 cup
Onions chopped	1 cup
Ginger chopped	1 Tbs
Garlic chopped	1 Tbs
Green chilies chopped	1 Tbs
Salt	to taste
Coriander seeds crushed	1 Tbs
Red pepper	1 tsp
Lemon juice	2 Tbs
Garam masala	1 tsp
Carom seeds (ajwain)	1 tsp
Pomegranate seeds powder	1 Tbs
Vegetable oil or ghee	2 Tbs
Coriander leaves chopped	2 Tbs
Baking powder	a pinch
Oil for frying	4 cups

METHOD

1. Mix together gram flour, salt, red pepper, *garam masala*, pomegranate seeds powder, and baking powder. Add water and lemon juice gradually to make a thick batter of the consistency of muffin mix or cake batter.

2. Add the clean and well drained chopped cabbage, chopped fenugreek leaves, chopped spinach, chopped ginger, garlic, green chilies, onions, carom seeds, chopped coriander leaves, oil or *ghee*, crushed coriander seeds. Mix everything into the batter and beat the batter gently to make it smooth. If the batter gets thin, add more gram flour as needed.

3. Heat the oil to 180°C or 350°F in a heavy-bottom wok or a fryer. Add the batter a large spoonful at a time into the hot oil. A number of *pakoras* can be cooked at a time. Do not overheat the oil and keep the same temperature. Fry the *pakoras* until light golden brown. Remove them with a slotted spoon on a paper towel and drain the oil.

4. They go great as appetizers or as a teatime snack and are served with mint *chutney* or tamarind *chutney*. This is one of the most commonly served snack in Indian cuisine.

Note: If crisper *pakoras* are desired, add 2 Tbs of rice flour to the batter.

A sadhu offering prayers to Sun at Ganga ghat in Varanasi

Plantain Fritters
Kela Pakora

Mangoes and bananas grow in abundance all over India. Raw bananas are curried and are also cooked to be served as appetizers. In this recipe peeled pieces of raw bananas are dipped in a spiced batter of gram flour and deep-fried and are served with a *chutney* of your choice. They make a crispy snack with any drink.

METHOD

1. Peel the raw bananas and slice them into about ½ inch thick pieces. Set them aside.
2. Mix the gram flour and rice flour with finely chopped onions, ginger, garlic and green chilies in a medium size mixing bowl and enough water to make a smooth batter.
3. Add the salt, baking soda, red pepper, *amchoor*, coriander powder, *garam masala*, chopped coriander leaves and mix them well.
4. Heat the oil to about 150°C or 300°F in a wok or a nonstick deep frying pan or a fryer on medium low heat. Dip the sliced banana pieces one at a time and fry them in hot oil until golden brown. Remove them from the hot oil with a slotted spoon into a bowl lined with a paper towel and drain the excess oil. Serve them hot with green coriander *chutney* or tomato ketchup or with any *chutney* of your choice.
5. They make a crunchy, spicy and delicious appetizer. Serve them with a *chutney* of your choice.

SERVES 6 – 8

Ingredients

Raw bananas peeled and sliced into ½ inch pieces	4
Gram flour	1 cup
Rice flour	1 cup
Salt	1 tsp
Baking soda	a pinch
Red pepper	1 tsp
Carom seeds	1 tsp
Cumin roasted	½ tsp
Coriander powder	1 tsp
Garam masala	1 tsp
Vegetable oil	1 Tbs
Amchoor	1 Tbs
Onions chopped	2 Tbs
Ginger chopped	1 Tbs
Green chilies chopped	1 Tbs
Garlic chopped	1 Tbs
Green coriander leaves chopped	2 Tbs
Vegetable oil (for frying)	4 cups
Water as needed	

APPETIZERS AND SNACKS

Green Pepper Fritters
Shimla Mirch Pakora

Large green wax peppers or Jalapeno peppers make great fritters especially when stuffed with mashed spiced potato filling. In India, they are deep-fried in spicy batter of gram flour and in western countries, the batter is of spicy all purpose flour. Both ways, they make a popular snack.

METHOD

1. Mix together gram flour with salt, red pepper, *ajwain* seeds, coriander powder and *garam masala,* and slowly add the water to make a smooth batter. Set it aside.

2. Mix together mashed potatoes with chopped onions, ginger, garlic, green chilies, salt, coriander powder, cumin powder, black pepper, a pinch of baking soda, coriander leaves, lemon juice, *garam masala* and raisins. Set the filling inside.

3. Split the washed wax peppers or Jalapeno peppers (if you like hot food) lengthwise all the way and take out the fiber and seeds. Chop some of it and mix them and cook it with onions, ginger and garlic to go in the filling, if you like. If the peppers are too large cut them half. Fill the peppers with about 1 Tbs of potato filling and line them in a plate and set them aside.

4. Heat the oil to about 180°C or 350°F in a fryer or a large wok. Dip the peppers and coat them completely with batter, making sure the filling is secure inside the peppers. Slide them slowly into the hot oil. Fry them until light golden brown. Remove them from hot oil and keep them on a platter lined with a paper towel and drain the excess oil.

5. Serve them hot with your mint or tamarind *chutney*.

Note: Gram flour can be substituted by all purpose flour. Small green wax peppers can also be made into fritters by first slicing them in half and rubbing their interior with a mixture of salt, black pepper and *amchoor*.

SERVES 6 – 8

Ingredients

Wax peppers or Jalapeno (mild and large)	6

Filling:

Mashed potatoes	2 cups
Onions chopped	2 Tbs
Garlic chopped	1 tsp
Ginger chopped	1 tsp
Hot green chillies chopped (optional)	1 tsp
Salt	to taste
Coriander powder	1 tsp
Cumin powder	1 tsp
Coriander leaves chopped	1 Tbs
Lemon juice	2 Tbs
Or	
Anaardana seeds ground (dry)	1 tsp
Baking soda	a pinch
Black pepper	1 tsp
Garam masala	1 tsp
Raisins	1 Tbs
Oil (for frying the peppers)	3–4 cups

Batter:

Gram flour	2 cups
Salt	1 tsp
Red pepper	½ tsp
Ajwain seeds	½ tsp
Coriander powder	1 tsp
Garam masala	½ tsp
Water to make a thick batter as needed	

The Exquisite World of Indian Cuisine

APPETIZERS AND SNACKS

Mushroom Fritters
Khumb Pakora

These *pakoras* are my favorite. The mighty mushrooms were a delicacy for the Pharaohs of Egypt, the Greeks believed they gave strength to the warriors and the Romans thought they were a gift from God. Chinese regard them as a treasure house of a health food. They are in fact anticancer, are a great source of potassium, riboflavin, niacin and selenium. Use medium to large mushrooms. Dip them in spicy batter of gram flour fry and serve.

METHOD

1. Wash the mushrooms and remove most of their stem. Slice the mushrooms about ½ inch thick and one inch long.
2. Boil them in a saucepan with lemon juice and ½ tsp of salt for 2 minutes and drain the water and refresh them with cold water.
3. In a mixing bowl mix gram flour, rice flour, red pepper, salt, carom seeds, a pinch of baking soda, dry fenugreek leaves, chopped ginger, garlic, green chilies, and *garam masala*. Add water to make a thick batter of pancake batter consistency.
4. Heat oil in a wok or fryer. Make sure the oil temperature is not more than 150°C or 300°F. Dip them in the batter and drop them into hot oil with help of a tablespoon. Few can be added at a time. Fry them until golden brown, about 2–3 minutes. These can be made ahead of time and reheated in the oven when needed.
5. Remove them from the oil with slotted spoon and transfer them onto a towel paper lined bowl. Drain the oil and serve hot with a *chutney* of your choice. Preferably tamarind or mint *chutney*. They make a yummy appetizer.

Note: Zucchini can be used instead of mushrooms. Peel a medium size zucchini and cut into half. Cut 4 pieces out of each piece by cross cutting them lengthwise. Dip them into gram flour and make the zucchini fritters.

SERVES 4 – 6

Ingredients

Mushrooms large	½ lb
Lemon juice	2 Tbs
Salt or to taste	1 tsp
Gram flour	1 cup
Rice flour	½ cup
Baking soda	a pinch
Ginger chopped	1 Tbs
Garlic chopped	1 Tbs
Green chilies chopped	1 Tbs
Fenugreek leaves dry	2 Tbs
Red pepper	1 tsp
Carom (*Ajwain*) seeds	1 tsp
Garam masala	1 tsp
Water	1 cup
Oil for frying	4 cups

The Exquisite World of Indian Cuisine

Baked Spinach and Fenugreek Fritters
Muthia

GUJARAT

A snack from the state of Gujarat to go with your tea. They make a very appetizing, nutritious and fat-free snack. They are also used in a vegetable curry of Gujarat called *undhiya*.

METHOD

1. In a large bowl mix together spinach and fenugreek leaves and sprinkle a little salt over them. Let them sit for about 5 minutes. Squeeze the leaves between your palms to remove any liquid and store them in a bowl. Save the squeezed liquid in a bowl.
2. Add to the bowl wheat flour, *suji*, gram flour, salt, sugar, baking soda, lemon juice, green chilies chopped, ginger, red pepper, and knead well to make a dough. Use some of the squeezed juices for kneading the dough if needed. Divide the dough into 4 equal parts.
3. Grease your hands and roll each part with a rolling pin into a 6 inch wide and about ¼ inch thick cylinder. Roll each piece into tight rolls.
4. Place these rolls in a greased glass dish and cover them for 5 minutes. Place the dish in a microwave and cook for 3 minutes. Leave the dish in the microwave for another minute before taking it out. Cool them.
5. Slice ½ inch pieces from these rolls and set them aside. These are called *muthia*.
6. Heat the oil in a large thick-bottom cooking pan, and add the sesame seeds and cumin seeds and as they start to pop add the asafoetida.
7. Add the *muthias* and stir well. Keep stirring until they are light brown (about 2 minutes).
8. Serve them with mint *chutney*. Makes a delicious fat free appetizer.

Note: *Muthias* can also be made from grated zuchini or cabbage in the same manner as above but, instead of baking the dough pieces, or they can be steamed and then garnished as above with grated *paneer* or sliced tomatoes.

SERVES 6 – 8

Ingredients

Spinach chopped	4 cups
Fenugreek leaves freshly chopped	2 cups
Wheat flour	3 Tbs
Gram flour	1½ Tbs
Suji (Cream of wheat from an Indian grocery store)	1½ Tbs
Green chilies chopped more as needed	1 tsp or
Ginger chopped	1 tsp
Salt	1½ tsp
Red pepper	½–1 tsp
Sugar	1½ tsp
Cumin seeds	½ tsp
Sesame seeds	1–2 tsp
Asafoetida	a pinch
Lemon juice	1½ Tbs
Oil for cooking	1½ tsp
Baking soda	¼ tsp
Oil for greasing the dish	

APPETIZERS AND SNACKS

Lentil Patties
Urad Dal Vada

TAMIL NADU

A very popular south Indian appetizer made with a base of split hulled black lentil (*urad dal*) batter. No festive occasion in south India is complete without them. They are usually served with *sambhar* and *chutney* to make a complete meal.

METHOD

1. Soak the *urad dal* in water (enough to cover 1 inch above the beans) for at least 2–3 hours or overnight. Drain the water and grind them with help of 2–3 cups of water and transfer the batter to a deep salad bowl. Keep the batter rather thick. Add rice flour to make batter thick to make patties. Mix well.

2. Add the chopped ginger, chopped green chilies, curry leaves, squeezed onions, a pinch of baking soda, garlic chopped, pepper corns, salt and asafoetida and whip it well to mix it (about 2–3 minutes). Heat the oil in a wok at 350°F.

3. Shape a patty 2" in diameter and ½ inch thick on the palm of your greased hand and stick a finger in the middle to make a hole (it looks like a small doughnut). Drop it in the hot oil with the help of an oiled spatula. Cook slowly on medium heat (2–3 minutes). Several of them can be cooked at the same time. Take care that they do not stick with each other.

4. Fry until golden brown. Remove them from the oil with a slotted large spoon and place onto a platter lined with paper towel to drain excess oil.

5. Serve hot with coconut *chutney*, *channa dal chutney*, or any *chutney* of your choice.

SERVES 4 – 6

Ingredients

Black eyed split and hulled beans soaked	1 cup
Onions chopped	2 Tbs
Rice flour as needed	
Water	2–3 cups
Green chilies fresh (medium hot) finely chopped	2–3
Ginger fresh chopped	1 Tbs
Garlic chopped	1 Tbs
Baking soda	a pinch
Curry leaves chopped	2 Tbs
Black pepper corns	½ tsp
Asafoetida powder	½ tsp
Salt	1 tsp

Note: These *vadas* are often stringed into a garland and offered to the lord Hanuman in temples and shrines in south India.

The Exquisite World of Indian Cuisine

Lentil Fritters
Channa Dal Vada

Delicious but light fritters made of ground lentils base mixed with chopped vegetables and spices result in crisp and light golden brown patties. A very popular coffee time and an all-time snack of south, east and west. Serve them with coconut *chutney*.

METHOD

1. Soak the split peas or *channa dal* in a large bowl of water for 4–6 hours or overnight. Drain the water. Grind the split peas smoothly small amounts at a time by adding as little water as possible to make a thick batter in a blender or a food processor.
2. Pour the batter in a deep mixing bowl and add the onions, ginger, garlic, green chilies, salt, coriander powder, cumin powder, asafoetida, red pepper, chopped spinach, and the green coriander leaves and mix well.
3. Add enough bread-crumbs to make the batter manageable, and make small balls of the size of golf balls. Flatten them into ½ inch thick patties. Increase or decrease the bread crumbs as needed.
4. Heat the oil at 150ºC or about 300ºF.
5. Deep-fry the patties in the heated oil until golden brown. The browning and cooking of patties should be slow and should take about 2 to 3 minutes.
6. Drain them on a paper towel and serve them with coconut *chutney* or any *chutney* of your choice. A very tasty snack.

SERVES 6 – 8

Ingredients

Yellow split peas or *channa dal* soaked, drained and ground	2 cups
Onions chopped	½ cup
Ginger chopped	1 Tbs
Garlic chopped	1 Tbs
Green chilies chopped	1 Tbs
Salt	1 tsp
Red pepper (optional)	1 tsp
Coriander powder	1 Tbs
Cumin powder	1 tsp
Coriander leaves chopped	1 Tbs
Bread crumbs (if needed)	1 cup
Fresh spinach chopped	1½ cup
Asafoetida powder	¼ tsp
Water as needed	

HINT

Cup of shredded carrots or a 1–½ cup of steamed cabbage can be substituted for chopped spinach.

Potato Croquettes
Bonda

These well spiced potato balls are dipped into a batter of gram flour, deep-fried and served with *chutney* of your choice. It is a great snack for any time. They are made with variations in different parts of the country. Made crunchy in the south by adding *urad dal* and mustard seeds, in Gujarat made sweet and sour with raisins and lemon juice, but in the north they like to add to this sweet and sour potato mixture, green coriander and cumin seeds that make it quite refreshing. Nevertheless they are light and delicious for any occasion.

METHOD

For Filling:

1. Boil and mash the potatoes and set aside.
2. Cook the onions, ginger, garlic, green chilies in 3 Tbs of oil for 2 minutes and add the cumin seeds* until they crackle and add the salt, red pepper, lemon juice, raisins, chopped green coriander leaves, cashew nuts (crushed), coriander powder and the mashed potatoes. Stir and cook the mixture for 2 minutes. Cool and make them into balls the size of walnuts and set them aside in a deep flat pan in a single layer and cover them with a plastic wrap.

Batter preparation:

3. Make a batter by mixing the gram flour, rice flour, salt, pepper, and the asafoetida powder and water. If the batter is too thick add a little more water.
4. Heat the oil in a deep wok at 325–350°F. Dip the mashed potato balls in the batter and fry them in the heated oil few at a time. Keep the temperature down so that they take about 3–5 minutes to turn golden brown.
5. Take them out with a slotted spoon and drain them out on a paper towel. Serve them with tomato *chutney*, tamarind *chutney*, mint *chutney* or any other *chutney* of your choice. Makes excellent teatime snack or an appetizer.

*****Note:** You can substitute the cumin seeds and raisins with *urad dal* and mustard seeds in the filling.

SERVES 8 – 10

Ingredient

For the filling:

Potatoes (medium) boiled and mashed	6
Onions chopped	1 cup
Ginger chopped	1 Tbs
Garlic	1 Tbs
Green chilies chopped (optional)	1 tsp
Salt	1 tsp
Red pepper (optional)	1 tsp
Coriander powder	1½ Tbs
Raisins	2 Tbs
Cumin seeds	1 tsp
Vegetable oil	3 Tbs
Green coriander leaves chopped	¼ cup
Asafoetida (optional)	¼ tsp
Lemon juice	1 Tbs
Or	
Amchoor	1 Tbs
Cashew nuts (crushed)	2 Tbs

For the batter:

Gram flour sifted	2 cups
Salt	½ tsp
Red pepper	½ tsp
Rice flour	½ cup
Oil for frying	4 cups
Water to make the batter	2 cups

The Exquisite World of Indian Cuisine

Cheese Puffs
Paneer Vada

These fried cheese balls flavored with chopped green chilies, salt, green coriander are easy to prepare and a quick fixing appetizer. A yummy addition for any occasion.

METHOD

1. Knead the cheese smooth and add the chopped chilies, coriander leaves, salt, arrow-root flour, *garam masala*, ground roasted cumin powder, lemon juice, baking soda and corn flour, and mix well into the cheese and make a ball of smooth consistency.

2. Divide the cheese ball into 12 equal parts and shape them into smooth balls. Set them aside. Heat the oil in a *karahi* or wok to 150°C or about 300°F and fry slowly, few at a time until golden light brown. Remove from the oil with a slotted spoon onto a plate lined with a paper towel and drain the excess oil. Serve them with tomato ketchup or your favorite *chutney*.

3. Make a great appetizer or a snack.

SERVES 4 – 6

Ingredients

Paneer or Ricotta cheese completely drained and grated	2 cups
Green chilies finely chopped	1 tsp
Salt	to taste
Garam masala	½ tsp
Red pepper	to taste
Cumin powder ground, roasted	¾ tsp
Lemon juice	2 Tbs
Baking soda	a pinch
Corn flour	2 Tbs
Arrow-root flour	2 Tbs
Coriander leaves chopped	1 Tbs
Vegetable oil for frying	4 cups

Corn Fritters
Makki ke Vade

MAHARASHTRA

These crunchy corn fritters are a very popular appetizer from the state of Maharashtra and have been adopted by almost everyone around the country, because of their light, fluffy and creamy taste. Corn is added to a dough of all-purpose flour flavored with roasted cumin, green onions, chopped bell pepper and fenugreek leaves and a few more spices.

METHOD

1. Mix together the all-purpose flour, rice flour, baking powder, and salt. Beat together with milk, egg, and *ghee* or oil in a separate bowl. Pour the milk and egg mixture into the flour mixture and beat it smooth with a fork or with hand and remove any lumps the batter may have.
2. Add the cumin seeds, *garam masala*, chopped bell pepper, fenugreek leaves, green chilies, thawed corn, green onions, cilantro leaves, and ginger and stir them well into the batter.
3. Heat the oil in a frying pan to 350°F and drop the batter in spoonfuls into the oil, few at a time. Fry them on medium-low heat until they are golden brown (about 2–3 minutes).
4. Take them out with a slotted spoon onto a paper towel and drain the excess oil.
5. Serve them with a mint *chutney* or tamarind *chutney* as an appetizer or with a meal.

SERVES 6 – 8

Ingredients

All purpose flour	1½ cups
Rice flour	½ cup
Milk	1½ cup
Egg beaten	1
Baking powder	2 tsp
Green onions chopped	½ cup
Ginger fresh chopped	1 tsp
Vegetable oil or *ghee* (melted)	2 Tbs
Frozen thawed corn	1 cup
Red bell pepper finely chopped	½ cup
Cumin seeds or powder roasted	1 tsp
Fenugreek leaves	1 Tbs
Salt	1 tsp
Garam masala	1 tsp
Cilantro leaves chopped	½ cup
Green chilies chopped	1 tsp
Vegetable oil (for frying)	4 cups

Tapioca Potato Puffs
Sabudana Vada

MAHARASHTRA

These potatoes patties rolled in freshly soaked tapioca and deep fried are crunchy and are native to Maharashtra. Try them – you will like them.

SERVES 6 – 8

Ingredients

Potatoes boiled	2 lb
Tapioca balls	1 cup
Paneer or Ricotta cheese completely drained and mashed	1 cup
Peanuts (dry) roasted crushed	2 Tbs
Green chilies chopped	1 tsp
Ginger chopped	1 Tbs
Garlic chopped	1 tsp
Poppy seeds	1½ Tbs
Salt	to taste
Red pepper	1 tsp
Raisins	1 Tbs
Lemon juice	1 Tbs
Green coriander chopped	2 Tbs
Garam masala	1 tsp
Vegetable oil (for frying)	3 cups
Bread crumbs	1 cup

METHOD

1. Soak the tapioca balls in warm water until soft (4 hours), drain and set them aside.

2. Peel the potatoes and mash them. Mix in them drained tapioca, bread crumbs, salt chopped ginger, red pepper, garlic, green chilies, poppy seeds, *garam masala*, lemon juice, green coriander, raisins, peanuts and cheese, and knead the mixture well to mix everything evenly.

3. Divide the mixture into 20 equal parts and roll them into balls. Insert a couple of raisins in the center of the ball and make the surface smooth. Flatten each ball into an oval shape. And set them all aside.

4. Heat oil in a *karahi* (wok) or a deep frying pan at about 150°C - 300°F and fry them, few at a time, turning them occasionally until golden brown. Take them out on a towel paper lined plate to drain the oil and serve them with your favorite *chutney* as an appetizer or a snack.

Note: *Karahi* is a wok that is a must in an Indian kitchen. Almost all vegetables are cooked in this *karahi*. It is metallic with a heavy-bottom and is a very versatile pan for Indian cooking. It comes in many sizes and has been in use in India from time immemorial. It has two handles and is used for roasting spices, tempering and cooking. (See picture)

APPETIZERS AND SNACKS

Yams in Peanut Sauce
Arbi Tikka Masala

KERALA

Boiled and peeled yam marinated in spicy peanut sauce and grilled or baked in the oven with a southern flavor of curry leaves and mustard seeds. It make a very nice addition to any dinner as an appetizer or an accompaniment. Yam leaves wrapped in a filling of spiced rice and pan-fried are a delicacy in the south.

SERVES 4 – 6

Ingredients

Boiled yam (medium size) peeled	12

Marinade:

Olive oil or *ghee*	1 Tbs
Peanuts	¼ cup
Yogurt	½ cup
Tamarind	½ tsp
Ginger chopped	1 tsp
Garlic chopped	1 tsp
Salt	1½ tsp
Turmeric powder	1 tsp
Red pepper	1 tsp
Coriander powder	1 Tbs

Tempering (*Tadka*):

Vegetable oil	2 Tbs
Mustard seeds	1 tsp
Cumin seeds	½ tsp
Curry leaves chopped	6–8
Red pepper (dry) crushed	1 tsp
Amchoor	1 tsp
Garam masala	½ tsp
Coriander leaves chopped	2 Tbs

METHOD

1. Boil the yam and peel them. Flatten them between your palms and set them aside. If the yam size is too large, cut them in ½ inch pieces and then flatten them between your palms. Blend yogurt, peanuts, tamarind, ginger, oil, garlic, salt, turmeric powder, red pepper, coriander powder, in a blender and grind smooth.

2. Add the yam to the above marinade and coat them well. Transfer them to the oven in a baking pan with a grilling rack and bake at 400°F for about 25–30 minutes, until they are light brown.

3. Remove from the oven and set them aside. Heat the oil in a non stick small frying pan and add the mustard seeds, cumin seeds and wait till they start popping. Then add the dry red pepper, curry leaves, and stir well. Add the *amchoor* and *garam masala*, and mix well. Add the cooked yam and stir to coat the yam *tikka* on both sides. Sprinkle with chopped coriander leaves. Serve as appetizer or a vegetable accompaniment.

The Exquisite World of Indian Cuisine

Stuffed Mushrooms
Bharvan Khumb

Mushrooms stuffed with mashed potatoes, spices and ricotta cheese make a tasty and a very quick fixing snack or an appetizer. They are light and delicious, and make great nibblers with a drink.

SERVES 4 – 6

Ingredients

Mushrooms (large)	1 lb
Water	4 cups
Salt	1 tsp
Red pepper	½–1 tsp
Lemon juice	1 Tbs
Potatoes boiled and mashed	½ cup
Ricotta cheese or *Paneer* (completely drained of water)	½ cup
Bread crumbs	1 Tbs
Ginger chopped	1 tsp
Garlic chopped	1 tsp
Green chilies chopped	1 tsp
Salt	¾ tsp
Fresh coriander leaves chopped	1 Tbs
Lemon juice (optional)	1 Tbs
Garam masala	½ tsp
Vegetable oil or *ghee* as needed	

METHOD

1. Wash the mushrooms and remove the stems. Clean the cavities and set them aside.
2. Boil 4 cups of water with 1 Tbs of lemon juice and 1 tsp of salt and add the mushrooms. Boil for 2 minutes, drain the water and run cold water over the mushrooms and drain them and set them aside.
3. Prepare the filling by mixing the mashed potatoes, ricotta cheese, salt, lemon juice, red pepper, bread crumbs, green coriander leaves, green chilies, chopped ginger and garlic. Stuff ¾ of the mushrooms with filling and arrange them on a baking sheet. Brush them with a little oil or *ghee*.
4. Bake them at 400°F until the top starts to turn light brown. Serve with a *chutney*.

In 'God's Own Country', Kerala – 'Puram', the elephant festival

Cream of Wheat with Vegetables
Uppama

KERALA

One of the most popular south Indian snacks made out of cream of wheat flavored with mustard seeds and cashew nuts. A wonderful way to turn plain cream of wheat into a wholesome meal. It is quite nutritious. It can be served as a light lunch with yogurt or *raita*.

METHOD

1. Heat one Tbs of *ghee* or oil in a large frying pan and add the mustard seeds. When they stop popping, add the *urad dal*, yellow split peas and the cashew nuts or peanuts and cook till they start turning brown. Remove with slotted spoon in a bowl and set them aside.
2. Add another 2 Tbs of *ghee* and transfer the cream of wheat (*suji*) into the frying pan and fry till light brown (about 10 minutes) on medium-low heat and set it aside.
3. Cook the onions, ginger, garlic, and green chilies in 1 Tbs of oil on medium-low heat in a wok and fry till the onions are soft. Add the chopped potatoes and peas. Fry 2–3 minutes and add the curry leaves, cumin seeds, broken whole red peppers, coriander powder, red pepper, and keep stirring to mix it well. Add the coconut powder and stir till it starts to turn slightly brown.
4. Add the fried *suji* and fried nuts mixture. Mix everything well. Add the boiling water slowly and keep stirring to mix until all the water is gone. Add more water if necessary. Stir in between to make sure that the cream of wheat is not sticking. Cook till it does not look grainy and all grains are soft and cooked.
5. Keep stirring until the mixture separates from the pan.
6. Remove from heat and serve topped with coriander leaves as a breakfast or teatime snack if you wish. It is usually served with *sambhar*, coconut, or *channa dal chutney*.

During my last visit to India I visited the famous Sai Center at Bangalore and there I tasted the best uppama ever, prepared by American volunteers. Uppama is popular all over the country.

SERVES 4 – 6

Ingredients

Uncooked cream of wheat from an Indian grocery store (*Suji*) Or	1 cup
5 minute Instant cream of wheat from your local store	1 cup
Fresh cubed potatoes chopped	½ cup
Onion chopped	½ cup
Ginger chopped	1 tsp
Garlic chopped	1 tsp
Green chilies chopped (optional)	1 Tbs
Vegetable oil or *ghee*	¼ cup
Mustard seeds	1 tsp
Cumin seeds	1 tsp
Urad dal	1 Tbs
Yellow spilt peas	1 Tbs
Curry leaves chopped	6–8
Red pepper dry (broken in half)	1
Vegetable oil or clarified butter	¼ cup
Cashew nuts or peanuts (crushed)	2 Tbs
Water preferably boiled	3½ cup
Green peas frozen	¼ cup
Salt to taste or	1–2 tsp
Red pepper	½-1 tsp
Coriander powder	1 tsp
Coconut powder	1 Tbs
Garam masala	½–¾ tsp
Coriander leaves chopped	1 Tbs
Lemon juice to taste	1 Tbs

HINT

You can also add ½ cup of shredded carrots with ½ cup of chopped tomatoes at the same time you are frying the potatoes. Cashew nuts can be substituted with fried unsalted peanuts or a tablespoon of raisins. Instant cooked cream of wheat from a local grocery store can be substituted for the *suji*. Less frying time will be needed to fry the cooked cream of wheat. Follow same steps as mentioned above.

Spiced Rice Flakes
Poha / Aval

MAHARASHTRA

Before cooking, the *poha* is soaked briefly and handled delicately to make a very delicious teatime snack. It is combined with cashew nuts or peanuts and shallots and is flavored with garlic, ginger, grated fresh coconut, green chilies, lemon juice, salt and other spices like asafoetida. The aroma of the preparation fills the environment. It can be served with a *raita*, *chutney* or a simple vegetable stir-fry. Try this specialty from the state of Maharashtra.

SERVES 4 – 6

Ingredients

Rice flakes or *poha* (from your local Indian grocer)	2 cups
Water (to soak the *poha*)	
Shallots finely chopped	½ cup
Mustard seeds	½ tsp
Ghee or clarified butter	3 Tbs
Cumin seeds	1 tsp
Potatoes (medium) finely chopped	1
Turmeric powder	½ tsp
Cashew nuts roasted, chopped	2 Tbs
Raisins	2 Tbs
Coriander powder	1 tsp
Red pepper	½ tsp
Garlic chopped	1 tsp
Ginger chopped	1 tsp
Green chilies chopped	1 tsp
Coconut freshly grated (optional)	½ cup
Or	
Coconut dry powder	2 Tbs
Asafoetida	½ tsp
Fresh lemon juice	2 Tbs
Salt	to taste
Curry leaves	4–6
Coriander leaves freshly chopped (optional)	1 Tbs

METHOD

1. Transfer the *poha* to a bowl and cover it with water for ½ minute.
2. Drain the water and set the *poha* aside (do not squeeze).
3. Heat the *ghee* in a non-stick large saucepan and when hot add the cumin seeds, mustard seeds and wait till they start popping and then add the shallots, ginger, garlic and green chilies. Add fine chopped potato.
4. Fry until they are light brown and add the cashew nuts, asafoetida, turmeric powder, coriander powder, red pepper, and curry leaves.
5. Stir-fry for ½ minute and add the drained *poha*. Mix gently to coat them with spices and add the salt and lemon juice, raisins and stir the mixture.
6. Cook until the flakes become drier, cooking on low heat stirring gently for about 3–5 minutes. Moisten the *poha* with a couple of tsp of water, if needed.
7. Fold in the grated coconut and coriander leaves and fry for a minute longer. Remove from heat. Serve warm.

Rice Flake Cutlets
Poha Patties

It is easy, quick fixing and low in calories. A popular appetizer or snack all over India. Serve them with *chutney* of your choice.

SERVES 4 – 6

Ingredients

Poha (cooked and flattened rice) soaked and drained	2 cups
Bread slices	2
Green coriander leaves chopped	½ cup
Ginger chopped	1 Tbs
Green chilies chopped	1 Tbs
Cashews or fried peanuts finely chopped	2 Tbs
Raisins	1 Tbs
Lemon juice	1½ Tbs
Red pepper	½ tsp
Salt	1 tsp
Cumin powder	½ tsp
Garam masala	½ tsp
Coriander powder	½ tsp
Cumin powder	½ tsp
Vegetable oil (for pan-frying)	¼ cup
Poppy seeds to coat	¼ cup

METHOD

1. Soak 2 cups of *poha* in water for 10 minutes and drain and squeeze the water out completely. Set it aside. Soak the bread slices in water to soften them, squeeze out the water and crumble into pieces and set the pieces aside.

2. Mix the ginger, green chilies, lemon juice, salt, green coriander leaves, red pepper, cumin powder, coriander powder, cashews, raisins, *garam masala*, and the bread pieces into the squeezed *poha* and mix well. Make small patties with *poha* mixture about 2–2½ inch in diameter and set them aside.

3. Pour the poppy seeds onto a large plate and coat the patties in the poppy seeds. In a large nonstick frying pan transfer the ¼ cup oil and heat it.

4. Fry the patties in the oil till they are light brown on both sides. Transfer them to towel paper lined dish to drain the excess oil.

5. Serve them with mint *chutney* or ketchup.

The Exquisite World of Indian Cuisine

Steamed Lentil Cake
Dhokla

GUJARAT

From the state of Gujarat, comes this very fluffy and delightful snack light in texture and with an appetizing look. Made by steaming the spiced and fermented ground *Toor dal* into small cakes. *Dhokla* is enjoyed all over India. This snack is very low in calories but rich in protein. You can serve *dhokla* at mealtime or teatime or with lunch.

METHOD

1. Soak the *dal* overnight and grind it in an electric blender the next morning with the green chilies and yogurt and little water to a thick batter consistency.
2. Add asafoetida, lemon juice, sugar, salt, and oil. Keep aside for three hours. Add the fenugreek leaves, Eno's fruit salt and blend to a thick pouring batter.
3. Pour the batter into greased small moulds for the desired shape or into a 1–2" deep stainless steel plate, with a 4–6 inch diameter that will fit into a large saucepan. Pour water about 2 inches deep in the saucepan and place a wire rack over it. Adjust the plate with the batter or a plate with the batter filled moulds on top of the rack inside the saucepan for steaming. Boil the water. Cover the saucepan with the lid and steam until *dhokla* is done (about 15–20 minutes).
4. Heat some oil in a skillet. Add a tsp of mustard seeds, sesame seeds and the whole red chilies to the oil, wait till the seeds start to pop. Pour the tempering over the *dhokla*. Cut it in desired shapes. Sprinkle with coriander leaves and serve the pieces with coconut, mint or any *chutney* of your choice. It makes a very light and appealing appetizer.

SERVES 8 – 10

Ingredients

Toor dal	1 cup
Fresh green methi leaves chopped	1 cup
Green chilies	6
Yogurt	2 cups
Asafoetida	¼ tsp
Sugar	1 Tbs
Eno's fruit salt	1 Tbs
Soya oil or any other vegetable oil	1 tsp
Lemon juice	2 tsp
Salt	1 tsp
Mustard seeds	1 tsp
Red whole chilies (broken)	3
Coriander leaves chopped	1 Tbs
Sesame seeds	1 tsp

Note: *Dhokla* is served in several decorative ways. You can serve them as sandwiches by coating one piece with mint or tamarind *chutney* and place the other piece over it. Sprinkle with coconut powder or grated fresh coconut and serve. A sprinkle of red pepper or paprika gives it a very colorful look too. Eno's fruit salt is available at your local Indian grocery store. It is somewhat like baking soda.

Cream of Wheat Cakes
Khaman Dhokla

GUJARAT

A traditionally Gujarati snack that cooks fast in the microwave too. It is so soft that it melts in your mouth. Makes a great appetizer.

SERVES 4 – 6

Ingredients

Gram flour (from your local Indian grocer)	2 cups
Fine *suji* or cream of wheat (Indian grocer)	¼ cup
Lemon juice	2 Tbs
Yogurt	2 cups
Asafoetida powder	¼ tsp
Ginger finely chopped	1 Tbs
Green chilies finely chopped	1 Tbs
Water as needed	
Eno's fruit salt (from your local Indian grocer)	3 tsp
Or	
Baking Soda	2 tsp
Citric acid	½ tsp
Sugar	1 Tbs
Salt	1 tsp
Tamarind *chutney*	½ cup
Ricotta cheese beaten smooth	½ cup
Red pepper	½ tsp
Green coriander leaves chopped	½ cup
Mustard seeds	1 tsp
Vegetable oil	2 Tbs
Green chilies (small) chopped	2
Sesame seeds	1 tsp
Curry leaves chopped	1 tsp

METHOD

1. Mix together fine cream of wheat, gram flour, lemon juice, ginger, green chilies, salt, asafoetida powder and yogurt in a deep bowl. Mix and set aside for ½ hour. Add 3 tsp of fruit salt or 2 tsp of baking soda and citric acid to the mixture.

2. Stir it well and pour one inch layer of it into a greased 2 inch thick aluminium pan or a stainless *thali*, 6–8 in diameter. Boil 2 cups of water in a large wide cooking pan. Place a small rack in it and place the greased pan with batter over it. Cover the cooking pan and let batter steam cook for 15–20 minutes or until the *dhokla* is done. (Insert a toothpick into the center and if it comes out clean then it is done). If using microwave oven then cook for 2 minutes in a small 5–6 inch diameter and 2 inch deep microwavable plate. Take it out of the oven. Leave it to cool for 2 minutes.

3. Transfer it onto a serving tray. Smear it with a thin layer of tamarind *chutney* and ricotta cheese. Bake another layer of *dhokla* in the same manner and put it on top of the first one. Heat the oil in a small frying pan and add a tsp of mustard seeds and when they start to crackle then add the sesame seeds. Add the asafoetida powder, green chilies. Remove this tempering from the fire and pour over the top of the *dhokla*. Sprinkle the top with chopped green coriander leaves. Cut them into 2 inch squares and serve them with drinks or as a snack with your evening tea.

Note: *Khaman dhokla* is different from regular *dhokla*

The Exquisite World of Indian Cuisine

Steamed Lentil Rolls
Khandvi

GUJARAT

A delicate appetizer. Originally from the state of Gujarat, it is popular all over India. Usually made with *gram* (chick peas) flour and yogurt but made here with freshly soaked *mung* beans paste, yogurt and flavored with chopped green pepper, ginger, asafoetida and salt. Cooked, rolled and stuffed with spicy Riccotta cheese and topped with a seasoning of hot buttered sesame seeds and mustard seeds.

METHOD

1. Wash and soak the *mung dal* in a large bowl overnight in at least 4 cups of water.

2. Drain the *dal* and grind it fine with ginger, green chilies, salt in a blender with couple of Tablespoons of water as needed to make a paste. Transfer the *dal* paste into a glass bowl and mix into it yogurt, turmeric powder, salt and asafoetida. Stir well to make a smooth paste. Cook this mixture in a microwave oven for 6-8 minutes and stir in between couple of times. When it gets thick and doughy remove from the oven.

3. Spread tin-foil on top of large smooth cutting stone or on the back of a large *thali*.

4. Roll the dough while it is warm and spread it with the sharp edge of a stainless steel spatula or rolling pin on the back of a *thali* or a stone which already has a lining of the tin-foil (use a little *besan* flour to help in rolling, if needed). Roll into very thin layer (½ cm thick). Let it cool for 5 minutes and prepare the filling.

5. Prepare the filling by mixing together *paneer* or crumbled ricotta cheese, carrots, lemon juice, coconut, red pepper, chopped coriander leaves and salt. Spread the filling on top of the thin layer of dough and cut the layer into 2 inch pieces. Gently roll the pieces and set them aside in a serving platter.

6. Prepare the tempering (*tadka*) by heating the oil in a small pan and add the mustard seeds. When they start popping, add the sesame seeds. Pour this tempering over the prepared *khandvi*.

7. Serve the rolls as an appetizer or as a snack at teatime.

Note: The time to cook in the microwave will vary, depending upon what kind of oven you are using. *Khandvi* can be made similarly with *besan* or gram flour.

SERVES 4 – 6

Ingredients

Pastry:

Skinless *mung dal* washed	1 cup
Yogurt	1 cup
Green pepper chopped	1 tsp
Ginger chopped	1 tsp
Salt	1 tsp
Asafoetida	½ tsp
Turmeric powder	½ tsp
Water (as needed)	½ cup

Filling:

Carrots finely grated	¼ cup
Drained and crumbled ricotta cheese or *Paneer*	¼ cup
Coriander leaves chopped	2 Tbs
Lemon juice	1 Tbs
Salt	1 tsp
Red pepper	½ tsp
Coconut (grated)	2 Tbs
Or dry coconut powder	1 Tbs

Tempering (*Tadka*):

Mustard seeds	1 Tbs
Sesame seeds	1 Tbs
Vegetable oil	2 Tbs

The Exquisite World of Indian Cuisine

Tortilla chips with Tamarind Sauce
Papri

These crisp discs of flour made at home with dough can easily be prepared here in the United States from the cooked or uncooked flour *tortillas available in general grocery stores. This appetizer is sure to please the crowd. They are served with tamarind *chutney*, boiled chopped potatoes, yogurt, canned chick-peas, salt, red pepper, *garam masala*, and ground roasted cumin powder. A counterpart of the Tortilla chips of Mexico.

METHOD

1. Cut squares or circles from fresh uncooked tortillas bought from the general grocery store. You can use a bottle cap with sharp edges as a cutter or cut them out with a knife in any shape but not bigger than one inch in size. Heat oil to about 180°C or 350°F in a deep skillet or a cooking pot and fry them until they are crisp and golden brown. Drain them on a paper towel and store them in a warm oven until ready to serve. They can be stored after cooling in zip lock bags for later use.
2. Serve them to the guests in a snack plate or large bowl as follows: 4 Tbs of the tortilla chips topped with 2 Tbs each of chopped boiled potatoes, washed and drained canned chick-peas, 1 Tbs each of chopped onions and tomatoes, *mung* bean sprouts, gram flour *bhiji*, chopped coriander leaves and 1 Tbs of yogurt.
3. Again top it all with *chaat masala,* salt, red pepper, ground roasted cumin powder, *garam masala* and tamarind *chutney* or any other *chutney* of your taste and serve.
4. Makes an excellent appetizer.

SERVES 10 – 12

Ingredients

Tortillas pkg of 8 inch cooked or uncooked twelve, cut into 2 inch squares	
Vegetable oil (for frying)	
Tamarind *chutney* chilled	1 cup
Boiled potatoes (small) chopped	2 cups
Chick peas washed and drained	1 can
Yogurt whisked and smooth	2 cups
Onions finely chopped	1 cup
Mint *chutney*	1 cup
Coriander leaves chopped	1 cup
Tomatoes chopped fine	1 cup
Mung bean sprouts	1 cup
Gram flour *bhiji* (available at your local Indian grocer)	1 cup
Yogurt	1 cup
A spice container with roasted ground cumin powder, salt, *garam masala*, and red pepper	
Or	
Chaat masala in a bowl	

Note: *Papris* and *golgappas* are usually sold in special shops or vendors in every region in India. These shops or the vendors are called *"Chaatwalas"*. To make uncooked tortilla, follows the method for preparing the dough as in the recipe for *samosa*.

Flour Puffs with Tamarind Water
Golgappa

Hollow small wafers of flour and cream of wheat are a definite party pleaser. Ready to eat *golgappas (paani poori)* are available at your local Indian grocery store. Here is a method to make them at home.

METHOD

1. Knead smooth dough with the three mixed flours using water. It takes a little time in kneading and making a smooth dough.
2. Leave it covered with a wet cloth for about 20 minutes.
3. Knead again for another 5 minutes and divide into 4 equal parts.
4. Knead one part as thin as possible and cut little circles of about 1–1½ inch diameter with the help of a round 1 inch cookie cutter.
5. Spread a piece of wet cloth and place these round circles or discs on this cloth and cover them with another wet cloth.
6. Deep-fry them in oil heated between 300°F–340°F, a few at a time. They become puffed up balls of light golden color. Remove them from the hot oil onto a large baking sheet lined with tin foil.
7. Warm the oven and place the tray in the warm oven. Leave them until they are dry.
8. Take them out of the oven and store in a cool dry place in zip lock bags. They can be stored at room temperature in these bags for a month and can be stored in the refrigerator for a few weeks.
9. Serve them to the guests, few at a time, in small snack plates with *zeera paani,* canned cooked chick-peas, boiled potatoes, and tamarind *chutney,* and/or mint *chutney* and yogurt.
10. *They are enjoyed as follows*: Make a small hole with your index finger at the top of the *golgappa* and add a small piece of cooked potato, couple of boiled chick-peas, and a slight bit of tamarind *chutney,* ½ tsp of yogurt and fill it up almost ¾ with *zeera paani.* Eat it whole without breaking it. They are a delicious appetizer and when served they always cheer up the crowd.

SERVES 6 – 8

Ingredients

Cream of wheat (3 oz)	½ cup
All purpose flour (3 oz)	½ cup
Urad flour	1 Tbs
Warm water to make pliable dough	1 cup
Vegetable oil (for frying)	
Flour (for dredging)	

To serve use:

Zeera paani	1 quart
Chick-peas (boiled) or from can	2 cups
Boiled potatoes chopped	2 cups
Tamarind sweet & sour *chutney*	1 cup
Mint *chutney*	½ cup
Yogurt	1 cup

Crunchy Rice Puffs with Salad
Bhelpoori

MAHARASHTRA

From the beaches of Bombay comes this snack or appetizer. Made with a mixture of rice puffs, *mung* bean sprouts, chopped onions, tomatoes, green chilies, boiled potatoes, fine salted gram flour vermicelli, tossed in tamarind *chutney* and topped with mint *chutney*, yogurt, salt, red pepper, *garam masala* and chopped coriander leaves, this is now popular all over the country.

SERVES 10 – 15

Ingredients

Rice puffs	6 cups
Tortillas deep fried and broken in pieces	2 cups
Gram flour *bhiji* (from an Indian grocery store)	1 cup
Mung bean sprouts	2 cups
Channa dal soaked overnight	1 cup
Onions chopped	2 cups
Tomatoes firmly chopped	2 cups
Green chilies chopped	½ cup
Tamarind *chutney*	2 cups
Red pepper	1 tsp
Salt	1 tsp
Potatoes (boiled) chopped	2 cups
Raw mango chopped	½ cup
Green coriander chopped	1 cup
Lemon juice	2 Tbs
Mint *chutney*	1 cup
Yogurt	1 cup
Garam masala	1 Tbs
Chaat masala (from your local Indian grocery store)	2 Tbs

METHOD

1. In large mixing bowl mix together rice puffs, crushed tortillas, gram flour *bhiji*.

2. Add *mung* bean sprouts, washed and soaked and drained *channa dal* and chopped boiled potatoes, chopped raw mangoes, onions and a cup of tamarind *chutney*. Toss the mixture well to coat everything in it.

3. Before serving to the guests, transfer 4 Tbs of the above mixture onto a snack plate and top it with chopped tomatoes, a little yogurt salt, red pepper, *garam masala*, lemon juice, mint *chutney* and more tamarind *chutney* if desired. *Chaat masala* can be used instead of the individual spices. Serve it on the side for preference.

4. Serve it with your favorite drink. Makes a great afternoon snack with your tea or coffee too.

Note: It can have variations in its contents from place to place in the country.

Yogurt dipped Lentil Fritters
Dahi Vada and Pakori

These lentil fritters are softened by soaking in warm water after cooking. Squeeze the water out and serve them in well-beaten smooth chilled yogurt and top them with ground roasted cumin, red pepper, salt and *garam masala* and chopped coriander leaves. They are then served topped with sweet and sour tamarind *chutney*. A great accompaniment at a festive occasion or a party.

METHOD

Dahi Vada:

1. Wash and grind the *urad dal* and add a pinch of baking soda to the batter.
2. Beat the batter well and set it aside. Keep the batter thick so that the *urad dal vadas* can be shaped into half circles with a cashew nut or a raisin placed inside before shaping.
3. Heat the oil to about 150°C or 300°F and fry on low heat until light golden brown.
4. Take them out of the oil with a slotted spoon and drain them on a paper towel.

Mung Pakori:

5. When making *mung dal pakoris*, grind the *dal* and prepare the batter as for *urad dal*, shape them round by dropping tablespoonfuls of dough into the hot oil and frying them until light brown. Make sure that the oil does not get too hot. Soak the *urad dal vadas* as well as *mung dal pakoris* for 5–7 minutes in warm salted water. Squeeze them gently to remove the water and excess fat.
6. Arrange them in a serving dish. Just before serving pour the whisked yogurt on top so as to almost cover them with yogurt. Sprinkle them with salt, red pepper, *garam masala* and ground roasted cumin powder. Before serving top it all with tamarind *chutney*, chopped coriander leaves. They are a stunning presentation for any party or festive occasion. Serve *chaat masala* on the side.

Note: Check the oil if it is ready to cook by dropping a small ball of dough into the oil. If it rises up instantly, the oil is ready to fry.

SERVES 8 – 10

Ingredients

Urad dal or *mung dal* (each) soaked overnight	1 lb
Salt, red pepper and *garam masala* (each)	1 tsp
Cumin seeds ground, roasted	1 Tbs
Vegetable oil (for frying)	
Yogurt well beaten	4 cups
Baking soda	$1/8$ tsp
Cashew nuts or raisins	2 Tbs
Tamarind chutney	1 cup
Coriander leaves chopped	2 Tbs
Chaat masala	4 Tbs

The Exquisite World of Indian Cuisine

Crunchy Lentils Wafers
Papadum

GUJARAT

Crunchy wafers made out of washed split *urad* and *mung dal* are always made commercially as their preparation requires great amounts of skill and experience. Purchased from an Indian grocery store and served either deep-fried or directly roasted on the fire. They are usually highly spiced with black pepper and red pepper though mild varieties are also available. They are usually served as an appetizer with some mild *chutney* or as a crunchy accompaniment to a full meal. A specialty of Gujarat where it is always served with a meal.

SERVES 6 – 8

Ingredients

Papadums (if large then broken in halves)	10
Vegetable oil (for frying)	4 cups

METHOD

1. Heat the oil to 300°F–340°F in a deep wide saucepan and make sure that the oil is ready by dropping a little piece of *papadum* into the hot oil to see if the piece rises to the top.
2. Once the oil is ready, drop the broken halves into the hot oil one by one.
3. They will expand in the hot oil and turn from yellow to golden brown rather quickly.
4. Take them out immediately with tongs on a paper towel and let the oil drain. Serve as an appetizer or with your meal.

Note: Lentil papadums can be cooked on direct flame also but they have to be browned carefully with the help of tongs. They can be cooked also in the microwave. Papadums bring very vivid memories of how my mother and her close friends who used to get together in our courtyard to roll and make fresh papadums, in the afternoons. They are not only made with *urad* and *mung* beans but are also made with potatoes and tapioca. Spiced just right according to your taste they have great flavor and aroma.

You will need tongs to fry the *papdums*.

APPETIZERS AND SNACKS

Rolled and Stuffed Wafers
Papad Rolls

GUJARAT

Papad is an ornament of the Gujarati meal. No meal is complete without it. This recipe presents it in an appetizer form with mashed potatoes rolled inside it.

METHOD

1. Boil the potatoes, peel them and mash them. Add ginger, green chilies, raisins, cooked rice, coriander powder, salt, green coriander leaves, lemon juice, red pepper and *garam masala*. Mix well and set aside.

2. Make a roll of the potato mixture about 3 inches long and an inch thick in diameter.

3. Wet the *papad* by immersing in water for a few seconds and then pick it up and spread it on the plate. Wait till it gets a little soft to roll. Put the roll of potato filling at the center of the *papad* and cover the potato roll by flapping the two sides of the *papad* over it. Cover the potato filling from the top with *papad* and start rolling the *papad* over it. Seal all the edges with gram flour paste.

4. Heat the oil in a wok at about 150°C–170°C or 300°F–350°F and fry the whole *papad* roll until light brown. Remove from oil with a large slotted spoon and place on paper towel lined plate to drain the excess oil. Cut one inch pieces. It goes best with fresh medium hot salsa. But it can also be served with sweet and sour mint *chutney* or sweet tamarind *chutney*. Makes a nice snack with tea or as an appetizer before a meal.

SERVES 4 – 6

Ingredients

Plain *papad* of *urad* or *mung dal*	4

Potatoes boiled and mashed	2 cups
Cooked rice	2 Tbs
Raisins	1 Tbs
Green chilies finely chopped (hot or mild according to preference)	1 tsp
Coriander leaves chopped	2 Tbs
Lemon juice	1 Tbs
Salt	1 tsp
Red pepper	½ tsp
Coriander powder	1 tsp
Ginger chopped	1 tsp
Garam masala	½ tsp
Vegetable oil (for frying)	4 cups

Note: *Papad* rolls look very much like egg rolls. You can use any filling of your choice.

The Exquisite World of Indian Cuisine

Rice Noodles Stir-Fried

The fine Chinese rice noodles when stir-fried with finely chopped carrots, finely chopped cabbage or French cut beans, fresh coconut and flavored with mustard seeds, dried chilies, curry leaves, coconut milk and salt make a very delicate but appetizing dish. It can be served for lunch or a dinner buffet; this dish can enhance any menu.

SERVES 6 – 8

Ingredients

Rice noodles thin Chinese or Thai 8 oz packet	1 pkt
Water to boil the noodles	4–6 cups
Carrots finely diced	¼ cup
Cabbage or french cut beans finely diced	¼ cup
Vegetable oil	3 Tbs
Coconut grated Or	1 cup
Dry coconut powder	2–4 Tbs
Cashew nuts (raw) chopped	2 Tbs
Mustard seeds	½ tsp
Urad dal	2 Tbs
Salt	to taste
Black pepper	½ tsp
Red pepper	¼ tsp
Coconut milk	½ cup
Curry leaves	8–10

METHOD

1. In a large saucepan boil 4 cups of water and add the noodles. Remove from heat and let the noodles sit in the hot water until softened – about 5 minutes. Drain the water and set the noodles aside.

2. In the same saucepan boil another 4 cups of water and add the chopped carrots and beans to cook. Leave in the water for a minute or two. Drain the water and cool the vegetables in the refrigerator.

3. In thick-bottom skillet add the 3 Tbs of oil. Heat it and add the mustard seeds and when they start popping add curry leaves and the *urad dal* and fry until the *dal* is light brown. Add the raw chopped cashew nuts, wait and fry and then add fresh or dry coconut. When it starts turning brown, add the noodles, coconut milk, salt, black pepper, red pepper and stir to mix. Cook until the coconut milk is all absorbed about 6–8 minutes. Fold in the cooked carrots and beans. Mix well and serve. Add more salt or coconut milk, if needed.

Note: 2 Tbs of coconut powder can be substituted for fresh coconut.

Lemon Rice Noodles

Homemade lemony rice noodles are a very common preparation in south India. They are quick fixing and tasty by themselves without any accompaniment. Therefore they make a very good teatime snack to take along with you when you are traveling or as a light lunch.

METHOD

1. Cook the noodles according to package directions and set them aside.
2. Heat the oil in a wok or heavy-bottom saucepan and add the mustard seeds. When they stop popping add the spilt peas, cashew nuts, and asafoetida and fry till the nuts start to turn light brown and the peas look done. Lower the heat.
3. Add the green chilies, curry leaves, and grated carrots and mix well.
4. Add the salt, red pepper, turmeric powder and cumin powder. Cover and cook for 2 minutes.
5. Add the cooked rice noodles and the lemon juice. Mix and coat the noodles well with the curry mixture. Heat them and serve, sprinkled with coriander leaves.

SERVES 4 – 6

Ingredients

Fresh rice noodles or packaged dry noodles (available at your local Indian grocery)	2 cups
Water to boil the noodles	6 cups
Dry yellow or green split peas	2 Tbs
Mustard seeds	1 tsp
Asafoetida powder	a pinch
Curry leaves chopped	1 Tbs
Vegetable oil	2 Tbs
Green chilies finely chopped hot or mild according to taste	2 Tbs
Carrots fresh and grated	½ cup
Salt	1 tsp
Red pepper	½ tsp
Cashew nuts or peanuts	¼ cup
Turmeric powder	¼ tsp
Cumin powder	½ tsp
Lemon juice	2–3 Tbs
Coriander leaves chopped	2 Tbs

The Exquisite World of Indian Cuisine

Spicy Fruit Salad
Fruit Chaat

India is known to have some of the most exotic fruits and vegetables. Vendors all over the country sell this mix (*chaat*) of fresh fruits like guavas, bananas, apples, pears, grapes, and fresh vegetables like cucumbers, tomatoes, boiled potatoes and boiled chick peas. The fruits and vegetables are chopped into bite size pieces and garnished with lemon juice, and *chaat masala* (black salt, ground roasted cumin, red pepper, *amchoor*, black pepper, *garam masala*) and the mint *chutney* or the tamarind *chutney*. This is a very healthy and delicious snack. *Chaat* is a term used for a snack and in this case the spices used make it a great appetizer too. This preparation brings back childhood memories when as a child or teenager, we looked forward to this snack from vendors near our homes.

METHOD

1. Wash and clean the fruits and the vegetables with fresh water and dry them.
2. Peel and chop the different fruits in bite size pieces in a large bowl. Cover and store in the refrigerator.
3. Chop the boiled potatoes, tomatoes, and cucumbers in different small size bowls and also transfer a can of washed and drained chick-peas in another bowl. Cover the bowls and also set them aside in the refrigerator. Just before snack time remove the bowls from the refrigerator and start serving as follows.
4. Transfer a cup of mixture of fruits onto the plate. Sprinkle a little *chaat masala* and mix it with tamarind *chutney* and serve or if you want to mix the vegetables with it. Then follow steps 5 and 6.
5. Add 1 Tbs each of boiled potatoes, tomatoes and cucumbers and 1 tsp of the chick peas onto the top of the fruit.
6. Squeeze about a tablespoon of lemon juice over the fruits and vegetable mix and sprinkle a tablespoon of mixture of the *chaat masala* and add a teaspoonful of mint *chutney* or sweet tamarind *chutney* (some people only like tamarind *chutney*) and serve.

Note: Ripe papaya, pomegranate, plums or peaches, kiwi fruits or *chikus* (sapodilla) can also be used for this salad.

SERVES 4 – 6

Ingredients

Guavas ripe – peeled and chopped into bite size pieces	2
Apples peeled and chopped	2
Bananas peeled and chopped	1
Pears peeled and chopped	2
Grapes	1 cup
Cucumber peeled and chopped	1 cup
Tomatoes ripe and firmly chopped	1 cup
Boiled peeled and chopped potatoes	1 cup
Cooked chick peas can (optional)	15 ozs
Chaat masala	¼ cup
Lemon juice from fresh lemons	4
Mint or Tamarind *chutney*	½ cup

Spiced Sweet Potatoes
Shakarkandi ki Chaat

Spiced baked sweet potatoes (*chaat*) is sold by the vendors in India around the major shopping areas. The sweet potatoes are baked in hot sand right on the vendor stand.

SERVES 4 – 6

Sweet potatoes	2 lbs
Chaat masala (from your Indian grocery store)	4 Tbs
Lemon juice fresh	4 Tbs

METHOD

1. Bake the sweet potato in an oven for 1 hour or until it is completely soft as a regular baked potato.

2. Peel and chop the baked sweet potato into one inch pieces in a large bowl. Cover and set aside.

3. Transfer a cup of chopped sweet potatoes to a serving plate and sprinkle with 1 Tbs of *chaat masala* (If *chaat masala*, is not available use salt, ground roasted cumin powder, black pepper, red pepper and *garam masala*) and 1 Tbs of lemon juice.

4. Toss the pieces well to coat with juice and *masala* and serve.

5. Makes an excellent healthy snack.

Note: Sweet potatoes are one of the unsung heroes of balanced diet. For a reasonable number of calories you get a bundle of nutrients. They stabilize blood sugar levels, and are top notch in fighting chronic ailments like cancers and heart disease. They are antiinflammatory and rich in potassium and vitamin C. They are packed with beta-carotene and have no cholesterol and no fat. An excellent food for children as well as adults.

Fruity Yogurt Poha
Payesh / Poha kheer

ASSAM

Rice is a staple food of Assam. Each meal has rice in one form or the other. Here is a delicious rice dish with fruits. It is served at breakfast or as an after school snack for children or as dessert. It is an easy last minute preparation, any time.

METHOD

1. Wash the *poha* in cold water in a small mixing bowl and drain the water completely. Add hot water slowly and let the *poha* soak in it for 5 minutes. Drain the water completely and set it aside.
2. Add yogurt to the drained *poha* in the bowl, and add chopped fruits. Mix them together gently. Add honey to your taste and mix it in. Transfer to a serving bowl and sprinkle with chopped almonds, raisins, coconut and a couple of sprigs of saffron. Sprinkle ½ tsp of cardamom and serve.

SERVES 2 – 4

Ingredients

Poha (flattened rice)	1 cup
Homemade yogurt	2 cups
Any seasonal fruit chopped	2 cups
Honey or molasses	2–4 Tbs
Almonds chopped	1 Tbs
Raisins and dates chopped	1 Tbs
Saffron	¼ tsp
Cardamom powder	½ tsp
Coconut grated (optional)	1 Tbs

APPETIZERS AND SNACKS

Tapioca Stir-Fried
Sabudana ki Khichdi

This fluffy preparation of softened tapioca is easy to make and looks very appetizing. It is one of my favorites for a light snack. Served mainly during festivals like *Shivratri*, and other fasting days when eating grain is not allowed.

METHOD

1. Wash and soak the Tapioca overnight in 2 cups of water. Drain and set it aside.
2. Heat the oil in a thick-bottom skillet and add to it mustard seeds and cumin seeds and wait till they start to pop.
3. Add the curry leaves, dry whole red pepper and wait till red pepper starts to sizzle.
4. Add the chopped onions, ginger and green chilies and stir. Cook until the ginger turns light brown and then add the garlic and let it cook for 2 minutes. Turn the heat on low.
5. Add the chopped potatoes, salt, red pepper, turmeric powder, black pepper, roasted peanuts and stir to mix. Add the drained Tapioca. Mix it well and heat it through. Remove from heat after a minute. Serve as a morning snack. Sprinkle lemon juice, *garam masala,* coriander leaves and mix to serve.

SERVES 2 – 4

Ingredients

Tapioca	1 cup
Peanuts roasted, crushed coarsely	¼ cup
Potato boiled peeled and chopped in small pieces	½ cup
Onions chopped	2 Tbs
Green chilies finely chopped	1 Tbs
Ginger finely chopped	1 Tbs
Garlic finely chopped (optional)	1 tsp
Curry leaves	6–8
Salt	1 tsp
Red pepper	½ tsp
Turmeric powder	½ tsp
Vegetable oil	2–3 Tbs
Mustard seeds	1 tsp
Cumin seeds	½ tsp
Red peppers whole (dry) broken	3
Black pepper	½ tsp
Coriander leaves chopped	1 Tbs
Lemon juice	1–2 Tbs
Garam masala	½ tsp

Note: Omit onions from the recipe, if cooking for a fasting devotee. This preparation is specially made for the devotees to break their fast on the day of *Maha Shivratri* (the Great Night of Shiva). It is believed that any person who recites the name of lord *Shiva* on this day with perfect devotion and concentration is set free from all past sins. He is also liberated from the cycle of births and deaths. In the *Hindu* religion there are three primary gods. *Brahma* – the Creator, *Vishnu* – the Keeper and *Shiva* – the Destroyer and Transformer, generally considered the supreme of all gods.

The Exquisite World of Indian Cuisine

Spicy Saltine Sticks
Mathri / Nimki

These crisp and crunchy spicy crackers are so yummy that it is hard to stop eating them once you start. When they are cut into one inch strips and fried, they are called *Nimki*. A great appetizer to go with drinks before the dinner, they make a perfect teatime snack too. They are very easy to make and can be enjoyed alone or with a pickle or sweet *chutney*.

METHOD

1. Mix all purpose flour, sesame seeds, ground roasted cumin seeds, *ajwain*, salt, red pepper, baking powder, and *ghee* or oil in a deep bowl and try to make a stiff but pliable dough with ¼ cup water. Add more water if needed.

For making Nimki:

2. Divide the dough into 2 inch balls and roll them real thin like a *chappati* about ⅛ inch thick and prick them all over with a fork. Cut them into strips with a sharp knife 2–3 inches long and ½ –¾ inch wide and set them aside. Cover them with a plastic wrap until ready to fry.

For making Mathri:

3. Cut a piece of dough as small as a walnut and roll it into a small patty about ⅛ inch thick with a diameter of 3 inches and prick it with knife or a fork at several places to prevent it from puffing up during frying. Set the patties aside covered with a plastic wrap.

4. Heat the oil to 300°F –340°F and deep-fry these strips and *Mathris* until golden brown and crisp on medium heat, few at a time. Drain them on to a paper towel and serve them with drinks or as a coffee snack.

5. Serve them with or without pickle or *chutney* of your choice.

SERVES 4 – 6

Ingredients

All purpose flour (*Maida*)	2 cups
Vegetable oil or *ghee*	4 Tbs
Salt	½ tsp
Baking powder	¼ tsp
Ajwain (carom seeds)	½ tsp
Cumin seeds ground roasted	½ tsp
Red pepper	½ tsp
Sesame seeds	½ tsp
Water as needed or	¼ cup
Oil (for frying) and more if needed	

Note: Sometimes whole black pepper corns are pressed into the discs or patties before frying to give them a spicy taste.

CHAPTER 3

Chicken

Chicken is extensively used all over India often with their regional variations. The Mughals introduced it into Indian cuisine in many magnificent ways. *Tandoori* (clay oven cooked) chicken from Lucknow in north India is famous all over the world. Every region of the country has developed its own version of chicken curry using their local produce. To name a few I would like to mention Chicken *Tikka Masala* and Chicken *Korma* from the north, Chicken in coconut gravy from Kerala, Chicken *Vindaloo* from Goa, *Dhansak* from Bombay and Chicken with cashew nut from Maharashtra. I have tried to present a sampling from each region to give the reader a glimpse of that region's cuisine. Cardamom chicken from Sri Lanka also gets a mention.

Chicken is preferred meat over all other meats because it has the least amount of fat that is also less saturated than in any other meat. It is much softer than other meats, and has very little odor of its own. Children love it with a little flavoring. It cooks fast and is lean as well as easy to digest.

The practice of raising chicken for food is ancient . If there is one word for chicken it is versatility. Roasted, broiled, grilled, or curried it is delicious, flavorful and nutritious. No wonder chicken is the primary source of proteins among the foods in the world. It is available throughout the year. It protects against bone loss and is rich in Vitamin B6. It can be used in soups, salads, sandwiches and main course dishes. It is the best source of animal proteins for infants and the elderly.

Chicken is a great source of proteins, selenium, Vitamin B, phosphorous, zinc, iron, riboflavin, thiamin and niacin.

It helps reduce the chances of Alzheimer's disease because it is rich in niacin. Chicken breast meat has the least amount of cholesterol. When buying chicken, make sure the skin is opaque and not spotted and it is solid frozen and that the 'sell by' date has not expired. It should be stored in the coldest section of the freezer and thaw the chicken preferably in the refrigerator. Wash the cutting board, utensils, and even your hands thoroughly with soap after chopping or handling chicken.

Chicken cooked with Lentils and Vegetables
Dhansak

A *Parsi* (Persians settled in India) speciality, wholesome and rich with a unique blend of chicken, legumes, and vegetables. It is a meal by itself, delicious and nutritious.

SERVES 8 – 10

Ingredients

Mung dal	¼ cup
Toor dal	½ cup
Masoor dal	¼ cup
Water	6 cups
Breast of chicken cut into 3" pieces	1 lb
Onions chopped	1 cup
Garlic chopped	1 Tbs
Ginger chopped	1 Tbs
Green chilies	1 Tbs
Tomatoes Fresh chopped	1 cup
Tamarind pulp	½ tsp
Vegetable oil	¼ cup
Coriander leaves chopped	1 Tbs
Dill freshly chopped	2 Tbs
Eggplant (medium) chopped	1
Potatoes chopped	½ cup
Spinach chopped	1 cup
Fenugreek leaves freshly chopped	½ cup
or dry	2 Tbs
Cardamom seeds	½ tsp
Turmeric powder	1 tsp
Curry leaves	4-6
Cumin seeds	2 tsp
Coriander seeds	1½ Tbs
Cinnamom sticks (small) pieces	2
Red pepper	1 tsp
Salt	to taste
Garam masala	1 tsp
Black pepper	1 tsp
Fresh pumpkin chopped	1 cup

METHOD

1. Wash and soak all three *dals* for ½ hour. Dry-roast 1 tsp of cumin seeds, coriander seeds, cinnamon sticks, cardamom seeds and grind them and set them aside.

2. In a large saucepan cook all the *dals* in 6 cups of water with ½ tsp turmeric, salt and the curry leaves for about 10 minutes on low heat and then add all the chopped vegetables, potatoes, pumpkin and eggplant.

3. Cook vegetables for 5–10 minutes and set the pan aside.

4. In another large saucepan cook the onions, ginger, garlic, and green chilies, and stir-fry for a few minutes until the onions are light brown. Add another teaspoon of cumin seeds. Wait till they pop.

5. Add the chicken pieces and coat them with this spice mixture while stirring for 5 minutes or until the chicken pieces turn white.

6. Add the remaining turmeric powder, ground spice mixture (see step 1), salt, red pepper, black pepper, chopped spinach, fenugreek leaves, *dill* leaves and chopped tomatoes. Stir-fry for 5–10 minutes on low heat until the tomatoes are softened and the sauce gets thick.

7. Now transfer the lentil mixture in to the chicken mixture. Cover the pan and cook until the chicken is tender (about 25–30 minutes) and add more water if the sauce is getting too thick.

8. Mix the tamarind pulp dissolved in a tablespoon of water and mix it into the meat and *dal* mixture. Simmer for 5 more minutes.

9. Top it with *garam masala* and coriander leaves and stir well while *dhansak* is cooking on low heat.

10. Serve with plain rice, *khus-khus, pulav* or *nan*.

Chicken Curry
Murg Curry

In this excellent preparation, chicken pieces or cubes of breast of chicken are marinated in yogurt and then curried. Marinating in yogurt makes the chicken pieces moist and flavorful. Serve it with plain rice or rice *pulav*. It makes a great meal.

SERVES 4 – 6

Ingredients

Marinade:

Yogurt	½ cup
Salt	1 tsp
Green chilies ground	1 tsp
Ginger ground	1 tsp
Garlic ground	1 tsp
Red pepper	½ tsp
Lemon juice	1 Tbs
Vegetable oil	1 Tbs

For the Curry:

Breast chicken cubed	2 lbs
Onions chopped	1 cup
Ginger chopped	1 tsp
Garlic chopped	1 tsp
Green chilies chopped (mild)	1 tsp
Cloves	½ tsp
Peppercorns	6
Cinnamon stick (small)	1
Cardamoms brown	2
Cumin seeds	1 tsp
Tomato sauce	1½ cup
Tomatoes medium chopped	2
Turmeric powder	1 tsp
Coriander powder	1 tsp
Red pepper	1 tsp
Salt	1 tsp
Vegetable oil	2 Tbs
Bell pepper medium chopped	2
Desiccated coconut (optional)	2 Tbs
Coriander leaves chopped	2 Tbs
Garam masala	1 tsp
Heavy cream	2 Tbs
Fenugreek leaves (dry)	1 Tbs

METHOD

1. In a bowl transfer yogurt and beat it smooth with a fork. Add salt, green chillies, ginger, garlic, red pepper, lemon juice and oil. Add the chicken cubes. Mix well to coat chicken pieces with spices and yogurt. Leave the chicken in the marinade preferably overnight or for at least 1 hour.

2. Heat the oil and fry the onions, garlic, green chillies and ginger until the onions turn brown. *Add all the whole spices, cloves, peppercorns, cinnamon sticks, cardamoms, cumin seeds, and wait till the cumin seeds star to pop, then add the tomato sauce, chopped tomatoes and all the ground spices like turmeric powder, coriander powder, red pepper, salt, desiccated coconut and dried fenugreek leaves.

3. Stir well to mix for a minute or two or until the oil separates from the sauce.

4. Add the marinated chicken along with the marinade and stir and cook for 5 minutes on medium, low heat. Cover the pan with a lid.

5. If thin curry is desired, then add ½ cup of water, otherwise simmer over medium heat till the chicken is tender (about 20–25 minutes). Now add the chopped bell pepper and stir well. Cook more for 5–10 minutes.

6. Add the cream, coriander leaves and garam *masala* and mix. Slow cook for another 2 minutes and bring it to boil.

7. Serve in a serving dish sprinkled with few chopped coriander leaves and *garam masala*.

Note: Dried fenugreek leaves are available at an Indian grocery store.
*Whole spices can be used in a *garni*.

The Exquisite World of Indian Cuisine

Chicken in Coconut Gravy
Murg Nariyal Masala

KERALA

Chicken cooked in a hot and spicy sauce of coconut milk and tamarind and flavored with mustard and fenugreek seeds give this curry a special south Indian touch. It goes very well with plain rice, *nan* or *chappati* and your special stir-fry vegetable and *raita*.

SERVES 8 – 10

Ingredients

Coriander seeds	2 Tbs
Mustard seeds	½ tsp
Fenugreek seeds	½ tsp
Cumin seeds	1 tsp
Coconut milk	1½ cups
Onions chopped	2 cups
Ginger chopped	1 Tbs
Garlic chopped	1 Tbs
Green chilies chopped (jalapeno)	1 tsp
Curry leaves	4–5
Cinnamon stick 1 inch	1
Cardamoms large	1
Red pepper whole (dry) broken	2
Tamarind pulp	1 tsp
Salt to taste or	1 tsp
Turmeric powder	1 tsp
Black pepper	½ tsp
Red pepper	1 tsp
Chicken breast 1–2 inch pieces or legs and thighs	2 lbs
Coconut grated Or	1 cup
Dry coconut powder	2 Tbs
Vegetable oil or *ghee*	¼ cup
Coriander leaves chopped	2 Tbs
Garam masala	1 tsp

METHOD

1. Heat a tablespoon of oil to coat the surface of a skillet and quickly roast the grated coconut or dry coconut powder and set it aside. Similarly roast the coriander seeds, mustard seeds, fenugreek seeds and the cumin seeds. Grind all the spices in a small coffee grinder with ½ cup of coconut milk and set this aside.

2. Fry the onions, ginger, garlic, and green chilies, in the remaining oil in a deep wok on medium-low heat or a Dutch oven and wait till the onions turn brown.

3. Lower the heat and add the curry leaves, cinnamon sticks, cardamoms, whole red pepper, the ground spices and fry until they start to separate from the oil.

4. Add the tamarind pulp dissolved in 1 Tbs of water, salt, turmeric powder, black pepper, red pepper and ¼ cup water and stir until the mixture is like a sauce.

5. Add the chicken and cook for 5 minutes on medium heat.

6. Add 1 cup of coconut milk and cook the mixture on low heat by covering the pan with the lid until the chicken is tender, about 20–25 minutes. Stir in between to prevent sticking.

7. Sprinkle *garam masala* and the coriander leaves and heat through. Serve with plain rice, *pulav, nan* or *chappati* and any stir-fry vegetable.

Goan Chicken Curry
Murg Vindaloo

GOA

Chicken cooked with vinegar and coconut milk from Goa, a former Portuguese colony along the west coast of India. Goa is known for its glorious past with its magnificent churches, groves of cashew, scenic beauty with palm and coconut trees swaying on the shiny sandy beaches of the Arabian sea. The dish is enriched by the use of coconut milk and tamarind. It really is very delicious.

METHOD

1. Dry roast the cumin seeds, poppy seeds, mustard seeds, cinnamon sticks, pepper corns, cloves, coriander seeds, cardamom seeds and whole dry red peppers on a hot skillet and grind them in a coffee grinder. *Vindaloo masala* or *Reiachado masala* (recipe in introduction) can be used for marinating, instead of the above *masala*.
2. Transfer the above *masala* to a bowl and mix it with the vinegar, tamarind pulp, salt, sugar, oil and set it aside. This is the marinade.
3. Wash and clean the chicken pieces. Make small cuts in the chicken thighs and legs or breast pieces and marinate them in the above marinade for at least 30 minutes.
4. Fry onions, garlic, ginger, and green chilies in 3 Tbs of oil in a Dutch oven or a deep heavy bottom saucepan until light brown and add the curry leaves, coriander powder, red pepper, turmeric powder and fry till they start sizzling.
5. Add the chopped tomatoes and stir-fry the mixture for few minutes or until the tomatoes are soft and mixture has turned into a sauce. Keep frying until the oil separates from the sauce.
6. Add the potatoes or the baby onions and coat them with the sauce for a couple of minutes and then add the marinated chicken, with the marinade and stir well. Cook for 25–30 minutes.
7. Add the coconut milk and simmer until the potatoes are tender and chicken is done. Takes another 5–10 minutes.
8. Top it off with chopped coriander leaves, *garam masala* and heat through.

SERVES 8 – 10

Ingredients

For the curry:

Onions chopped	2 cups
Ginger chopped	1 Tbs
Garlic chopped	1 Tbs
Green chilies chopped	1 Tbs
Curry leaves	5–6
Vegetable oil	¼ cup
Boiled potatoes (small)	8–10
Or	
Canned small baby onions in vinegar (reduce vinegar in the marinade)	8–10
Turmeric powder	1 tsp
Red pepper	1 tsp
Coriander powder	2 tsp
Tomatoes chopped	1 cup
Coconut milk canned (unsweetened)	½ cup
Coriander leaves chopped	1 Tbs
Garam masala	½ tsp

For the marinade:

Skinless chicken thighs or legs or 2 inch pieces of breast of chicken	2 lbs
Coriander seeds	1 tsp
Cinnamon whole	1 inch
Cloves and peppercorns each	1 tsp
Red pepper whole	2
Green cardamom seeds	2
Mustard seeds	1 tsp
Poppy seeds	1 Tbs
Cumin seeds	1 tsp
Salt	1 Tbs
Vegetable oil	2–3 Tbs
Sugar	1 tsp
Vinegar (use only 1 Tbs if using canned onions in vinegar)	2 Tbs
Tamarind pulp	1 tsp

Chicken in Creamy Sauce
Murg Korma

ANDHRA PRADESH

Chicken cooked in creamy sauce of nuts and cream is rich and very special. It is usually made at parties or weddings. *Korma* is a delightful addition to any meal and is always found in a menu of an Indian restaurant. This is how the Mughals cooked and served. Sometimes turmeric and tomato sauce is omitted to keep this dish white to make it look elegant.

SERVE 6 – 8

METHOD

1. Soak the poppy seeds in ½ cup of water for ½ hour.
2. Grind the poppy seeds, almonds and cashew with water in an electric blender or a coffee grinder into a paste and set it aside.
3. Similarly grind the onions, ginger, garlic and green chilies and set it aside.
4. Heat the *ghee* in a pan and fry the above ground mixture in a deep thick bottom saucepan or a Dutch oven. Add the bay leaves, ground cardamoms, ground cloves, and ground cinnamon and cook for 2 minutes. Then add the tomato sauce, salt, red pepper, coriander powder, cumin powder and stir well. Cook until the tomato sauce get mixed well into the spice mixture keeping the heat low. Cook till the sauce separates from the oil.
5. Add the ground paste of nuts. Stir-fry for five more minutes.
6. Add the chicken pieces and stir them well. Cook for 5 minutes on slow heat and keep stirring.
7. Add the yogurt and mix.
8. Add a cup of water and simmer for 25–30 minutes or until the pieces are soft and done.
9. Sprinkle *garam masala* and chopped coriander leaves and continue cooking for a minute more.
10. Remove from heat and serve with *nan, chappati*, pea *pulav* or vegetable stir-fry of your choice.

Note: When making pistachio *korma* substitute the almonds and cashew with ½ cup ground shelled pistachios.

Ingredients

Cashew nuts	¼ cup
Poppy seeds	2 tsp
Almonds slivered and chopped	¼ cup
Onions chopped	1 cup
Ginger chopped	1 Tbs
Garlic chopped	1 Tbs
Green chilies chopped	1 tsp
Bay leaves	4–5
Cardamoms (ground)	¼ tsp
Cloves (ground)	¼ tsp
Cinnamon (ground)	¼ tsp
Tomato sauce (optional)	1 cup
Water	½ cup
Red pepper	1 tsp
Coriander powder	1½ tsp
Cumin powder	½ tsp
Yogurt	½ cup
Garam masala	1 tsp
Vegetable oil or *ghee*	⅓ cup
Salt	1 tsp
Coriander leaves chopped	1 Tbs
Chicken breasts chopped into 1 inch pieces	2 lbs

Chicken Stew
Kolhapuri Murg

MAHARASHTRA

This recipe comes from Kolhapur, the coastal region of the state of Maharashtra, where coconut grows in abundance. Chicken stew cooked with boneless pieces or breast pieces, vegetables and potatoes in the gravy of coconut milk and aromatic spices is a popular dish in the Malabar Hills of Karnataka and Kerala. It is usually served with rice pancakes but goes very well with the plain rice too.

SERVE 6 – 8

Ingredients

Breast or boneless thigh meat chicken pieces	1½ lbs
Onions chopped	2 cups
Ginger chopped	1 Tbs
Garlic chopped	1 Tbs
Green chilies chopped (mild)	1 Tbs
Coriander leaves	½ cup
Grated coconut	1 cup
Curry leaves	8–10
Salt	to taste
Turmeric powder	1 tsp
Red pepper	1 tsp
Malwani masala (see recipe in Introduction)	2 Tbs
White potatoes (small)	10
Carrots chopped into horizontal pieces	½ cup
Frozen peas	½ cup
Coconut milk	1½ cups
Water	½ cup
Vegetable oil or *ghee*	4 Tbs

METHOD

1. Cook 1 cup of onions, ginger, garlic and green chilies in 2 Tbs of vegetable oil in a thick bottom saucepan and wait till they turn light brown. Remove them from the oil and grind them in the blender along with ¼ cup of coriander leaves. Set aside this onion paste.

2. Cook the remaining onions in the remaining oil until light brown and add the grated coconut and curry leaves and brown it. Add the salt, red pepper, turmeric powder, ground onions paste and the *malwani masala* and stir to mix well.

3. Add the chicken pieces and sauté in this spices mixture for 3–5 minutes.

4. Add the potatoes, carrots and peas and stir well to coat them with these spices.

5. Add coconut milk and water. Mix in well and let it simmer on medium-low heat for 20–30 minutes or until the chicken is done. Add more water if needed. Sprinkle with ¼ cup of chopped coriander leaves. Mix and serve.

The Exquisite World of Indian Cuisine

Fine in-lay work in marble from Agra, Uttar Pradesh

Clay Oven Grilled Chicken
Murg Tikka

UTTAR PRADESH

A delightful dish from the royal kitchen of the *Nawabs* of Lucknow in north India. It is one of the most favorite non-vegetarian main courses in the menu of most Indian restaurants. Delightfully tender, juicy and flavorful. It is popular in the western countries too.

SERVES 8 – 10

Ingredients

For the marinade:

Green chilies chopped	1 tsp
Garlic chopped	1 Tbs
Ginger chopped	1 Tbs
Turmeric powder	½ tsp
Salt	1 tsp
Chicken pieces or breast halves	2 lbs
Lemon juice	2 Tbs
Oil for the marinade	2 Tbs
Coriander powder	1 tsp
Cumin powder	1 tsp
Red pepper	½ tsp
Tomato sauce	¼ cup
Yogurt	½ cups

For sprinkling over:

Amchoor (powdered raw mango powder)	1 Tbs
Melted *ghee* or clarified butter	2 Tbs
Fenugreek leaves dry (*kasuri methi*)	1 Tbs
Cumin powder (ground roasted)	1 Tbs
Lime juice	1 Tbs
Salt	to taste
Garam masala	1 tsp
Paprika as needed	

To garnish:
Sliced onions, green chilies, mint leaves or chopped coriander leaves

METHOD

1. Make cuts over the chicken pieces. Mix the chopped green chilies, ginger, garlic, turmeric powder, salt, lemon juice, oil, coriander powder, cumin powder, tomato sauce and red pepper into the yogurt and rub this yogurt mixture onto the chicken pieces and leave in this marinade for at least an hour.

2. Remove them one at a time from the yogurt and sprinkle them with tomato coloring or paprika and keep on arranging them in a large dish with a grilling pan in it. Broil them in the oven and brush them with oil or *ghee* before you put them in the oven and cook until chicken is starting to turn brown on both sides.

3. Take them out of the oven and sprinkle with *amchoor*, dry fenugreek leaves, ground roasted cumin powder, lime juice and the *ghee* and broil again for another 5–10 minutes or until the chicken starts to turn darker brown. *Amchoor*, dry roasted cumin powder and *garam masala* can be substituted by 1 Tbs of *tandoori masala* (see Introduction).

4. Serve the chicken pieces sprinkled with *garam masala* in a platter garnished with sliced onions, green chilies, lemon wedges, and mint leaves or coriander leaves.

5. It makes one of the excellent main courses in a formal dinner.

Note: *Tandoori masala* is also available at your local Indian grocery store.

The Exquisite World of Indian Cuisine

Grilled Chicken in Gravy
Murg Tikka Masala

PUNJAB

Marinated chicken pieces baked in the oven and then dressed with thick curry sauce are a great preparation. They go very well as a main dish, and to serve at formal parties with pea *pulav* and *nan*. It is an excellent dish to order in a restaurant.

METHOD

1. Prepare the marinade by mixing the yogurt with lemon juice, salt, red pepper and oil. Transfer the chicken pieces in the marinade overnight or for at least a couple of hours. Broil them in the oven in a grilling pan or on an outdoor grill until light brown and set it aside.
2. Cook the onions in *ghee* and add the ginger, garlic and green chilies, and fry until light brown. Add the cumin seeds and wait till they pop.
3. Add the tomato sauce and water and mix.
4. Add the turmeric powder, coriander powder, dry fenugreek leaves, red pepper, ground roasted sesame seeds and salt. Cook the mixture for 5 minutes till the oil starts to separate from the sauce.
5. Add the chicken pieces and cook them for about 5 minutes on low heat and coat them well with sauce. Add ¼ cup of cream and cook for another 5 minutes.
6. Serve garnished with *garam masala*, ground roasted cumin powder and green coriander leaves.

Note: Use leftover pieces of the *Murg Tikka* (see recipe), It will be a perfect use of the leftover chicken.

SERVES 8

Ingredients

For the marinade:

Chicken breast, legs or thighs (skinned)	2 lbs
Yogurt	1½ cup
Lemon juice	2 Tbs
Salt	1 tsp
Red pepper	1 tsp
Vegetable oil	2 Tbs

For curry sauce:

Onions chopped	2 cups
Ginger chopped	1 Tbs
Garlic chopped	1 Tbs
Green chilies	1 tsp
Cumin seeds	1 tsp
Tomato sauce (15 ozs can)	1
Coriander powder	1 Tbs
Sesame seeds ground, roasted	2 Tbs
Red pepper	1 tsp
Salt	to taste
Cumin powder ground, roasted	1 Tbs
Fenugreek leaves (dry)	1 Tbs
Turmeric powder	1 tsp
Garam masala	1 tsp
Water	¼ cup
Cream (for garnish)	¼ cup
Green coriander chopped	2 Tbs
Vegetable oil or *ghee*	2 Tbs

Chicken with Cashew Nuts
Bombay Murg Korma

MAHARASHTRA

Along the west coast of India, Maharashtra, in Mumbai and even in Hyderabad, the chicken is cooked in thick-hot gravy of grated coconut, cashew, and dark *masala* to give it a special nutty and creamy taste. It is delicious and is worth the effort.

SERVES 6 – 8

Ingredients

Cumin seeds	1 tsp
Coriander seeds	2 Tbs
Black pepper (corns)	½ tsp
Freshly grated coconut.	½ cup
Or dry coconut	2 Tbs
Cloves	½ tsp
Red pepper whole, dry	2 or 3
Cashew nuts	3 Tbs
Onions chopped	2 cups
Ginger chopped	1 Tbs
Garlic chopped	1 Tbs
Green chilies chopped	1 tsp
Chicken breast pieces or thighs or legs	3 lbs
Cinnamon sticks (small)	2
Cardamoms green	4
Tomatoes chopped	1½ cup
Turmeric powder	1 tsp
Red pepper	1 tsp
Salt	1½ tsp
Curry leaves	3–4
Cashew whole	½ cup
Raisins	2 ozs
Coconut milk	½ cup
Coriander leaves chopped	1 Tbs
Vegetable oil	¼ cup
Water (for grinding spices)	¾ cup

METHOD

1. Pan fry cumin seeds, coriander seeds, peppercorns, cloves, whole dry red pepper, grated coconut, and 3 Tbs of the cashew for a few minutes with no oil until light brown and aromatic. Grind them to fine paste in a blender with ¾ cup of water and set it aside (or use 2 Tbs of *goda masala*) (see Introduction). Fry coconut powder or fresh coconut at the end of frying and mix.
2. Fry the onions in oil in a thick bottom 2–3 quart saucepan with ginger, garlic, and green chilies, and wait till the onions turn brown. Add the curry leaves, cinnamon and cardamoms.
3. Add the ground cashew and spices mixture and stir-fry for 5 minutes.
4. Add the tomatoes, turmeric powder, red pepper, salt and mix on low heat until the tomatoes become mushy and the mixture looks like a sauce. As soon as the sauce separates from the oil add the chicken pieces.
5. Cover with a lid and let chicken cook in its own juices for 5 minutes and add the whole cashew and raisins and mix.
6. Add the coconut milk, water and let it simmer until the chicken is tender and starts to separate from the bone (about 25–30 minutes). If the gravy is thick add more boiled water as needed. Sprinkle the chopped coriander leaves.
7. Serve with lemon rice or plain rice, *chappati* and stir-fry vegetable of your choice.

The Exquisite World of Indian Cuisine

Onion Chicken
Murg Do Pyazaa

Chicken pieces are baked with halves of onions, small whole potatoes, whole and ground spices, and the sauce of tomatoes and yogurt and topped with chopped fried onions and curry leaves. This wholesome, appetizing dish has become very popular in many restaurants also. All you need to fix with it is some bread or rice and the meal is complete.

METHOD

1. Fry the chopped onions in a heavy thick bottom saucepan on medium-low heat in 2 Tbs of oil and remove into a bowl with a slotted spoon and set them aside.
2. In the same oil fry the ginger, garlic, and green chilies, and add the cardamoms, cloves, cinnamon, black pepper corns and whole red pepper.
3. Sauté them for a minute or two.
4. Add the chicken pieces, and the potatoes and fry them with the whole spices for at least 5 minutes.
5. Now fry the onion halves in another frying pan and sauté for another 2 minutes, gently, so that the layers of the onion halves stay intact.
6. Lower the heat and add to the pan chicken pieces, chopped tomatoes, yogurt, salt, turmeric, coriander powder, red pepper, sugar, and stir and coat the pieces in the sauce for another 5 minutes. Add ½ cup of water and stir to mix.
7. Lay down the onion halves and chicken pieces flat into the baking dish along with the potatoes and pour the sauce over them.
8. Cover with thin foil and bake in the oven at 425°F for 25–30 minutes or until the potatoes and chicken are done. Top the dish with *garam masala*, fried onions and the curry leaves.
9. Serve with *pulav*. Makes a very appealing presentation.

SERVES 6 – 8

Ingredients

Onions chopped	1 cup
Ginger chopped	1 Tbs
Garlic chopped	1 Tbs
Green chilies chopped	1 Tbs
*Cardamoms brown	2
Cloves	½ tsp
Black pepper corns	1 tsp
Red pepper whole	2
Chicken legs, thighs or breast pieces cut in half	2–2½ lbs
Potatoes (washed and peeled)	8 small
Onions (medium) cut in halves	6
Tomatoes chopped	2 cups
Yogurt smoothly beaten	½ cup
Salt	1 tsp
Coriander powder	1 Tbs
Turmeric powder	1 tsp
Red pepper	1 tsp
Cinnamon stick	1 inch
Sugar	1 Tbs
Curry leaves	8–10
Vegetable oil or *ghee*	3 Tbs
Garam masala	1 tsp
Water	½ cup

*Whole spices are added only for flavor. Omit them if you wish.

The majestic Jama Masjid in Delhi. Commissioned by the Mughal Emperor Shah Jehan, it is the largest and one of the finest mosques in India

Cardamom Chicken Curry
Kukul Mas Curry

Chicken pieces marinated in ground mixture of roasted spices, cashew nuts, rice, grated coconut, coriander seeds, cumin seeds, dry red chilies and curried in onions and coconut milk. It is simply aromatic and uniquely different.

METHOD

1. Transfer the rice grains, coriander seeds, black pepper corns, cumin seeds, red peppers, cinnamon sticks and cardamom seeds into a wok and dry roast them slowly on medium-low heat until they start to turn brown and become aromatic. Store them in a bowl.
2. Now roast the cashew nuts and transfer them also into the bowl. Lastly roast the coconut powder. It will roast very fast. Mix that also into the mixture in the bowl. Grind all the spices and nuts in a coffee grinder and set it aside.
3. Wash the chicken pieces and remove the skin. Coat the pieces with spice mixture one by one and set all of them in a baking dish. Cook them on a broil for 10–15 minutes turning them once or bake them in a oven for 20–25 minutes at 400ºF. Brush them with the oil while cooking and broiling. Set them aside.
4. Heat the oil in a large saucepan or a frying pan and add the chopped onions, ginger, and garlic and fry the onions until light brown and add the tomato sauce and the curry leaves.
5. Stir-fry and add the salt, and turmeric powder. Fry until the oil separates from the sauce. Stir well and lower the heat. Add the baked chicken pieces and coat them with tomato sauce mixture. Add 1 cup coconut milk. Let it cook for 5 minutes. Stir in between to make sure it is not sticking. Add ½ cup of water, if the curry is too thick.
6. Add curry leaves. Stir them in. Put the cover back on and let it cook for another 5 minutes. Serve with plain rice and simple vegetable stir-fry.

SERVES 6 – 8

Ingredients

Chicken legs or thigh pieces	12–14

For marinade:

Rice grains	1 Tbs
Coriander seeds	1 Tbs
Cumin seeds	1 Tbs
Red chilies (dry) crushed	4
Black pepper corns	½ tsp
Cinnamon stick 1 inch piece	1
Cardamom seeds	1 tsp
Cashew nuts	¼ cup
Coconut powder grated sweetened	2 Tbs
Oil (for brushing) Or	2 Tbs
Clarified butter (for brushing)	2–3 Tbs

Ingredients for sauce:

Onions chopped	1 cup
Ginger and garlic each chopped	1 Tbs
Tomato sauce	1 cup
Salt	1½ tsp
Turmeric powder	1 tsp
Oil	3 Tbs
Coconut milk	½–1 cup
Curry leaves	6–8
Oil (for cooking)	3 Tbs

The Exquisite World of Indian Cuisine

Butter Chicken
Murg Makhani

PUNJAB

Boneless or on bone pieces of chicken are marinated in yogurt and spices. These are then barbecued or simply cooked with the marinade in a creamy sauce of tomatoes, butter or heavy cream. Try this delightful Punjabi style chicken dish.

SERVES 8 – 10

Ingredients

Chicken legs, thighs or breast (cut into 1 inch pieces)	2 lbs
Oil to cook the chicken	3 Tbs

Ingredients for the marinade:

Yogurt	1 cup
Ginger chopped	1 Tbs
Garlic chopped	1 Tbs
Green chilies chopped	1 tsp
Red pepper	1 tsp
Coriander powder	1 Tbs
Lemon juice	2 Tbs
Salt	1 tsp
Cumin powder	1 tsp
Vegetable oil or *ghee*	2 Tbs
Garam masala	1 tsp
Fenugreek leaves dry (powdered)	2 Tbs
Turmeric powder	½ tsp

Ingredients for the sauce:

Butter melted	¼ cup
Tomato sauce	2 Tbs
Heavy cream	½ cup
Garam masala	½ tsp
Green coriander leaves chopped	1 Tbs
Tandoori color or paprika (available at an Indian grocery store)	½ tsp
Cumin seeds	½ tsp
Red pepper whole dry (optional)	a few

METHOD

1. Beat the yogurt smooth. Mix the ingredients for the marinade into it and then add the chicken pieces. If using legs and thigh pieces make cuts into the meat with a knife. Leave the chicken for at least an hour in the marinade. Leave longer preferably overnight to get better results.

2. Heat 3 Tbs of oil in a medium size heavy bottom deep saucepan for half a minute and slowly transfer the chicken with the marinade into it. Cook on medium-low heat for 25–30 minutes covered. Cook it open on low heat for another 10 minutes until the sauce thickens and chicken is almost done. Set it aside.

3. In a small saucepan mix melted butter and heat it. Add cumin seeds and when they start to pop, add tomato sauce and cook on low heat. Add heavy cream and the *garam masala* and more salt (if needed) and also add the *tandoori* color or paprika.

4. Add another ½ tsp of red pepper, if desired.

5. Cook for 5 more minutes and transfer the sauce to the cooked chicken and mix well. Boil and cook until the sauce thickens. Add the chopped coriander leaves and serve with pea *pulav*, *nan*, *chappati* or rice.

Chicken in Fenugreek Sauce
Methi Murg

Chicken cooked with mixture of ground spinach, fenugreek leaves and coriander leaves has a unique combination of greens with a creamy sauce. It has excellent flavor, is very nutritious and delicious.

SERVES 6 – 8

Ingredients

Fresh cilantro leaves chopped	1½ cup
Fenugreek leaves (dry)	¼ cup
Dill leaves	¼ cup
Green chilies	5–6
Spinach leaves chopped	1 cup
Or	
Spinach leaves frozen	½ cup
Cinnamon stick	1 inch
Brown cardamoms	2
Red dry peppers (whole), broken	2
Cumin seeds	1 tsp
Onions chopped	1 cup
Ginger chopped	1 Tbs
Garlic chopped	1 Tbs
Tomato sauce	1 cup
Turmeric powder	1 tsp
Red pepper	1 tsp
Salt	1½ tsp
Coriander powder	1 Tbs
Chicken pieces or breast of chicken	2 lbs
Heavy cream	2 Tbs
Vegetable oil or *ghee*	3 Tbs
Garam masala	1 tsp

METHOD

1. Wash coriander leaves, dill leaves and green chilies and grind them in a blender. Add the dry fenugreek leaves and the frozen and thawed spinach leaves to the ground mixture and grind again. Add ½ cup of water, if needed, and set the paste aside.

2. Heat the oil in a deep thick-bottom saucepan and add the cinnamon sticks, cardamoms, dry red pepper and cumin seeds. Wait till the seeds start popping and then add the onions, ginger. Fry them until the onions start to turn brown and then add the garlic and the ground green spinach and chilies mixture and stir-fry for few more minutes. Add the tomato sauce, turmeric powder, red pepper, coriander powder and salt and mix well. Turn down the heat and cook the sauce for 3–5 minutes or until the oil separates from the sauce.

3. Add the chicken and stir well to cover the pieces with the sauce. Keep the heat medium-low and cover with a lid and let it simmer for 30 minutes or until the chicken is tender, stirring in between to prevent any sticking.

4. Gently stir in the cream and *garam masala*. Heat it through.

5. Serve with plain rice or pea *pulav*, and or *nan*. This chicken preparation meets the requirement for both meat and vegetables. You do not have to serve another vegetable with it, but if there is one it is all the better.

Note: The dish does not have traditionally looking yellow sauce, it is green but quite delicious. It has a creamy and herbaceous taste.

Chicken Pickle Style
Achaari Murg

PUNJAB

In Punjab, pickling spices are also used sometimes to make chicken or a lamb curry. The aroma of this curry is unparalleld.

SERVES 4 – 6

Ingredients

Chicken breast or lean lamb meat cut in cubes (1½ inch pieces)	2 lbs
Achaari masala	3–4 Tbs
Coconut grated (dry)	2 Tbs
Sesame seeds roasted (crushed)	2 Tbs
Salt	1 Tbs
Onions chopped	3 cups
Ginger chopped	2 Tbs
Green chilies chopped	2 Tbs
Garlic chopped	2 Tbs
Turmeric powder	1 tsp
Red pepper	1–2 tsp
Yogurt smoothly beaten	1¼ cup
Extra virgin olive oil or clarified butter	4 Tbs
Coriander leaves chopped	3 Tbs
Garam masala	1 tsp

METHOD

1. Clean and chop the breast of chicken in 1½ inch pieces (legs and thighs of chicken can be used too) and sprinkle with *achaari masala*, ½ tsp *garam masala*, grated coconut and ground roasted sesame seeds and 1 tsp of salt. Set this aside.

2. Heat 4 Tbs of oil in a heavy-bottom cooking pan and transfer the onions, green chilies, ginger, and garlic into it. Fry the onion until it has turned light brown. Remove the onion mixture from the pan and save in a bowl.

3. Add the *masala* coated chicken into the same pan and fry and cook the chicken until the pieces have turned completely white (5–10 minutes).

4. To the above add the onion mixture, turmeric powder, red pepper, and 1 tsp of salt. Stir to fry the chicken in this mixture for 2–3 minutes. Add the yogurt. Stir well to mix. Lower the heat and cover the pan. Let it simmer for 15–20 minutes or wait till the oil separates from the chicken and its sauce. Add the coriander leaves and ½ tsp of *garam masala* and mix well. Let it simmer another 2 minutes and serve with plain rice or pea *pulav*. It is absolutely delicious.

Fried Chicken
Tala hua Murg

Fried chicken is not so popular in India as it is in North America and Europe. In this recipe, pieces are marinated in a spicy paste of ground red dry chilies, onions, ginger, garlic, green chilies, rice, yogurt, salt and eggs. It is then coated with bread crumbs or cornflakes crumbs and baked in the oven. Serve it with salad, French fried potatoes, sweet and sour sauce or any sauce of your choice. It is pretty hot and tangy.

METHOD

1. Grind ginger, garlic, green and red chilies, yogurt and rice grains into a paste in a blender. Add salt, 1 Tbs of oil, *garam masala* and 1 egg to the paste. Add coriander leaves and stir to mix them well. Set aside the marinade.
2. Make small cuts in the chicken pieces and marinade them in this marinade mixture for at least 1–2 hours.
3. Grease a large baking dish with ¼ cup of oil.
4. Transfer fine dry bread crumbs to a large dish and add a teaspoon of black pepper, red pepper and salt to it. Mix well. Roll the pieces in the bread crumbs and lay them flat in the baking dish. *Bake them in the oven at 425°F. Turn them couple of times to make sure they are evenly brown.
5. Bake for 20–25 minutes or until the pieces are crisp and have turned golden brown. Serve with sliced onions, tomato wedges and *chutney* of your choice. Makes a great lunch or dinner when served with a salad, French fried potatoes, rolls or buns.

SERVES 6 – 8

Ingredients

Chicken breast cut in half or legs and thighs pieces skinless	10
Bread crumbs	1½ cups
Egg beaten	1
Ginger chopped	2 Tbs
Garlic chopped	2 Tbs
Green chilies chopped	2 Tbs
Red chilies (dry)	3–4
Red pepper powder	1 tsp
Yogurt	2 Tbs
Rice	2 Tbs
Salt	1 Tbs
Black pepper	1 tsp
Coriander leaves	½ cup
Vegetable oil	¼ cup
Garam masala	1 tsp

Note: If you wish, the bread crumbs coated chicken pieces can be fried in hot oil ½ to 1 inch deep skillet. For deep frying: Roll the chicken pieces first in all purpose flour, then in beaten egg with water and then in fine dry bread crumbs.

The Exquisite World of Indian Cuisine

Twice Cooked Chicken
Bhune hue Murg ki Curry

Among all the chicken dishes this recipe is my favorite. Rotisserie chicken provides already cooked meat. Just stir-fry it with chopped onions, tomato sauce, spices, lemon juice and fresh coriander. Even children love it.

METHOD

1. Remove the cooked chicken meat from Rotisserie chicken like legs, thigh, and breast of chicken and transfer all to a large mixing bowl. Make all pieces 1–1½ inch in size.

2. Heat the oil in a large wok or a frying pan and add the onions, ginger, and green chilies. Cook till the onions turn light brown, add the garlic and cook for another minute or so and add the cumin seeds. As soon as they stop popping add the mustard seeds and wait till they stop popping. Add the coconut powder and wait till it starts to turn brown and add the dry red peppers. Wait one minute. Add the tomato sauce, salt, turmeric powder, coriander powder, red pepper, dry fenugreek leaves and stir to mix. Stir to cook until the oil separates from the sauce, about 5 minutes, on medium-low heat.

3. Add the cooked chicken and coat the chicken pieces well with the sauce gently. Add ½ cup of water and lower the heat. Let it simmer for 5–10 minutes on medium-low heat until the chicken heats through. Add the lemon juice and *garam masala*. Stir well and heat it through. Sprinkle it with green coriander leaves. Serve with mushroom curry, plain rice and *poori*. Makes a very tasty chicken dish. It is fast and far less cumbersome.

Note: Omit red pepper if cooking for children.

SERVES 6 – 8

Ingredients

Onions chopped	3 cups
Ginger, garlic and green chilies chopped (each)	2 Tbs
Vegetable oil or *ghee*	3 Tbs
Cumin seeds	1 tsp
Mustard seeds	1 tsp
Coconut powder (unsweetened)	2 Tbs
Dry red pepper (crushed)	2
Tomato sauce	2 cups
Salt	1 tsp
Turmeric powder	½–1 tsp
Coriander powder	2 Tbs
Red pepper	½–1 tsp
Fenugreek leaves (dry)	3 Tbs
Rotisserie chicken or whole roasted chicken	1
Water	½ cup
Garam masala	1 tsp
Asafoetida powder	¼ tsp
Curry leaves chopped	6–8
Lemon juice	2–3 Tbs
Coriander leaves chopped	3 Tbs

Hot Chicken Curry with Almonds
Bangladeshi Murg Curry

Pieces of breast of chicken, thighs or legs simmered in hot sauce of tomatoes, onions and red pepper make this dish very special because of its beautiful red color and when garnished with coriander leaves it makes a great presentation. It is usually served with rice.

SERVES 6 – 8

Ingredients

Onions chopped	2 cups
Ginger chopped	1 Tbs
Garlic chopped	1 Tbs
Vegetable oil	3 Tbs
Almonds (grounded)	2 Tbs
Cardamom seeds from pods	3–4
Cinnamom sticks	1–2
Panchphoran masala	2 tsp
Tomatoes chopped	1 cup
Tomato sauce (8 oz can)	1
Turmeric powder	1 tsp
Kashmiri red pepper	2 tsp
Coriander powder	2 Tbs
Chicken stock	2 cups
Chicken legs, thighs or breast	2 lbs
Salt	to taste
Cream	2 Tbs
Coriander leaves chopped	¼ cup
Saffron	½ tsp

METHOD

1. Fry the onions, ginger and garlic in oil, in a thick bottom saucepan of medium size and wait till the onions turn light brown. Dry roast the almond, cardamom seeds and cinnamom and grind them. Set them aside.

2. Add 1 tsp *panchphoran masala* and wait till it starts to simmer. Add the tomatoes and tomato sauce. Mix them well.

3. Add the turmeric powder, salt, coriander powder, and the Kashmiri red pepper, ground almonds and spices mixture and stir to mix the spices well into the onions and tomato mixture. Wait till the oil separates from the sauce.

4. Add the chicken pieces and mix well to coat them with the spices mixture.

5. Cook the chicken in the spices mixture on low heat for 5 minutes and then add the chicken stock, stir well and cover with a lid to simmer on medium heat until the chicken is done (about 25–30 minutes). Add the cream. Stir and heat through. Sprinkle coriander leaves, and the dissolved saffron. Boil again and serve. Goes very well with rice.

The Exquisite World of Indian Cuisine

Madras Chicken Curry
Murg Chettinad

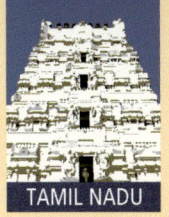
TAMIL NADU

The Chettiar people of Tamil Nadu come up with this great chicken curry prepared in a sauce of ground roasted poppy seeds, fennel seeds, grated coconut, tomatoes, cayenne pepper and a touch of star anise. It is hot but good and is usually served with flavored rice preparations like lemon and tamarind rice.

SERVES 6 – 8

Ingredients

Ingredient	Amount
Poppy seeds	1 Tbs
Fennel seeds	1 tsp
Freshly grated coconut	2 cups
Or	
Coconut powder (dry)	¼ cup
Cinnamon stick	½ inch
Cloves	½ tsp
Cardamoms (large)	2
Onion (large) chopped	1 cup
Ginger chopped	1 Tbs
Garlic chopped	1 Tbs
Star anise	2
Turmeric powder	1 tsp
Black pepper	3 tsp
Cayenne pepper (optional)	1 tsp
Salt	1 tsp
Curry leaves	6–8
Tomatoes chopped	1½ cup
Chicken pieces on bone or without bone	2 lbs
Coconut milk	1 cup
Garam masala	1 tsp
Lemon juice	1 Tbs
Vegetable oil	3 Tbs
Cilantro leaves chopped	½ cup
Water as needed	

METHOD

1. Roast the poppy seeds, fennel seeds on a hot skillet and grind them with grated coconut, cinnamon, cloves and cardamom into a paste with the help of 1 Tbs of water or more. Set aside.

2. In a deep-thick bottom saucepan, fry the onions, ginger, garlic in 3 Tbs of oil, till the onions turn light brown and then add the star anise.

3. Add the turmeric powder, black pepper, salt and the coconut paste, and cook on low heat until the oil starts to separate from the paste.

4. Add the curry leaves, tomatoes, salt and stir-fry for few minutes and then add the chicken pieces. Sauté the chicken pieces in this gravy for about 2 minutes.

5. At this point add 1 cup of coconut milk and let it simmer on medium heat until the chicken is done about 25–30 minutes. Add another ½ cup of water in between the cooking, if curry is too thick.

6. Sprinkle the *garam masala*, lemon juice and mix it into the curry. Remove from heat and transfer to a serving dish sprinkled with cilantro leaves. Serve it with plain rice.

CHAPTER 4

Sea Food & Fish

Indian seacoast that stretches from the southern tip of Kerala northward on the western side beyond the former Portuguese colony of Goa to the state of Gujarat, and on the eastern side to Kolkata is rich and brims with sea life. Coconuts, tropical fruits, fish and seafood have been the staple food of the people along this coastline from times unknown. States like Kerala, Maharashtra and Goa also regard sea food as an essential part of their every day meal. In Bengal, people call fish the *'jaltori'* or the squash of the sea.

In the central states people do not have fish on their menu everyday and it is cooked only occasionally unlike in the coastal states. Fish is cooked in many ways: depending upon which part of the country you are in. In Kerala, the fish curry is cooked with coconut milk and flavored with tamarind. In Bengal, mustard fish is their speciality. Maharashtrians cook it highly spiced and Punjabis and north Indians like to grill it and make *kormas* and *kebabs* from it. It is sometimes deep-fried as *pakoras* dipped in the batter of gram flour and served with *chutney* or ketchup as an appetizer too.

Shrimp is quite common in coastal states. It is served as Shrimp Curry rich with coconut milk or pan-fried after marinating in tamarind sauce, ground black pepper and ground coconut. Lobster is grilled or baked in the oven. Crab meat is also used to make *koftas* or croquettes and their curry is delicious. Squids and scallops are not so popular as seafood and one does not find them on a menu in a regular Indian restaurant. Sometimes these are curried and served with rice.

Seafood like fish, shrimp, lobster or crab is very lean meat without any saturated fat and is very rich in Omega 3 fatty acids. These polyunsaturated fatty acids protect you from heart diseases. Certain varities of fish strengthen your immune system and reove symptoms of arthritis and depression. Essential fatty acids found in seafood, prevent Alzheimer's disease, cancer and lowers the risk of asthma. It seems that these wonderful sea creatures are a powerhouse for your health benefits.

Fish baked in Coconut Sauce
Bhuni hui Machhli

Karnataka

This fish recipe is common along the west coast of India. The fish cooked in the sauce of tomatoes and coconut milk is mild, delicious with a creamy refreshing taste.

SERVES 6 – 8

Ingredients

Fish fillets, Halibut, Salmon or Cod in 2 inch pieces	2 lbs
Lemon juice	2 Tbs
Salt to taste or	1 tsp
Onions chopped	1½ cup
Garlic chopped	1 Tbs
Green chilies	1 tsp
Curry leaves	6–8
Ginger chopped	1 Tbs
Cardamoms (large)	1 or 2
Cloves	½ tsp
Peppercorns	½ tsp
Coriander leaves chopped	1 Tbs
Tomatoes chopped	1 cup
Turmeric powder	1 tsp
Red pepper	1 tsp
Coriander powder	2 Tbs
Cumin powder	1 tsp
Vegetable oil	¼ cup
Coconut milk	1¼ cup
Garam masala	1 tsp

METHOD

1. Rub the fish in salt, lemon and 1 Tbs oil and set it aside for at least half an hour. Pan-fry the fillets in a little oil for 2 minutes. Remove any tough skin from the fillets. Set them aside.
2. Fry the onions, ginger, garlic, green chilies in the remaining oil in a deep saucepan and wait till the onions turn light brown.
3. Add the curry leaves, cardamoms, cloves, peppercorns, and the tomatoes and fry till the tomatoes are soft.
4. Add the turmeric powder, salt, red pepper, coriander powder, and cumin powder and stir the mixture. Add 1 cup of the coconut milk and simmer for few minutes and wait till the oil separates from the sauce.
5. Arrange the fillets in a baking dish. Pour the sauce over the fish and cover it tight with a tin foil.
6. Bake the fish in the oven at 425°F for 10–15 minutes or until the fish is done. Remove from the oven. Serve topped with cilantro leaves, *garam masala* and plain rice.

Fish Curry

PUNJAB

Fish fillets are marinated and rubbed with lemon juice and red pepper. They are then fried after coating them with delicately spiced gram flour batter. These when cooked in a curried tomato sauce make a superb dish. Serve with your favorite rice preparation or a meal of your liking.

METHOD

Clean and rub the pieces with salt, pepper and lemon juice and leave for ½ hour.

Prepare the batter

1. Mix gram flour with salt, carom seeds, black pepper, ½ Tbs of oil and water and gently beat it into a batter. Keep the batter thick.
2. Add a pinch of baking powder just before frying.
3. Roll the fish pieces one by one into the batter and deep fry in hot oil heated to about 300°F until slightly brown on both sides.
4. Remove from oil with a slotted spoon and drain the pieces in a plate lined with a paper towel.

Prepare the sauce

5. Cook and simmer the chopped onions, ginger, garlic and green chilies in 2 Tbs of hot *ghee* or oil till light brown and add turmeric powder, salt, red pepper, tomato sauce and chopped tomatoes. Stir to mix and cook until the oil separates from the sauce.
6. Add 1 cup of water, simmer and bring it to a full boil for 3–5 minutes. Add the fried fish pieces gently.
7. Cook and simmer for 2–5 minutes until well coated with sauce.
8. Stir only once very gently while cooking.
9. Serve sprinkled with chopped green coriander and 1 tsp of *garam masala*.

SERVES 8

Ingredients

For rubbing over:

Firm fillet of fish of your choice cut in 2–3 inch pieces weighing over	2 lbs
Salt	1 tsp
Red pepper	½ tsp
Lemon juice	1 Tbs

For a thick batter to coat and fry the Fish:

Salt	½ tsp
Gram flour	1 cup
Black pepper	½ tsp
Vegetable oil	1 Tbs
Carom seeds	1 tsp
Baking powder	a pinch
Water (as needed)	½–¾ cup
Oil (for frying) as needed	

For the sauce:

Onions chopped	1 cup
Ginger chopped	2 Tbs
Starch (optional)	2 tsp
Coriander powder	1 Tbs
Garlic chopped	1 Tbs
Ginger chopped	1 Tbs
Green chilies chopped	1 Tbs
Vegetable oil	3 Tbs
Salt	1 tsp
Turmeric powder	1 tsp
Red pepper	½ tsp
Tomatoes (medium) chopped	4
Tomato sauce	1 cup
Coriander leaves green chopped	2 Tbs
Garam masala	1 tsp
Water	½–1 cup

The Exquisite World of Indian Cuisine

Fish Curry with Vegetables

WEST BENGAL

This is a recipe inspired by the popular light, sometimes almost bland, *Macher Jhol* from the state of Bengal. I have adapted the traditional preparation to transform it into a complete meal when served with rice.

SERVES 8 – 10

Ingredients

Firm fillets of any fish cut 4 inch pieces	2 lbs
Lemon juice	2 Tbs
Salt	1 tsp
Onions chopped	1 cup
Garlic chopped	1 Tbs
Ginger chopped	1 Tbs
Green chilies chopped	1 tsp
Panchphoran masala	1 tsp
Red peppers whole, dry	2–3
Bay leaves	4–5
Turmeric powder	1 tsp
Red pepper	1 tsp
Coriander powder	1 Tbs
Tomatoes chopped	1 cup
Tomato sauce	1 cup
Cauliflower floret	1 cup
Potatoes peeled and chopped	1 cup
Carrots chopped in small bite size pieces	½ cup
Coriander leaves chopped	2 Tbs
Chicken stock	1½ cup
Mustard oil for cooking the sauce and frying the fillets	4 Tbs

METHOD

1. Rub the fish pieces with ¼ tsp of salt and lemon juice and set them aside.
2. Fry the onions, ginger, garlic and green chilies in 2 Tbs of oil and wait till the onions turn brown. Add the *panchphoran masala* and wait till they pop and add the bay leaves, whole red pepper, tomato sauce, tomatoes, turmeric powder, salt, red pepper and coriander powder and stir-fry for 5 minutes on low heat. Wait till the oil separates from the sauce.
3. Add the vegetables and fry them in this sauce for 5 minutes on low heat.
4. Add one cup of chicken stock, reduce the heat. Simmer for another 5 minutes.
5. While the sauce is cooking pan-fry the fish in 2 Tbs of mustard oil in a large skillet until light brown (2 minutes). Drain on a paper towel and set them aside.
6. Lower the heat. Simmer the sauce or the gravy for a few minutes and add the other ½ cup of chicken stock. Stir and let it come to a boil. Gently add the fried pieces of fish into the gravy and let it simmer for another 5–10 minutes.
7. Add the *garam masala* and sprinkle the coriander leaves and serve with plain rice or *pulav*.

Fish in Fenugreek Sauce
Methi Machhi

Fish prepared in the green sauce of fenugreek leaves, spinach and coriander leaves is very appealing and has a very special taste. The use of greens makes this preparation very healthy and nutritious. Fenugreek is very good for diabetes, high blood pressure and has numerous other health benefits.

METHOD

1. Rub the fish with ½ tsp of salt and 1 Tbs of lemon juice. Heat 2 Tbs of oil in a skillet and fry the fillets until light brown, about 2 minutes.
2. Wash and grind the fresh fenugreek leaves, spinach leaves, coriander leaves and green chilies together and set them aside.
3. Fry the onions, ginger, garlic in 2 Tbs of oil and wait till the onions turn light brown.
4. Add the cumin seeds and wait till they start popping. Lower the heat and add the curry leaves, turmeric powder, red pepper, coriander powder and salt and stir the mixture and add the tomatoes and ½ cup of fish stock. Cook until the tomatoes are soft (about 5 minutes) and the oil separates from the sauce.
5. Add the green leaves mixture and mix. Cook on the low heat for another 5–10 minutes till the oil separates. Gently add the fillets of fish and coat the fillets with the sauce. Simmer on low heat for 5–10 minutes or more and add more stock if needed. Sprinkle with *garam masala* and serve with your favorite rice dish or as a side dish of a meal.

SERVES 8 – 10

Ingredients

Fish fillets of Halibut, Salmon, Cod or any fish with firm fillets	2 lbs
Lemon juice	1 Tbs
Fenugreek leaves fresh (if dry use 2 Tbs) chopped	1 cup
Spinach leaves chopped	1 cup
Green chilies chopped	1 Tbs
Green coriander leaves chopped	1 cup
Cumin seeds	1 tsp
Curry leaves	3–4
Onions chopped	1 cup
Ginger chopped	1 Tbs
Garlic chopped	1 Tbs
Vegetable oil	¼ cup
Turmeric powder	1 tsp
Red pepper	1 tsp
Coriander powder	1 Tbs
Salt	1 tsp
Garam masala	1 tsp
Tomatoes chopped	2 cups
Fish stock or chicken stock	½–1 cup

The Exquisite World of Indian Cuisine

Fish Curry with Yogurt
Doi Machh

WEST BENGAL

Fish cooked in yogurt and sautéed in mustard oil brings out the typical taste of a dish cooked Bengali style. It is finger licking and is mostly served with plain rice.

SERVES 6 – 8

Ingredients

Onions chopped	1 cup
Ginger chopped	1 Tbs
Garlic chopped	1 Tbs
Green chilies chopped (mild)	1 tsp
Yogurt whipped	1¼ cup
Mustard oil	¼ cup
Panchphoran masala	1 Tbs
Red peppers whole, dry	2–3
Bay leaves or curry leaves	4–6
Turmeric powder	1 tsp
Red pepper	½ tsp
Coriander powder	1 Tbs
Fish fillets of Salmon, Halibut or any fish with good flesh	2 lbs
Lemon juice	1 Tbs
Salt	1 tsp
Garam masala	1 tsp
Sugar	1–2 tsp
Vegetable oil or *ghee*	1 Tbs
Water	½ cup
Coriander leaves chopped	2 Tbs
Cashew nuts chopped	1 Tbs
Raisins	1 Tbs

METHOD

1. Rub the fish fillets with lemon juice and salt and set them aside.
2. In a skillet heat 2 Tbs of the mustard oil and fry the fish fillets few at a time until slightly brown, and set them aside on a paper towel.
3. In a large heavy bottom saucepan heat 2 Tbs of the left over mustard oil and sauté the onions, ginger, garlic, and the green chilies and fry till light brown.
4. Add the *panchphoran masala*, red pepper whole and bay leaves and fry until the seeds start to pop.
5. Add the turmeric powder, coriander powder, red pepper, salt and sugar and lower the heat. Add the yogurt and mix well. Add nuts and raisins and mix well. Fry until the oil separates from the sauce.
6. Add the fish fillets and gently coat them well with the yogurt mixture. Add ½ cup of water and simmer on low heat till cooked (about 5–10 minutes).
7. Serve topped with chopped coriander leaves, *garam masala* and 1 Tbs of melted *ghee*. It is delicious. Serve with rice.

Fish Curry with Nuts
Fish Korma

ANDHRA PRADESH

Fish cooked in creamy sauce of poppy seeds and yogurt and flavored with almonds and raisins. The dish is really special. Serve it with pea *pulav* or plain rice. It is delightful and delicious. The Mughlai influence is noticeable in the use of the nuts and raisins.

METHOD

1. Rub the fish fillets with lemon juice and salt and set aside for an hour.
2. Heat 2 Tbs of oil in a skillet and fry the fillets light brown and set them aside. It takes about 2 minutes. Grind the poppy seeds and 2 Tbs of almonds and 1 tsp of black pepper corns in a coffee grinder and set them aside.
3. Fry the onions, ginger, garlic and green chilies in 2 Tbs of oil until the onions are light brown and add the bay leaves and fry for a minute and add the tomato sauce, the ground almond and poppy seeds, turmeric powder, red pepper, coriander powder, cumin powder, salt, ½ cup of stock and stir-fry for 5 minutes.
4. Wait until the oil starts to separate from the gravy and then lower the heat.
5. Whisk ½ cup yogurt in 1 cup of the stock and add it to the cooked gravy.
6. Add the remaining nuts and raisins and stir them well into the sauce and cook for a few minutes.
7. Gently add the fish fillets to the saucepan and simmer the fish *korma* for 5–10 minutes.
8. Sprinkle chopped coriander leaves with *garam masala*, and bring the sauce to a boil once.
9. Serve with plain rice or pea *pulav* or other side dishes of your choice. Makes an excellent dish for formal dining.

SERVES 4 – 6

Ingredients

Fish fillets of Sole, Trout, Salmon or Flounder	2 lbs
Lemon juice	2 Tbs
Salt	1 tsp
Almonds or cashews	4 Tbs
Poppy seeds	1 Tbs
Black pepper corns	1 tsp
Onions chopped	1 cup
Ginger chopped	1 Tbs
Garlic chopped	1 Tbs
Green chilies (mild) chopped	1 tsp
Bay leaves	2 or 3
Vegetable oil	4 Tbs
Tomato sauce	1 cup
Turmeric powder	1 tsp
Red pepper	1 tsp
Salt	1 tsp
Cumin powder	1 tsp
Coriander powder	1 tsp
Raisins	2 Tbs
Yogurt	½ cup
Chicken or fish stock	1½ cup
Coriander leaves chopped	1 Tbs
Garam masala	1 tsp

The Exquisite World of Indian Cuisine

Fried Fish
Tali hui Machhli

Fish is very commonly deep-fried in America and all over Europe with a coating of egg and then rolled in bread crumbs. But in India, it is prepared by marinating it in a mixture of spices, yogurt, lime juice, dredged in flour mixture and then deep-fried or pan-fried in a couple of teaspoons of oil, so it is not so oily but very tasty.

METHOD

1. Prepare a paste by combining yogurt, butter, 1 Tbs of lemon juice, salt, peppers, coriander powder, onions, ginger, garlic, *garam masala*, *ajwain* and rub the fish fillets with this paste. Cover and transfer them to the refrigerator for an hour. Roll the marinated fish fillets in the flour and then beaten egg mixed with little water, and then roll them in a mixture of corn flour and all-purpose flour and set them aside.

2. Heat ½ cup of the oil in a frying pan for about 2 minutes on medium heat and fry the fish fillets few at a time until light brown and drain them on a paper towel or deep fry them couple of pieces at a time in 4 cups of heated oil (300°F–340°F) until crisp brown.

3. Serve them sprinkled with chopped fresh onions, slices of hot green peppers, mint leaves and *chaat masala*. The fish is mouth watering good. Serve with any vegetable curry, *raita* or any bread of your choice.

SERVES 6 – 8

Ingredients

For marinade:

Yogurt	¼ cup
Butter	2 Tbs
Eggs beaten	2
Lemon juice	1 Tbs
Red pepper	½ tsp
Black pepper ground	1 tsp
Salt	1 tsp
Pomfret fish fillets about 8 pieces	1 lb
Onions finely chopped	3 Tbs
Ginger chopped	1 Tbs
Garlic finely chopped	1 Tbs
Garam masala	1 tsp
Coriander powder	1 Tbs
Ajwain	1 tsp

For frying the fish:

Corn meal	½ cup
All purpose flour	½ cup
Vegetable oil	4 cups
Salt	½ tsp
Black pepper	½ tsp
Chaat masala	1–2 Tbs

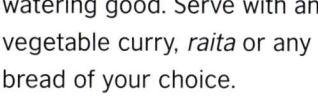

Note: Fried fish can be served with French fries (deep fried potato slices).

Clay Oven Grilled Fish
Tandoori Machhli

Fish marinated in spiced yogurt and then grilled or baked in an oven is also a speciality of India. Here in the west, we usually grill it on an electric or a kitchen grill to give it a dark brown texture. When baked in the oven, it may not have that dark brown texture, but it is still a delicacy that you will always remember.

METHOD

1. Make several superficial cuts in the fish fillets and rub them with lemon juice and salt mixture and set them aside in a refrigerator for at least ½ hr.
2. Prepare a paste by grinding chopped ginger, garlic, onions, *garam masala* and vinegar. Add yogurt, butter, salt, coriander powder, paprika, peppers and dry fenugreek leaves to the ground mixture. Rub the marinated fish fillets with this paste and leave them in the refrigerator for two hours.
3. Broil them in the oven in a baking dish that has little grilling pan in it. Baste it with butter occasionally while in the oven. Turn it once gently and broil until lightly brown (about 5–10 minutes).
4. Similarly it can be grilled on an open gas/grill turning it gently couple of times with a spatula and occasionally basting it with butter until dark brown.
5. Serve sprinkled with *tandoori masala* and chopped fresh onions and mint leaves. A really delicious preparation that can be served with grilled or sir-fried vegetables and rice.

SERVES 2 – 4

Ingredients

For rubbing over the fish:

Pomfret fillets	4
Lemon juice	1 Tbs
Salt	1 tsp

For marinade:

Onions finely chopped	3 Tbs
Ginger finely chopped	1 Tbs
Garlic finely chopped	1 Tbs
Vinegar	1 Tbs
Yogurt	¼ cup
Butter	2 Tbs
Red pepper	1 tsp
Black pepper ground	½ tsp
Salt	1 tsp
Garam masala	1 tsp
Coriander powder	1 Tbs
Fenugreek leaves (dry)	1 Tbs
Paprika	1 tsp

For sprinkling after:

Vegetable oil or *ghee*	1 Tbs
Mint leaves	1 Tbs
Tandoori masala (from your local Indian grocer)	1 Tbs
Lemon juice	2 Tbs

The Exquisite World of Indian Cuisine

Madras Fish Curry

TAMIL NADU

Fish preparation, that is hot for you. Marinaded in vinegar, lime juice and cooked in the sauce of freshly grated coconut, poppy seeds, tamarind water and hot pepper.

METHOD

1. Marinade the fillets with ½ tsp salt, vinegar and ½ tsp of red pepper for an hour.
2. Grind the coconut, ginger, garlic, green chilies and poppy seeds in a blender with the help of water and set the paste aside.
3. Fry the onions in oil and when they turn brown add the mustard seeds, cumin seeds, fenugreek seeds and *urad dal* and wait till the mustard seeds start to pop and *urad dal* starts to turn brown.
4. Add the curry leaves, coriander powder, turmeric powder, black pepper and red pepper, ½ tsp of salt and stir.
5. Add the coconut paste and chopped tomatoes and mix. Add the tamarind pulp dissolved in 1 Tbs of water. Stir-fry until the tomatoes are soft (about 5 minutes) or till the oil separates from the sauce.
6. Add another cup of water and keep stirring and boil for 5 minutes. Add less water if you want the curry thick.
7. Add the fish fillets gently and turn the heat to low and cook for 5–10 minutes or cook until the fish is done.
8. Remove from heat, sprinkle the chopped coriander leaves and *garam masala* and serve with plain rice or any other meal or as one of the main courses.

SERVES 8 – 10

Ingredients

Fish fillets	2 lbs
Salt	1 tsp
Vinegar	1½ Tbs
Onions	1 cup
Coconut grated	2 cups
Or	
Dry coconut powder	¼ cup
Ginger chopped	1 Tbs
Garlic chopped	1 Tbs
Green chilies chopped	1 Tbs
Tomatoes chopped	2 cups
Poppy seeds	3 Tbs
Tamarind pulp	1 Tbs
Mustard seeds	1 tsp
Urad dal	½ tsp
Cumin seeds	1 tsp
Fenugreek seeds	½ tsp
Turmeric powder	1 tsp
Coriander powder	2 Tbs
Red pepper	2 tsp
Black pepper	1 tsp
Vegetable oil	3 Tbs
Curry leaves	10–15
Water	1 cup
Garam masala	1 tsp
Coriander leaves chopped	1 Tbs

Fish in Tamarind Sauce

KERALA

This fish curry is made in a tangy tamarind and coconut milk sauce and is a speciality of south India. Firmer fillets are suggested as the fillets tend to fall apart very easily.

SERVES 6 – 8

Ingredients

Onions chopped	1 cup
Ginger chopped	1 Tbs
Garlic chopped	1 Tbs
Green chilies chopped (mild)	1 Tbs
Vegetable oil	3 Tbs
Fenugreek seeds	1 tsp
Mustard seeds	1 tsp
Cumin seeds	1 tsp
Red pepper dry (whole) broken	2–3
Tamarind pulp	1–2 tsp
Curry leaves	5–6
Turmeric powder	1 tsp
Red pepper	1 tsp
Salt	to taste
Black pepper	1 tsp
Ground coriander	1 tsp
Coconut milk	1 cup
Water	½ cup
Garam masala (optional)	½ tsp
Green coriander leaves chopped	1 Tbs
Fish fillets of Cod, Salmon, or Halibut in 2 inch pieces	2 lbs

METHOD

1. Marinade the fish fillets in 1 tsp of lemon juice and 1 tsp of salt. After half an hour pan-fry them in 1 Tbs of oil for 2 minutes and remove any skin that the fillets might have. Set them aside. Fry the onions, ginger, garlic and green chilies in oil in a deep thick-bottom cooking pot or a dutch oven till light brown and add the fenugreek seeds, mustard seeds, cumin seeds, and wait till they pop. Add the whole red pepper and curry leaves.

2. Turn heat down and add the turmeric powder, red pepper, black pepper, coriander powder, salt and the tamarind paste dissolved in ¼ cup water. Fry till it all becomes a paste.

3. Add 1 cup of coconut milk and simmer until well mixed.

4. Add the fish pieces gently and line them at the bottom of the cooking pan and let them simmer in this sauce for another 5–10 minutes.

5. Gently transfer them to a serving dish and serve it with sprinkled *garam masala* and chopped coriander leaves. Makes a delicious addition to any meal.

6. It is served ideally with plain rice or any kind of *pulav*.

Note: This is a rather hot curry. So please adjust the use of red peppers according to taste.

The Exquisite World of Indian Cuisine

Fish in Mustard Sauce

The state of Bengal is famous for its fish curries. Its rivers provide a rich harvest of sweet-water fish like *rahu* and *hilsa*. From the Bay of Bengal comes an abundance of seafood. Mustard and coconut grows along the sea shores of the state. One can see the influence of these in Bengali cuisine. This recipe is inspired by the popular *Shorshe Machh* from Bengal.

METHOD

1. Marinade the fish pieces in lemon juice and salt for at least an hour. Pan-fry the pieces in 1 Tbs of oil in a non-stick frying pan for few minutes and set them aside.
2. Roast the poppy seeds on a hot griddle and grind them with a rolling pin and set them aside.
3. Fry the onions, ginger, garlic and green chilies in 2 Tbs of mustard oil in a deep saucepan and wait till the onions turn light brown.
4. Add the onion seeds (*Nigella*) and the coarsely ground mustard seeds and curry leaves and fry them for 2 minutes.
5. Add the grated coconut and stir-fry until light brown (takes 1–2 minutes) and then add the tomatoes, turmeric powder, red pepper, salt, coriander powder and ground poppy seeds. Lower the heat and add 1 cup of water and simmer for 5 minutes, or till the oil separates from the sauce.
6. Arrange the fish pieces in a layer in a heavy bottom 2–3 quart cooking pan and pour the sauce over the pieces.
7. Simmer for another 5–10 minutes on low heat.
8. Sprinkle with *garam masala* and chopped coriander leaves and serve.
9. Handle the fish pieces gently and serve. Plain rice is recommended or with *chappati* or bread of your choice.

SERVES 8 – 10

Ingredients

To marinate:

2 inch fillets of salmon, cod or halibut	2 lbs
Lemon juice	2 Tbs
Salt	1 tsp

For gravy:

Onions chopped	2 cups
Ginger	1 Tbs
Garlic chopped	1 Tbs
Green chilies chopped (mild)	1 Tbs
Tomatoes chopped	1 cup
Tomato sauce	1 cup
Mustard oil	½ cup
Curry leaves	5–6
Coconut grated	¼ cup
Or dry coconut powder	1 Tbs
Poppy seeds	2 Tbs
Mustard seeds coarsely ground	2 Tbs
Onion seeds (Nigella seeds)	1 tsp
Turmeric powder	1 tsp
Red pepper	1 tsp
Salt	to taste
Garam masala	½ tsp
Green coriander leaves	2 Tbs
Coriander powder	1 Tbs
Water (as needed)	1 cup

Lobster Delight

This grilled lobster recipe makes a lovely presentation and is very delectable too.

METHOD

Place the lobsters in the freezer for at least 2 hours to completely immobilize them.

1. Cut open the immobilized lobster in half with help of a sharp knife or a cleaver, remove the meat carefully in one piece from the shell. Cut the meat into 1½ inch pieces and set them aside. Wash the shells clean and set them aside.
2. Prepare the marinade by mixing together chick pea flour, onions, garlic, ginger, whipping cream, lemon juice, brown sugar, beaten eggs, salt, red pepper, 1 tsp *garam masala* and the carom seeds in a bowl and beat the mixture into a smooth paste. Add the lobster pieces into a bowl and coat them with this marinade. Transfer the bowl into the refrigerator for a couple of hours.
3. Preheat the oven to broil. Skewer the lobster pieces onto metal skewers and transfer them into the oven by placing them onto a grilling pan. Broil for 5 minutes. Turn and brush them with melted butter, and cook for another 3–5 minutes.
4. Remove the skewers from the oven. Set them aside onto a platter and roast the cleaned shells for a few minutes in the same oven until they turn red. Remove the shells from the oven and fill them up with the roasted lobster pieces by taking them off the skewers.
5. Put the shells filled with lobster pieces onto a platter and sprinkle them with ½ tsp of *garam masala*, roasted cumin powder, lemon juice and chopped coriander leaves before serving. Makes an elegant presentation.

SERVES 6 – 8

Ingredients

Large lobster (immobilized)	2
Or	
Lobster meat	1½–2 lbs

Marinade:

Onions chopped	¼ cup
Ginger chopped	1 Tbs
Garlic chopped	1 Tbs
Whipping cream	¼ cup
Lemon juice	1 Tbs
Brown sugar	2 Tbs
Chick-peas flour	¼ cup
Eggs beaten	2
Red pepper	½ tsp
Garam masala	2½ tsp
Carom seeds	½ tsp
Cumin powder ground, roasted	1 Tbs
Coriander leaves chopped	2 Tbs
Salt	1 tsp
Ghee or melted butter for brushing as needed	

Note: Can be served as an appetizer with a mild *chutney* or serve them with baked potatoes or grilled vegetables for an outdoor dinner with rolls and salad.

The Exquisite World of Indian Cuisine

Shrimp Curry
Jhinga Curry

GOA

Shelled fresh or frozen shrimp can be curried beautifully. Shrimp curry is authentically prepared in the coastal states rich in sea food like Tamil Nadu, Goa and Maharashtra. Curry prepared here is primarily from Goa where *kokum* is the real king of the local cuisine.

SERVES 6 – 8

Ingredients

Onions	1 cup
Ginger chopped	1 Tbs
Garlic chopped	1 Tbs
Red peppers whole (dry) crushed	1 Tbs
Fresh grated coconut	¼ cup
Or dry coconut powder	2 Tbs
Vegetable oil	4 Tbs
Cumin seeds	1 tsp
Mustard seeds	1 tsp
Tomatoes chopped	1½ cup
Cumin powder	½ tsp
Coriander powder	3 tsp
Salt	to taste
Red pepper	1 tsp
Turmeric powder	1 tsp
Kokum	4–6
Coconut milk canned	½ cup
Green coriander leaves	¼ cup
Tamarind paste	1 tsp
Water	¾–1 cup
Shrimp shelled and deveined	2 lbs
Garam masala	1½ tsp

METHOD

1. Heat 4 Tbs of oil in a large saucepan and cook onions, ginger, garlic, whole dry red peppers, until the onions are tender. Add the grated coconut and fry for 2 minutes until slightly brown. Remove the mixture with a slotted spoon and grind them with the help of ½ cup of water in a blender and pour it into a bowl. Marinade the shrimp in this sauce.
2. In the same saucepan, in the remaining oil, add the mustard seeds, cumin seeds and wait till the seeds start to pop.
3. Add the chopped tomatoes, and stir-fry for few minutes until they are soft. Fry till the oil separates.
4. Add the cumin powder, coriander powder, red pepper, turmeric powder and salt and mix it well. Add the coconut milk, *Kokum* and 1 tsp of tamarind paste and mix well.
5. Add the water, cook and simmer until the sauce is smooth and the oil separates from the sauce (about 5 minutes).
6. Now add the marinated shrimp along with the marinade and simmer for at least 5 minutes or until the shrimp is transparent. Add some water, if the sauce is too thick.
7. Add *garam masala* and chopped green cilantro and cook for 2 more minutes.
8. Serve with plain rice or *pulav*, vegetable stir-fry and bread of your choice.

Note: In this dish shrimp can be substituted with pork, chopped crabmeat or with prawns.

Shrimp Stir-Fried

Freshly shelled and deveined shrimp when tossed and cooked with chopped onions, ginger, garlic, green chilies and flavored with mustard seeds, spices and lemon juice becomes a very delicious main course. It is quick fixing, nutritious and can go with any vegetable curry, rice and bread.

METHOD

1. Wash the shrimp and dry them on the paper towel. Sprinkle 1 Tbs of lemon juice over them and coat them with a mixture of salt, turmeric powder, red pepper, coriander powder, ginger, garlic and cumin powder.
2. Let them marinade in the spices for at least an hour.
3. Cook the onions in a skillet in 2 Tbs of oil until light brown, and add the mustard seeds and wait till they pop and then add the grated coconut and toast it lightly and add the curry leaves and the chopped coriander leaves.
4. Fry for few minutes and set the onions and curry leaves mixture in a bowl on one side.
5. In the same skillet add 2 Tbs of oil and heat it. Add the shrimp and gently stir-fry them until they change their color and get cooked.
6. Transfer them to a serving dish and pour the onion mixture on top of the fried shrimp. Using a large spoon toss the shrimp into the coconut and onion mixture and serve topped with a little sprinkle of *garam masala* and remaining lemon juice.
7. Makes an excellent presentation with the flavor of *garam masala*. Squeeze the remaining lemon juice over them. The green curry leaves give nice texture and color to the dish.

SERVES 8 – 10

Ingredients

Deveined shelled shrimp or frozen ready to cook shrimp	2 lbs
Lemon juice	2 Tbs
Salt	to taste
Turmeric powder	1 tsp
Red pepper	1 tsp
Garlic chopped	1 Tbs
Vegetable oil	3–4 Tbs
Cumin powder	1 tsp
Coriander powder	1 Tbs
Onions sliced	¾ cup
Ginger chopped	1 Tbs
Mustard seeds	1 tsp
Curry leaves (small)	8–10
Freshly grated coconut	¼ cup
Or	
Dry coconut powder	2 Tbs
Coriander leaves chopped	2 Tbs
Garam masala	½ tsp

The Exquisite World of Indian Cuisine

Fried Shrimp

Shrimp marinated in tamarind sauce, deep fried and served with tartar sauce or cream sauce makes a great main meal at any dinner

SERVES 6 – 8

Ingredients

Shrimp large, shelled, deveined or frozen	2 lbs
Onions chopped	2 Tbs
Ginger chopped	2 Tbs
Garlic chopped	2 Tbs
Green hot chillies	2 Tbs
Salt	2 tsp
Red pepper	1–2 tsp
Turmeric powder	1 tsp
Tamarind pulp	1 Tbs
Black pepper	1 tsp
Cream of wheat	2 cups
Vegetable oil	2 cups
Egg beaten	2
Corn starch	2 tsp
Onion slices	4-5
Lemon wedges	4-5
Chilies green	a few

METHOD

1. Grind onions, ginger, garlic, green chillies, salt, red pepper, turmeric powder, tamarind pulp, black pepper, with little water, if needed and set it aside in a bowl. Transfer the shrimp to marinate in this sauce for at least an hour.
2. Transfer the cream of wheat onto a plate. Beat eggs and corn starch together in a bowl.
3. Roll the shrimp in beaten egg and corn starch mixture and coat the marinated shrimp one at a time in the cream of wheat.
4. Pour 2 cups of oil into a wok or thick-bottom skillet and heat it moderately. Fry the coated shrimp in the oil, few at a time, until they are evenly browned on both sides. Remove them from the oil with a slotted spoon and drain them on a paper towel lined dish. Serve them with some sliced onions and lemon wedges, French fries or mashed potatoes.

Fishermen setting up the nets along a coast in Kerala

SEA FOOD AND FISH

Scallops & Squid Curry

Cleaned fresh scallops or squid when curried with freshly chopped fenugreek leaves and coconut milk make a very pleasant addition to any meal.

SERVES 6 – 8

Ingredients

Fresh or frozen cleaned squid pieces or scallop	2 lbs
Lemon juice	1 Tbs
Oil	4 Tbs
Mushrooms sliced	1 cup
Or	
Red or yellow bell pepper chopped	1 cup
Mustard seeds	1 tsp
Onions chopped	1 cup
Ginger chopped	2 Tbs
Garlic chopped	2 Tbs
Green chillies chopped	1 Tbs
Turmeric powder	¾ tsp
Red pepper	1 tsp
Salt	1½ tsp
Coriander powder	1 Tbs
Fenugreek leaves freshly chopped	2 cups
Or	
Fenugreek leaves dry (*kasuri methi*)	4 Tbs
Tomato sauce	1 cup
Coconut milk	½ cup
Fresh coriander leaves chopped	2 Tbs
Garam masala	1 tsp
Green spring onions chopped	1 Tbs
Water	½ cup

METHOD

1. Mix together lemon juice, ½ tsp of salt and a table spoon of oil in a salad bowl and transfer the scallop or squid pieces and mushrooms sliced into it. Let them marinade for an hour.

2. Heat 2 Tbs of oil in a thick-bottom cooking pan and add the mustard seeds and when they start to pop add the onions, ginger, garlic, green chillies and cook until the onion is turning slightly brown.

3. Add the turmeric powder, salt, red pepper, coriander powder, and dry fenugreek leaves. Stir-fry for 2 minutes. Add the tomato sauce and ½ cup of coconut milk. Gently boil for 5 minutes and wait till the oil separates from the sauce.

4. Add the marinated pieces of squid and mushrooms and gently mix them in. Add ½ cup of water and simmer for another 25–30 minutes or until the squids are done. Add more water, if needed.

5. Serve sprinkled with chopped coriander leaves, chopped spring green onions and *garam masala*. Serve with plain rice or *pulav*.

The Exquisite World of Indian Cuisine

Crab Stir-Fried

MAHARASHTRA

Crab meat preparations from the coastal states of India are very popular. Cooked with spicy *malwani masala*, tamarind pulp and coconut, this is a tangy and appetizing dish. The recipe is from the western coastal state of Maharashtra.

METHOD

1. Crack the claws of the crabs and take out the meat. Cut the meat into large pieces.
2. Fry the chopped onions, ginger, garlic, and green chillies, in 2 Tbs of oil. Wait till the onions are brown. Add the mustard seeds. As soon as the mustard stop popping add the dry coconut powder and wait till it turns slightly brown.
3. Add the chopped crab meat pieces. Add the turmeric powder, salt and the *malwani masala*.
4. Stir to mix. Fry them in the onion mixture for few minutes. Add the tamarind pulp dissolved in one cup of water. Stir to mix.
5. Cook for 5-10 minutes on low heat till the meat gets cooked.
6. Add the coriander leaves, lemon wedges and serve with rice or bread as an accompaniment to a meal.

SERVES 6 – 8

Ingredients

Crabs	4
Or	
Crab meat	1 lb
Onions chopped	½ cup
Garlic chopped	1 Tbs
Ginger chopped	1 Tbs
Green chillies (mild)	1 Tbs
Mustard seeds	1 tsp
Dry coconut powder	2 Tbs
Turmeric powder	¾ tsp
Salt	1 tsp
Malwani masala	2 Tbs
Tamarind pulp	1 tsp
Vegetable oil	2 Tbs
Coriander leaves chopped	2 Tbs
Water	1 cup
Lemon wedges	a few

Crab Croquettes Curry
Kekra Curry

Cooked crab meat balls, made by mixing in ground nuts, onions and spices are curried in a creamy sauce. They are mouth-watering, good and delicious. Serve them with just your favorite rice preparation, or any other meal of your choice. This curry makes a great accompaniment to any dinner.

SERVES 8

Ingredients

For *koftas*:

Cooked crab meat (available at your local Indian grocery store)	2 lbs
Onions chopped	¼ cup
Ginger chopped	2 Tbs
Garlic chopped	2 Tbs
Almonds ground	¼ cup
Whipping / heavy cream	2 Tbs
Eggs	2
Gram flour	¼ cup
Lemon juice	2 Tbs
Green chilies chopped (mild) Or	1 Tbs
Red pepper	
Salt	1 tsp
Vegetable oil for frying	3–4 cups
Baking soda	a pinch

For curry:

Olive oil or any cooking oil	2–3 Tbs
Tomatoes chopped or tomato sauce	2 cups
Onions chopped	1 cup
Cumin seeds	1 tsp
Turmeric powder	1 tsp
Red pepper whole, dry broken	2
Coriander powder	1 Tbs
Salt	1–2 tsp
Red pepper	½–1 tsp
Garam masala	1 tsp
Coconut milk	1 cup
Coriander leaves chopped	2 Tbs
Water, if needed	½–1 cup

METHOD

1. Mix together crab meat, whipping cream, onions, ginger, green chilies chopped, garlic, red pepper, eggs, gram flour, lemon juice, ground almonds, baking soda and salt and make one inch balls of the mixture. Add more gram flour if needed. Heat the oil in a deep skillet and fry the balls to make *koftas* on medium heat by gently turning them, until the *koftas* are light brown. Make sure the oil is not over heated. Remove from oil and drain them on a paper towel in a bowl and set them aside.

2. Fry one cup of onions in 3 Tbs oil, in a deep heavy bottom saucepan, until light brown. Add the cumin seeds and the whole red peppers broken and wait till the cumin seeds start to pop. Add the tomatoes, turmeric powder, coriander powder, salt, red pepper (as desired) and stir well. Cook the mixture for 3–5 minutes stirring regularly. Wait till the oil separates from the sauce and then add the coconut milk, stir and boil the curry for 2–3 minutes. Add the *koftas* and simmer on very low heat to cook for 5 minutes. Add the *garam masala*, coriander leaves and let them sit in the sauce for another 15 minutes and then serve with your favorite meal.

The Exquisite World of Indian Cuisine

Shrimp in Mango Sauce

Shrimp marinated in the spicy sweet and sour sauce of yogurt, mango pulp, cashew and jalapenos is mouth-watering good. It can be served with mint *raita* or tamarind *chutney* and it is a perfect idea for a summer afternoon grill.

METHOD

1. Mix together yogurt with finely chopped ginger, garlic, jalapeno and mango pulp in a medium size bowl and add to it the roasted cumin and mustard seeds, salt, red pepper, *garam masala*, *ghee*, lemon juice, fenugreek leaves, salt and cashew nuts. Blend the mixture in a blender into a smooth paste and set aside.
2. Add the shrimp to the marinade and put it in a refrigerator for a couple of hours.
3. When ready to grill, skew the shrimp from the marinade onto the skewers and grill them on until lightly browned and charred, or broil them in the oven until light brown and roasted.
4. Serve with plain yogurt flavored with mint *chutney* or tamarind *chutney*.
5. Makes a excellent appetizer or can be served on top of a bed of lettuce leaves as a main course.

SERVES 4 – 6

Ingredients

Shrimp shelled and deveined	1 lb
Raw cashews	¼ cup
Yogurt	1 cup
Ginger, garlic and jalapeno (each) chopped	1 Tbs
Mango pulp	½ cup
Mustard seeds roasted	1 tsp
Cumin seeds roasted	1 tsp
Garam masala	1 tsp
Salt	1 tsp
Ghee or clarified butter or Vegetable oil	2 Tbs
Lemon juice	2 Tbs
Red pepper	1 tsp
Fenugreek leaves dry	1 tsp

CHAPTER 5

Exotic Vegetables

Indian culinary traditions are rooted in vegetarianism, mainly because of religion and of the cornucopia of vegetables available to the cook. With this incentive they have generated a great treasure of beautiful aromatic vegetable dishes. There is a major emphasis on freshness in Indian cooking. People cook fresh bread, use fresh vegetables, fresh lentils, and fresh yogurt for every meal each day. Vegetables and legumes substitute for the staple meat of the west. There is a great effort made to make at least two vegetable dishes for a fairly decent meal every day in an Indian household. Vegetables are ornamented with spices in as many different ways as you can imagine. They are stir-fried, curried, roasted as in eggplant (*bharta*), grilled like in *kebabs*, or steam cooked like in *undiya*. Sometimes several of these vegetables are curried together. Vegetables are immersed in a spicy batter to make delicious *fritters* and *koftas* (croquettes). Several kinds of croquettes are curried in exotic, aromatic and creamy gravies to be served with *nans* and home made fresh *chapattis*. The gravy of these vegetable curries is similar to the meat curries in terms of appearance and content.

Even the most ordinary vegetable can be turned into a delightful and appetizing accompaniment to a meal. Many different kinds of spice powders are used to make the vegetable curries like *podi masala* in the south, *panchphoran masala* in Bengal, *garam masala* and *achari masala* in north India, *tandoori masala* for making vegetable *kebabs*, *goda masala* mix in Maharashtra, *malwani masala* in the Malabar coast of India and *pathare prabhu masala* in Bombay. All vegetables in the north of India are cooked with tempering of cumin seeds and flavored with *garam masala* (a mixture of 5 spices) and freshly chopped coriander leaves whereas in the southern and western regions tempering is done with mustard seeds and their regional spice powders.

Most of the vegetables are now available all round the year. Vegetables that grow in the tropics like *bottle gourd, pointed gourd, round gourd, bitter melon, Japanese eggplant, yam, arrowroot* have to be purchased from your local Indian grocery store. Even *okra, coriander leaves, fenugreek leaves, ginger, coconut, papaya, hot chili peppers* are fresher and economical to purchase from the Indian grocers.

Vegetables should always be washed before chopping. They can be steam cooked with salt and pepper for a few minutes on the stove and frozen for future use. The seasoning of onions, ginger, garlic and green chilies for a vegetable stir-fry can be prepared ahead of time by chopping them in the food processor and can be frozen or refrigerated till the day of use. You can also make the curry masala-mixture of chopped onions, garlic, ginger, green chilies, tomatoes and the spices ahead of time and stored in the freezer in small bags. These will stay good for a couple of weeks and can be used as needed for making curries. All Indian cooking should be done on medium to low heat in a heavy-bottom, preferably nonstick, metal pan. High heat usually destroys the flavor and nutritive value.

Stuffed Mushrooms in Pomegranate Sauce
Kandhari Khumb Curry

Mushroom stuffed with *paneer* or Ricotta cheese, fresh pomegranate seeds and crushed cashew. Served in a curry sauce made thick with milk and pomegranate juice. Recipe shows influence of Afghanistan in use of nuts and pomegranate. It also gives this curry a unique tangy taste and a beautiful color.

METHOD

1. Get the mushrooms ready by washing them in cold water. Remove their stalks and save them in a bowl.
2. Boil them in water with 1 Tbs each of lemon juice and a tsp of salt for 2 minutes. Drain the water and wash them again with cold water, pat them dry and set them aside.

Filling

3. Cook ½ cup of onions, 1 tsp each of chopped ginger, garlic and green chilies in 2 Tbs of oil until light brown. Mix in ½ cup of ricotta cheese or *paneer* crumbled, chopped cashew nuts, 4 Tbs of fresh pomegranate seeds, ½ tsp black pepper, 1 tsp of salt and 3 Tbs of freshly chopped coriander leaves.
4. Fill up each mushroom with the filling. Bake them at 400ºF for 10 minutes. Remove from the oven. Arrange them in large but deep serving dish and set them aside.

Kandhari Sauce

5. Grind 1 cup of chopped onions, mushrooms stalks, ginger, 1 tsp each of chopped green chilies and garlic in an electric blender to smooth paste with the help of ½ cup of water and set it aside.
6. Heat 2 Tbs of oil in a thick-bottom large size cooking pan on low heat and add the ground onions and mushroom stalks mixture. Cook until oil separates from the onion mixture (about 5–8 minutes). Add cumin seeds and when they stop popping add turmeric powder, red pepper, coriander powder and salt, and mix the spices well into the onions. Cook and stir for 2 minutes and add the pomegranate juice. Stir it well. Boil the gravy for 4–5 minutes and add 1½ cups of milk. Simmer for 5 minutes. Now the gravy is ready to be poured over the mushrooms.
7. Pour the gravy gently around the baked mushrooms in a serving dish and sprinkle with 1 Tbs of remaining green coriander leaves, ground roasted cumin powder and ½ tsp of *garam masala*. Heat and serve with *pulav* or as a vegetable accompaniment for your favorite dinner.

SERVES 8 – 10

Ingredients

Mushrooms (large)	20
Lemon juice	2 tsp
Salt	2 tsp
Onions chopped	1½ cups
Ginger chopped	2 tsp
Garlic chopped	1 tsp
Green chilies chopped (mild)	2 tsp
Cashew nuts	¼ cup
Paneer or ricotta cheese drained and crumbled	½ cup
Fresh pomegranate seeds	1½ cup
Black pepper	½–1 tsp
Coriander leaves chopped	4 Tbs
Turmeric powder	1 tsp
Cooking oil	4–5 Tbs
Red pepper	½–1 tsp
Garam masala	1 tsp
Coriander powder	1 Tbs
Pomegranate juice	1 cup
Milk	1½ cups
Cumin powder ground, roasted	1 Tbs
Cumin seeds	1 tsp

Eggplant Stir-Fried
Baingan Dum

Eggplant pieces are first fried and then curried in a typical Mughlai style of cooking. It is a little time consuming but is elegant and exceptionally delicious.

SERVES 4 – 6

Ingredients

Small eggplants or couple of large ones sliced	2 lbs
Yogurt	1 cup
Onions chopped	½ cup
Vegetable oil	¼ cup
Garlic chopped	1 Tbs
Ginger chopped	1 Tbs
Green chilies chopped	1 Tbs
Dry fenugreek leaves (from your local Indian grocer)	1 Tbs
Turmeric powder	1 tsp
Coriander powder	1 tsp
Red pepper	1 tsp
Salt	to taste
Tomatoes chopped	1 cup
Cumin seeds	1 tsp
Garam masala	1 tsp
Cilantro leaves freshly chopped	2 Tbs

METHOD

1. Chop the eggplants into ½ inch thick and 4 inches long slices. Heat 2 Tbs of oil in a saucepan and fry the eggplant pieces golden brown and set them aside on a plate lined with paper towel. If small egg plants are used then just cut them twice crosswise starting from the bottom and leave them attached at the top end.

2. In a thick-bottom saucepan, heat the rest of the oil and add the onions, ginger, garlic and green chilies, and cook until light brown.

3. Add the cumin seeds and wait till they pop. Add the turmeric powder, salt, coriander powder, red pepper, *garam masala*, fenugreek leaves and stir to mix.

4. Turn the heat low and add the whisked yogurt and stir well to blend the spices into it. Let it simmer for a minute and add the fried eggplant pieces. Fold them gently into the yogurt sauce.

5. Lower the heat and cover the pan partially with a lid and let it cook until the eggplant pieces are tender (about 5 minutes). Cook 5 minutes open without a lid until most of the moisture is gone.

6. Add the chopped tomatoes and stir them in. Cover the pan with the lid and let it cook for another 5–10 minutes. Add 2 Tbs of coriander leaves and stir them in.

7. Serve topped with rest of the chopped coriander leaves.

Roasted Eggplant Curried
Bharta

An eggplant preparation made by roasting the eggplant under broiler in the regular oven until soft and the skin is dark brown. The skin is then peeled off and pulp of the eggplant is mashed and cooked with spices, tomatoes and some cream, topping it with butter and cilantro. Here is a delicious vegetable addition to any meal.

METHOD

1. Rub a little oil over the eggplants before wrapping them in aluminum foil. Transfer them to a regular oven in a rectangular baking pan and broil for 30 minutes or longer until they turn brown and get soft. Turn them a couple of times to get uniform browning. Remove from the oven. The eggplants will shrink considerably. Wait until they cool down. Peel the skin and mash the pulp with a fork or a potato masher.
2. In a large skillet, fry the onions, ginger, garlic, and green chilies until the onions turn light brown.
3. Add the cumin seeds and wait until they pop and then add the tomatoes and the tomato sauce.
4. Cook for a few minutes stirring on low heat. Add the turmeric powder, red pepper, coriander powder, cumin powder and salt, and cook till oil separates from the sauce mixture.
5. In ¼ cup of water boil peas separately for 5 minutes.
6. Add peas to the sauce mixture.
7. Mix well and add the mashed eggplants. Mix thoroughly. Cook on low heat until the mixture is absolutely smooth (about 20–25 minutes) stirring occasionally. Cooking time will depend on how well roasted are the eggplants.
8. Add the cream and cook another 2 minutes.
9. Top it with *garam masala* and green coriander leaves.

SERVES 8 – 10

Ingredients

Eggplants (large)	2
Onions chopped	1½ cup
Ginger chopped	2 Tbs
Garlic chopped	2 Tbs
Green chilies chopped	2 tsp
Vegetable oil	3 Tbs
Cumin seeds	1 tsp
Tomatoes chopped	2 cups
Tomato sauce	1 cup
Turmeric powder	1 tsp
Red pepper	1 tsp
Coriander powder	1 Tbs
Cumin powder	½ tsp
Salt	to taste
Water	¼ cup
Heavy cream	1 Tbs
Cream (optional)	2 Tbs
Garam masala	1 tsp
Green coriander or cilantro leaves chopped	2 Tbs
Peas frozen	1 cup

1

2

3

Egg Curry
Anda Curry

In north India, boiled eggs are popularly smothered in a creamy tomato sauce. Eggs are a good source of protein. The curry is nutritious and can be made any time as eggs are always there in the house. In south India coconut milk is also added to the curry to make it creamier. Serve it topped with fried onions or grated coconut and accompany with rice or a bread of your choice. It is delicious with both.

METHOD

1. Fry the sliced onions crisp and light brown in 3 Tbs of oil in a thick-bottom saucepan. Using a slotted spoon remove the fried onions and set them aside.
2. In the same oil, add the finely chopped onions, ginger, garlic and green chilies. When onions turn light brown lower the heat and add the turmeric powder, coriander powder, red pepper, salt, cumin powder and mix the spices into the onions.
3. Add the tomatoes, fenugreek leaves and stir well. Lower the heat and let it simmer for 2–3 minutes while stirring. Add the potatoes and mix them in.
4. Add the water and coconut milk and let the curry sauce thicken for at least 10 minutes and make sure that the potatoes are tender. Gently lay the egg halves at the bottom of the pan with the yellow facing up and let them simmer in the sauce for 5 minutes.
5. Add the lemon juice and *garam masala* and cook the gravy for another 2 minutes.
6. Serve the curry by gently ladling out the egg halves first into serving dish and pouring the gravy on top. Sprinkle with fried onions or grated coconut, if you desire. Serve it with rice, or bread of your choice.

SERVES 4 – 6

Ingredients

Onions finely chopped	2 cups
Vegetable oil or *ghee*	3 Tbs
Sliced onions	½ cup
Ginger chopped	1 Tbs
Garlic chopped	1 Tbs
Green serrano peppers chopped	1 Tbs
Turmeric powder	1 tsp
Coriander powder	2 tsp
Cumin powder	1 tsp
Red pepper	1½ tsp
Tomatoes chopped	2 cups
Water	2 cups
Coconut milk	1 cup
Lemon juice	1 Tbs
Grated coconut or dry coconut powder	2 Tbs
Medium peeled half boiled eggs cut in halves	6
Boiled potatoes chopped	1 cup
Fenugreek leaves (dry)	2 Tbs
Salt	to taste
Garam masala	1 tsp

Scrambled Eggs with Vegetables/Italian Frittata
Anda Bhurjee

Scrambled eggs when flavored with chopped shallots, green serrano peppers, tomatoes, green coriander leaves, salt, red pepper and cumin seeds are delicious. For a quick and complete meal, serve it with toast at breakfast or with a *parantha* and enjoy it for lunch.

SERVES 4

Ingredients

Eggs	6
Zucchini grated	½ cup
Shallots finely chopped	1 cup
Tomatoes finely chopped	1 cup
Serrano peppers green, finely chopped	1 Tbs
Garlic chopped	½ tsp
Olive oil or *ghee*	2–3 Tbs
Cumin seeds	1 tsp
Salt	to taste
Coriander leaves chopped	4 Tbs
Lemon juice	1 Tbs
Red pepper	1–2 tsp
Garam masala	1 tsp

METHOD

1. Beat the eggs with salt, lemon juice, pepper, *garam masala*, coriander leaves and set them aside.
2. In a thick-bottom skillet heat the oil and add the cumin seeds. When they start popping add the shallots, green peppers, and stir to mix.
3. When the onions turn light brown add the zucchini and tomatoes and garlic, and after lowering the heat stir to mix. Cover with a lid and let it cook for five minutes or until the zucchini is softened. Remove the lid.
4. Add the beaten eggs and stir to mix. Keep mixing until the eggs get cooked (about 2–3 minutes).
5. Transfer the cooked eggs with the vegetables to a platter and garnish with fresh mint.
6. Serve with lemon or mango pickle and *parantha* or just with a warm toast if you wish. It makes a hearty lunch, a breakfast or a quick snack.

Note: Zucchini can be replaced by any of the following vegetables: chopped red, yellow and green bell peppers, tender bits of asparagus or chopped baby spinach and grated processed cheese or *paneer*.

Eggplant in Tamarind Sauce
Bhagara Baingan

ANDHRA PRADESH

In southern India, especially in the Hyderabad region, eggplants are deep fried and then cooked in a sauce of dissolved tamarind, chopped tomatoes, ground roasted poppy seeds, sesame seeds, grated coconut, and spices like powdered fenugreek and cumin etc. It is a very regal dish.

SERVES 8 – 10

Ingredients

Eggplants small size	2 lbs
Vegetable oil to fry the eggplants	2–3 cups
Sesame seeds lightly roasted and ground	2 Tbs
Poppy seeds roasted and ground	2 Tbs
Peanuts lightly roasted and ground	2 Tbs
Fresh coconut grated	½ cup
Vegetable oil to cook	3 Tbs
Ginger chopped	1 Tbs
Green chilies chopped	1 Tbs
Tomatoes chopped	2 cups
Turmeric powder	1 tsp
Red pepper	1 tsp
Salt	to taste
Fenugreek leaves dry	2 Tbs
Cumin powder	1 tsp
Coriander powder	1 Tbs
Tamarind paste soaked in 2 Tbs of water Or according to taste	1–2 Tbs
Onions chopped	2 cups
Garlic chopped	1 Tbs
Curry leaves (small)	10
Garam masala	1 tsp
Coriander leaves chopped	2 Tbs

METHOD

1. Wash and cut the eggplants crosswise leaving them attached at the top. Pat them dry and set them aside.

2. In a deep wok heat the oil and fry the eggplants, a couple at a time, until lightly browned and set them aside on a platter lined with a paper towel and allow the oil to drain off.

3. In a clean skillet dry roast the sesame seeds, poppy seeds, peanuts and coconut until just turned brown and grind them in a food chopper along with the onions and set the paste aside.

4. In a deep-thick bottom saucepan fry the onion paste in 2 Tbs of oil with ginger, chopped green chilies, chopped tomatoes, garlic, turmeric powder, red pepper, salt, fenugreek leaves, cumin and coriander powders, and the dissolved tamarind until well blended. Add 2–3 cups of water and cook on low heat until the sauce is uniformly thick and the oil separates from the sauce.

5. Add the fried *baingans* (eggplants) and the curry leaves and cook for another 5 minutes. Remove from heat and serve sprinkled with *garam masala* and chopped coriander leaves. It makes an excellent vegetable side dish for a formal occasion.

The Exquisite World of Indian Cuisine

Eggplant in Sweet & Sour Sauce
Khatte-Mithe Baingan

Khatte-Mithe Baingan is mostly served this way in Bombay and other parts of Maharashtra. Eggplants are deep-fried and then cooked in tamarind sauce flavored with brown sugar and chilies. The curry is tangy, delicious and hot to the palate. It makes an excellent vegetable side dish to serve with any main meal.

METHOD

1. Make a crosswise slit in the eggplants and leave it attached at the top. If using large eggplant, chop it into 2 inch pieces and set them aside.
2. Heat the oil for frying in a wok and fry the eggplants light brown and drain them on to a plate lined with a paper towel.
3. In a medium saucepan heat the oil for cooking and fry the onions, ginger and green chilies on medium low heat until the onions are light brown. Add the cumin seeds, fenugreek seeds and the fennel seeds and wait until they start to pop.
4. Add the chopped tomatoes and stir to mix.
5. Add the turmeric powder, coriander powder, red pepper and salt, and stir-fry for a few minutes.
6. Add the potatoes and stir to fry for few more minutes. Add 2 cups of water and let the potatoes cook for about 8 minutes.
7. Transfer the eggplants into the pan and stir to mix. Add the dissolved tamarind and the brown sugar and stir well.
8. Add another cup of water and boil the curry for 5 more minutes. Make sure the potatoes are done.
9. Serve sprinkled with *garam masala* and chopped coriander leaves.

SERVES 8 – 10

Ingredients

Eggplants small or a large one chopped into 2 inch pieces	2 lbs
Oil (for frying)	4 cups
Oil (for cooking)	3 Tbs
Onions chopped	2 cups
Ginger finely chopped	1 Tbs
Garlic finely chopped	1 Tbs
Green chilies finely chopped	1 Tbs
Cumin seeds	1 tsp
Fennel seeds	1 tsp
Fenugreek seeds	½ tsp
Tomatoes chopped	2 cups
Ground coriander powder	1 Tbs
Turmeric powder	1 tsp
Red pepper	1 tsp
Salt	to taste
Water	3 cups
Potatoes cut into 2 inch pieces	1 cup
Garam masala	1 tsp
Coriander leaves chopped	2–5 Tbs
Tamarind pulp dissolved in 2 Tbs of water	1 Tbs
Brown sugar	1 Tbs or more to taste

Mixed Vegetable Curry
Navratan Korma

Several vegetables can be mixed to make a delicious colorful curry with a creamy sauce of tomatoes and small amount of coconut milk or heavy cream. It is mouth-watering, flavory and appetizing.

SERVES 8 – 10

Ingredients

Onions chopped	2 cups
Ginger chopped	1 Tbs
Garlic chopped	1 Tbs
Green chilies chopped	1 Tbs
Vegetable oil	¼ cup
Cumin seeds	1 tsp
Mustard seeds	1 tsp
Whole red pepper broken	2 or 3
Potatoes chopped	1 cup
Cauliflowerets	1 cup
Tomatoes fresh chopped	2 cups
Or canned	2 cups
Turmeric powder	1 tsp
Coriander powder	1 Tbs
Red pepper	1 tsp
Salt	to taste
Carrots chopped	½ cup
Beans chopped	½ cup
Peas fresh or frozen	½ cup
Zucchini chopped	½ cup
Curry leaves (small)	6
Heavy cream	1–2 Tbs
Or coconut milk	½ cup
Green coriander leaves chopped	3 Tbs
Garam masala	1 tsp
Water	2 cups

METHOD

1. Cook the onions, ginger, garlic, green chilies in the oil till light brown on medium heat in a deep heavy-bottom saucepan or a *Dutch oven.
2. Add the cumin seeds, curry leaves, mustard seeds and whole red pepper broken into pieces and wait till the cumin and mustard seeds start popping.
3. Lower the heat and add the tomatoes, turmeric powder, coriander powder, red pepper, salt and stir well.
4. Add the potatoes and carrots first and let them cook for 5 minutes and then add all the vegetables and stir well to coat them with all the spices. Add 2 cups of water and cover with the lid. Simmer for 10 minutes stirring in between by removing the lid. Add the coconut milk. Mix the curry well and let it simmer by occasionally stirring to check that there is no sticking to the bottom of the pan.
5. Cook until the potatoes get tender and carrots look softened.
6. Sprinkle with *garam masala* and chopped coriander leaves and simmer for another 2 minutes and serve.

Note: In this preparation ½ cup each of chopped daikon, radish, broccoli or red, green or yellow bell peppers can be added. Two Tbs each of chopped fenugreek leaves and coconut powder will really enhance the flavor of the curry. If frozen vegetables are used in the cooking, then use less cooking time. *Dutch oven is a deep heavy bottom cooking pan with an opening and is used in the west for cooking stews and chilli.

The Exquisite World of Indian Cuisine

Potatoes and Onions Stir-Fried
Aalu Pyaz ki Sabzi

Boiled, peeled and chopped potatoes when stir-fried with chopped onions, tomatoes and spices make a very delicious accompaniment to go with any meal but specifically with *masala dosa*. It is quick to fix and quite yummy.

SERVES 6 – 8

Ingredients

Potatoes boiled	2 lbs
Onions medium sliced	2 cups
Ginger chopped	1 Tbs
Garlic chopped	1 Tbs
Green chilies chopped	1 Tbs
Tomatoes chopped	2 cups
Cooking oil	2–3 Tbs
Cumin seeds	1 tsp
Mustard seeds	1 tsp
Red pepper (whole) dry, broken	2
Asafoetida powder	1/8 tsp
Urad dal	1 tsp
Turmeric powder	¾ tsp
Salt	1 tsp
Red pepper powder	1 tsp
Coriander powder	1½ tsp
Fenugreek leaves (dry)	2 Tbs
Water	½ cup
Green coriander leaves chopped	2 Tbs

METHOD

1. Boil the potatoes in a 4 quart saucepan with plenty of water to cover the potatoes. Cover and cook until the skin on the potato tears open (about 25–30 minutes). Slowly drain the water from the potatoes into the sink and cover them with cold water. Wait to peel until they are cool and easy to peel. Chop them into about one inch cubes. Set them aside in a bowl.

2. On medium heat, cook the sliced onions, chopped ginger and pepper in oil in a deep large skillet and wait until they turn light brown. Move the onion mixture to one side and add the whole dry red pepper, cumin seeds, mustard seeds and *urad dal,* and wait till the seeds start to pop.

3. Add the chopped garlic, turmeric powder, red pepper, coriander powder, dry fenugreek leaves, and the asafoetida powder. Stir and cook for half a minute and mix them into the onion mixture.

4. Add the chopped tomatoes and the salt. Stir and cook for few minutes until the tomatoes get mixed into the onion and spices mixture and oil starts separates from the sauce. Add the chopped potatoes and mix and coat them with the spice mixture. Add 1–2 cups of water and lower the heat. Cover them with a lid and cook for 5 minutes. Remove the lid and sprinkle with the chopped coriander leaves and stir.

5. Transfer to a serving bowl and serve it with your favorite meal.

Note: 1 quart is equal to 4 cups.

Bottle Gourd Croquettes Curry
Ghia Kofta Curry

Indians love vegetables and they can transform any vegetable with spices and curry sauce to turn it into a delicacy. This curry is a perfect example of that. Bottle gourd or Chinese squash is grated and mixed with gram flour and spices to make balls. These balls are then deep fried and cooked in a creamy tomato sauce.

METHOD

1. Mix 1 tsp of salt into the 2 cups of grated *ghia* or bottle gourd and let it sit for 1 hour. Squeeze the *ghia* and save the squeezed juices to be used later for the sauce. Add to the drained *ghia*, ginger, garlic, green chilies, red pepper, coriander powder, *garam masala*, baking soda, chopped pistachio, raisins, *anaardana* powder or 1 Tbs of *amchoor* and knead with help of gram flour into balls (*koftas*). Add more gram flour if needed. Fry them, few at a time, in a deep wok or *karahi* in oil heated to about 300°F until golden brown (about 5 minutes). Take them out on a plate lined with paper towel with a slotted spoon. Keep the heat low to maintain steady temperature.

2. In a heavy bottom 2–3 quart cooking pan, fry the onions, ginger, garlic, and green chilies in 2 Tbs of oil and wait till they turn light brown. Add the cumin seeds and whole red pepper. Wait for the cumin to start popping and add the turmeric powder, coriander powder, red pepper, salt, and mix well. Add the tomatoes, tomato sauce and mix the sauce in.

3. Cook on low heat for 3–5 minutes and add the water and the saved liquid from the grated *ghia*. Simmer the sauce for 15–20 minutes. Add gently the *koftas* and stir them in.

4. Cover with a lid and let it simmer for another 2 minutes. Turn off the heat, check to see if *koftas* are soft and plump but not broken. Add the cream and mix it in. Let the *koftas* sit in hot sauce for at least 20–30 minutes before serving.

5. Heat for another 2 minutes and add the *garam masala*, chopped coriander leaves and gently stir.

6. Remove from fire and serve by lading out the *koftas*. They can be served with rice, *pulav* or bread of your choice or any other meal. This dish is always a special addition to any meal.

Note: Lotus root, cauliflower and spinach are also very frequently used to make *koftas*. Same procedure as *ghia koftas* will work very well for spinach but lotus root and cauliflower after chopping would have to be boiled in water until soft.

SERVES 4 – 6

Ingredients for the *koftas*:

Bottle gourd (*ghia*) peeled and grated or finely chopped	2 cups
Gram flour	1 cup
Coriander powder	1 tsp
Red pepper	½ tsp
Salt	½ tsp
Garam masala	½ tsp
Ginger chopped	1 tsp
Green chilies chopped	1 tsp
Garlic chopped	1 tsp
Baking soda	a pinch
Amchoor	1 Tbs
Or	
Anaardana powder	1 tsp
Pistachio very finely chopped	1 Tbs
Raisins	1 Tbs
Vegetable oil for frying	3 cups

Ingredients for the curry sauce:

Onions chopped	1 cup
Ginger chopped	1 Tbs
Red pepper	1 tsp
Cumin seeds	1 tsp
Turmeric powder	1 tsp
Red pepper (dry)	2 broken
Garlic chopped	1 Tbs
Green chilies chopped	1 tsp
Vegetable oil or *ghee*	2 Tbs
Salt	to taste
Coriander powder	1 Tbs
Garam masala	1 tsp
Tomato sauce	1 cup
Fresh tomatoes chopped	2 cups
Cream	2 Tbs
Coriander leaves chopped	2 Tbs
Water	2 cups

1

2

3

4

169

EXOTIC VEGETABLES

Potato Curry
Aalu ki Sabzi

A perfect accompaniment with *poori* for a Sunday lunch. Quick and delicious, in fact it is a perfect side dish for any occasion.

METHOD

1. Cook the onions, ginger, garlic and green chilies in oil in a deep thick-bottom saucepan and wait till the onions turn light brown.
2. Add the cumin seeds, mustard seeds, whole red pepper and sauté until the seeds crackle.

3. Add the curry leaves and tomatoes.
4. Add the red pepper, turmeric powder, coriander powder, dry fenugreek leaves and the salt. Stir-fry for 5 minutes until the tomatoes are soft and the oil separates from the sauce. Lower the heat.
5. Add the potatoes and mix them well into the mixture. Add the water and simmer for 10–15 minutes or until the potatoes are tender. The amount of water to be used is at your own decision depending on how thick a curry you want.
6. Top it with *garam masala* and the chopped cilantro leaves. Mix well into the curry and boil once.
7. Serve with *raita* and *poori*.

SERVES 4 – 6

Ingredients

Boiled potatoes chopped into cubes	2 lbs
Onions chopped	½–1 cup
Ginger chopped	1 Tbs
Garlic chopped	1 Tbs
Green chilies chopped	1 tsp
Tomatoes chopped	2 cups
Red pepper whole	2 tsp
Cumin seeds broken and crushed	1 tsp
Mustard seeds	1 tsp
Red pepper powder	1 tsp
Coriander powder	1 Tbs
Turmeric powder	1 tsp
Salt	to taste
Garam masala	1 tsp
Cilantro leaves chopped	2 Tbs
Water	1 cup
Curry leaves	5–6
Dried fenugreek leaves (optional)	2 tsp or more
Coconut milk canned and unsweetened (optional)	½ cup

The Exquisite World of Indian Cuisine

Mustard Greens Curried
Sarson ka Saag

PUNJAB

One of the very famous mustard greens speciality from the state of Punjab. It can be made in advance and freezes very well. One can add to the mustard greens, spinach, broccoli, and sometimes small amounts of fenugreek leaves. It is invariably served with buttered corn bread.

SERVES 8 – 10

Ingredients

Mustard greens	2 lbs
Spinach leaves washed and chopped	½ lb
Broccoli washed and chopped	½ lb
Fenugreek leaves	1 cup
Ginger chopped	2 Tbs
Garlic chopped	1 Tbs
Green chilies chopped	2 Tbs
Whole dry red peppers broken (if green chilies not available)	2–3
Onions chopped	1 cup
Cumin seeds	1 tsp
Turmeric powder (optional)	½ tsp
Coriander powder	1½ Tbs
Cumin powder	½ tsp
Red pepper (if desired)	1 tsp
Garam masala	1 tsp
Vegetable oil or *ghee*	4 Tbs
Water	4 cups
Salt	1 tsp
Corn meal	3–4 Tbs

METHOD

1. Wash thoroughly all the greens in several changes of water. Drain the greens and chop them.
2. In a large thick-bottom saucepan or a bean pot add the greens with the water, salt, green chilies, garlic, ginger, and cook on low heat until very tender (takes about 1 hour) or pressure-cook them for 30 minutes.
3. Remove the pressure and mash the greens with a potatoes masher or cool them and blend them in a blender. Transfer them again into the saucepan and lower the heat.
4. Add the corn meal and mix vigorously until well blended. Cook and simmer while stirring for 10 minutes.
5. Heat 4 Tbs of the *ghee* in small saucepan and brown the onions. Add the cumin seeds and when they start popping add the turmeric powder, coriander powder, *garam masala*, cumin powder and whole red peppers. Mix the sautéed onions and spice mixture to the greens. Simmer and cook. If it starts to get thick add ½–1 cup of hot water and keep stirring. Remove from heat and add the *garam masala* and mix. Top it with a dash of butter and serve it with buttered hot corn bread.

Note: Use of green chilies is at your discretion, depending on how hot you want this curry to be.

EXOTIC VEGETABLES

Golden hues of a mustard field

Okra Stir-Fried
Bhuni hui Bhindi

Okra is widely enjoyed all over India. It is mostly stir-fried with onions, green chilies and spices and it becomes crunchy and very flavorful. It is also served whole stuffed with spices on special occasions.

METHOD

1. Wash and dry the okra and chop them horizontally into ¼–½ inch pieces. Coat an 10–13 inch baking dish with 2 Tbs of the oil or use oil spray to coat the pan with grease and spread the okra evenly in the dish in a layer. Bake at 425°F in the oven for 15–20 minutes or until they starts to turn brown. Turn them occasionally during baking with a spatula for even browning.

2. Fry the onions, ginger and green chilies in a wok or large heavy-bottom skillet in 2 Tbs of oil until the onions are a shade of brown and then add the garlic. Fry till the garlic turns light brown.

3. Add the cumin seeds and curry leaves and wait till the cumin seeds stop popping. Mix it well. Transfer the baked okra into the wok and stir gently to mix it with the onion mixture. Making sure that okra pieces do not get crushed.

4. Add the turmeric powder, red pepper, coriander powder and the salt, and gently fold in the spices.

5. Turn the heat low and add the *amchoor* and the *garam masala*. Mix it in gently.

6. Serve topped with chopped green coriander leaves.

SERVES 6 – 8

Ingredients

Fresh okra cut and trimmed in ¼ inch pieces	2 lbs
Onions chopped	½ cup
Ginger chopped	1 Tbs
Garlic chopped	1 Tbs
Green chilies chopped	1 Tbs
Vegetable oil	3–4 Tbs
Curry leaves	6–8
Cumin seeds	1 tsp

Spice mixture:

Red pepper	1 tsp
Turmeric powder	1 tsp
Coriander powder	1 Tbs
Salt	to taste
Garam masala	1 tsp
Amchoor (dried mango powder) or *anaardana* powder	1 Tbs

Note: Baking the okra in the oven is done only because the okra pieces will not crush. Okra can be fried gently in the frying pan on direct heat. Making sure it is done gently.

The Exquisite World of Indian Cuisine

Flavored Zucchini
Tori ki Sabzi

This simple but delicious dish is a delight in itself. Enjoy its delicate taste. When it is cooked with fresh tomatoes, onions and spices. Makes a very rich and flavorful accompaniment to any dinner.

SERVES 6 – 8

Ingredients

Fresh zucchini peeled and chopped	2 lbs
Onions chopped	½ cup
Ginger chopped	1 tsp
Garlic chopped	1 tsp
Green chilies chopped	1 tsp
Tomatoes chopped	1 cup
Cumin seeds	1 tsp
Dill leaves chopped (optional)	1 tsp
Turmeric powder	¾ tsp
Coriander powder	1½ tsp
Cumin powder	½ tsp
Red pepper	1 tsp
Garam masala	1 tsp
Coriander leaves chopped	2 Tbs
Vegetable oil	2 Tbs

METHOD

1. Heat the oil and cook the onions, ginger, and the green chilies on medium low heat until the onions are tender and then add the garlic. Fry for another minute.
2. Add the cumin seeds and fry them until they crackle.
3. Add the tomatoes and the dill leaves and stir-fry until the tomatoes are softened. Lower the heat.
4. Add the turmeric powder, red pepper, coriander powder, cumin powder and the salt and stir the mixture well. Add the chopped and sliced (¼ inch pieces cut horizontally or into cubes) zucchini and again stir well and cover the pan.
5. Let it simmer until the zucchini is tender (about 10–15 minutes). Stir and remove the lid and cook for another 5–10 minutes so that some of the moisture dries up.
6. Add the *garam masala* and green coriander leaves and mix.
7. Cook for another 2 minutes and serve.

Note: To make this dish special in step 1, as soon as the onion is done, add *badian* (dried spiced lentil balls) and fry them in oil until light brown. Addition of *badian* will make it much more appetizing. *Badians* are available at your local Indian grocery store.

Tofu Curry
Soya Meat Curry

Tofu is cooked in several ways in Indian cuisine. It is sometimes curried and sometimes stir-fried. It is also being used in the *pulavs*. It has become very popular in India as it provides some protein to the meatless diet of its majority vegetarian population. The easy to cook quality has also made it a very well liked preparation. Try it, it is quite delicious.

METHOD

1. In a skillet pour 1 cup of oil and heat it to pan-fry the Tofu cubes. Fry them until they are slightly brown. Remove and drain them on a paper towel.
2. Fry the onions, ginger, garlic, and green chilies in 2 Tbs of oil and add whole dry red pepper, curry leaves and cumin seeds.
3. When the cumin seeds start to pop, add the tomatoes, turmeric powder, red pepper, salt, coriander powder, cumin powder and the tomato sauce.
4. Mix well and cook for 5 minutes on low heat. When the oil starts to separate, add the potatoes, and fry stirring constantly for 2 minutes.
5. Add the peas and 1 cup of water and simmer for 5–10 minutes and add the Tofu gently and mix. Lower the heat.
6. Let it simmer until the potatoes are tender. Lower the heat a little more and add the yogurt and stir gently on low heat and slowly bring to a boil.
7. Remove from heat and add the chopped coriander leaves and *garam masala* and serve with plain rice or any *pulav* and *chappati*.

SERVES 4 – 6

Ingredients

Tofu firmly drained and cubed in 1 inch cubes	2 lbs
Vegetable oil	2 Tbs
Onions chopped	1 cup
Ginger chopped	1 Tbs
Garlic chopped	1 Tbs
Green chilies	1 Tbs
Red pepper (dry)	2–3
Curry leaves	5–6
Cumin seeds	1 tsp
Tomatoes chopped	1 cup
Tomato sauce	½ cup
Turmeric powder	1 tsp
Coriander powder	2 tsp
Salt	1½ tsp
Cumin powder	½ tsp
Garam masala	1 tsp
Yogurt whipped	½ cup
Or	
Coconut milk	½ cup
Coriander leaves chopped	2 Tbs
Peas frozen	¼ cup
Potatoes peeled and cubed	½ cup
Vegetable oil (for frying the Tofu)	1 cup
Water	1 cup

The Exquisite World of Indian Cuisine

Turnip Stir-Fried
Shalgam ki Sabzi

PUNJAB

Turnips are cooked with tomatoes and garnished with green coriander and *garam masala*. A vegetable accompaniment to any meal.

METHOD

1. Wash peel and chop the turnips into small cubes and set aside.
2. In a wok or non-stick skillet heat the *ghee* and add the chopped onions, ginger, garlic, and the green chilies, and fry the onions until light brown.
3. Add the cumin seeds and wait till they start to pop and then add the chopped turnips. Stir and add the turmeric powder, salt, red pepper, coriander powder, cumin powder and the fennel seeds. Mix and coat the turnips with these spices.
4. Add the tomatoes and stir-fry for 2 minutes. Lower the heat and cover the turnips tight with a lid. Let them cook for at least 10 to 15 minutes or until the turnips are tender. Mash the turnips and add sugar and yogurt. Mix well.
5. Remove from heat and add the *garam masala*, roasted ground mixture of sesame seeds, poppy seeds and coconut powder and the chopped coriander leaves and mix well. Adjust seasonings.
6. Heat it through and serve.

SERVES 8 – 10

Ingredients

Sesame seeds, poppy seeds, coconut powder ground, roasted	1 tsp each
Turnips washed, peeled and chopped	2 lbs
Onions chopped	1 cup
Ginger chopped	1 Tbs
Garlic chopped	1 Tbs
Green chilies chopped	1 Tbs
Vegetable oil or *ghee*	2 Tbs
Cumin seeds	1 tsp
Fennel seeds	½ tsp
Turmeric powder	1 tsp
Red pepper	1 tsp
Coriander powder	1 Tbs
Cumin powder	½ tsp
Salt	1 tsp
Yogurt	½ cup
Brown sugar	1 Tbs
Garam masala	1 tsp
Tomatoes chopped	2 cups
Coriander leaves chopped	1 Tbs

EXOTIC VEGETABLES

Cheese and Mushroom Curry

Mushrooms with tomatoes, peas and cheese cubes curried in a creamy tomato sauce are a delightful addition to any meal. They are very easy to fix and a very presentable accompaniment.

SERVES 6 – 8

Ingredients

Mushrooms (preferably portabella) washed and sliced	1 lb
Tomato sauce 8 oz can	1
Fresh tomatoes chopped	2 cups
Onions chopped	1 cup
Frozen peas or chopped red or yellow bell peppers sliced lengthwise	1 cup
Paneer cubes fried	1 cup
Ginger chopped	1 Tbs
Garlic chopped	1 Tbs
Green chili chopped	1 Tbs
Vegetable oil or *ghee*	3 Tbs
Salt	1½ tsp
Turmeric powder	½ tsp
Red pepper	1 tsp
Coriander powder	1 Tbs
Garam masala	¾ tsp
Half and Half or cream	2 Tbs
Coriander leaves chopped	2 Tbs

METHOD

1. Wash the mushrooms and remove the stalks or stems. Slice them into 4 pieces and set them aside. If Portabella mushrooms are used, slice them in ½ inch thick slices.
2. Cook the onions and ginger in 2 Tbs of oil or *ghee* in a wok or a thick-bottom deep frying pan for 2 minutes and add the tomato sauce.
3. Lower the heat, add salt, turmeric powder, red pepper, coriander powder, *garam masala* and mix well.
4. Stir-fry for 2 minutes and add the chopped mushrooms and the cheese cubes and stir to mix. Cook for 5 minutes.
5. Add the frozen peas, or the peppers, garlic, green chilies and chopped tomatoes. Cook for another 2–5 minutes.
6. Remove from heat, and just before serving heat and add the cream. Mix it well, sprinkle with coriander leaves and *garam masala*, and serve with any dinner or meal as a vegetable accompaniment.

The Exquisite World of Indian Cuisine

Peas & Cheese Curry
Matar Paneer

PUNJAB

Green peas are cooked with fried pieces of ricotta cheese in creamy sauce of tomatoes, cream and onions. It makes a great dish to be served with *nan*, *chappati* or *paranthas*, particularly for a formal occasion. A very delightful savory vegetable dish from the state of Punjab.

SERVES 4 – 6

Ingredients

Frozen peas or fresh peas	1 cup
*Fried cubes of *paneer* (see Introduction) (If the *paneer* is made at home, add ½ tsp of saffron to the milk that is being used to make the *paneer*.)	2 cups
Onions chopped	1 cup
Ginger chopped	1 Tbs
Garlic chopped	1 Tbs
Green chilies chopped	1 Tbs
Tomatoes chopped	2 cups
Tomato sauce	1 cup
Turmeric powder	1 tsp
Red pepper	1 tsp
Coriander powder	2 tsp
Cumin seeds	1 tsp
Cumin powder	½ tsp
Salt	to taste
Garam masala	1 tsp
Vegetable oil	2 Tbs
Cream	2 Tbs
Water or more	1 cup
Coriander leaves chopped	2 Tbs
Saffron	½ tsp

METHOD

1. Fry the onions, ginger and garlic in 2 Tbs of oil till the onions are light brown in a heavy-bottom cooking pan on medium-low heat.
2. Add the cumin seeds and when they start popping add the turmeric powder, red pepper, coriander powder, salt, cumin powder and stir well.
3. Add the chopped tomatoes, tomato sauce and salt. Mix well. Fry for 5 minutes.
4. Add the peas and stir to mix. Cook the peas in the sauce for 5 minutes.
5. Add the water and bring the curry to a full boil. Simmer for 5 minutes.
6. Add the fried ricotta cheese cubes and stir them in gently. Cover with a lid and let it simmer for at least 10 more minutes.
7. Add more water, if the sauce is looking too thick.
8. Add the cream, mix and let it simmer for 5 more minutes. Sprinkle with saffron, chopped coriander leaves and *garam masala* and bring the curry to a boil and serve with *nan*, *roti*, *pulav* or plain rice.

Note: Sometimes boiling the fried *paneer* pieces prior to adding them into the curry makes the pieces softer.

Paneer can be purchased at your local Indian grocery store. Completely drained ricotta cheese (see Introduction) can be substituted for *paneer*. Fried cheese cubes can also be purchased at your local Indian grocery store.

Baked Cauliflower
Bhuni Gobhi

Cauliflower coated with spices and butter and then baked whole is easier and is more tasty. Try it and you will love it. It makes a great presentation.

SERVES 8 – 10

Ingredients

Cauliflower head medium size	1
Onions chopped	1 cup
Ginger chopped	1 Tbs
Garlic chopped	1 Tbs
Green chilies chopped (mild)	1 Tbs
Salt	1 tsp
Turmeric powder	1 tsp
Red pepper	1 tsp
Cumin powder	½ tsp
Ground coriander	1 Tbs
Amchoor	1 Tbs
Garam masala	1 tsp
Vegetable oil or *ghee*	3–4 Tbs
Lemon juice	1 tsp
Coriander leaves chopped	2 Tbs

METHOD

1. Wash and remove the loose leaves of the head of the cauliflower and dry it with a paper towel and set it aside.

2. Grind the ginger, onions, garlic and green chilies in a blender or a food processor and add a little water to facilitate the grinding. Remove the mixture from the blender into a bowl and add the turmeric powder, red pepper, coriander powder, salt, cumin powder and *amchoor,* and mix well.

3. Coat the cauliflower head with this *masala* mixture completely and pour 2 Tbs of *ghee* or choice of your oil over the *masala* coated head of the cauliflower and bake at 425°F in the oven in a shallow baking pan.

4. Cover the pan for 30–40 minutes. Remove the cover and pour 2 Tbs of melted butter or *ghee* over the cauliflower again and bake for another 10–15 minutes or until it starts to turn brown.

5. Remove from the oven and sprinkle *garam masala*, lemon juice and chopped coriander leaves and serve as a vegetable accompaniment to any meal.

The Exquisite World of Indian Cuisine

Fried Potato Curry
Dum Aalu

Potatoes cooked whole in a creamy sauce of yogurt, ground poppy seeds, coconut, almonds, onions, ginger, garlic, green chilies and spices, are delightfully tasty because they are completely smeared with the sauce.

METHOD

1. In a medium size thick-bottom saucepan fry the potatoes in ¼ cup oil or *ghee* and sprinkle ½ tsp of salt while frying. Remove them from the cooking pan with a slotted spoon and set them aside.
2. In a skillet roast the cumin seeds, poppy seeds, almonds, black pepper, cloves, brown cardamom seeds and coconut powder and grind them in the blender with ginger, garlic, green chilies, in ¼ cup of water to make a fine paste and set aside.
3. In the same saucepan, used for frying the potatoes, fry the onions, in the remaining *ghee* until the onions turn golden brown.
4. Lower the heat and add the bay leaves, turmeric powder, red pepper, coriander powder, salt and the ground paste and stir. Add the tomato sauce and mix well. Cook for 2 minutes and lower the heat and add 1 cup of yogurt and stir-fry for 5 minutes, or until the sauce separates from the oil.
5. Add the fried potatoes and stir to coat them with the sauce. Cook on slow heat for 5 minutes and add the remaining yogurt and the remaining water and let it simmer until the potatoes are tender (about 20–30 minutes).
6. Sprinkle with *garam masala* and mix well. Cook for another minute. Sprinkle with green coriander leaves.
7. Serve with *poori*, *nan* or *chappati*.

SERVES 8 – 10

Ingredients

Potatoes small peeled and washed 1–1½ inch diameter	2 lbs
Onions chopped	1 cup
Ginger chopped	1 Tbs
Garlic chopped	1 Tbs
Green chilies chopped	1 tsp
Cumin seeds	1 tsp
Poppy seeds	1½ tsp
Almonds	1 Tbs
Coconut powder unsweetened	1 Tbs
Cloves	½ tsp
Brown cardamom seeds	½ tsp
Black peppercorns	½ tsp
Salt	1 tsp
Tomato sauce	1 cup
Bay leaves	4–6
Turmeric powder	1 tsp
Red pepper	1 tsp
Yogurt	1½ cup
Coriander powder	1 Tbs
Vegetable oil or *ghee*	¼ cup
Water	2 cups
Fresh green coriander leaves chopped	2 Tbs
Fenugreek leaves dry	1½ Tbs

Note: Cut the potatoes in half, if they are more than 1 inch in diameter.

EXOTIC VEGETABLES

Fenugreek Leaves and Potatoes
Methi Aalu

Stir-fry chopped fenugreek leaves and potatoes make a very healthy vegetable accompaniment to any meal. Fenugreek leaves have numerous health benefits and are cooked in several ways. I find this the easiest.

METHOD

1. Heat the oil in a deep 1 quart saucepan and sauté the onions and garlic, ginger and green chilies.
2. As soon the onions are light brown add the cumin seeds. As they start to pop, add the whole red peppers.
3. Add the potatoes and stir the mixture and stir-fry them until light brown.
4. Add the salt, coriander powder, red pepper, turmeric powder and mix well. Add the chopped fenugreek leaves and stir again. Lower the heat. Add 2 Tbs of water.
5. Cover the pan with a tight lid and let it cook for 10 minutes stirring a couple of times to prevent any sticking. Add more water, if needed to soften the potatoes, if the stir-fry is too dry.
6. Remove the lid and let it simmer until most of the water evaporates and potatoes are tender. Mix in the *garam masala* and the chopped coriander leaves and stir to mix. Serve it with *chappatis*, *dal* and *raita*.

SERVES 4 – 6

Ingredients

Fenugreek leaves washed and chopped	3 cups
Potatoes peeled and chopped in ½ inch cubes	1 cup
Vegetable oil	2 Tbs
Onion chopped	½ cup
Garlic copped	½ tsp
Red dry pepper (whole)	2
Cumin seeds	1 tsp
Salt	½ tsp
Turmeric powder	1 tsp
Water	2 Tbs
Garam masala	½ tsp
Coriander leaves chopped	2 Tbs
Ginger chopped	1 tsp
Green chilies	1 tsp
Coriander powder	1 tsp
Red pepper	½ tsp

Kerala Vegetable Curry
Aviyal

KERALA

This mixed vegetable curry is made with fresh coconut and tamarind. They grow abundantly in this part of the country. The curry has many variations depending on what is available in that season. Tamarind is often replaced by buttermilk or yogurt. It is very mild but rich, creamy and delicious.

SERVES 6 – 8

Ingredients

Ingredient	Amount
Water	3 cups
Salt	1½ tsp
Tamarind pulp dissolved in 1 tsp of water	1 tsp
Fresh peeled and chopped carrots cut into 2 inch long thin pieces	½ cup
Fresh French beans (cleaned and cut in half) or frozen	1 cup
Fresh peeled potatoes cut in at least 2 inch pieces lengthwise	1 cup
Lima beans or peas frozen or fresh	½ cup
Bell pepper cut lengthwise into 2 inch pieces	½ cup
Or a medium cucumber piece cut in cubes	1 cup
Fresh coconut grated	1 cup
Or	
Dry coconut powder	¼ cup
Green chilies	2 Tbs
Garlic chopped	2 Tbs
Ginger chopped	2 Tbs
Coconut milk	½ cup
Onions chopped	1½ cup
Cumin seeds	1 tsp
Mustard seeds	1 tsp
Curry leaves	6–8
Turmeric powder	1 tsp
Coriander powder	1 Tbs
Vegetable oil	3–4 Tbs
Red pepper	1 tsp
Fenugreek leaves dry	1 Tbs

METHOD

1. Boil 2 cups of the water with 1 tsp of salt, 1 tsp of tamarind pulp in a 4 quart heavy-bottom saucepan and add chopped carrots, and beans and cook for 5 minutes.
2. Add the potatoes, and boil for another 5 minutes.
3. Add the frozen peas, bell pepper and cook for 2 more minutes and set them aside.
4. Grind in the blender the coconut, onion, green chili, garlic, ginger, ½ tsp salt, with ½ cup of water and ½ cup of coconut milk. Set it aside.
5. Add the onions and coconut mixture to the cooked vegetables in the cooking pan and simmer on low heat for at least another 5 minutes and add 1 cup of water. Cook until the curry sauce is thickened and vegetables are tender.
6. Fry the cumin seeds, mustard seeds, curry leaves, turmeric powder, coriander powder, dry fenugreek leaves, red pepper in 2 Tbs of oil and transfer the tempering on to the vegetables aviyal in the cooking pan. Stir the mixture well and serve. Check for salt and seasoning and add more, if needed.
7. Serve hot as a vegetable accompaniment in any meal.

Note: 1 cup boiled yams, or raw bananas or plantains or pumpkin chopped into cubes can be substituted for 1 cup of boiled potato cubes. Add more coconut milk if you wish it to be a thicker curry.

Paneer & Potatoes in Coconut Sauce
Paneer-Aalu Nariyalwale

A friend of mine from the Pathare Prabhu community of Bombay uses *Pathare Prabhu Masala* for her curries. The *masala* has rich and tangy ingredients and they give this curry a unique taste.

SERVES 6 – 8

Ingredients

Paneer slab cut in 1 inch long and ½ wide and thick pieces	2 cups
Cooking oil	¼ cup
Onions (medium) chopped	1 cup
Potatoes pieces cubed	1 cup
Frozen peas	½ cup
Ginger chopped	1 Tbs
Garlic chopped	1 tsp
Pathare Prabhu *masala*	2 Tbs
Turmeric powder	1 tsp
Cumin seeds	1 tsp
Red pepper	1 tsp
Asafoetida	¼ tsp
Tamarind dissolved in 1½ cups of water	1 tsp
Coconut milk	1 cup
Cashew nuts	¼ cup
Sugar	1 tsp
Salt	1 tsp
Coriander leaves chopped	1 Tbs

METHOD

1. Heat 2–3 Tbs of oil and add the onions, ginger and garlic until the onions are light brown. Lower the heat.

2. Add the cumin seeds by moving the onion mixture to one side with a cooking spoon and wait till they start to pop. Add the asafoetida, turmeric powder, red pepper, salt and sugar and stir to mix.

3. Add the frozen peas and chopped potatoes and cashew nuts. Mix well and add the Pathare Prabhu *masala* and keep stirring. Add the tamarind water. Mix and cover the pan and let it simmer for 8–10 minutes or until the potatoes get soft. Add more water, if needed.

4. Add the coconut milk and stir well. Let it simmer for 2 minutes and add the fried cheese cubes, and let it simmer until the cheese cubes are soft and plump (about 10 minutes). Lower the heat and add the chopped coriander leaves. Boil and serve garnished with freshly grated coconut, if possible. Check and season the curry, if needed.

Note: *Paneer* cubes can be substituted by cauliflower florets or its *koftas*.

Spinach with Fried Cheese
Palak Paneer

A nutritious dish of spinach with deep fried cubes of homemade cheese or ricotta cheese makes a very popular north Indian curry. It is served in restaurants also as *saag paneer*. *Paneer* is popularly used in Indian cooking as a good source of digestible protein. This is a favourite vegetable accompaniment to a meat curry.

METHOD

1. Transfer freshly chopped spinach or frozen spinach with 2 cups of water, into a pressure cooker and add 1 tsp of salt, 1 Tbs of ginger and garlic each and 1 Tbs of green chilies, and pressure cook for at least 15–20 minutes. Cool and blend the spinach mixture in the blender to a smooth mixture with the help of ½ cup of water and set it aside.
2. Fry the cheese pieces in the oil, at 350–375°F until slightly brown (5 minutes). Transfer with a slotted spoon onto a paper towel and drain the oil. Set it aside.
3. In a large saucepan, cook onions in oil over medium heat until tender and light brown.
4. Add the red whole chilies (optional) and cumin seeds and wait till the seeds start popping.
5. Add the tomatoes, red pepper, coriander powder, turmeric powder, cumin powder and mix. Cook until the tomatoes are softened and the mixture looks like a thick sauce and the oil separates from the sauce. Add ¼ cup of water and bring the sauce to a boil.
6. Now add the pressure cooked spinach and ½ cup of water and cook on low heat for about 10 more minutes.
7. Add the fried pieces of *paneer* or ricotta cheese and cook for another 10 minutes or until the *paneer* pieces get soft. Add more water, if needed, depending on the thickness of curry you want. Add more salt, if needed.
8. Add the heavy cream, *garam masala* and chopped coriander leaves and simmer for about 2 more minutes. Serve with *chappatis* or *nan*.

SERVES 8 – 10

Ingredients

Frozen chopped baby spinach	15 oz
Or	
Spinach freshly chopped	1 lb
Salt	1 tsp
Ginger chopped	1 Tbs
Garlic chopped	1 Tbs
Green chilies (mild)	1 Tbs
Water	1½ cup
*Paneer or well drained ricotta cheese cut in 1½ inch pieces	1 lb
Oil for frying the cheese	3–4 cups
Onions chopped	2 cups
Red chilies (whole) broken	3
Cumin seeds	1 tsp
Fresh tomatoes chopped	2 cups
Red pepper	1 tsp
Coriander powder	1 Tbs
Vegetable oil	¼ cup
Turmeric powder	1 tsp
Cumin powder	1 tsp
Garam masala	1 tsp
Heavy cream	1–2 Tbs
Coriander leaves chopped	2 Tbs

Creamy Cheese Croquettes in Curry Sauce
Malai Kofta

These deep fried balls of mashed potatoes and cheese are curried and usually served with rice *pulav* but can be served with *chappati* or *nan*. It is one of the gourmet dishes in Indian cooking and takes a little effort to make than the regular curry but it is all worth it.

METHOD

1. Boil the potatoes and mash them.
2. Mix the cheese and the bread crumbs into the mashed potatoes.
3. Add ginger, garlic, green chilies, a pinch of baking soda, salt, red pepper, coriander powder, green coriander leaves, *garam masala* and *amchoor*. Mix well to make thick dough.
4. Make small 1 inch diameter balls/croquettes (*koftas*) and insert a piece of pistachio or a piece of almond in the center of each of them and fry few at a time in oil heated at 325–350°F on medium low heat until light brown. Do not overheat the oil. Takes about 2–3 minutes.
5. Take *koftas* out with slotted spoon. Drain on a paper towel lined bowl and set them aside.
6. Grind the onions, ginger, garlic, and green chilies in a blender. Fry the ground *masala* in 2 Tbs of oil in a heavy-bottom 2 quart cooking pan on medium low heat.
7. Move the onions mixture to one side and add the cumin seeds and wait till they start popping.
8. Add the whole red chili peppers, wait till they start sizzling. Add turmeric powder, red pepper, coriander powder, salt, tomatoes and tomato sauce. Keep frying until the tomatoes become soft, and the oil separates from the *masala*. Lower the heat.
9. Add the yogurt and stir well on low heat.
10. Add the 2 cups of water and cook the sauce for 5 minutes.
11. Add the *koftas* and stir them gently in the sauce.

SERVES 6 – 8

Ingredients

For *Koftas*:

Potatoes boiled and mashed	2 cups
Paneer or ricotta cheese completely drained of moisture	1 cup
Bread crumbs	1 cup
Ginger	1 tsp
Garlic	1 tsp
Green chilies	1 tsp
Salt	½ tsp
Baking soda	a pinch
Red pepper	½ tsp
Coriander powder	1 tsp
Garam masala	½ tsp
Amchoor	1 Tbs
Coriander leaves chopped	1 Tbs
Almonds or pieces of pistachio chopped	2 Tbs
Oil for frying	

For the curry:

Onions chopped	2 cups
Ginger, garlic and green chilies (each) chopped	1 Tbs
Cumin seeds	1 tsp
Turmeric powder	1 tsp
Red pepper	1 tsp
Coriander powder	1 Tbs
Red pepper (whole) broken	2 or 3
Tomatoes chopped	1 cup
Tomato sauce	1 cup

Note: Instead of bread crumbs, 1–2 Tbs of arrow-root flour can be mixed with mashed potatoes and *paneer* (available only at your local Indian grocery store) to make the *koftas* or croquettes.

The Exquisite World of Indian Cuisine

UTTAR PRADESH

12. Cover the pan with a lid and simmer on low heat for 2 minutes. Add the heavy cream and stir it in gently. Cook a minute longer. Let the *koftas* sit in the gravy for at least ½ hour before serving.
13. Sprinkle with *garam masala* and coriander leaves and serve with *pulav*, *nan*, *chappati* or *poori*.

Plain whipped yogurt	1 cup
Salt	1½ tsp
Garam masala	1 tsp
Heavy cream	2 Tbs
Coriander leaves chopped	2 Tbs
Oil	3 Tbs
Water	2 cups

EXOTIC VEGETABLES

Cabbage and Peas Stir-Fried
Patta Gobhi aur Matar ki Sabzi

Convert the ordinary cabbage into great vegetable side dish. Serve it with bread, rice, a meat curry or lentils. Its crunchy and delicate taste is quite unique and appealing.

METHOD

1. Fry the ginger, garlic, and green chilies in a thick-bottom skillet on low heat in 2 Tbs of oil. Wait till they are light brown and then add the mustard seeds, and the *urad dal*. Wait till they start popping and *urad dal* starts to turn brown. Add the asafoetida powder. Mix well.

2. Add the cabbage and mix completely to coat the cabbage with the spice mixture. Lower the heat.

3. Add salt, turmeric powder, coriander powder, red pepper and stir the vegetable well. Cover it tight with a lid and cook for 5 minutes. Add the peas and mix them in. Again cover with a lid and cook another 2 minutes, stirring in between to prevent sticking to the bottom of the pan.

4. Add the curry leaves and coconut and fry the vegetable on low heat till the moisture is somewhat gone.

5. Remove from heat and sprinkle chopped coriander leaves, *garam masala* and lemon juice. Stir well and serve. Makes an excellent vegetable accompaniment to any meal.

SERVES 8 – 10

Ingredients

Ginger chopped	1 Tbs
Garlic chopped	1 Tbs
Green chilies chopped	1 Tbs
Mustard seeds	1 tsp
Urad dal (dry)	1 Tbs
Asafoetida powder	$\frac{1}{8}$ tsp
Cabbage (*patta gobhi*) washed chopped and shredded	4 cups
Or	
A bag of fresh Cole Slaw	4 cups
Turmeric powder	1 tsp
Salt	1 tsp
Red pepper	1 tsp
Coriander powder	1 Tbs
Frozen peas	½ cup
Curry leaves chopped	2 Tbs
Fresh grated coconut	1 cup
Or	
Dry unsweetened coconut powder	¼ cup
Vegetable oil	2 Tbs
Lemon juice	1 Tbs
Coriander leaves	2 Tbs
Garam masala	½ tsp

HINT
Gujarati style cabbage stir-fry will use 2 Tbs of sugar and substitute the peas with ½ cup roasted chopped peanuts.

The Exquisite World of Indian Cuisine

Eggplant, Potatoes and Tomatoes Stir-Fried
Baingan, Aalu aur Tamatar ki Sabzi

PUNJAB

This eggplant, potatoes and tomatoes stir-fried dish is a delicious vegetable accompaniment to any dinner. Fresh eggplants are cooked with onions, tomatoes, green chilies and flavored with fresh coriander and *garam masala*. This dish goes with any meal.

SERVES 8

Ingredients

Onions chopped	1 cup
Ginger chopped	1 Tbs
Garlic chopped	1 Tbs
Green chilies chopped	1 Tbs
Vegetable oil	¼ cup
Cumin seeds	1 tsp
Potatoes peeled and chopped	1 cup
Fresh tomatoes chopped or canned chopped tomatoes	1 cup
Fresh eggplants chopped	2 lbs
Turmeric powder	1 tsp
Coriander powder	1 Tbs
Cumin powder	1 tsp
Red pepper	1 tsp
Salt	1 tsp
Garam masala	1 tsp
Green coriander leaves chopped	2 Tbs
Sesame seeds ground, dry roasted	1 Tbs

METHOD

1. Cook the onions, ginger, garlic and green chilies in a deep skillet or a wok and wait till they are light brown. Sauté with cumin seeds, and add the chopped eggplant, potatoes and stir the mixture well.
2. Add the turmeric powder, salt, coriander powder, cumin powder and the red pepper, and coat the vegetable mixture.
3. Add the tomatoes and stir them well into the curry.
4. Lower the heat and cover the vegetable tight with a lid. Cook for 15 minutes or more and stir two or three times in between by removing the lid to make sure there is no sticking. If the stir-fry is too dry, add a couple of Tbs of water and stir in it.
5. Cook until the potatoes are tender.
6. Add the *garam masala,* dry roasted sesame seeds and sprinkle with green coriander leaves. Stir and serve as a side dish with lentils, bread, rice and meat curry.

Mixed Vegetable Curry Baked
Gujarati Undiya

GUJARAT

Gujaratis make this select mixed vegetable dish which has a great flavor because it is baked. A group of selected vegetables are mixed with different spices, onions, ginger, garlic, green chilies which are then baked in a inverted clay pot called *undu* with burning coal on top of it and around it. The pot is completely sealed and the vegetables cook in their own steam under pressure.

SERVES 8 – 10

Ingredients

Potatoes peeled and chopped	1 cup
Plantain (raw banana) peeled and chopped	½ cup
Beetroot chopped	½ cup
Tomatoes chopped	2 cups
Sweet potatoes peeled and chopped	½ cup
Carrots peeled and chopped	½ cup
Green frozen *toovar* or snow pea pods	1 cup
Eggplant chopped	1 cup
*Fenugreek leaves (*kasuri methi*)	1 cup
Muthia	1 cup
Spinach washed and chopped	1 cup
Water	½ cup
Onions chopped	2 cups
Green chilies chopped (mild)	2 Tbs
Ginger chopped	2 Tbs
Garlic chopped	2 Tbs
Salt	2 tsp
Turmeric powder	½ tsp
Vegetable oil or *ghee*	6 Tbs
Coriander powder	2 Tbs
Red pepper	1 tsp
Cumin powder	1 tsp
Sugar	1½ Tbs
Mustard seeds	1 tsp
Cumin seeds	1 tsp
Curry leaves	8–10
Carom seeds	1 tsp
Green coriander leaves chopped	2 Tbs
Garam masala	1 tsp
Fresh coconut grated	½ cup
Or	
Coconut powder	2 Tbs
Kashmiri chilies dry, broken	2–3
Asafoetida	½ tsp

METHOD

1. Chop all the vegetables in large pieces. Mix the vegetables (except tomatoes and *muthias**) together in large deep baking dish and add onions, ginger, garlic, green chilies, salt, red pepper, Kashmiri chilies, turmeric, 4 Tbs of *ghee*, coriander powder, cumin powder, sugar, water and mix well until blended. Cover the pan with a lid.

2. Bake covered in an oven at 425°F for 30 minutes or microwave until the vegetables are tender. Add the *muthias* and tomatoes and bake for another 15 minutes or until all the vegetables are tender and cooked. Add more water, if needed.

3. Heat 2 Tbs of oil in a large thick-bottom cooking pan and add the mustard seeds, cumin seeds, curry leaves and carom seeds. Wait till the seeds start to pop, then add the fresh coconut or dry coconut powder and asafoetida powder. Stir and transfer the tempering on cooked vegetables into the pan. Stir to mix.

4. Top it with chopped coriander leaves and *garam masala*.

5. Undiya serves best with *poori*.

*See the *Muthia* recipe in the Appetizers section.

The Exquisite World of Indian Cuisine

Bread Croquettes in Curry
Bread Kofta

Bread *koftas* in a delicious white gourd sauce with tomatoes and curd are mouth watering. The dish makes a excellent accompaniment to any dinner.

METHOD

1. Boil the chopped or grated *ghia* (bottle guard) in 2 cups of water with ½ tsp of salt. As soon as the *ghia* becomes transparent and soft, purée it in a blender. Set it aside.
2. Prepare the *koftas* by mixing together yogurt, pieces of bread slices (remove the crust), chopped green coriander, chopped green chillies, chopped ginger, garlic, onions, all purpose flour, baking soda, and salt in a deep salad bowl. Knead it well to make a soft dough and make small balls of the size of a walnut. Add more flour if needed.
3. Heat the oil in a wok at 325–350°F and fry the *koftas* light brown. Do not overheat the oil. Drain them on a paper towel and set them aside.
4. Grind onions, ginger, garlic and green chilies together in a blender.
5. Heat 3 Tbs of *ghee* in a medium size thick-bottom cooking pan and add the puréed onions, ginger and garlic mixture. Add the cumin seeds and when they start to pop, add the tomato sauce, turmeric, cumin powder, red pepper, coriander powder and salt. Mix and fry the *masala* until the *ghee* separates from the *masala*. Add the puréed squash, sour cream, cooked potatoes and ½ cup of water and cook for 5 minutes on medium heat.
6. Just before serving, make sure the sauce is not too thick because after adding *koftas* it is going to thicken as the *koftas* will absorb water. Add more boiling water, if needed, and mix it well. Add the *koftas* to the sauce and bring it to a boil and simmer for 2 minutes. Remove from heat. Wait till the *koftas* swell up (15 – 20 minutes) and then serve by first lading out the *koftas* in a serving dish. Serve it sprinkled with green coriander and *garam masala*.

SERVES 6 – 8

Ingredients

Koftas:

Bread slices	6–8
Fresh yogurt	½ cup
All purpose flour	¼ cup
Coriander leaves chopped	2 Tbs
Green chilies chopped	1 Tbs
Ginger chopped	1 tsp
Salt	½ tsp
Garlic chopped	1 tsp
Baking soda	$\frac{1}{8}$ tsp
Vegetable oil (for frying)	4 cups

Curry sauce:

Bottle gourd (*ghia*) or pumpkin grated	½ lb
Water	2 cups
Tomato sauce	1 cup
Onions chopped	1½ cup
Ginger and garlic chopped	2 Tbs
Green chilies	1 Tbs
Sour cream or heavy cream	½ cup
Red pepper	1 tsp
Turmeric powder	1 tsp
Salt	1 tsp
Coriander powder	1 Tbs
Cumin seeds	1 tsp
Cumin powder	1 tsp
Potatoes small cooked and peeled	1 cup
Vegetable oil or *ghee*	3 Tbs
Garam masala	1 tsp
Coriander leaves chopped	½ cup

Mixed Vegetable Croquettes Curry
Kofta Curry

Cooked vegetable when mashed with gram flour can be formed into balls and deep-fried. These balls when curried make a dish, which is called *Kofta* Curry. It is usually served with rice or your favorite bread. Highly recommended for a formal occasion.

METHOD

1. Boil peas and cauliflower in 2 cups of water until soft. Drain the water from the vegetables and save to be used later. Mash the vegetables. Store them. Boil the 3 potatoes until soft (the skin starts to break on the potato) and peel them. Mash potatoes and mix them with mashed vegetables in the mixing bowl.

2. Add 1 Tbs each of ginger, garlic, 1 tsp of green chilies, ½ cup of onions, gram flour, a pinch of baking soda, ground roasted cumin and coriander, ½ tsp of *garam masala*, ½ tsp of red pepper, ½ tsp of salt, 2 Tbs of chopped coriander leaves and mix well. Make 1 inch balls (*Koftas*) from the mixture. Add more gram flour, if needed.

3. Make a depression in the center and place a raisin and $1/8$ tsp of pistachio in each ball. Heat the oil to 325–350°F. Do not overheat. Fry *koftas* until light brown and remove them from oil with a slotted spoon. Drain them on a paper towel and set aside.

4. Grind 1 cup of onions, remaining ginger, garlic and green chilies in a blender and fry in 2 Tbs of oil in a deep, thick-bottom saucepan. Cook till the oil starts to separate from the onion mixture.

5. Add the tomato sauce, tomatoes, turmeric, coriander powder, 1 tsp each of red pepper, salt and fry till the tomatoes are completely soft. The mixture should look like a sauce and the oil separates from the sauce. Add 1½ cups of water plus the saved water from the boiled vegetables and boil the sauce for 5–10 minutes. Gently add the *koftas* and cover the pan and let it simmer on low heat for 2 minutes. Add the cream and stir it in gently. Turn off the heat and leave the *koftas* in sauce for ½ an hour before serving.

6. Add the *garam masala* and chopped coriander. Remove the *koftas* onto the serving dish first and then pour the gravy over them. It can be served with rice, *pulav*, *nan* or *chappatis*.

SERVES 8 – 10

Ingredients

Cauliflower florets boiled and mashed (medium size head)	½
Peas cooked and mashed	½ cup
Potatoes boiled and mashed (medium)	3
Ginger chopped	2 Tbs
Garlic chopped	2 Tbs
Green chilies chopped	1 tsp
Onions chopped	1½ cup
Gram flour	2 cups
Baking soda	a pinch
Cumin seeds ground roasted	1 tsp
Coriander seeds ground roasted	1 Tbs
Garam masala	1 tsp
Red pepper powder	1 tsp
Salt	1½ tsp
Coriander leaves chopped	2 Tbs
Raisins (lightly pan-fried in a tsp of oil)	1 cup
Pistachio chopped (lightly fried in a pan along with raisins)	1 Tbs
Vegetable oil (for frying)	2–4 cups
Ghee or oil	3 Tbs
Tomato sauce	1 cup
Tomatoes chopped	1 cup
Turmeric powder	1 tsp
Coriander powder	1 tsp
Cream	½ cup
Water	1½ cups

EXOTIC VEGETABLES

Beans with Coconut
Nariyalwali Sem ki Phali

Beans lightly flavored with *podi* powder. The grated coconut give it that crunchy crispy taste which is quite different from the other beans preparations.

SERVES 8

Ingredients

String beans fresh	1½ lbs
Or	
Frozen French cut beans	15 oz
Mustard seeds	1 tsp
Podi powder	2 Tbs
Salt to taste or	1 tsp
Turmeric powder	¾ tsp
Garlic chopped	1 Tbs
Ginger chopped	1 Tbs
Green chilies chopped	1 Tbs
Lime juice	2 Tbs
Coriander leaves chopped	¼ cup
Curry leaves	5–7
Vegetable oil	3 Tbs
Grated fresh coconut	1 cup
Or	
Coconut powder dry	2–3 Tbs
Garam masala	½ tsp

METHOD

1. Wash and dry the beans and chop them into 1 inch long pieces and set them aside.
2. Heat the oil in a skillet and add the mustard seeds and wait till they pop and then add the garlic, ginger, green chilies and cook for 2 minutes and then add the chopped beans. Add 2 Tbs of *Podi* powder and stir well to completely coat the beans. (If using fresh beans add a little water and cook longer).
3. Add salt and turmeric powder. Lower the heat and cover the pan.
4. Let it cook while stirring occasionally to prevent the sticking until the beans are tender. It will take about 8–10 minutes.
5. Sprinkle the coconut over the beans and stir well.
6. Turn off the heat and sprinkle with the lime juice, chopped coriander leaves and *garam masala* and serve.

Note: If *podi* powder is not available, add in step 2 right after adding mustard seeds, ½ tsp each of *urad dal*, *channa dal* and cumin seeds. When they start to sizzle and the *dal* turns light brown, add a pinch of asafoetida, and 1 Tbs of coconut powder. Immediately add the 1 tsp of sesame seeds and red pepper. Stir to mix in the beans. If using fresh beans, add extra cooking time.

Bitter Gourd Stir-Fried
Karele ki Sabzi

Bitter gourd stir-fry is very easy to make. It is crunchy, and its hot and sour taste makes it very appetizing. The natural bitterness is removed by sprinkling salt over it before cooking and then squeezing out the bitter water. Bitter gourd lowers blood sugar and maintains normal body functions. This vegetable is rich in all the essential vitamins and its regular use prevents hypertension and the body's resistance against infection. Particularly rcommended, if you have diabetes.

SERVES 4 – 6

Ingredients

Bitter gourd (*karela*) peeled, sliced and salted	1 lb
Onions chopped	½ cup
Oil	2 Tbs
Ginger chopped	1 tsp
Garlic	1 tsp
Green chilies chopped	1 tsp
Salt	1½ tsp
Turmeric powder	1 tsp
Coriander powder	1 tsp
Cumin powder	½ tsp
Red pepper	1 tsp
Cumin seeds	1 tsp
Amchoor (dried mango powder)	1 tsp
Or	
Lemon juice	1 Tbs
Garam masala	½ tsp
Green coriander leaves chopped	2 Tbs

METHOD

1. Peel and slice the bitter gourd (*Karela*) in ¼ inch thick slices and sprinkle 1 Tbs of salt on them and leave them in a bowl for 2–3 hours or longer. It can be covered and can be left in the refrigerator overnight.
2. Remove from the bowl, wash and squeeze the bitter water out and put them aside.
3. Fry the onions in the oil until golden brown and set them aside.
4. Heat the oil in a deep skillet and fry the bitter gourd on medium heat until light brown and add the ginger, garlic and green chilies and keep stirring until the ginger turns brown too. Add the turmeric powder, red pepper, salt, and cumin seeds and wait till they start to pop. Add the fried onions, the cumin powder, and coriander powder. Stir and add the lemon juice, or the *amchoor*, *garam masala* and chopped coriander leaves.
5. Cook while stirring for 2 more minutes. Serve with *dal* and *chappati*.

Bitter Gourd Stuffed
Bharwan Karela

Peeling them and soaking them in lemon juice and salt for an hour ahead of cooking takes out the bitterness of bitter gourd. This vegetable has tremendous health benefits, helps cure diabetes, high blood pressure and increases body's resistance against infection. They taste best when stuffed with a mixture of mashed potatoes, or crumbled up ricotta cheese, ground onions, garlic, ginger, tamarind pulp and all the other spices used in the curries. This makes them really delicious and palatable.

METHOD

1. Peel the bitter gourds and make a slit lengthwise in them and soak in lemon juice and salt at least an hour or overnight. Wash them well the next morning and scoop out the pulp and any tough seeds you may have. Squeeze to take out all the bitterness from the bitter gourds and set them aside.

2. Fry the onions, ginger, garlic and green chilies in *ghee* until light brown. Add the turmeric powder, coriander powder, cumin seeds, ground anise seeds, red pepper and salt. Stir well and add the tamarind pulp. Fry till the water dries up.

3. Add the crumbled up cheese or mashed potatoes and mix. Cook another 2 minutes and add the *garam masala*. Stir the mixture well and let it cool. Stuff the *karelas* with this stuffing and wrap a thin thread around it 3–4 times to cover the opening of the bitter gourd.

4. Grease generously an 8 or 10 inches wide, two inches deep baking dish and arrange the bitter gourds in a layer. Bake them in an oven at 425°F and cover them for 20–25 minutes. Remove the lid and bake for another 15–20 minutes. Keep turning them occasionally to brown all sides. It may take more or less time depending on the number and size of bitter gourds. They can be pan fried in the oil coated frying pan, turning them occasionally until light brown.

5. Serve them with any wet curry, *dal* and bread of your choice. Remove the thread before eating.

SERVES 6

Ingredients

For soaking to remove bitterness:

Bitter gourds medium sized	6
Salt	2 tsp
Lemon juice	2 tsp

Ingredients for stuffing:

Onions chopped	½ cup
Ginger chopped	1 Tbs
Garlic chopped	1 Tbs
Mashed potatoes	½ cup
Or	
Crumbled up ricotta cheese or *paneer*	½ cup
Coriander powder	1 Tbs
Cumin seeds	1 tsp
Red pepper	1 tsp
Green chilies chopped (mild)	1 Tbs
Turmeric powder	1 tsp
Tamarind pulp	1 tsp
Salt	1 tsp
Garam masala	1 tsp
Ghee (for frying)	2 Tbs
Ghee (for frying the stuffing)	1 Tbs
Anise seeds ground	1 Tbs
Coriander leaves chopped	1–2 Tbs

The Exquisite World of Indian Cuisine

Carrots and Potatoes Stir-Fried
Gaajar-Aalu ki Sabzi

Chopped carrots and potatoes stir-fry is one of the quick fixing (and my favorite) vegetables. It is very healthy and delicious. Serve it with *chappati* and your favorite curry.

SERVES 8

Ingredients

Carrots peeled and chopped	3 cups
Potatoes chopped	1 cup
Onions chopped	1 cup
Ginger chopped	1 Tbs
Garlic chopped	1 Tbs
Green chilies chopped	1 tsp
Cumin seeds	1 tsp
Oil	2 Tbs
Whole red dry pepper (broken)	2–3
Turmeric powder	1 tsp
Coriander powder	1 Tbs
Salt	1 tsp
Red pepper	1 tsp
Garam masala	½ tsp
Chopped coriander leaves	1 Tbs
Water	¼ cup
Fresh fenugreek leaves chopped Or	1 cup
Fenugreek leaves dry	2 Tbs

METHOD

1. Fry the onions in oil in a deep thick-bottom skillet and add the ginger, garlic and green chilies. Cook until the onions turn light brown.

2. Add the cumin seeds and wait till they pop. Add the whole red peppers and wait till they turn color.

3. Add the chopped vegetables and stir. Lower the heat and add the turmeric powder, red pepper, salt, coriander powder, and coat the vegetables with the spices. Cover the carrots with a tight fitting lid and add fenugreek leaves and ¼ cup of water. Stir and cook until the potatoes are tender. About 15 minutes. Keep stirring in between to avoid any sticking. Add more water, if needed. Sprinkle with *garam masala* and chopped green coriander leaves. Transfer to a serving dish and serve with *chappati*, *poori* or *nan* along with your favorite curry.

Note: Potatoes are sometimes replaced by 1 cup of fresh or frozen peas. It is your choice, and you can use ½ cup of each of them.

Whole Stuffed Okra
Bharwan Bhindi

It is a very special north Indian preparation. Whole okra is slit open on one side and is stuffed with ground spices and is then pan-fried in oil. It is crisp and delicious and is usually served as a vegetable side dish with a meat curry or just lentil and bread and is one of the very popular vegetables to be served in a formal setting.

SERVES 8 – 10

Ingredients

Whole okra washed and ends trimmed	2 lbs
Onions chopped	1 cup
Ginger chopped	1 Tbs
Garlic chopped	1 Tbs
Green chilies	2–3
Turmeric powder	1 tsp
Red pepper	1 tsp
Coriander powder	1 Tbs
Cumin powder	1 tsp
Fenugreek leaves (dry)	1 tsp
Salt	1 tsp
Garam masala	¾ tsp
Amchoor or *Anaardana* powder	1 Tbs
Oil (for frying)	5 Tbs
Coriander leaves chopped	2 Tbs

METHOD

1. Grind the onions, ginger, garlic and green chilies in a blender. Add turmeric powder, red pepper, cumin powder, coriander powder, salt, *garam masala* and *amchoor* or *anaardana* powder and dry fenugreek leaves. Mix and fry the *masala* in 2 Tbs of oil for 5 minutes and set it aside.

2. Make a single lengthwise slit into the okras to make a pocket and open the slit wide. Fill up the opening with 1 tsp of the fried *masala*. Set them aside.

3. Take a large cookie sheet and oil it generously. Arrange the stuffed okra in single layer on the cookie sheet and bake them at 425°F for 40–45 minutes until they are dark brown and crisp. Turn them once or twice and brush them with oil or *ghee*.

4. Remove from the oven, sprinkle *garam masala* and chopped coriander and bake again for 2 minutes. They should be crunchy and delicious.

5. Serve them with a meat curry, *dal* and any bread of your choice.

The Exquisite World of Indian Cuisine

Okra and Peanuts
Bhindi aur Moongphali ki Sabzi

Chopped and fried okra and peanuts cooked with coconut powder makes a very appetizing accompaniment and is quite presentable.

SERVES 6 – 8

Ingredients

Okra (*bhindi*)	2 lbs
Oil for frying the okra (*bhindi*) and peanuts	2 Tbs
Oil or *ghee* (for cooking)	2 Tbs
Onions chopped	1 cup
Ginger chopped	1 Tbs
Garlic chopped	1 Tbs
Green chilies chopped	1 tsp
Coconut grated dry	2 Tbs
Mustard seeds	1 tsp
Peanuts (roasted)	½–1 cup
Cumin seeds	1 tsp
Tomato sauce	1 cup
Turmeric powder	1 tsp
Coriander powder	1 Tbs
Salt	1–1½ tsp
Garam masala	¾ tsp
Red pepper	½–1 tsp
Coriander chopped	2 Tbs

METHOD

1. Wash the okra and chop it diagonally into 1–1½ inch pieces. Set it aside.

2. Heat the oil in a wok (*karahi*) and fry the okra for 10–15 minutes till it is lightly browned. Remove them from the oil on a plate lined with paper towel. Fry the peanuts in the same hot oil till golden brown. Take them out from oil in a bowl lined with a paper towel and set them aside.

3. In the same wok heat 2 Tbs of oil and add the mustard seeds and cumin seeds. When they start popping add the coconut powder and cook till it turns brown. Add the onions, ginger, garlic, green chilies, and cook till light brown. Add the tomato sauce and stir to mix. Add the turmeric powder, coriander powder, red pepper, salt and stir to cook till the oil starts to separate from the wok (*karahi*). Add the *garam masala* and the chopped coriander leaves. Stir it in.

4. Just before serving add the fried okra and peanuts. Mix well gently and serve as a accompaniment to any dinner.

Bell Pepper, Potatoes and Tomatoes Stir-Fried
Shimla Mirch, Aalu aur Tamatar ki Sabzi

Bell peppers and potatoes go very well together and the tomatoes give it the extra tangy taste needed to make this a delicious stir-fry vegetable special.

METHOD

1. Cook the onions in oil and add the ginger, garlic and green chilies. Fry until light brown in a deep-heavy bottom saucepan or a wok.
2. Add the cumin seeds and wait till they pop. Add the potatoes and all the spices – turmeric powder, red pepper, salt, cumin powder, coriander powder, and stir well. Add ¼ cup of water, lower the heat and cover and cook for 10 minutes.
3. Add the chopped peppers, the tomatoes and the tomato sauce, stir well. Cover with a tight lid on a low heat and simmer for another 5 minutes or until the potatoes are tender.
4. Keep stirring to make sure the vegetables do not stick to the bottom of the pan.
5. Sprinkle with *garam masala* and chopped coriander leaves and mix.
6. Cook for another 2 minutes and serve.

SERVES 8

Ingredients

Bell pepper fresh, medium size washed, deseeded and chopped	4
Potatoes peeled, washed and chopped	1 cup
Tomatoes chopped	1 cup
Tomato sauce	½ cup
Onions chopped	1 cup
Ginger chopped	1 Tbs
Garlic chopped	1 Tbs
Green chilies chopped	1 tsp
Vegetable oil	2 Tbs
Cumin seeds	1 tsp
Turmeric powder	1 tsp
Coriander powder	1 Tbs
Cumin powder	½ tsp
Red pepper	1 tsp
Garam masala	1 tsp
Coriander leaves chopped	1 Tbs
Water	¼ cup

Stuffed Bell Peppers
Bharwan Shimla Mirch

Stuffed vegetables are usually made when the meal is special. They are easy to make and look elegant too. The stuffing is made of cooked mixture of boiled potatoes, onions, core of the peppers, fresh herbs, rice and spices.

SERVES 6 – 8

Ingredients

Green bell pepper (small size)	8
Boiled potatoes, peeled and cubed or small fried *paneer* cubes	2 cups

METHOD

1. Wash and dry the peppers. Boil them in water for 5 minutes, drain the water and dry them. Remove the top – going in a circle with a sharp knife, so that the top comes out like a cap with a little handle that is the stem of the pepper. Set it aside for use later. Remove the seeds and center flesh and brush the outside of the pepper with oil. Set them aside.

2. Cook the onions, ginger, garlic and green chilies in 2 Tbs of oil until light brown and add the cumin seeds. Wait till they pop and add the chopped potatoes, or small paneer cubes, fried and freshly chopped flesh from the interior of the peppers leaving any firm seeds behind. Add also ½ cup of cooked rice. Stir well.

3. Add the turmeric powder, poppy seeds, red pepper, coriander powder and salt, and mix well. Lower the heat and cook while stirring for 2 minutes.

4. Add the lemon juice, chopped green coriander, *garam masala* and the cream of coconut. Stir and cover the pan with a lid and let it simmer for 3–5 minutes or until the potatoes become a little soft. The stuffing is ready. Let it cool and set it aside.

5. Fill the pepper shells with the stuffing leaving a little space at the top and cover them with the top of the pepper that was removed and stored for this purpose only.

6. Bake at 425°F in an 8–10 inch baking dish that has been greased with the remaining oil. Cover the pan for the first 15 minutes and then remove the cover and bake open for another 10 minutes. Remove them from the oven and serve. Great vegetable accompaniment to any meal.

Cooked rice	½ cup
Onions chopped	½ cup
Green hot chilies chopped	1 Tbs
Ginger chopped	1 Tbs
Garlic chopped	1½ tsp
Salt	to taste
Turmeric powder	1 tsp
Vegetable oil	¼ cup
Cumin seeds	1 tsp
Poppy seeds	1 tsp
Red pepper	1 tsp
Ground coriander	1 Tbs
Salt	1½ tsp
Coriander leaves chopped	2 Tbs
Lemon juice	2 Tbs
Garam masala	1 tsp
Cream of coconut	¼ cup

Note: If large size peppers are used, cut them in half and fill the cavities in the same way and bake them.

Stuffed Whole Tomatoes
Bharwan Tamatar

Tomatoes stuffed with mashed boiled potatoes, diced carrots, peas, onions and spices and tiny fried cheese cubes baked in oven. Makes a delicious preparation with a beautiful presentation.

METHOD

1. Wash and dry the tomatoes. Remove the top of tomato by going in a circle around the top with a sharp knife so as to make a cap with any stem it may have and brush the outside of the tomatoes with oil and set it aside.
2. Scoop out the center pulp of the tomato and store in a bowl, leaving the sides intact.
3. Fry the onions in a thick-bottom skillet. Add the ginger with green chilies and wait till the onions turn a shade of brown. Add the garlic. Stir and add the cumin seeds, carom seeds and wait till they start popping. Add the potatoes, peas and carrots, the center of the tomato pulp and the tiny fried cheese (*paneer*) cubes and mix well.
4. Add the turmeric powder, red pepper, coriander powder, coconut powder, salt, and stir to cook. Lower the heat, cover the skillet with a lid and cook the stuffing for 8–10 minutes.
5. Add the chopped up coriander leaves, *garam masala* and mix it in.
6. Remove from heat and cool.
7. Stuff the shell of the tomatoes with the stuffing leaving a little space at the surface and place the cap on top.
8. Pour the remaining oil into an 8–10 inch baking dish and arrange the tomatoes in the pan. Bake at 425°F in a conventional oven for 10–15 minutes. Sprinkle chopped coriander leaves. Remove from the baking dish gently with a spatula and serve as a vegetable accompaniment to any dinner or a meal. Make sure that you do not overcook the tomatoes.

Note: Either potatoes or cheese can be replaced by chopped cabbage that has been drained of all moisture. Water can be removed by sprinkling salt over the cabbage. Let it sit for an hour or so and squeeze out the water.

SERVES 6 – 8

Ingredients

For stuffing:

Tomatoes (medium) fresh, firm	8
Onions chopped	½ cup
Potatoes boiled chopped	2 cups
Tiny fried cheese (*paneer*) cubes	½ cup
Peas and finely diced carrots (fresh or frozen)	½ cup
Vegetable oil	¼ cup
Ginger finely chopped	1 Tbs
Green chilies finely chopped	1 Tbs
Garlic finely chopped	1 Tbs
Cumin seeds	1 tsp
Carom seeds	1 tsp
Coriander powder	1 Tbs
Turmeric powder	1 tsp
Red pepper	1 tsp
Salt	to taste
Coconut powder	1 Tbs
Garam masala	1 tsp
Green coriander leaves chopped	2–4 Tbs

The Exquisite World of Indian Cuisine

Stuffed Eggplants
Bharwan Baingan

Small Japanese eggplants are stuffed with a mixture of spices, ground onions, ginger, garlic, tamarind pulp and pan-fried or baked in the oven. They make a very tasty, great looking vegetable presentation.

SERVES 8

Ingredients

Japanese eggplants	2 lbs
Onions ground	1 cup
Ginger ground	1 Tbs
Garlic ground	1 Tbs
Green chilies ground	1 tsp
Turmeric powder	1½ tsp
Goda masala	4 Tbs
Tamarind pulp	1 tsp
Salt to taste or	1 tsp
Oil	½ cup
Green coriander leaves chopped	4 Tbs

METHOD

1. Wash the eggplants and make two crosswise slits on the smooth side of the eggplants, ¾ inch down the length of the eggplant. Set them aside.

2. Mix the onions, ginger, garlic, green chilies, turmeric powder, salt, 4 Tbs of *goda masala* and 1 tsp of tamarind pulp dissolved in 1 Tbs of water in a small bowl. Add 2 Tbs of the oil to a skillet and heat it a little and transfer everything from the bowl into it. Fry for 5 minutes or until the water dries up. Set it aside.

3. Cool and stuff the *masala* mixture in between the slits of the eggplants and press to close them. Put them in a shallow baking dish that has already been greased generously with oil.

4. Cover the dish with a foil and bake at 425°F for 30 minutes. Remove the foil and bake them open for another 15–20 minutes turning them once or twice or until the skin turns golden brown. Remove them to a serving dish and sprinkle with coriander leaves and serve.

Note: Japanese eggplant are slender with thinner skins and a more delicate, sweeter flavor and can be green, pink, white, lavender and purple. One American eggplant equals about 3 Japanese eggplants.

EXOTIC VEGETABLES

Colourfully attired Ragni folk singers and musicians from Haryana at a local fair

The Exquisite World of Indian Cuisine

Yam Curry
Raswali Arbi

Here is another example of a very ordinary vegetable turned into a delicious preparation by cooking it in a creamy tomato sauce and flavoring it gently with spices.

METHOD

1. Wash the yams in tap water and boil them in water in a saucepan.
2. As soon as you see a spilt in the skin on the yams turn the heat off and cool them in running water. Peel the skin, chop them and slightly pan-fry them for 2 minutes in oil in a skillet. Set aside.
3. In the same saucepan heat the oil. Add the cumin seeds and the carom seeds. As soon as they start to pop, add the onions, ginger, garlic and green chilies. Fry till the onions start to turn light brown.
4. Lower the heat and add the turmeric powder, coriander powder, red pepper and salt. Stir to mix. Add the tomato sauce and mix it in. Cook until the oil separates from the sauce. Add the chopped yams. Stir them in the sauce and add the water. Cover the saucepan with a lid and let it simmer for 5–10 minutes or until the sauce becomes creamy and thick. Add the cream and heat it through.
5. Sprinkle with *garam masala* and chopped coriander leaves and serve it with your favorite bread.

SERVES 8 – 10

Ingredients

Yams boiled, peeled, chopped into cubes	2 cups
Onions chopped	1 cup
Ginger chopped	1 Tbs
Garlic chopped	1 Tbs
Green chilies chopped (mild)	1 Tbs
Vegetable oil	2 Tbs
Tomato sauce	1 cup
Turmeric powder	1 tsp
Cumin seeds	1 tsp
Carom seeds	1 tsp
Red pepper	1 tsp
Coriander powder	1 tsp
Garam masala	½–1 tsp
Salt to taste or	1 tsp
Heavy cream	2 Tbs
Coriander leaves chopped	2 Tbs
Water	2 cups

The Exquisite World of Indian Cuisine

Dry Yam Curry
Dum Arbi

Here is another great preparation of yams. The curry is drier than the wet curry and the pieces of yam are first deep-fried and then curried. It has its own unique and rich taste. It goes very well as a side dish with meats and other vegetable curries.

SERVES 6–8

Ingredients

Yams washed, boiled, peeled and chopped	2 cups
Oil for frying	4 cups
Onions chopped	1 cup
Ginger chopped	1 Tbs
Green chilies chopped	1 Tbs
Garlic chopped	1 Tbs
Carom seeds	1 tsp
Cumin seeds	1 tsp
Amchoor	1 Tbs
Coriander leaves chopped	2 Tbs
Vegetable oil or *ghee*	2 Tbs
Coriander powder	1 Tbs
Garam masala	1 tsp
Salt	1 tsp
Turmeric	½ tsp
Red pepper	1 tsp
Lemon juice	1–2 Tbs
Water	¼ cup

METHOD

1. Peel and chop yams about ½ inch pieces. Heat the oil in a deep wok or a thick-bottom saucepan between 300°F–340°F and fry the chopped up yam pieces until they are golden brown (about 5 minutes) or pan fry them in ½ cup of oil, gently turning them until slightly brown. Remove them from the oil with a slotted spoon on to a paper towel lined bowl and set them aside.

2. Heat the 2 Tbs of *ghee* or oil in a heavy thick-bottom saucepan or a wok and add the carom seeds, cumin seeds, and wait till the cumin seeds start to pop. Add the onions, ginger, garlic and green chilies. Fry them until the onions are light brown. Lower the heat and add the fried pieces of yam. Add the coriander powder, turmeric, red pepper, salt and *amchoor*.

3. Stir to mix. Add ¼ cups of water and mix well. Cover the pan with a lid and cook on very low heat for 5–10 minutes. Remove from fire, stir well and serve sprinkled with chopped coriander leaves, *garam masala* and the lemon juice.

Plantain Curry
Kele ki Sabzi

Bananas grow in abundance in India and plantains make a wonderful curry. Sliced plantains are first deep fried and then curried in a sauce of tomatoes and cream.

SERVES 6 – 8

Ingredients

Raw bananas (plantain) deep fried	2 cups
Paneer cubes or ricotta cheese cubes	1 cup
Onions chopped	1 cup
Ginger chopped	1 Tbs
Garlic chopped	1 Tbs
Green chilies chopped	1 tsp
Tomato sauce	1 cup
Yogurt beaten smooth	1 cup
Turmeric powder	1 tsp
Red pepper	1 tsp
Cumin powder	1 tsp
Vegetable oil or *ghee*	2 Tbs
Coriander powder	1 Tbs
Curry or Bay leaves	4–6
Cumin seeds	1 tsp
Coriander leaves chopped	2 Tbs
Salt	to taste
Water	2 cups
Garam masala	1 tsp
Oil for frying	2 cups

METHOD

1. Peel the plantains and slice them about ½ inch thick.
2. In a skillet heat the oil to about 300°F–340°F and fry them light brown. Drain them on a paper towel and set them aside. Fry the *paneer* cubes in the same oil and set them aside.
3. In a thick-bottom saucepan fry the onions, ginger, garlic and green chilies in 2 Tbs of oil until the onions are light brown and add the cumin seeds. When they start to pop, add the curry leaves and stir.
4. Add the turmeric powder, coriander powder, cumin powder, red pepper, and salt. Mix well and add the tomato sauce and stir the mixture. Cook till the oil separates from the sauce. Add water. Mix and bring it to a full boil.
5. Add the fried bananas and fried cheese cubes. Lower the heat. Let it simmer on low heat until the bananas are tender but still firm and not mushy (10–15 minutes).
6. Lower the heat and add the yogurt. Mix well and cook for 3–5 minutes. Bring the curry to a boil.
7. Add the *garam masala* and the chopped coriander leaves. Mix well and remove from heat and serve with rice, *chappati* or any bread of your choice.

Note: Yogurt can be replaced by 2 Tbs of cream.

The Exquisite World of Indian Cuisine

Beans and Potatoes Stir-Fried
Beans Aalu

Green beans curried and stir-fried with potatoes make a great vegetable side dish.

SERVES 4 – 6

Ingredients

Green beans cut in ½ inch pieces (washed)	2 lbs
Or	
Frozen French cut beans	15 oz pkg
Potatoes washed peeled chopped into 1 inch cubes	1 cup
Onions chopped	1 cup
Ginger chopped	1 Tbs
Garlic chopped	1 Tbs
Green chilies chopped (mild)	1 Tbs
Vegetable oil or *ghee*	¼ cup
Channa dal	¼ cup
Urad dal	2 Tbs
Sesame seeds	2 Tbs
Mustard seeds	1 tsp
Asafoetida	¼ tsp
Turmeric powder	1 tsp
Coriander powder	1½ tsp
Cumin powder	1 tsp
Red pepper	1 tsp
Salt to taste or	1 tsp
Garam masala	1 tsp
Green coriander leaves chopped	2 Tbs
Water	½ cup

METHOD

1. Fry the onions in oil and add the ginger, garlic and green chilies. When the onions start to turn light brown add the turmeric powder, red pepper, cumin powder, coriander powder and salt. Add the chopped potatoes. Stir well and add ¼ cup of water.

2. Turn the heat low and cover it tight with the lid. Cook for about 10 minutes. Remove the lid to stir and check if the potatoes are sticking to the bottom of the pan and add a couple of teaspoons of water. Add the beans and stir well and cover the pan again. Cook for another few minutes until the potatoes are tender.

3. In a wok heat ¼ cup of oil, add the *channa dal, urad dal*, sesame seeds and fry till golden brown. Add the mustard seeds and asafoetida powder and wait till the mustard seeds start to pop. Add this tempering over the cooked beans.

4. Sprinkle with the *garam masala* and the chopped coriander leaves and mix well. Heat again for a minute and serve.

Cauliflower and Potatoes Stir-Fried
Aalu Gobhi

The cauliflower florets are flavored with onions, cumin and *garam masala* and the potatoes give it an extra creamy taste. Truly a delicious vegetable preparation.

METHOD

1. Fry the onion in a Dutch oven or a deep saucepan in oil. Add ginger, garlic and green chilies. Fry until light brown, move onion mixture to one side with a large serving spoon.
2. Add 1 tsp of cumin seeds and wait until they start popping and then add the potatoes. Stir-fry them for 5 minutes.
3. Add cumin powder, coriander powder, salt, red pepper and turmeric. Stir the mixture well and add 3 Tbs of water. Cover it tight with a lid for about 8–10 minutes. During cooking turn the heat on medium-low. Add the washed cauliflower florets after draining them well. Stir gently to coat them with spices and cover the stir-fry with lid again for 5 minutes. Stir gently not to break the florets. Remove the lid and cook open for few minutes so that any extra moisture will evaporate, about 5 more minutes.
4. If the potatoes are still firm, cook for a few more minutes on low heat while covering the stir-fry with the lid.
5. Sprinkle with *garam masala* and chopped coriander leaves and heat through before serving.
6. This is a side dish suitable to serve with main course with rice or *chappatis*, or any other kind of dinner.

SERVES 8

Ingredients

Vegetable oil	3 Tbs
Onions chopped	1 cup
Cauliflower head chopped into 1 inch florets	2 lbs
Medium potatoes chopped into 1 inch cubes	2
Ginger chopped	2 Tbs

Garlic cloves chopped	1 Tbs
Green hot chilies chopped (mild)	1–2 tsp
Coriander powder	1½/2 tsp
Cumin powder	¾ tsp
Red pepper	1 tsp
Cumin seeds	1 tsp
Salt	1 tsp
Turmeric powder	1 tsp
Garam masala	¾ tsp
Coriander leaves chopped	3 Tbs

HINT

½ cup of fresh or frozen peas can be added to this stir-fry.

The Exquisite World of Indian Cuisine

Cauliflower with Figs
Phool Gobhi aur Anjeer ki Sabzi

Cauliflower coated with sauce of chopped onion *masala* and ground figs is a unique way to fix this dish. Figs give it a little crunchy, sweet and sour taste which makes it very appetizing.

METHOD

1. Fry the cauliflower florets in a thick-bottom frying pan in 2 cups of oil until light brown (or pan-fry them in 2 Tbs of oil). Remove them with a slotted spoon from the oil on to a platter lined with paper towel and set aside.
2. Grind the figs with yogurt in a blender and set aside.
3. Fry the onions with ginger, garlic and green chilies in a large wok or a frying pan in 3 Tbs of *ghee* or oil till the onions turn light brown.
4. Add the cumin seeds and wait till they start popping. Add the turmeric powder, red pepper, coriander powder and salt. Mix well and add the ground figs and yogurt mixture. Keep stirring and cooking till the sauce gets a little thick and the oil separates from the sauce.
5. Add the fried cauliflower florets and stir to coat them well with the spicy fig sauce. Serve hot as an accompaniment of a vegetable dish at a dinner.
6. Sprinkle with *garam masala* and coriander leaves before serving.

SERVES 6 – 8

Ingredients

Cauliflower head separated into small florets (large head)	1
Oil to fry the florets	2 cup
Cumin seeds	1 tsp
Turmeric powder	1 tsp
Red pepper	1 tsp
Coriander powder	1 Tbs
Garam masala	1 tsp
Vegetable oil or *ghee*	3 Tbs
Salt	2 tsp
Figs dried (small)	8–10
Yogurt	1 cup
Onions chopped	1 cup
Ginger chopped	1 Tbs
Garlic chopped	1 Tbs
Green chilies chopped	1 tsp
Coriander leaves chopped	2 Tbs

Pumpkin Stir-Fried
Kaddu ki Sabzi/Dry Petha Curry

In India, pumpkin is usually served highly flavored with spices and a little sugar. The flavor and aroma of spices makes this one of my very favorite dishes. The sweet and sour taste of this dish goes very well with *pooris*.

METHOD

1. Heat the oil in a deep, thick-bottom cooking pan of medium size and add the onions, green chilies and ginger. Wait till they turn slightly brown. Add the cardamoms, cinnamon sticks and curry leaves. Cook for a minute. Add the nigella seeds, and fenugreek seeds. When the seeds start to crackle, add the turmeric, red pepper, coriander powder and cumin powder mixture, asafoetida, and salt. Lower the heat. Stir well and add the tomato sauce.
2. Mix all the ingredients well and fry for 2–3 minutes on medium low heat.
3. Add ½ cup water and stir. Cover the pan and let the sauce cook for 2 minutes. Add the chopped pumpkin. Cover it with a lid and let it simmer and cook until the pumpkin gets soft. Add the sugar, coconut powder and the yogurt. Stir well and cook until the sugar completely mixes in. Heat it through.
4. Remove from heat. Sprinkle a little *garam masala*, chopped coriander leaves and serve.

SERVES 6 – 8

Ingredients

Vegetable oil or *ghee*	3–4 Tbs
Onions chopped	1 cup
Green chilies chopped	1 Tbs
Ginger chopped	1 Tbs
Brown cardamom pods half open	2
Cinnamon sticks (small)	2
Curry leaves	4–6
Nigella seeds	½ tsp
Fenugreek seeds	½ tsp
Turmeric powder	1 tsp
Red pepper	1 tsp
Coriander and cumin powder mixture	1 Tbs
Asafoetida powder	½ tsp
Salt	1 tsp
Tomato sauce	1 cup
Pumpkin peeled and grated	4 cups
Sugar	1 Tbs
Coconut fresh grated	1 cup
Or	
Coconut dry powder	2 Tbs
Water	2 Tbs
Garam masala	1 tsp
Fresh coriander leaves chopped	2 Tbs
Yogurt	½ cup

Assam Vegetable Curry

ASSAM

Assam is famous for growing rice, tea and coconuts. Therefore it is no surprise that coconut milk and ground rice make the base or the thickening agent for this curry.

METHOD

1. Grind the green chilies, ginger, curry leaves, garlic and dry rice in a blender to a smooth paste and set it aside.

2. Transfer the coconut milk to a medium size, thick-bottom cooking pan and start to heat it. Add the grated paste to it and mix it well. Add all the vegetables, chopped onions, turmeric powder, red pepper, salt and a cup of water and cook the vegetables for a few minutes. Add the tomato sauce and *garam masala* and cook for another 4–5 minutes.

3. Just before serving, add the lemon juice, chopped coriander leaves, stir and serve hot with rice. Adjust the taste of salt and pepper.

SERVES 4 – 6

Ingredients

Mixed vegetables frozen (peas, carrots, and beans)	1 cup
Potatoes cooked and cubed	½ cup
Frozen cauliflower or broccoli florets	1 cup
French cut beans	½ cup
Coconut milk	1 cup
Water	1 cup
Rice	2 Tbs
Turmeric powder	¾ tsp
Salt	to taste
Red pepper	1 tsp
Onions chopped	½ cup
Green chilies chopped	1 tsp
Fresh ginger chopped	1 Tbs
Garlic cloves	5
Curry leaves	4–5
Tomato sauce	½ cup
Or	
Tomatoes chopped	1 cup
Lemon juice	1 tsp
Garam masala	1 tsp
Coriander leaves fresh	1 Tbs

Sinhalese Vegetable Curry

SRI LANKA

Sri Lanka is further south of the Indian state of Tamil Nadu separated by the Indian Ocean. The curries here are mainly cooked and flavored with curry leaves and very hot chilli pepper, Maldive fish flakes (available at your local Indian grocers) and coconut milk.

SERVES 4 – 6

Ingredients

Vegetable oil	2–3 Tbs
Spring onions or red onions chopped	1 cup
Green chilies (cayenne) chopped	1 Tbs
Curry leaves	6–8
Ginger chopped	1 Tbs
Garlic chopped	1 Tbs
Cumin seeds	1 tsp
Turmeric powder	¾ tsp
Maldive fish or Bonito flakes	2 Tbs
Salt	1 tsp
Water	1 cup
Fenugreek leaves (dry)	2 Tbs
Mixed frozen vegetables bag	16 oz
Cooked potatoes cubed (small)	½ cup
Tomatoes chopped	2 cups
Coconut milk	1¼ cup
Tomato sauce	½ cup

METHOD:

1. Heat the oil in heavy-bottom medium size saucepan and add the onions, green hot (cayenne) pepper, curry leaves, chopped ginger, garlic and fry till the onions turn light brown.

2. Add the cumin seeds and, when they start to pop, add the turmeric powder, Maldive fish flakes, salt and fenugreek leaves. Stir to mix. Lower the heat and add 1 cup of water and simmer for 5 minutes. Add mixed vegetables, cooked potatoes and chopped tomatoes with tomato sauce. Cover the pan and cook for 10 minutes.

3. Add the coconut milk and simmer on very low heat for another 5 minutes and serve with grilled meats, rice and hot and spicy Ceylonese *sambol chutney*.

Note: Mixed vegetables and potatoes can be replaced by chopped okra. The curry recipe uses hot chilies but you can use mild peppers if you wish.

The Exquisite World of Indian Cuisine

Sweet Potato and Spinach Curry
Shakarkandi Curry

Sweet potato, a very nutritious vegetable, is very common among Gujarati and south Indian stir-fries and mixed vegetable curries. In north India, it is mostly enjoyed as a baked vegetable with lemon, spices and *chutney*.

METHOD

1. Peel and chop the sweet potatoes in cubes and set them aside. Heat the oil in a wok or frying pan on medium heat.
2. Add the onions, ginger and green chilies. Brown them a little and add the *urad dal*, mustard seeds and the sesame seeds. As they start popping add the asafoetida powder and the curry leaves. Wait for a few seconds and add chopped sweet potatoes, and cook. Stir well.
3. Add salt, turmeric powder, coriander powder, red pepper and mix. Add the water. Cover tight with a lid and keep the heat on low.
4. Let it cook and simmer for 15–20 minutes and add the chopped spinach and cook until the sweet potatoes are tender but not mushy. Remove from heat and serve as vegetable accompaniment with any meal. Garnish with the fresh chopped coriander leaves and *garam masala* and serve..

- SERVES 4– 6

Ingredients

Large sweet potatoes peeled and cut into cubes	2 cups
Onions chopped	2 Tbs
Green chilies chopped	1 tsp
Turmeric powder	¾ tsp
Mustard seeds	1 tsp
Sesame seeds	2 Tbs
Asafoetida powder	¼ tsp
Curry leaves chopped	2 Tbs
Salt	1 tsp
Coriander powder	1 Tbs
Vegetable oil or *ghee*	2 Tbs
Urad dehusked *dal* or channa dal	2 Tbs
Red pepper	1 tsp
Ginger chopped	1 tsp
Water	¼ cup
Spinach chopped	1 lb pkg
Fresh coriander leaves chopped	1 Tbs
Garam masala	½ tsp

Sweet Corn and Beans

Plain corn comes to life in this stir-fry when mixed with green beans, coconut, fresh cilantro, green chilies and spices.

METHOD

1. Transfer 2 Tbs of oil or clarified butter into a thick-bottom medium size cooking pan and put it on medium heat.
2. Add the cumin seeds and when they start to pop add the ginger, green chilies, garlic and cook till ginger turns slightly brown.
3. Add the corn, beans and mix them well. Add the turmeric powder, coriander powder, salt, red pepper and mix it in. Cover it with a lid and let it simmer for 10 minutes.
4. Add the coconut, chopped fresh coriander leaves and *garam masala*.
5. Stir and serve.

SERVES 6 – 8

Ingredients

Vegetable oil or clarified butter	2 Tbs
Ginger chopped	1 Tbs
Garlic chopped	1 Tbs
Green chilies chopped	1 Tbs
Fresh or frozen corn kernels	2 cups
Beans frozen or fresh chopped in 1 inch pieces	2 cups
Turmeric powder	1 tsp
Coriander powder	1 tsp
Salt	1 tsp
Cumin seeds	1 tsp
Red pepper	1 tsp
Coconut fresh grated	1 cup
Or	
Dry unsweetened coconut powder	½ cup
Fresh coriander leaves chopped	¼ cup
Garam masala	1 tsp

The Exquisite World of Indian Cuisine

Carrots and Peas Stir-Fried

WEST BENGAL

This vegetable accompaniment, cooked Bengali style, can be made very special when cooked in a sauce base of poppy seeds, cashew nuts and yogurt instead of onions.

SERVES 6 – 8

METHOD

1. Heat a Tbs of mustard oil in a wok or heavy-bottom skillet on medium heat. Add the cashew nuts and poppy seeds. Fry them light brown and blend them in a blender with yogurt, salt, ginger and green chilies. Set them aside.

2. Heat another Tbs of oil and add the *panchphoran* seeds and wait till they stop popping. Add the curry leaves, turmeric, coriander powder and red pepper. Stir to mix. Add the peas and the carrots mixture and cook for a minute or two until they are thawed. Add the yogurt sauce and stir to mix well. Add water.

3. Cover with a lid and let it simmer on medium low heat for 10–15 minutes until the carrots are tender. Keep stirring in between to prevent it from sticking to the bottom of the pan. Serve sprinkled with freshly chopped coriander. Makes a yummy vegetable accompaniment to any meal.

Ingredients

Frozen carrots and peas (pkg)	16 oz
Yogurt	½ cup
Green chilies chopped (mild)	1 tsp
Ginger chopped	1 tsp
Mustard oil or clarified butter	2 Tbs
Cashew nuts (raw)	½ cup
Poppy seeds	1 Tbs
Red pepper	½ tsp
Salt	1 tsp
Coriander powder	¾ tsp
Turmeric	½ tsp
Curry leaves	2–4
Green coriander chopped	2 Tbs
Panchphoran masala	1 Tbs
Water	½ cup

Note: Smoking mustard oil is usually used in all Bengali cooking but in western countries it is hard to find. For authentic preparation the mustard oil will be available at an Indian grocery store. Use of green chilies is optional.

EXOTIC VEGETABLES

Round Gourd Stuffed
Bharwan Tindey

Native to India, this vegetable is from the cucumber family. It has a soft very green and tender exterior and is rich in vitamins. Stuffed with spices and pan-fried, they make a delicious and pleasing presentation.

METHOD

1. Mix all the spices salt, turmeric powder, coriander powder, 1 tsp *garam masala*, red pepper, garlic powder, ginger powder, cumin powder and *amchoor* in a small mixing bowl and set them aside.

2. Cut and peel fresh round gourd (*tinda*) and cut them twice crosswise from the top with one-third bottom intact. Brush the outside with oil or *ghee*. *Tindas* can be stuffed as described in the Note below.

3. Coat the cut sides of each *tinda* with mixture of spices (at least using ½–1 tsp) using a spoon and set them on a plate.

4. Heat 3–4 Tbs of oil in a wok or a heavy-bottom skillet on medium low heat. Arrange the round gourd in a layer in the skillet. Cook them, covered on low heat for 5–8 minutes. Remove the cover, turn them over and cook them uncovered until the sides and the bottom starts to turn dark brown. Keep turning them to avoid burning (about 15–20 minutes).

5. Instead of cooking on direct heat, bake them in an 8–12 rectangular 2 inch deep baking pan at 425°F in the oven. Bake covered for 5–10 minutes and then uncovered for another 15–20 minutes until they turn golden brown. Turn them once or twice in between to avoid burning the bottom of the round gourd. Remove them from heat and serve them with any meal as a vegetable accompaniment. Brush them with a little *ghee* during baking.

6. Serve, sprinkled with chopped coriander leaves and *garam masala*.

SERVES 6 – 8

Ingredients

Round gourd fresh (*Tinda* medium size)	10–12
Turmeric powder	1 tsp
Coriander powder	2 Tbs
Ginger powder (or chopped ginger)	1 tsp
Garlic powder (or chopped garlic)	1 tsp
Red pepper	1 tsp
Garam masala	1½ tsp
Amchoor	2 Tbs
Salt	1½ tsp
Vegetable oil	3–4 Tbs
Cumin seeds	1 tsp
Cumin powder	1 tsp
Coriander leaves chopped	1 Tbs
*Cooked rice Or	½ cup
Grated *paneer*	½ cup

Note: For stuffing the round gourd (*tindas*), scoop out the center of the gourd. Chop the center flesh finely. Heat some oil, add cumin seeds and when they stop popping add cooked rice, chopped central flesh of the *tindas* and all the spices. Cook for 5 minutes stirring. Fill the empty shells of round gourd with the filling and follow step 3 onwards.

Pointed Gourd Curry
Parwal aur Aalu ki Sabzi

Pointed Gourd (*parwal*) a good source of vitamins A and C is native to India. It is usually imported into the U.S. and sold only in Indian vegetable stores. This is the north Indian or Punjabi style of cooking it but in other parts of the country it is stuffed with spiced mashed potatoes or grated coconut. Pointed Gourd belongs to the squash or zucchini family.

METHOD

1. Heat the oil or clarified butter in a wok or a thick-bottom frying pan on medium heat and add the cumin seeds. As they stop popping add the chopped onions, ginger, garlic and green chilies.
2. Fry until the onions start turning light brown and then add the chopped potatoes. Lower the heat. Stir them well and add the salt, coriander powder, turmeric powder, red pepper and stir well again. Cook covered for 5 minutes.
3. Add the chopped round gourd and mix. Add ¼ cup of water and stir well. Cover the vegetable with a tight lid and keep the heat medium low. Add the coconut after 5 minutes. Let it cook for another 5–10 minutes or until the potatoes are soft. Stir in between to prevent stocking.
4. Sprinkle the *garam masala* and the coriander leaves. Mix well and serve. A welcome vegetable accompaniment to any meal.

SERVES 4 – 6

Ingredients

Pointed Gourd (*parwal*) washed and cut length wise into ½ inch strips	2 cups
Onions chopped	1 cup
Ginger and garlic chopped each	1 Tbs
Green chilies chopped	1 Tbs
Vegetable oil or clarified butter	2–3 Tbs
Potatoes peeled and cubed	1 cup
Cumin seeds	1 tsp
Turmeric powder	½–1 tsp
Coriander powder	1 tsp
Red pepper	1 tsp
Salt	1 tsp
Coconut fresh grated	½ cup
Or	
Coconut powder	2 Tbs
Water	¼ cup
Garam masala	¾ tsp
Coriander leaves chopped	2 Tbs

Note: Pointed Gourd is available at your local Indian grocery store in season.

Soyabean and Carrots Curry
Soyabean aur Gaajar ki Sabzi

Packed with proteins and minerals this vegetable is very much in demand. It is a very good substitute for proteins in a typical vegetarian Indian meal. This curry delicately prepared in yogurt sauce is a good substitute for meat.

METHOD

1. Boil the soyabeans and the carrots in 4 cups of water with ½ tsp of salt for 15–20 minutes until the beans are tender. Set them aside along with water.

2. Heat the oil in a heavy-bottom, medium size pan on medium-heat and add the cumin seeds and the mustard seeds. When seeds stop popping add the chopped onions, green chilies and ginger mixture and stir to cook. Wait till the onions turn light brown. Lower the heat.

3. Add the tomato sauce and mix well. Add the turmeric powder, cumin powder, red pepper, coriander powder and salt. Stir and cook until the oil separates from the sauce. Add the beaten yogurt and gently mix it in. Cook for 2 minutes, or until the oil separates.

4. Add the boiled soyabeans and the carrots mixture with its water to the sauce. Mix well and simmer another 5–10 minutes until the gravy thickens and the beans and carrots are tender.

5. Add the *garam masala*, coriander leaves, stir them in and serve with rice or any other meal as an accompaniment.

SERVES 4 – 6

Ingredients

Soyabeans	2 cups
Onions chopped	1 cup
Ginger, green chilies and garlic finely chopped	2 Tbs
Curry leaves chopped	6–8
Carrots frozen chopped Or fresh cut lengthwise	1 cup
Mustard seeds	1 tsp
Cumin seeds	1 tsp
Yogurt	½ cup
Turmeric powder	1 tsp
Cumin powder	½ tsp
Red pepper	1 tsp
Salt	1 tsp
Coriander powder	1 Tbs
Tomato sauce	½–1 cup
Water	4 cups
Coriander leaves	2 Tbs
Garam masala	¾ tsp

The Exquisite World of Indian Cuisine

Corn Curry with Spinach
Makki aur Palak ki Sabzi

Sweet corn comes alive in this delicious sauce of ground poppy seeds, green chilies, coriander leaves and coconut milk.

SERVES 4 – 6

Ingredients

Onions chopped	½ cup
Ginger, garlic and green chilies chopped	1 Tbs each
Coconut powder	1 Tbs
Poppy seeds	1 Tbs
Cumin seeds	1 tsp
Mustard seeds	1 tsp
Fenugreek leaves (dry)	1 Tbs
Salt	1 tsp
Red pepper	1 tsp
Coriander powder	1 tsp
Tomato sauce	1 cup
Spinach chopped frozen or fresh	8 ozs
Corn frozen or fresh	2 cups
Coconut milk	1 cup
Green coriander leaves	2 Tbs
Garam masala	1 tsp

METHOD

1. Grind together chopped onions, ginger, garlic, green chilies, coconut powder and poppy seeds.

2. Heat oil or *ghee* in a heavy-bottom saucepan on medium-heat. Add the cumin and mustard seeds. When they stop popping add the ground onions mixture, fenugreek leaves, salt, red pepper and coriander powder. Add the tomato sauce. Stir well. Cook till the oil separates from the mixture. Lower the heat.

3. Add the spinach and cook for 3–4 minutes. Add the corn and mix well. Add the coconut milk and mix it again. Let it simmer for 10–15 minutes.

4. Add the *garam masala*. Mix it in and bring it to a boil again. Add the coriander leaves and serve as a vegetable accompaniment to any meal.

Baby Vegetables Curry

Baby corn, Brussel sprouts, baby carrots, baby onions, cherry tomatoes and potatoes come alive in this stir-fry with yogurt, curry leaves, grated coconut, *garam masala* and onion tomato sauce. They make a great vegetable accompaniment for any meal especially for meat barbecue or a pot-roast.

METHOD

1. In a large saucepan, heat 6 cups of water and add the Brussel sprouts, baby corn, baby carrots with a little salt for 2–3 minutes. Drain the water and wash them in cold water. Set them aside in a large mixing bowl with the frozen beans, peas and cherry tomatoes.
2. Grind chopped onions, garlic, ginger and green chilies to a smooth paste in a blender and set it aside.
3. Heat oil or clarified butter in a large wok on medium heat and add cumin seeds, mustard seeds and dry red pepper. Wait till the seeds stop popping and then add the ground paste of onions mixture. Cook for 2–3 minutes and add the chopped curry leaves, turmeric powder, cumin powder, salt, red pepper and coconut powder, and stir well. Add the tomato sauce and mix it in. Cook till the oil separates from the curry. Add baby onions and stir-fry them for 2 minutes. Add all the vegetables and mix well. Lower the heat and simmer for 10 minutes.
4. Add the beaten yogurt, and stir it in. Cook covered for 5 minutes on low heat. Add the boiled chopped potatoes and stir gently. Add 1 cup of water and mix well. Cover the pan with lid and simmer for 3–5 minutes. Remove from heat, add the lemon juice and sprinkle the *garam masala* and the coriander leaves.
5. Mix gently and serve.

SERVES 6 – 8

Ingredients

Baby Brussel sprouts	5–6
Baby corn	7–8
Baby carrots	10–12
Onions chopped	2 cups
Ginger chopped	2 Tbs
Green chilies chopped	2 Tbs
Garlic chopped	2 Tbs
Cumin seeds	1 tsp
Mustard seeds	1 tsp
Red chilies (whole) dry	2–3
Curry leaves chopped	6–8
Turmeric powder	1 tsp
Cumin powder	1 tsp
Salt	1 tsp
Red chilli powder	1 tsp
Baby onions (optional)	8–10
Cherry tomatoes	14–16
Peas frozen	1 cup
Green beans frozen sliced	½ cup
Yogurt	1 cup
Potatoes boiled and chopped into cubes	1 cup
Water	1 cup
Lemon juice	2 Tbs
Garam masala	1 tsp
Coriander chopped	¼ cup
Coconut powder	2 Tbs
Tomato sauce	2 cups
Clarified butter or olive oil	3–4 Tbs

The Exquisite World of Indian Cuisine

Dakshineswar Temple, near Kolkata, West Bengal

Spinach and Potatoes Stir-Fried
Aalu Palak ki Sabzi

Chopped spinach flavored with mustard seeds and *garam masala*. Adding a few potatoes really makes these greens far more appetizing and tasty. Even a fussy eater who dislikes spinach in your family may start liking it.

SERVES 4 – 6

Ingredients

Spinach chopped fresh or frozen	1 lb
Onions chopped	½ cup
Ginger and garlic chopped	1 Tbs
Green chilies chopped (not hot)	1 Tbs
Potatoes chopped (medium)	1 cup
Mustard seeds	1 tsp
Cumin seeds	1 tsp
Urad dal	2 Tbs
Whole red dry pepper broken in two	2
Salt	1 tsp
Turmeric powder	½ tsp
Red pepper (optional)	1 tsp
Coriander powder	1 Tbs
Vegetable oil or *ghee*	2 Tbs
Rice flour (optional)	2 Tbs
Water	2–4 Tbs

METHOD

1. Heat the oil in a medium size thick-bottom wok or a cooking pan. Add the cumin seeds, mustard seeds, *urad dal* and whole dry red pepper. Wait till they start to pop. Add the onions, ginger and green chilies and stir to cook for 2–3 minutes. Add the garlic and cook till the onions start turning brown.

2. Add asafoetida, turmeric powder, salt, red pepper, coriander powder and mix well. Add the chopped potatoes and stir to mix. Fry them for 5 minutes. Add the spinach. Stir and cover the vegetable mixture with a tight lid and let it simmer for 15–20 minutes or until the potatoes are tender. Add water (¼ cup), if needed. Stir in between to prevent sticking.

3. Cook for 2–3 minutes and add the rice flour (blended already in 2 Tbs of water). Mix and cook for another 5 minutes. Remove from heat, sprinkle the *garam masala* and serve.

The Exquisite World of Indian Cuisine

Bean Sprouts Stir-Fried
Ankur Dal ki Sabzi

This has become a favourite breakfast snack of vegetarians in India, as it is healthy, nutritious and tasty. Any kind of beans, black grams, chickpeas or *mung* beans can be used. *Mung* beans are the easiest of all. These will sprout in your kitchen in a warm dry place overnight. Cook them with freshly chopped scallions, fresh chopped tomatoes, green chilies, ginger, garlic, salt, lemon juice, red pepper, chopped fresh cilantro and crushed roasted peanuts.

METHOD

1. Wash the *mung* beans and soak them in 2–3 cups of water in the morning. Drain the water in the evening completely and cover them with a cloth. Put them in a dark place overnight. In the morning you will notice tender little sprouts have grown on these beans.
2. Heat the oil in a saucepan and add the cumin and mustard seeds, and wait till they stop popping. Add the onions and green chilies and fry until onions are light brown. Then add the chopped ginger and garlic. Fry for 2 minutes. Stir to mix and set the pan aside.
3. Transfer the bean sprouts and ½ cup of water to a small pressure cooker and add salt, red pepper and black pepper. Pressure cook for 2–5 minutes and transfer the bean sprouts to a bowl and add the sugar, chopped tomatoes and the ingredients from the saucepan. Stir to mix well.
4. Transfer them to a serving dish. Mix in the lemon juice, roasted peanuts, *garam masala* and sprinkle with chopped coriander leaves and serve.

SERVES 4 – 6

Ingredients

Mung beans (whole)	1 cup
Onions chopped	½ cup
Tomatoes chopped	½ cup
Ginger chopped	1 tsp
Garlic chopped	1 tsp
Green coriander chopped	2 Tbs
Green chilies chopped (mild)	1 Tbs
Vegetable oil	1 Tbs
Mustard seeds	1 tsp
Cumin seeds	½ tsp
Garam masala (optional)	½ tsp
Lemon juice	2–3 Tbs
Salt	to taste
Red pepper to taste or	1 tsp
Black pepper	½ tsp
Sugar	2 tsp
Roasted peanuts	2 Tbs

Lotus Root and Mushroom Curry
Kamal Kakadi aur Khumb ki Sabzi

Crunchy lotus roots with creamy and soft mushrooms together make two perfect ingredients to make a curry. They are very popular and can be curried in many different ways. Lotus root croquettes curry is a delicacy in northern India. Lotus roots are also pickled with raw mangoes and other vegetables to make a great mixed vegetable pickle.

SERVES 4 – 6

Ingredients

Lotus roots chopped and drained frozen or canned cooked	8 oz pkg
Mushrooms chopped	1 cup
Peas frozen	¼ cup
Tomato sauce	1 cup
Onions chopped	½ cup
Tomatoes fresh chopped	1 cup
Ginger chopped	1 Tbs
Garlic chopped	1 Tbs
Green chilies chopped	1 Tbs
Vegetable or sesame oil	2 Tbs
Cumin seeds	½ tsp
Salt	1 tsp
Turmeric powder	½ tsp
Red pepper	½ tsp
Coriander ground	1 Tbs
Heavy cream	1–2 Tbs
Garam masala	1 tsp
Coriander leaves chopped	2 Tbs

METHOD

1. Heat the oil in a heavy-bottom saucepan and add the chopped onions, ginger, garlic and green chilies. Boil the lotus roots in a separate pan until tender and set aside.

2. Stir-fry the onions until they are light brown. Add the cumin seeds and when they stop popping, add the tomato sauce, turmeric powder, coriander powder, red pepper and salt.

3. Stir to mix. Fry the sauce on low heat until the oil separates from the sauce. Add one cup of water and stir to mix. Boil the sauce for 5 minutes and add the cooked lotus roots. Mix well. Cover the pan and cook for 5–10 minutes. Add the peas and mushrooms. Stir to mix. Simmer for 5 minutes and add the fresh tomatoes, *garam masala* and the chopped coriander. Lower the heat.

4. Cook for 3–5 minutes more. Remove from heat and add 1 Tbs of cream. Stir to mix and serve with any meal as a vegetable accompaniment.

Note: Lotus root is available at your local Indian grocery store.

The lotus plant has long stem with very beautiful aromatic flowers with floating leaves. It can regenerate after thousands of years untouched by the mud and muddy water it grows in. Therefore, it symbolizes the triumph and purity of heart and mind. It has been a auspicious symbol of Indian culture since time immemorial. It also represents long life, honor, good fortune, divinity, knowledge and enlightenment to the people of India that is why the founding fathers enshrined it as the **national flower of India**.

Asparagus Stir-Fried
Shatwar ki Sabzi

NEPAL

You will not find Asparagus (*Musli*) easily with vegetable vendors in India. It grows in the Himalayas, in Nepal and is abundant here in Europe and North America in spring time. When curried like any other vegetable, it is delicious and creamy. It can be served as a vegetable accompaniment to any meal of your choice.

SERVES 4 – 6

Ingredients

Tender sprigs of chopped asparagus	1 lb
Mushrooms chopped in ½ inch pieces	½ cup
Onions chopped	½ cup
Ginger chopped	1 tsp
Garlic chopped	1 tsp
Green chilies chopped	1 tsp
Vegetable oil or mustard oil	2 Tbs
Fenugreek leaves fresh	1 cup
Or	
Fenugreek leaves dry	2 Tbs
Coriander leaves chopped	1 Tbs
Garam masala	½ tsp
Sesame seeds	1 tsp
Or	
Sesame dry leaves	2 Tbs
Cumin seeds	½ tsp
Turmeric powder	½ tsp
Red pepper	½ tsp
Coriander powder	1 tsp
Salt	1 tsp
Water or more as needed	2 Tbs

METHOD

1. Slice the asparagus into ½ inch pieces after cutting off the lower harder part of the asparagus shoots. Set it aside.

2. Heat the oil in a saucepan and add the onions, ginger, garlic and green chilies. Cook until the onions turn light brown and then add the sesame seeds. Wait till they stop popping and add the cumin seeds. Give it a minute and add the fenugreek leaves. Stir to mix.

3. Add the asparagus and stir well. Add the dry spices, turmeric powder, salt, coriander powder and red pepper. Stir-fry on low heat until the asparagus is well coated with spices. Add the water, cover the saucepan, and cook for 5–7 minutes or until the asparagus is soft. Add the mushrooms and stir. Cook for 5 more minutes. Sprinkle with green coriander leaves, *garam masala* and serve.

Himalayan peaks of Bander Poonch and Yellow Tooth with the glacier (in foreground), Uttarakhand, India

Beetroot Curry
Chukandar ki Sabzi

Beets are a great source of minerals and vitamins. As I remember, they used to ornament salads but in this dish from Sri Lanka, they are curried with hot pepper in coconut milk. The dish is colorful, delicious and makes a healthy addition to any meal.

SERVES 4 – 6

Ingredients

Beetroots julienne strips	1 lb
Sesame oil	2 Tbs
Onions red	½ cup
Mustard seeds	1 tsp
Fenugreek seeds	1 tsp
Jalapenos chopped	2
Ginger chopped	1 Tbs
Garlic chopped	½ tsp
Water (for boiling the vegetables)	2–2½ cups
Carrots julienne strips	2 Tbs
Rice vinegar	1 Tbs
Salt	1 tsp
Sugar	1 tsp
Curry leaves	6–8
Water	½ cup
Coconut milk canned	½ cup
Ceylonese spice powder	2 Tbs

METHOD

1. Boil the beet roots and carrots in 4 cups of water until tender. Set aside.

2. Heat the oil in a wok or heavy-bottom saucepan of medium size. Add the red chopped onions, green chilies and ginger. Stir to cook until the onions are slightly brown.

3. Add the mustard seeds and as they start to pop add the fenugreek seeds, and as the fenugreek seeds change color, lower the heat and add the salt, sugar and vinegar. Slowly stir and add the cooked vegetables along with water.

5. Cover the pan and let it cook (about 10 minutes).

6. Add the coconut milk and the curry leaves. Cook for another 5 minutes and bring it to a boil. Sprinkle the Ceylonese spice powder (*garam masala* will be good substitute), before serving. Serve it as a vegetable accompaniment with any meal.

Okra Curry
Bhindi ki Sabzi

Usually okra is served as a dry vegetable stir-fry but in the southern parts of India it is also served as a curry. Here is a recipe I got from a friend of mine. A curry sauce made from tomatoes, tamarind and coconut milk.

SERVES 6 – 8

METHOD

1. Heat the oil in a wok and fry the okra until light brown for about 10 minutes and set aside.
2. In the same pan heat another 1 Tbs of the oil and add the onions, ginger, and fry till the onion is brown. Add the chopped garlic. Fry for 2 minutes and move the onion mixture to one side and add the mustard seeds, cumin seeds and the split peas and fry till they start to pop and start to turn slightly brown. Add the curry leaves. Stir them in.
3. Add the turmeric powder, coriander powder, red pepper and fenugreek leaves and fry for a minute or two. Add the coconut powder and fry until it turns slightly brown. Add the tomato sauce and the tamarind pulp dissolved in water and stir to mix. Keep stirring until the oil begins to separate from the sauce (5 minutes).
4. Add the okra. Coat it gently in the sauce and lower the heat.
5. Add the coconut milk and salt, and stir it in well. Cover the pan and let the curry simmer for another 5–10 minutes or until the okra is cooked. Remove from heat and serve as a vegetable accompaniment to any meal.

Ingredients

Okra chopped in 1 inch pieces	1 ½ lbs
Or	
Frozen okra chopped	16 oz pkg
Onions chopped	1 cup
Ginger chopped	1 Tbs
Garlic chopped	1 Tbs
Green chilies (mild)	1 Tbs
Tomato sauce	1½ cup
Coconut milk	1½ cup
Mustard seeds	1 tsp
Cumin seeds	1 tsp
Curry leaves	6–8
Split yellow or green peas	1 tsp
Fenugreek dry leaves (*Methi*)	1 Tbs
Coconut dry powder	1 Tbs
Tamarind pulp or *kokum* powder	½ tsp
Salt	1 tsp
Coriander powder	1 Tbs
Red pepper	½ tsp
Turmeric powder	1 tsp
Vegetable oil or *ghee*	3–4 Tbs
Oil for frying	4 cups

Note: *Kokum* powder can be substituted for Tamarind pulp.

Mushrooms in Spinach Sauce
Palak aur Khumb Curry

This is a special recipe which I really like to make to entertain friends. Tender mushrooms in a creamy spinach sauce consisting of fresh tomatoes, gram flour and cream.

SERVES 4 – 6

Ingredients

Clarified butter (*ghee*) or vegetable oil	3–4 Tbs
Onions chopped	1 cup
Ginger chopped	1 Tbs
Garlic chopped	1 Tbs
Green chilies chopped (mild)	2 Tbs
Cumin seeds	1 tsp
Fenugreek leaves (dry)	2 Tbs
Red pepper (whole dry) broken	2
Red pepper (optional)	1 tsp
Tomatoes chopped (medium)	3
Turmeric powder	1 tsp
Coriander powder	2 Tbs
Salt	to taste
Water	1 cup
Spinach frozen	16 oz
Gram flour	2–3 Tbs
Cashew nuts or almonds ground	¼ cup
Mushrooms (large) sliced in ¼ inch thickness	½ lb
Heavy cream	1–2 Tbs
Garam masala	1 tsp
Fresh coriander leaves chopped	2 Tbs

METHOD

1. Start to heat the oil or *ghee* on low heat in a thick-bottom 4 quart cooking pan and add the onions, ginger, garlic and green chilies and keep frying until the onions start to turn light brown. Add the cumin seeds and wait till they start to pop. Add the dry red pepper, dry fenugreek leaves and the tomatoes. Stir to mix. Add turmeric, coriander powder, red pepper and salt. Mix it well and cover the pan with lid for 2 minutes to soften the tomatoes.

2. Remove the lid and add the spinach. Stir to mix and cover it with the lid again and let it simmer for at least 10 minutes. Stir in between, and if it is getting dry, add ½ cup of water. Remove from heat and cool it. Transfer the spinach mixture into a blender and blend it for 2–3 minutes with water (if it is too thick) to a smooth mixture. Transfer it back to the cooking pan and add the gram flour (pre-mixed smoothly in a cup of spinach purée) and ground cashew nuts. Keep the heat low and keep stirring. Add the sliced mushrooms. Mix them in and cover the pan with a lid and let it simmer for at least 10 minutes stirring in between to prevent sticking. Add the cream, *garam masala* and chopped coriander leaves.

3. Stir to mix. Remove from heat and serve as a vegetable accompaniment to any meal.

Jackfruit Stir-Fried
Kathael ki Sabzi

A tropical plant native to India, Myanmar, Sri Lanka and southern China. The tree bearing Jackfruit is tall and stately and the fruit can weigh upto 60 lbs or more. The interior of the fruit consists of large bulbs of banana flavored flesh with a core that can be cooked in the form of curries, *koftas* and with meats to make delicious gourmet preparations. It has large edible seeds that are not used in cooking. *Kathael* is a popular food ranking next to the mango and banana in southern India. It is available in the Indian grocery stores in cans as well as frozen.

METHOD

1. If using fresh jackfruit (*kathael*), oil your hands and then peel it. Cut it in quarters and chop the core into cubes. Marinade it in oil, lemon juice, salt and chilli pepper for atleast 2 hours and deep fry the pieces in hot oil till light brown. Set it aside.

2. Heat the *ghee* on medium-low heat in a heavy-bottom large cooking pan and fry the chopped onions, ginger and garlic till the onions are light pink. Add the cumin seeds and wait till they start popping. Add the curry leaves, cardamom powder and stir them well into the onion mixture. Set aside.

3. Beat together yogurt with turmeric powder, coriander powder, red pepper, salt and vegetable stock in a bowl and add to the fried onions and garlic mixture. Stir well and add the tomato sauce. Cook the gravy till the *ghee* separates from the gravy. Add the potatoes and stir to mix.

4. Add the fried jackfruit (*kathael*) to the sauce and cook on slow heat till it is tender and cooked. Add stock, if needed. Sprinkle *garam masala* and chopped coriander leaves and serve. Serves well with rice *pulav*.

SERVES 4 – 6

Ingredients

Jackfruit peeled and cut in pieces	2 lbs
Potatoes chopped	½ cup

Marinade:

Lemon juice	2 tsp
Oil	1 Tbs
Salt	1 tsp
Chili powder	1 tsp

Gravy:

Onions chopped	1 cup
Ginger and garlic chopped (each)	1 Tbs
Green chilies chopped	1 Tbs
Oil to fry jackfruit (*kathael*)	2 cups
Curry leaves	4–5
Vegetable oil or *ghee*	3 Tbs
Cumin seeds	1 tsp
Turmeric powder	1 tsp
Red pepper	1 tsp
Coriander powder	1 Tbs
Yogurt	½ cup
Tomato sauce	½ cup
Vegetable stock	2 cups
Cardamom powder	½ tsp
Garam masala	1 tsp
Coriander leaves chopped	2 Tbs
Salt to taste	

Note: Marinade the lamb chops along with jackfruit in the same marinade and grill them in the oven or open grill. Make the above curry with grilled pieces of jackfruit and pour the hot jackfruit curry over grilled lamb chops and serve. This makes a great meal. If you are cooking this jackfruit (*kathael*) curry to pour over the grilled meats, then omit potatoes from the recipe.

CHAPTER 6

Legumes

Lentils (*dal*) are one of the staple foods in the everyday meal of an Indian household. For thousands of years Indians have practiced Hinduism and meat was generally taboo in a land that propagates a vegetarian diet. Over a period of time, Indians have developed a very delicious vegetarian cuisine and they relied heavily on legumes as a source of protein in their daily diet.

Legumes are prepared in many different ways. These are enjoyed by the rich and poor alike and are an integral part of every formal and informal meal. The traditional method to prepare them used to be in a slow cooker or in a fairly large heavy-bottom pan and then season them.

It used to take hours to cook them but now, pressure cooking has made things a lot easier and these delicious preparations can be made in no time.

Among the well-known lentil preparations from north India are Chick-peas in Tamarind Sauce (*Chholey*), *Dal Makhni*, *Dal Panchratan* and *Rajmah*. In every part of the country, the preparation varies a little. *Gujarati Dal*, a little sweet and sour *Dal Vadodra* and *Dal Dhokli*, Oriya *Dal Dalma*, made with small pieces of eggplant, plantain and flavored with coconut, the southern delicious *Dal Sambhar* and Rajasthani *Dal Bati* are worth mentioning.

Lentil flours are used to make many different kinds of appetizers like *dhokla*, *khandvi*, *vadas* and *muthias*. The flour of the lentils is also used to make many different kinds of fritters like *palak pakoras*, *planktain pakoras*, *papadums*, *dahi vadas* and *vadas*. Bean sprouts are used in breakfast and as an ingredient of *chaat*. In southern India, at breakfast time or as snacks, lentil prepaprations like *idli*, *dosa* with *sambhar* are very common. In the north of India lentil preparations are served for lunch and dinner as a *dal* with rice. A very delicious curry called *Besan curry* is prepared with yogurt and chick-pea flour all over India.

Many desserts are also prepared with lentil flours like *Besan Ladoos*, *Pinnis* and lentil fudge as *Besan ki Burfi*. The flour is also used as a binding agent to make many different kinds of *koftas* (croquettes), cutlets and *kebabs*. Lentils like *urad, channa, arhar* and *mung* are only available at your local Indian grocery store. These can be boiled ahead of time, frozen and can be seasoned at the time of preparation.

Legumes are a great source of proteins needed by the human body without the fat. They are also richer in complex carbohydrates and provide plenty of fiber.

Chick-peas Curry
Kabuli Channa

PUNJAB

A spicy chick-peas preparation. It is proteinaceous and makes a very good meal when served with just plain rice and *raita*. It is also served as a side dish for a formal dinner.

SERVES 8

Ingredients

Chick-peas drained and washed (15 oz cans)	2
Vegetable oil or *ghee*	3 Tbs
Onions medium chopped	1 cup
Ginger chopped	2 Tbs
Garlic	2 Tbs
Green chilies chopped	1 Tbs
Cinnamon sticks very small	2
Bay or curry leaves	4–6
Red pepper whole	2–4
Cloves whole	½ tsp
Cumin seeds	1 tsp
Red pepper	1 tsp
Turmeric powder	1 tsp
Salt	1 tsp
Coriander powder	2 tsp
Tomato sauce	1 cup
Potatoes peeled and chopped	½ cup
Tamarind pulp (dissolved in ¼ cup of water)	1 tsp
Water	3 cups
Garam masala	1 tsp
Coriander leaves chopped	2 Tbs

METHOD

1. In a deep 4 quart saucepan, heat the oil and transfer onions, ginger, garlic, green chilies, and cook till light brown.
2. Add the cinnamon sticks, cloves, bay leaves, cumin seeds, and whole red pepper, and wait till the cumin seeds start popping.
3. Add the tomato sauce, turmeric powder, red pepper, salt, coriander powder, and stir for another 2 minutes. Add the potatoes and stir-fry for five minutes.
4. Now add the drained, cooked chick-peas and stir for 2 minutes.
5. Add water and let them simmer for 20–25 minutes so that the flavor of the spices penetrate the chick-peas and potatoes are tender. Add the tamarind dissolved in ¼ cup of water and stir to mix. Add more water, if the curry is too thick, and cook for another 5 minutes.
6. Serve sprinkled with *garam masala*, and top it with chopped coriander leaves. It makes a great dish to be served with rice only but enhances its appeal when served with vegetable curry, *chappati*, *poori*, or *nan*.

Note: The whole spices are usually put together in a small porous container (*garni*). It is dropped in the beginning into the pot while cooking chick-peas, so that the flavor of the spices penetrates the chick-peas. A Punjabi speciality introduced to India by Afghan traders, chick-peas are also one of the major staple foods in Mediterranean countries as Humus. Humus is ground chick-pea paste flavored with sumac, lemon and spices. Chick-peas are packed with proteins and nutrients. Indians love to eat the fresh chick-peas sold by the vendors roasted or grilled with spices. They make a perfect snack and they are delicious. If using uncooked chick-peas, see notes of recipe "*Chick-peas in Tamarind Sauce*" next page.

Chick-peas in Tamarind Sauce
Khattey Kabuli Channe

PUNJAB

A spicy chick-peas preparation, which is simply delicious with *bhaturas* (a kind of fried bread). The combination of these two specialities makes one of the most popular and favorite meals in Punjab, a stunning presentation with the wonderful aroma of spices.

METHOD

1. In a deep 4–quart sauce pan heat the oil and transfer onions, ginger, garlic, green chilies, and cook till light brown. Add the cumin seeds and wait till they pop.

*2. Add the cinnamon sticks, cloves, cardamoms and bay leaves, black pepper corns and whole red pepper. Fry them for 2 minutes. You can also use spice bag or *garni* (see Note).

3. Add the ground red pepper, salt, coriander powder, and stir-fry for a few minutes.

4. Add the drained chick-peas (*channa*) and 4–5 cups of water and let them simmer for half an hour or so till the flavor of the spices penetrate the chick-peas and they get blend completely with the sauce. Add more water, if needed.

5. Now, add the ground roasted pomegranate seeds (*anaardana*), 1 Tbs of ground roasted cumin seeds, *garam masala* and the tamarind paste. Stir well to mix the ingredients. Simmer for another half an hour adding water, if it gets too thick.

6. Serve sprinkled with remaining dry, ground, roasted cumin seeds, *garam masala*, and top it with wedges of tomatoes and slices of onions, pieces of chopped boiled potatoes and chopped coriander leaves.

7. Best served with *bhaturas* and *raita* but can also be served with *pooris* and *nans*, if desired.

Note: If using dry chick-peas wash them and pressure cook them in 5 cups of water in a pressure cooker with small pieces of ginger, garlic and green chilies. *Put the whole spices like whole red pepper, cinnamon stick, cardamoms, cloves, black pepper in a little porous bag (*garni*) and add this bag with the chick-peas in the pressure cooker. Add ¼ tsp of baking soda. Pressure cook the chick-peas for 45 minutes. Follow the recipe from 1–7 but omit step 2. Discard the bag of spices after pressure cooking is done.

SERVES 6 – 8

Ingredients

Vegetable oil or *ghee*	4 Tbs
Onions chopped	2 cups
Ginger chopped	2 Tbs
Garlic chopped	2 Tbs
Green chilies chopped	2 Tbs
Cumin seeds	1 tsp
Cinnamon sticks (very small)	2
Cloves whole	1 tsp
Bay leaves	4–6
Red pepper powder	1 tsp
Salt to taste Or	1–2 tsp
Black pepper corns	1 tsp
Red pepper (whole)	4
Cardamoms whole (large)	2
Coriander powder	2 Tbs
Chick-peas (15 oz cans) drained and washed Or	4 cans
Dry chick-peas	2½ cups
Garam masala	1 tsp
Water	4–5 cups
Pomegranate seeds ground Or *Amchoor*	1 Tbs
Gram flour to thicken the gravy (optional)	2 Tbs
Cumin seeds ground roasted	1½ tsp
Tamarind paste dissolved in 2 Tbs of water	1½ tsp

To garnish:

Dry roasted cumin powder	1 tsp
Garam masala	1 tsp
Coriander leaves chopped	2 Tbs
Tomatoes (sliced)	2
Onions fresh (sliced)	1
Small boiled potatoes chopped	2
Green chilies (small)	a few

HINT

Instead of tamarind paste 1 Tbs of *amchoor* can be used in case tamarind is not available.

The Exquisite World of Indian Cuisine

Andhra Dal
Palakura Pappu

ANDHRA PRADESH

This preparation is deliciously different from northern preparations as it has a special garnish of grated coconut and mustard seeds. Chopped eggplant, okra and tomatoes can also be added to this *dal*.

METHOD

1. Wash the beans in water and set them aside soaking in water.
2. Boil the water in heavy-bottom saucepan and add the drained *dal* along with salt, turmeric, pkg of chopped spinach and curry leaves. Cook in a saucepan or pressure cook it (for about 5–10 minutes) in a pressure cooker. Set aside.
3. In a non-stick skillet, fry the onions, green chilies, ginger in oil until the onions turns lightly brown. Add the cumin seeds, mustard seeds and fenugreek seeds; wait till they pop.
4. Add the garlic and dry chilies, freshly grated coconut and fry for 2–3 minutes until the coconut starts to turn brown.
5. Add the coriander powder and red pepper, and quickly transfer this seasoning to the cooked *dal* and mix. Add the tamarind pulp dissolved in 1 Tbs of water and stir to mix.
6. Cook and simmer for 5 minutes on low heat, stirring to make sure it is not sticking to the bottom. Add more water, if desired. Add the chopped green coriander and stir to serve with rice or as an accompaniment to your meal.

Note: 1 cup of chopped eggplant or okra or tomatoes can be added in step 2 in the last 10 mins of cooking.

SERVES 6 – 8

Ingredients

Arhar dal (*toor dal*) or split yellow or green peas	1 cup
Water	4 cups
Curry leaves	4–5
Onions chopped	1 cup
Green chilies chopped	1 tsp
Ginger chopped	1 Tbs
Garlic chopped	1 tsp
Frozen spinach chopped pkg	10 oz
Cumin seeds	1 tsp
Mustard seeds	½ tsp
Fenugreek seeds	1 tsp
Dry red chilies broken	2
Freshly grated coconut Or	¼ cup
Dry coconut powder	2 Tbs
Coriander powder	1 Tbs
Red pepper	1 tsp
Turmeric powder	1 tsp
Salt	1 tsp
Tamarind pulp to taste Or	1 tsp
Green coriander leaves chopped	1 Tbs
Vegetable oil	2 Tbs

The Exquisite World of Indian Cuisine

Lentils and Vegetables in Tamarind Sauce
Sambhar

TAMIL NADU

A spicy *toor dal* preparation from southern India with fresh chopped vegetables and is garnished with fresh curry leaves, tamarind paste and mustard seeds. This lentil preparation goes best with *idli*, *dosa* and rice preparations.

SERVES 6 – 8

Ingredients

Toor dal	1 cup
Water	8 cup
Curry leaves	4–6
Turmeric powder	1 tsp
Salt	1 tsp
Red pepper as needed	1 tsp
*Zucchini peeled and chopped	2 cups
Or	
Mixed vegetables	2 cups
Tomatoes chopped (large)	2
Onions chopped (medium)	2
Green chilies chopped	1 Tbs
Ginger chopped	1 Tbs
Garlic chopped	1 Tbs
Fenugreek leaves (dry)	2 Tbs
Tomato sauce	1 cup
Tamarind sauce	1 tsp
Mustard seeds	1 tsp
Coriander seeds	2 Tbs
Urad dal	1 tsp
Vegetable oil	3 Tbs
Red chilies (whole)	4
Cumin seeds (whole)	1 tsp
Asafoetida powder	¼ tsp
Coconut powder dry unsweetened (available at the Indian grocery store)	1 Tbs
Garam masala	1 tsp
Coriander leaves chopped	2 Tbs

METHOD

1. Wash and soak the *toor* (*arhar*) *dal* in 6 cups of water and transfer it into a deep thick-bottom pan. Cook for 15 minutes with curry leaves, turmeric, salt and red pepper or pressure cook for 5 minutes and then let the pressure down.
2. Add the zucchini, chopped tomatoes, onions, green chilies, chopped ginger, chopped garlic, fenugreek leaves and cook till the zucchini is tender and vegetables are well blended (15–20 minutes).
3. Add the tomato sauce and tamarind paste dissolved in a tablespoon of water. Add more water if needed. Cook and simmer for 5 more minutes or longer, until the *dal* has a uniform consistency. Set it aside.
4. Heat the oil in small skillet and add mustard seeds, cumin seeds, coriander seeds, whole red pepper and the *urad dal*. Wait until the mustard seeds, coriander seeds, and cumin seeds stop splattering and *urad dal* turns light brown. Add the coconut powder, fry till it is light brown (1 minute). Now add the asafoetida powder and wait till it changes color. Grind the mixture in a little coffee grinder and transfer it to the cooked *dal* mixture. Stir well.
5. Add 1 tsp of *garam masala* and coriander leaves, mix it well. Cook the *sambhar* for another 2 minutes. It is ready to be served with rice, *idli* or *dosa*.

Note : Instead of chopped zucchini, you can also use eggplants, potatoes with bell pepper, white radish with carrots, okra or simply mixed vegetables in the preparation of *sambhar*. It can also be prepared with lima beans or blackeyed beans. Frozen vegetables can be used but if fresh vegetables are used they should be chopped into medium size pieces.

Whole Black Beans with Cream
Dal Makhni

PUNJAB

Legumes are cooked for everyday meals in India and are served with rice or bread. Whole black *urad dal* is very popular in north India. It is sometimes cooked with a handful of kidney beans (*rajmah*) but when cooked alone it is as good. Curried with fresh herbs, spices and cream, it is wholesome and very flavorful.

METHOD

1. Wash the beans and add them to 4-5 cups of boiling water. Add salt, 1 tsp each of garlic, ginger and dry red chilies. Simmer until the *dal* is soft or pressure cook (25–30 minutes) until the *dal* is cooked and then let the pressure drop. Make sure the beans are still holding their shape but are soft and mushy.
2. Drain and wash the cooked red kidney beans and add 1 cup to the cooked *urad dal*.
3. Heat the oil in a deep saucepan. Add chopped onion, 1 tsp each of garlic and ginger, and add the green chilies and fry till the onions turn golden brown
4. Cook on low heat for a few minutes. Move the onion mixture to one side and add the cumin seeds until they pop. Now, add the coriander powder, dry fenugreek leaves, red pepper, turmeric powder and salt. Add the fresh tomatoes. Cook a little and add the tomato sauce. Stir well. Cook till the sauce separates from the oil.
5. Add the cooked *dal* to the onions and tomatoes mixture and mix well. Add ½ cup or more of water, if the *dal* is too thick. Add 2 Tbs of heavy cream and mix.
6. Cook for 5–10 minutes on low heat. Stir and bring to a boil. Add *garam masala* and chopped coriander leaves. Mix well and serve with rice, *chappati* and vegetables of your choice.

Note: *Dry fenugreek leaves are available at your local grocery store.

SERVES 8

Ingredients

Urad dal whole	8 oz
Water as needed or	4–5 cups
Red kidney beans cooked from a can	1 cup
Salt	2–3 tsp
Vegetable oil or *ghee*	3 Tbs
Onions chopped	½–1 cup
Garlic chopped	2 tsp
Ginger finely chopped	2 tsp
Green chilies	1 Tbs
Cumin seeds	1 tsp
Coriander powder	1 tsp
*Fenugreek leaves (dry)	2 Tbs
Dried red chilies (optional)	4
Turmeric powder	1 tsp
Red pepper	1 tsp
Tomatoes chopped	1 cup
Tomato sauce	½–1 cup
Garam masala	1½ tsp
Coriander leaves	2 Tbs
Heavy cream	2 Tbs

The Exquisite World of Indian Cuisine

Black Split Beans Curried
Urad aur Channe ki dal

PUNJAB

Urad (split) and *channa dal* when cooked together is richer, especially when garnished with cumin, freshly chopped tomatoes, ginger, garlic and green chilies. A little cream can be added at the end of the cooking to give that special creamy taste. It is a very common lentil preparation of Punjab.

SERVES 8

Ingredients

Urad dal split	8 oz
Split gram (*channa dal*)	4 oz
Water as needed or	6 cups
Vegetable oil or *ghee*	2½ Tbs
Onions chopped	1 cup
Ginger fine chopped	2 tsp
Red chilies dried (optional)	4
Garlic chopped	2 tsp
Green chilies	1 Tbs
Turmeric powder	1 tsp
Coriander powder	1 Tbs
Cumin seeds	1 tsp
Red pepper	1 tsp
Salt	1–2 tsp
Tomato sauce	2 cups
Heavy cream (optional)	2 Tbs
Garam masala	1 tsp
Coriander leaves	2 Tbs

METHOD

1. Wash the beans and add them to 6 cups of boiling water. Add salt, 1 tsp of garlic, ginger. Simmer until the *dal* is of saucey but grainy consistency or pressure cook (about 30 minutes) until *dal* is cooked and then let the pressure drop.

2. Heat the oil in a deep saucepan and then add the chopped onion, 1 tsp each of garlic and ginger and add the green chilies and fry till the onions turn golden brown and then add the dry red chillies.

3. Cook on low heat for a few minutes. Move the onion mixture to one side and add the cumin seeds until they pop. Now add the coriander powder, red pepper, turmeric powder and salt. Cook a little and add tomato sauce and cook for 2 minutes. Stir well and add the cooked *dal* and a little water, if *dal* is too thick. Mix well.

4. Cook for 2–5 minutes on low heat and then add the heavy cream. Stir and bring to a boil. Add *garam masala* and chopped coriander leaves. Mix well and serve with rice, *chappati* or *nan*.

Bhangra from Punjab, the most virile, vigorous and captivating dances of India

Legume Stir-Fried
Dal Sookhi

Lentils are always cooked to a consistency of a thick soup but in north India it is sometimes cooked dry (without any sauce) garnished similarly with fresh onions, ginger, garlic, green chilies and dry spices. Serve it topped with fresh coriander leaves and *garam masala* with another wet curry and *chappati* or *nan*.

METHOD

1. Transfer the *urad dal* from the soaked water into a heavy-bottom large cooking pan with (3–3½ cups) of water. Add turmeric powder and salt and cook on the fire, until the grains are soft but not mushy and water is completely absorbed or pressure cook for 5–10 minutes. Set aside.
2. Cook the onions, ginger, garlic and green chilies in oil and fry till light brown. Add the whole red pepper, cumin seeds, and wait for them to start popping.
3. Add the tomatoes, and stir well.
4. Lower the heat and add the coriander powder, red pepper, and add the chopped pumpkin or bottle gourd. Cover the pan and cook for 10 minutes or until the pumpkin pieces get soft. Add the cooked *dal*. Stir well and cook for 2–3 minutes making sure the grains do not get mushy.
5. Add the *garam masala*, chopped coriander leaves and the lemon juice. Mix the *dal* gently but thoroughly.
6. Serve with meat or vegetable wet curry, rice or any kind of bread.

Note: *Mung dal* will take less water (2–2½ cups) and less time to cook (5 minutes) in the pressure cooker. If *dal* has been soaking overnight then it will require lesser amount of water to cook.

SERVES 4 – 6

Ingredients

Urad or *mung dal* split without skin (washed and soaked in water for ten minutes)	2 cups
Water	3 cups
Turmeric powder	1 tsp
Salt	to taste
Vegetable oil or *ghee*	¼ cup
Onions chopped	1 cup
Ginger chopped	1 Tbs
Garlic chopped	1 Tbs
Green chillies chopped	1 tsp
Red pepper broken (whole)	2–3
Cumin seeds	1½ tsp
Red pepper	1 tsp
Coriander powder	1 Tbs
Tomatoes chopped	1 cup
Bottle gourd or zucchini chopped	1 cup
Garam masala	1 tsp
Coriander leaves chopped	¼ cup
Lemon juice	1 Tbs

Royal Mix Legume
Dal Baati/Dal Panchratan

RAJASTHAN

Lentils are the nerves of a daily meal in a common household of India because they are the source of proteins in the mainly vegetarian diet of an Indian. It is usually served with a vegetable curry, yogurt and freshly made bread to complete a meal. To a hungry north Indian 'Dal Roti' (chappati and dal) sounds as familiar and homely as probably 'meat and potatoes' to an American or a European. This *dal* is made by mixing five different kinds of lentils and is unlike any other lentil preparation. It is very easy to make the famous Rajasthani *Dal Baati* from this recipe.

METHOD

1. Pick and wash the *dals* and soak them in 6 cups of water.
2. Transfer them to a Dutch oven or a slow cooker, add one tsp each of ginger, green chillies, garlic and salt, and cook until the lentils are tender or pressure cook them (for 15–20 minutes). Let the pressure down. Set aside.
3. Heat 3 Tbs of oil or *ghee* and fry the rest of onions, ginger, garlic and the green chilies. When they are golden brown add the cumin seeds, mustard seeds and wait till they start to pop and then add the whole red pepper. Fry for half a minute and add the turmeric powder, salt, coriander powder and red pepper.
4. Add the tomato sauce and a cup of water. Turn the heat low. Cook and simmer this mixture for 5 minutes.
5. Add this tempering to the cooked lentils. Mix the tempering well into the cooked *dal*, bring it to a boil and simmer for 2 more minutes.
6. Add the *garam masala* and lemon juice (if tomato sauce is not used) and the chopped coriander.
7. Cook a minute longer and remove from heat and serve with just rice or bread and vegetables as a daily meal.

SERVES 8

Ingredients

Toor dal (*Arhar dal*)	⅓ cup
Urad dal split washed	⅓ cup
Split gram (*Channa dal*)	⅓ cup
Green *mung dal* split	⅓ cup
Masoor dal	⅓ cup
Vegetable oil or *ghee*	¼ cup

Onions chopped	1 cup
Ginger chopped	2 Tbs
Garlic chopped	2 Tbs
Green chilies chopped	1 Tbs
Cumin seeds	1½ tsp
Mustard seeds	¾ tsp
Red pepper (dry)	2–3
Turmeric powder	1½ tsp
Salt	2 tsp
Coriander powder	2 Tbs
Water	6 cups
Red pepper powder	1 tsp
Lemon juice	2 Tbs
Or	
Tomato sauce	1½ cup
Garam masala	1 tsp
Green coriander leaves chopped	2 Tbs

Note: Make *baatis* as follows:

Wheat flour	1 cup	Milk	½ cup	*Rawa* or *suji*	½ cup
Ghee or oil	¼ cup	Gram flour	2 Tbs	Salt	to taste

Mix together flour, *rawa*, gram flour, oil and salt. Knead it into a tight dough with the help of milk. Make lemon size balls and bake in the electric oven for 15–20 minutes, then grill until golden brown. Pour and smear them with oil / *ghee* and serve with the *panchratan dal*.

The Exquisite World of Indian Cuisine

Master craftsmanship reflects in this intricately carved haveli in Jaisalmer, Rajasthan

Dal Vadodara
Gujarati Dal/Dal Dhokli

GUJARAT

Split *mung* or *Masoor dal* is quick and easy to cook and is very light on the digestive system. This preparation from Gujarat uses brown sugar, asafoetida, freshly chopped tomatoes and mustard seeds. Try it with rice or *chappati*. It is very easy to make *dal dhokli* from this recipe.

METHOD

1. In a heavy-bottom saucepan of medium size boil 3–4 cups of water. Add the washed and soaked beans with salt and turmeric, and cook until a little grainy but smooth and not soupy or pressure cook for 5 minutes. Let the pressure down and set aside.
2. In a small skillet on medium heat, cook the onions, ginger and green chilies in 2 Tbs of peanut oil and cook until light brown.
3. Add the cumin seeds, mustard seeds, dry whole red pepper and wait till the cumin seeds start to pop. Add the asafoetida powder.
4. Add the chopped garlic, tomatoes, coriander powder, red pepper, turmeric powder and cumin powder. Mix well. Cook until the tomatoes get a little soft. Mix and stir for 2–3 minutes and add this sauté to the cooked beans. Stir to mix and add sugar, salt, tamarind pulp and a cup or more of water as needed. Add the boiled peanuts, omit them if making *dal dhokli*. Stir well. Let it simmer for another 5 minutes.
5. Add the chopped green coriander leaves and heat through.
6. Serve with *chappati*, vegetable stir-fry and rice of your choice. It is really wholesome and tasty.

SERVES 4 – 6

Ingredients

Water	4–5 cups
Mung beans split or *masoor dal* or *toor dal*	1 ½ cup
Onions chopped	1½ cup
Ginger chopped	2 tsp
Garlic chopped	2 tsp
Green chilies chopped	2 tsp
Peanut oil	3 Tbs
Cumin seeds	1 tsp
Mustard seeds	1 tsp
Red pepper whole (dry) broken	2–3
Asafoetida powder	¼ tsp
Turmeric powder	1 tsp
Freshly tomatoes chopped	1 cup
Coriander powder or *dhania* powder (mixture of coriander and cumin powder)	2 tsp
Cumin powder	½ tsp
Red pepper	1 tsp
Brown sugar	1 Tbs
Salt	1 tsp
Peanuts boiled (optional)	½ cup
Tamarind pulp dissolved in water	1 tsp
Coriander leaves chopped	2 Tbs

Dal Dhokli: Sift together 1 cup wheat flour, ½ tsp salt and add ½ tsp each of chilli powder, ½ *ajwain* and 4–5 Tbs oil. Knead the flour into dough with water. Roll the dough into large *chappati*. Cut 1½ x 1½ inch pieces and drop them into boiling *dal* in Step 4 right after adding tamarind pulp and water. Cook for another 10 minutes. Proceed to Step 5 and serve with rice. It is the traditional *dal dhokli* of Gujarat.

Oriya Dal
Dalma

ORISSA

The varied cooking of Orissa is centuries old and uses locally grown ingredients. The state is rich with sea food as well as tropical vegetables. The cuisine offers rather subtle and delicately spiced curries unlike the fiery curries typical of Indian cuisine. Lentils here are cooked with raw mango pieces but small pieces of small eggplants plantain, papaya and small pieces of potato can also be used. The lentils are seasoned with *panchphoran*, asafoetida, coconut powder, brown sugar and chopped coriander leaves.

SERVES 4 – 6

Ingredients

Channa dal and *Toor dal*	1 cup
Salt	1 tsp
Water	4 cups
Raw mango chopped	½ cup
Cinnamon stick	1 inch
Cardamom seeds, black pepper (each)	½ tsp

METHOD

1. Wash *dals* in plenty of water and set them aside.
2. Boil 4 cups of water in a pressure cooker and add the drained *dals*. Add the salt, turmeric powder, ginger and pressure cook them until tender. Remove the pressure and add the chopped mango and cook for another 5–8 minutes on the stove until the mango is tender. Set aside. Dry roast on a hot skillet the cinnamon, cardamom seeds and black pepper until aromatic, and grind them with mortar and pestle and set aside.
3. Heat 2 Tbs of oil in a nonstick skillet until light brown and then add the ground spices. Add the *panchphoran* and coconut powder. Wait till the *panchphoran* seeds start popping and coconut powder is light brown. Add the asafoetida, red pepper and sugar, and mix well.
4. Add this seasoning to the cooked *dal* and mix in well. If *dal* is too thick add ½ cup–1 cup of water and bring it to a boil. Let it simmer on low heat for 3–5 minutes.
5. Add the chopped coriander leaves. Stir it in and serve with just rice or as an accompaniment to a meal.

Panchphoran masala	1 Tbs
Dry coconut powder	2 tsp
Vegetable oil or *ghee* or more	2 Tbs
Ginger chopped	1 Tbs
Turmeric powder	1 tsp
Asafoetida powder	½ tsp
Red pepper	1 tsp
Brown sugar	1 tsp
Coriander leaves chopped	2 Tbs

Note: Half cup each of chopped plantain and egg plant can also be added to this *dal* instead of only raw mango.

Gram Dal
Dal Channa

PUNJAB

The split and washed *Channa dal* is cooked in several ways. This lentil is highly recommended for people who have diabetes because it does not raise the sugar level of your blood. This Punjabi style preparation is cooked with bottle gourd (*ghia*) or dried spicy ground lentil balls (*badian*) available at Indian grocery stores only. It is quite a different preparation from that of other states of the country where it is enriched with greens, dry fruits, raisins, coconut and brown sugar etc.

METHOD

1. Transfer the soaked split gram with ginger, turmeric powder and salt into a pressure cooker with 4–6 cups of water. Cook till the grains become soft under pressure
2. Add the chopped bottle gourd or zucchini or (dry lentil balls) *Badian* into the *dal* after pressure cooking.
3. Cook without pressure for another 10–15 minutes or until the squash or *ghia* or the lentil balls (*badis*) are well softened. Add more water if needed.
4. In a small skillet heat the oil and add the onions and green chilies, and wait till the onions start to get brown. Add the garlic and fry a little.
5. Add the cumin seeds and dry red pepper and wait till the cumin starts to pop. Add the tomatoes, tomato sauce, coriander powder, red pepper and salt. Cook until the tomatoes become mushy and well blended.
6. Add this sauté to the cooked *dal* and mix well. Add water, if needed.
7. Add the *garam masala* and chopped coriander leaves and mix well.
8. Add the lemon juice and wait till the *dal* comes to a boil. Remove from heat and serve with plain rice, *chappati*, stir-fry vegetable and *raita*.

Note: *Badian* (dried spicy lentil balls) can be substituted for the squash. Use them if you want your *dals* really hot and spicy. Available at a your local Indian grocer.

SERVES 8 – 10

Ingredients

Split Gram (*Channa dal*) washed and soaked	1 cup
Water	4–5 cups
Ginger	1 Tbs
Turmeric powder	1 tsp
Salt	1 tsp

Zucchini or *ghia* (Indian squash) or *badian* (dried spicy lentil balls)	1 cup
Vegetable oil or *ghee*	3 Tbs
Onions chopped	1 cup
Garlic chopped	1 Tbs
Green chilies	1 tsp
Whole dry red pepper broken	2 or 3
Cumin seeds	1 tsp
Tomatoes chopped	½ cup
Tomato sauce	1 cup
Coriander powder	1½ tsp
Red pepper	1 tsp
Garam masala	1 tsp
Coriander leaves chopped	2 Tbs
Lemon juice	1 tsp

Matar Dal with Meat

WEST BENGAL

Split peas when cooked with chopped chicken liver or bacon gives an entirely different flavor to this preparation. Garnish it with *ghee*, *panchphoran masala*, ginger, mustard and coconut powder. It is really good and wholesome.

SERVES 4 – 6

Ingredients

Yellow *dal* split	1 cup
Water	4–5 cups
Vegetable oil or *ghee*	3 Tbs
Onions chopped	½ cup
Ginger chopped	1 Tbs
Garlic chopped	1 Tbs
Green chilies chopped	1 tsp
Salt	1 tsp
Red pepper	1 tsp
Sugar	1 tsp
Turmeric powder	½ tsp
Panchphoran masala	1 tsp
Coconut powder	2 Tbs
Mustard seeds	1 Tbs
Liver or bacon chopped	1 cup
Coriander leaves chopped	2 Tbs

METHOD

1. Wash the peas and set them aside. Fry the bacon or liver in a nonstick frying pan until light brown and drain the fat. Set aside in a bowl to be used later.
2. Boil 4-5 cups of water in a heavy-bottom saucepan and add the washed peas, turmeric powder, ginger, garlic, green chilies, salt and red pepper. Cook till the peas are tender (about 40–45 minutes: the time may vary). Add the sugar to the cooked peas and set aside. Grind the mustard seeds to a powder and mix in 2 Tbs of water and set the paste aside.
3. Cook the onions in 3 Tbs of oil or *ghee* in a medium size saucepan until light brown and add the *panchporan masala*. As soon as the seeds stop crackling add the coconut powder and stir well, fry till light brown. Add the paste of mustard powder and stir to mix. Add the chopped liver or bacon and fry for 2–3 minutes.
4. Transfer the cooked peas to the onions and the meat mixture and stir well. Add more water, if the dal is too thick, and simmer on low heat for 5 minutes. Serve sprinkled with chopped coriander leaves with rice or as an accompaniment to a regular meal.

Note: Liver and bacon pieces can be replaced by fried pieces of okra, cauliflower or eggplant.

Spinach Dal
Dal Palak

UTTAR PRADESH

A very healthy legume and spinach preparation from Uttar Pradesh. It is a nutritious main course as it meets the requirements of proteins and vegetables in one preparation.

SERVES 8 – 10

Ingredients

Mung dal spilt washed and soaked	1 cup
Water	6 cups
Fresh spinach chopped	2 cups
Or	
Frozen (10 ozs)	½-1 pkg
Curry leaves	4
Onions chopped	1 cup
Ginger	1 Tbs
Garlic	1 Tbs
Green chilies	1 Tbs
Tomato sauce (8 oz can)	1
Vegetable oil or *ghee*	3 Tbs
Red whole chilies broken	2
Cumin seeds	1 tsp
Mustard seeds	1 tsp
Red pepper	1 tsp
Salt	1 tsp
Turmeric powder	1 tsp
Fenugreek leaves (dry)	1 Tbs
Coriander powder	2 tsp
Cumin powder	½ tsp
Garam masala	1 tsp
Coriander leaves chopped	2 Tbs
Tomatoes chopped	1 cup

METHOD

1. Drain the water from the soaked *dal* and transfer it into a deep saucepan with 6 cups of water and frozen spinach and let it cook on medium to low heat.
2. After 20 minutes add the ginger, garlic, tomatoes, green chilies, and the curry leaves while it is cooking.
3. Cook until it is smooth but grainy and has the consistency of a thick soup or pressure cook the *dal* with water, frozen spinach, ginger, garlic, green chilies, tomatoes, and curry leaves for 10 minutes and set it aside.
4. In a small skillet cook onions in 3 Tbs of oil until they are light brown and add the cumin seeds, mustard seeds and the red whole chilies. Fry till the cumin seeds and mustard seeds are popping.
5. Add the turmeric powder, dry fenugreek leaves, red pepper, coriander powder, cumin powder, salt and stir well. Add the tomato sauce. Stir to mix and cook for another 3–5 minutes.
6. Pour this sauté over the *dal* mixture and mix well. Add more water, if *dal* is too thick.
7. Add the *garam masala* and the chopped green coriander leaves. Stir well and serve. It can be served with just plain rice to make a quick meal or as an accompaniment with other main courses.

Note: The amount of water in cooking the *dal* will increase if unsoaked *dal* is used.

Curried Kidney Beans
Rajmah

PUNJAB

This red kidney bean preparation is very popular in the state of Punjab. It is a wholesome and a complete meal when served with rice.

METHOD

1. Drain the liquid from the cans of cooked kidney beans in a colander and wash the beans in tap water and set them aside. If using uncooked beans wash the beans and transfer them into a pressure cooker with 6 cups of water, cinnamon sticks, cloves, black pepper corns, cardamoms, and the whole red chilies. Pressure cook them until tender. Let the pressure down and set them aside.

2. Cook the onions in oil in a deep heavy-bottom saucepan and add the onions, ginger, garlic, and the green chilies till the onions become light brown.

3. Add the cumin seeds and fry till they pop (if cooking with the canned beans then add the cinnamon sticks, cardamoms, cloves, and red whole chilies. Wait till chilies are turning color) and then add the tomatoes, turmeric powder, coriander powder, red pepper, cumin powder, tomato sauce and the salt and cook until the tomatoes are mushy and the *ghee* separates from the sauce.

4. Add the potatoes and stir-fry them in the sauce. Add the water and cook the potatoes for about 10 minutes. Add the kidney beans. Stir them in the sauce well and cook for 15–20 more minutes or until the sauce is thick and kidney beans are pretty soft. Add more or less water as the consistency requires.

5. Add the *garam masala* and coriander leaves, heavy cream and simmer for 2 more minutes and serve with rice or as side dish to any main course meal.

Note: Whole spices like cinnamon, cloves, black pepper corns, and cardamoms can be enclosed in a small piece of muslin cloth. Tie the ends together with a piece of thread and then add this little bag (*garni*) to the curry. After cooking this bag can be discarded. These spices are added only to flavor the beans. Sometimes fried pieces of tofu or *paneer* can be added alongwith kidney beans and that would make the curry more wholesome.

SERVES 8 – 10

Ingredients

Vegetable oil	¼ cup
Red kidney beans uncooked	2 cups
Red kidney beans cooked 16 ozs cans	2
Onions chopped	1 cup
Ginger chopped	1 Tbs
Garlic chopped	1 Tbs
Green chilies chopped	1 tsp
Cumin seeds	1 tsp
Cinnamon stick one inch	1
Cardamoms dark brown	2
Cloves	½ tsp
Black pepper corns	½ tsp
Red whole chilies (dry)	2 broken
Tomatoes chopped	1 cup
Turmeric powder	1 tsp
Coriander powder	1 Tbs
Red pepper	1 tsp
Cumin powder	1 tsp
Tomato sauce	8 oz
Salt	1 tsp
Potatoes chopped	½ cup
Water	2–3 cups
Garam masala	1 tsp
Coriander leaves chopped	2 Tbs
Heavy cream (optional)	1 Tbs

Gram Flour Curry
Karhi

PUNJAB

A curry made of a mixture of curd and gram flour is made in all parts of India. The aroma of this dish fills the kitchen when you are cooking it. It takes some time to prepare, but is worth the effort. It is a complete meal when served with plain rice but can also be served as a side dish or with other vegetables and bread.

METHOD

1. Beat yogurt, salt, red pepper, turmeric powder and water together and cook on low heat and bring to boil stirring consistently in a large heavy-bottom cooking pan.
2. Add the onions, ginger and garlic.
3. Cook until the mixture thickens (10 minutes) on medium-low heat stirring occasionally to make sure the mixture does not stick to the bottom. Set aside.
4. Make the dumplings.
5. Mix all the ingredients for the dumplings, gram flour, salt, soda, carom seeds, green chilies and yogurt, and beat to make a smooth but thick batter using water as needed.
6. Heat the oil to 325–350°F for frying.
7. Drop the dough by spoonfuls into the hot oil and fry to golden brown.
8. Remove and set aside in a pan lined with paper towel to drain excess oil.
9. Add these dumplings and fenugreek leaves to the curry and cook the curry for another 20 minutes on low heat.
10. Add the coriander leaves and the *garam masala* and mix.
11. Transfer this mixture to serving bowl and set aside.
12. In a deep small skillet heat the 4 Tbs of oil and add the cumin and mustard seeds, and sauté till they crackle. Then add the whole red chilies and the asafoetida. Remove from fire and pour this tempering over the cooked curry.
13. Mix well and serve with plain rice.

SERVES 6 – 8

Ingredients

Gram flour	½ cup
Yogurt beaten smooth	2 cups
Salt	to taste
Red pepper	1 tsp
Turmeric powder	1 tsp
Onions chopped in ¼ inch rounds	1
Ginger chopped	1 Tbs
Garlic chopped	1 Tbs
Cumin seeds	1 tsp
Mustard seeds	1 tsp
Red chilies (whole)	2
Fenugreek leaves dried	1 Tbs
Vegetable oil	4 Tbs
Garam masala	1 tsp
Water	6-8 cups
Asafoetida	a pinch
Green coriander leaves chopped	2 Tbs

For the dumplings:

Gram flour	1 cup
Yogurt	½ cup
Salt	to taste
Baking soda	a pinch
Green chilies chopped	1 tsp
Carom seeds	1 tsp
Oil (for frying)	4 cups
Water enough to make a thick batter	

The Exquisite World of Indian Cuisine

LEGUMES

Whole Mung Dal
Mung Sabut

Whole *mung* is very popular in northern India and is very delicious and nutritious when cooked well. Mostly flavored with onions, cumin and fresh coriander leaves and served with rice and *chappati*. One of the easy lentils to cook and easy to digest, it has a very pleasing taste.

METHOD

1. Wash and soak the beans in 2 cups of water.
2. Boil 6–8 cups of water in a large saucepan and transfer the washed and drained beans into the pan.
3. Add the salt, turmeric powder and *kokum,* and let the beans cook on the medium heat until the beans are completely soft and the *dal* has a smooth but grainy look to it (one hour or more) and add more water, if needed. Preferably pressure cook the *dal* in 4–6 cups of water until soft. Let the pressure down and set it aside. Time of pressure cooking may vary from one place to another.
4. Cook the onions, ginger, garlic, and green chilies in 2 Tbs of oil and fry the onions till they are brown.
5. Add the cumin seeds and pieces of dry pepper and wait till the cumin starts to pop and then add coriander powder, cumin powder, red pepper, dry fenugreek leaves, salt, and transfer the sauté to the *dal*. Add more (1–2 cups) boiling water as needed and mix well. Let it simmer for 5 more minutes.
6. Add the *garam masala*, chopped coriander leaves and the cream and let it simmer for another 2 minutes. Serve with rice, vegetable curry of your choice and any bread.

SERVES 6 – 8

Ingredients

Whole *Mung* beans or *dal*	2 cups
Water	6 cups
Salt	to taste
Turmeric powder	1 tsp
Kokum pieces	4–5
Onions chopped	1 cup
Ginger chopped	1 Tbs
Garlic chopped	1 Tbs
Green chilies chopped	1 Tbs
Vegetable oil or *ghee*	¼ cup
Cumin seeds	1 tsp
Red pepper whole (dry) broken	2
Coriander powder	2 tsp
Cumin seeds	1 tsp
Red pepper	1 tsp
Garam masala	1 tsp
Green coriander leaves chopped	2 Tbs
Cream (optional)	2 Tbs
Fenugreek leaves (dry)	1 Tbs

Note: *Dry mung dal* is also very delicious. Add enough to cook in step 3; see that the beans are soft and then follow the rest of the steps except that no more water is added.

The Exquisite World of Indian Cuisine

Dal with Coconut Milk

SRI LANKA

In Sri Lanka, and in some parts of Bengal, *dal* is dry roasted first and then cooked and flavored not only with onions, ginger and green chilies but also with coconut milk. This gives it somewhat the same creamy texture as adding the cream to *Dal Makhani*.

METHOD

1. Wash the *dal* in clean water. Drain the water and wipe it dry on a paper towel.
2. In a heavy-bottom cooking pan of medium size heat 2 Tbs of the oil and start to fry the *dal* on medium low heat until the beans are light brown. Add the water with salt, turmeric and the curry leaves. Cook on medium heat until the *dal* is soft (about 15–20 minutes) and set aside.
3. In a small sauce-pan fry the onions, ginger and garlic in 1 Tbs of oil and add the cumin seeds and red dry chillies. As the seeds stop popping add the coriander powder, and red pepper powder. Stir to mix, add the coconut milk. Mix well and bring to boil. Add some *garam masala*.
4. Add the cooked *dal* to the above mixture and bring to boil. Simmer on low heat until it takes the uniform consistency of a thick soupy texture but the beans still retain their shape somewhat and are not completely mushed. Add more water, if *dal* is too thick, sprinkle coriander leaves and *garam masala*.
5. Serve hot with rice and *chappatis*.

SERVES 4 – 6

Ingredients

Vegetable oil or *ghee*	3 Tbs
Masoor dal or *mung dal* washed dehusked	1 cup
Water	3 cups
Salt	1 tsp
Turmeric powder	½ tsp
Curry leaves	6–8
Onions chopped	1 cup
Cumin seeds	1 tsp
Coriander powder ground	1 tsp
Garlic and ginger finely chopped (each)	1 Tbs
Red chilies broken	2–3
Red pepper	½ tsp
Canned coconut milk	1 cup
Sprinkle of coriander leaves	1 Tbs
Garam masala	½ tsp

CHAPTER 7

Rice and Pulav

India is one of the largest producers of grains and produces the best varieties of rice. Rice is the staple food of millions of Indians and is served daily in one form or another for breakfast, lunch or dinner.

In southern India it is served as *idli*, *dosa*, and *appam* besides as plain rice. Other states of India like Bengal, Maharashtra, Tamil Nadu, Karnataka, Gujarat use rice daily for their three major meals of the day.

The state of Tamil Nadu is known for its outstanding rice dishes like *Coconut Rice, Tamarind Rice, Yogurt Rice, Lemon Rice,* and from Maharashtra comes the *Masala Bhat,* whereas from Karnataka comes their famous *Shrimp Masala Rice* and *Bisi Bele Masala Rice.*

Northern India also has some very splendid rice preparations called *pulavs*. Among the famous *pulavs* are *Shahi Pulav*, *Navratan Pulav*, *Biryani*. These colorful aromatic *pulavs* decorated with nuts, fried onions, spices enhance the beauty of any dinner table when they are served surrounded by colorful meat and vegetables curries, lentils and bread preparations. Indians really know what to do with this versatile grain, and have transformed the plain grain of starch to beautiful aromatic and stylish dishes. Several appetizers like *Dhokla*, *Poha*, and some breads are the preparations using rice as the major component.

Rice is not only the staple food of the Indian sub-continent but feeds over three billion people all over the world. It is inexpensive, easily prepared, delicious and nutritious food that benefits humans all over the world. It is easy to digest and has non-allergic properties. It reduces hypertension and lowers cholestrol.

Plain Cumin Rice
Zeera Chawal

Rice is one of the main staple foods of India and there are numerous varieties of rice found and consumed all over the country. The most sought after and aromatic variety is *Basmati* rice. It is most frequently used in the northern parts of India as well as in open market restaurants. All varieties can be cooked using this recipe.

SERVES 4 – 6

Ingredients

Basmati rice	2 cups
Water	4 cups
Salt	½ tsp
Cumin seeds	1 tsp
Vegetable oil	2-4 Tbs

METHOD

1. Wash the rice and soak in water. Set aside.
2. Heat the oil in a heavy-bottom medium size saucepan. Add the cumin seeds, wait till they start popping.
3. Drain the water from soaked rice and transfer them to the cooking pan. Lower the heat and stir-fry the rice for a minute or so until the grains start sticking to the bottom. This frying is important as it hardens the outer covering of the rice and that prevents the grains from sticking to each other once they are cooked. Add 4 cups of water and salt. Boil it uncovered until almost all the water on the top of the rice is gone. Adjust the heat to low and cover with a lid.
4. Cook on low heat until rice has absorbed all the water. Turn the heat off, check the rice if it is not done, then cover it with a lid and again let it cook in its steam for another 5 minutes. Remove the lid and check the rice again. It should be done.
5. Serve it with any curry or *dal* and include it in a full meal with a stir-fry vegetable, *dal* and any kind of bread.

HINT
This rice can be made in a conventional rice cooker also.

Peas and Cheese Pulav
Matar-Paneer Pulav

Rice *pulav* made with fried pieces of *paneer* is wholesome and makes a beautiful presentation with peas and nuts. A popular rice dish.

METHOD

1. Wash and soak the rice in 2 cups of water and set aside.
2. Fry onions and cashew to garnish in a tablespoon of oil in a skillet on low heat and set aside.
3. Cook the onions in 2 Tbs of oil in a thick-bottom saucepan of a medium size and add the ginger, garlic and green chilies, and wait till the onions are light brown. Add the cinnamon, cardamoms, cloves and cumin seeds. Wait till the cumin seeds start popping. Add the drained rice, and fry them with the spices for 2 minutes.
4. Add the peas and *paneer* cubes and stir-fry for 2 minutes.
5. Add the water and mix. Raise the heat and bring the rice to a full boil and then reduce the heat. Cover and cook till the water is completely absorbed.
6. Remove from heat and leave covered with the lid. The rice cooks further in the steam, and 5 minutes later check the rice. It should be done.
7. Transfer the *pulav* to a serving dish and just before serving garnish the center with cashew nuts, onions, and go around in a circle with tomatoes and cucumber slices alternating with each other. Sprinkle with little *garam masala* and dissolved saffron.
8. Serve just with yogurt, or as an accompaniment to a full meal with vegetable curry, meat curry, salad and bread of your choice.

SERVES 8 – 10

Ingredients

Basmati rice	2 cups
Water	4 cups
Onions chopped	1 cup
Cinnamon sticks ½ inch piece	1
Brown cardamoms broken	2
Cumin seeds	1 tsp
Cloves	¼ tsp
Salt	½ tsp
Peas shelled or frozen	½ cup
Paneer cubes fried	1 cup
Ginger chopped	1 tsp
Garlic chopped	1 tsp
Green chilies chopped	½ tsp
Red pepper	½ tsp
Vegetable oil	2-4 Tbs

To garnish:

Cashew nuts	2 Tbs
Onions chopped and fried	1 Tbs
Cucumber and tomato slices	½ cup
Vegetable oil for frying	2 Tbs
Garam masala	½ tsp
Saffron (dissolved in 1 Tbs of water)	¼ tsp

The Exquisite World of Indian Cuisine

Royal Pulav
Shahi Pulav

Rice cooked with meat, nuts and raisins makes an elegant rice dish called the *Shahi Pulav* "worth serving to a king". No Indian meal is complete without a rice dish and no rice dish is as magnificent as this.

METHOD

1. Fry the meat cubes in a small skillet till slightly brown. Drain the fat and set them aside.
2. Heat 3 Tbs of oil in a heavy-bottom pan and fry, one by one, ½ cup of onions, cashews and raisins. Remove them from the oil with a slotted spoon and set them aside.
3. In the same oil, fry ½ cup of onions, ginger and garlic, and as soon as the onions are brown add the salt, red pepper, coriander powder and stir to mix. Add the tomato sauce and fry the sauce until the oil separates. Add the cooked meat, and fry the meat in the onion mixture on medium low heat. Add 1 cup of water and cook the meat until it is tender and almost all the water dries up. Add *garam masala* and stir to mix. Set it aside in a bowl.
4. Heat the leftover *ghee* or oil in a large deep saucepan for a minute and add a stick of cinnamon, few cloves, ½ tsp of peppercorns and salt. Fry for few minutes and add the cumin seeds.
5. When cumin seeds start popping, add the stock.
6. Add the drained rice to it and cook on low heat until all the water dries up and the rice is tender but not done. In a dish, lay down a layer of rice and pour 2 Tbs of cream, and a layer of cooked meat.
7. Keep layering until all the meat is gone.
8. Finish with a top layer of rice.
9. Put it in the oven covered with thin foil at 350°F for 5–10 minutes. Remove from the oven and garnish it with fried raisins, cashew, and onions. Serve sprinkled with *garam masala*, chopped green coriander and shredded green chilies and dissolved saffron. Makes a very elegant presentation.
10. Serve with *nan*, *poori* or *chappati* and vegetable curry or any meal.

SERVES 8 – 10

Ingredients

Beef or goat meat cubed	1 lb
Rice washed and soaked in water	2 cups
Onions chopped	1 cup
Mixture of heavy cream and whipped yogurt	¾ cup
Red pepper	¾ tsp
Ginger chopped	¾ tsp
Garlic chopped	¾ tsp
Melted *ghee* or oil	¼ cup
Lean lamb meat or beef chopped into small cubes	2 cups
Beef stock or chicken stock	3¾ cups
Cinnamon stick (½ inch)	1
Cloves and black pepper each	½ tsp
Salt	½ tsp
Coriander powder	1 tsp
Tomato sauce	1 cup
Garam masala	½ tsp
Saffron to sprinkle (dissolved in 1 Tbs of water)	½ tsp

Ingredients for garnishing:

Sliced onions	½ cup
Raisins	2 tsp
Cashew nuts	2 Tbs
Green chilies shredded	2 tsp
Coriander leaves chopped	1 Tbs
Garam masala	½ tsp

Peas Pulav
Matar Pulav

A rice dish garnished with peas, onions, almonds and raisins. It is usually served with all curries and is one of most widely served rice dishes in Indian restaurants. It is simple but quite elegant.

METHOD

1. Clean and wash the rice and set them aside.
2. Fry ½ cup of onions and all the almonds in the oil using a frying pan till brown. Set these aside to garnish.
3. In the same oil add the remaining onion and fry till brown. Move the onion to one side and add the cumin seeds and wait until they start popping, then add cinnamon stick, cloves, peppercorns, bay leaves and the cardamoms.
4. Add the peas, raisins and stir-fry for a few minutes.
5. Then add the drained rice and continue stirring the rice for about 2–3 minutes in the spices.
6. Add salt and 4 cups of water to the rice. Stir to mix.
7. Cook on medium heat till half the water dries up. Reduce the heat to low and tightly cover the pan until the grains are soft and all the water dries up. If the rice is still not done then leave covered with the lid for a few more minutes so that the rice can cook in its steam.
8. Serve in an oval dish. Cover the center with fried onions, almonds and garnish with saffron.
9. The *pulav* can be garnished with the slices of cucumbers, tomatoes, slices of boiled egg and coriander leaves. This is optional.

SERVES 6 – 8

Ingredients

Basmati rice	2 cups
Boiled eggs (sliced or cubed)	1 or 2
Vegetable oil or *ghee*	2-4 Tbs
Cloves	6–8
Pepper corn	10–12
Peas frozen	⅔ cup
Onion chopped	1 cup
Brown cardamoms	2
Cinnamon stick	1
Cumin seeds	1 tsp
Bay leaves	4
Salt	1 tsp
Saffron	½ tsp
Water	4 cups
Almonds chopped and slivered	2 Tbs
Raisins	1 Tbs

The Exquisite World of Indian Cuisine

Mushroom Pulav
Khumb Pulav

Mughlai influence in Indian cuisine is very evident in this rice preparation. Royals used *guchian** (a kind of lichen) similar to mushrooms. Actually in north India, lichens curry preparation was very popular. *Guchians* are quite expensive and are considered a delicacy. It is hard to find a good quality in the market. Mushrooms make a good replacement.

SERVES 4 – 6

Ingredients

Basmati Rice	2 cups
Onions chopped	2 Tbs
Cumin seeds	1 tsp
Cardamom brown (whole) crushed	2
Cinnamon sticks (small)	2
Clove whole	½ tsp
Black pepper corns	½ tsp
Bay leaves	2–3
Vegetable oil or *ghee*	3 Tbs
Mushrooms chopped into slices ½ inch thick and ½ long	1 cup
Salt	¾ tsp
Red pepper	½ tsp
Water or chicken broth	4 cups
Peas frozen	¼ cup
Fenugreek leaves freshly chopped	½ cup
Or dry leaves	2 Tbs
Garam masala to garnish	½ tsp
Saffron	¼ tsp

METHOD

1. Wash and soak the rice. Set it aside.
2. Heat the oil in a thick heavy-bottom pan of at least 4–quart capacity.
3. Add the onions, and fry them till they are slightly brown. Add the cumin, cardamoms, cinnamon sticks, bay leaves, cloves and black pepper, and after a minute add the cumin seeds. When the seeds stop popping, add the mushrooms, fenugreek leaves and peas. Fry them for 5–10 minutes and add the rice.
4. Fry the rice stirring gently. Lower the heat. This frying is important because it prevents the rice from sticking to each other when fully cooked as the outer surface of rice gets a little hardened.
5. Add the water or broth. Add salt and red pepper and stir to mix. Let it cook partially open until all water on the top of the rice is gone. Lower the heat and cover the pan and simmer until all the loose moisture is gone and the rice grains are fluffy and non sticky. Turn the heat off and let them stay covered in the cooking pan for a few minutes before serving.
6. Serve garnished with a sprinkle of *garam masala*, saffron and freshly chopped coriander leaves. They will go well with chicken *makhani*, any vegetable stir-fry and *raita*.

***Guchhian** (a kind of lichen) can also be curried with peas and is mainly found in the valley of Kashmir.

Multicolored Pulav
Navratan Pulav

Multicolored rice cooked with *paneer*, peas, nuts, and tomatoes. Another great dish inherited from the court of the great Mughal King, Akbar. It is colorful, delicious and unique. Though it is a little time consuming, it is a gem among the *pulavs*, and a complete meal by itself.

METHOD

1. Heat the *ghee* and fry the onions, ginger, garlic and green chilies. When the onion mixture is light brown, add cinnamon sticks, cloves, cardamoms, black pepper corns, and the cumin seeds. When the cumin starts to pop, add the rice. Stir well and lower the heat and fry the rice in this mixture for 2–3 minutes. Add the water and cook the rice until all the water is absorbed. Turn the heat off and let the rice cook in its steam for another 2–5 minutes.
2. Divide the rice into three parts and set aside in separate bowls.
3. To the first part add the green color by dissolving 6 drops of green food color in 1 Tbs of water and mix it well. Use only few drops of this colored water to give rice a light green color. Add the fried peas to it and stir them in.
4. Color the second part of the rice red by adding 4 drops of tomato coloring in 1 Tbs of water. Use only few drops of this colored water to turn the rice light red. Add the salted tomato cubes with *garam masala* and mix the rice well.
5. The third part can be left white and to that just add the cheese cubes with the salt and black pepper in it.
6. Fry the onions in 2 Tbs of oil until golden brown. Take them out of the *ghee* with slotted spoon and set aside. Now, fry the almonds, pistachio, raisins, cashew and chilies, and set them aside in a bowl.
7. Serve the rice by layering each color on top of the other in a large and elegant serving dish and topping the three layers with chopped eggs in the center and surround them with all the fried nuts and raisins, saffron, chopped green coriander leaves and shredded green chilies. Serve with chicken curry, beef curry or any vegetable curry of your choice.

Note: Moulds can be used to shape different colored rice, instead of layering them as the layers tend to fall apart.

SERVES 8 – 10

Ingredients

Rice	2 cups
Water	4 cups
Vegetable oil or *ghee*	2-4 Tbs
Onions chopped	1 cup
Ginger chopped	1 tsp
Green chilies chopped	1 tsp
Garlic chopped	1 tsp
Cinnamon stick ½ inch	1
Cloves	½ tsp
Whole green cardamoms	½ tsp
Pepper corns	½ tsp
Cumin seeds	½ tsp

To mix in rice :

Green food color	6 drops
Water	2 Tbs
Peas fried in 1 tsp of *ghee* with ¼ tsp each of salt and black pepper	½ cup
Tomato coloring	4 drops
Chopped tomatoes mixed with ¼ tsp each of red pepper, salt and *garam masala*	¼ cup
Fried *paneer* pieces or ricotta cheese + ¼ tsp each of salt and black pepper	¼ cup

To garnish the *pulav* :

Onions chopped	½ cup
Vegetable oil or *ghee*	1 Tbs
Almonds chopped	2 Tbs
Cashew chopped	2 Tbs
Raisins	2 Tbs
Green chilies finely cut	2–3
Coriander leaves chopped	2 Tbs
Full boiled eggs chopped	2
Pistachio nuts	2 Tbs
Red pepper	1 tsp
Saffron	¼ tsp

The Exquisite World of Indian Cuisine

The famous Chaar Minar (the gateway with four minarets) in Hyderabad, Andhra Pradesh

Biryani

A Mughal cuisine of great elegance.

METHOD

1. Prepare the Peas *pulav* by following the Peas *Pulav* recipe except that one must keep the rice slightly crisp by using less water for this recipe than is needed to cook the *pulav*. Set aside.
2. Prepare the chicken curry by following the Chicken Curry recipe but give less cooking time than required in that recipe also. Set aside.
3. Fry the cashew nuts, onions and raisins in 2 Tbs of clarified butter until light brown and keep aside in a bowl.
4. Brush the bottom of a casserole with oil and layer the pan in the following manner:
    - Put all the chicken pieces at the bottom of the pan but save the sauce.
    - Put a layer of Peas *Pulav* on top of these chicken pieces and then spread a layer of the chicken curry gravy on the top of this rice.
    - Put the rest of the rice *pulav* on the top and sprinkle 1 Tbs of *ghee* or oil on these layers and tightly close the lid of the casserole and bake for 15–20 minutes at 300°F.
5. Take it out of the oven and serve sprinkled with fried nuts first, then the fried onions and then top all this with the chopped coriander leaves *garam masala* and sprinkle the saffron water.

SERVES 8 – 10

Ingredients

Peas *pulav*	4 cups
Chicken curry	4 cups
Vegetable oil or clarified butter	2-4 Tbs
Raisins	2 Tbs
Cashew nuts	2 Tbs
Onions chopped	½ cup
Coriander leaves chopped	½ cup
Garam masala	1 tsp
Saffron dissolved in water	¼ tsp

Cauliflower Pulav
Gobhi Pulav

A rice preparation flavored with chunks of fried cauliflower florets, almonds and cooked with water and cream. It makes an elegant presentation and is very delicious and nutritious.

METHOD

1. Wash and soak the rice and set it aside.
2. Heat the oil in a large heavy-bottom saucepan and fry the onions and almonds for garnish. Remove them from oil and set them aside. In the same oil, fry the cauliflower florets by sprinkling salt and pepper over them. As soon as they turn light brown remove them from the oil and set them aside.
3. In the same oil, add the cardamoms, cloves, black pepper, and cinnamon and fry for ½ minute and then add the onions, garlic, ginger and green chilies, and fry until onions turn light brown. Add the cumin seeds, and when they start to pop add the red pepper, salt, and the drained rice. Fry for a few minutes until the water dries up and rice begins to stick to the bottom. Add 4 cups of water and the cream.
4. Cover and let it cook on medium to low heat. Partially cover with lid and cook till all the water is gone. Turn the heat off, and if the rice is not done, leave it covered with the lid for another 5–10 minutes to cook in its own steam.
5. Serve topped with fried cauliflower in the center, and arrange chopped tomatoes and slices of cucumber, saffron, fried onions, almonds or fried potato vermicelli around it.
6. Serve with yogurt or a curry.

SERVES 6 – 8

Ingredients

Basmati rice	2 cups
Ginger chopped	1 Tbs
Garlic chopped	1 Tbs
Green chilies chopped	1 Tbs
Cinnamon sticks small	1 inch
Cloves and black pepper each	¼ tsp
Cardamoms	4
Water	4 cups
Vegetable oil or *ghee*	¼ cup
Onions chopped	½ cup
Cloves and black pepper corns each	½ tsp
Cardamoms green	½ tsp
Cinnamon sticks ½ inch	1
Cumin seeds	1 tsp
Red pepper	½ tsp
Salt	1 tsp
Heavy cream	3 Tbs
Cauliflower florets about 1 inch size	1 cup

To garnish:

Onions chopped	¼ cup
Potato vermicelli (optional) (available at an Indian grocery store)	½ cup
Tomatoes and cucumber slices	2 Tbs
Roasted blanched almonds	1 Tbs
Saffron	¼ tsp

Note: Fried chopped jackfruit can also be used to make jackfruit pulav. It is delectable.

Yogurt Rice
Dahi Chawal

This dish goes very well with drier curries. Try it with dry chicken curry, fried fish, any dry meat curry or any vegetable stir-fry.

METHOD

1. Cook rice in four cups of water and set them aside. Follow the plain rice recipe.
2. In a large skillet heat the oil and add the mustard seeds, red pepper and curry leaves, and wait until the mustard seeds start popping.
3. Add the split peas, *urad dal* and nuts and wait till they are all light brown. Remove them with a slotted spoon and set them aside.
4. To the same oil, add the onions, ginger, bell pepper, green pepper, red pepper and salt.
5. Cook and stir until the onions and pepper look cooked and transparent (about 5 minutes).
6. Remove from heat and transfer and mix the buttermilk and yogurt into this onions and spices mixture and stir well. Mix in the fried nuts mixture.
7. Gently fold in the cooked rice into this mixture and mix well. Be careful not to mash the rice.
8. Top it with chopped coriander leaves and serve.

SERVES 8 – 10

Ingredients

Basmati rice	2 cups
Water	4 cups
Salt	1½ tsp
Red pepper to taste or	½ tsp
Onion chopped	1 cup
Ginger	1 tsp
Green chilies	2 tsp
Mustard seeds	1 tsp
Urad dal	2 Tbs
Yellow or green split peas	2 Tbs
Fresh cashew nuts or peanuts chopped	½ cup
Bell pepper yellow or green	1 cup
Vegetable oil	2–4 Tbs
Red pepper (dry)	4
Curry leaves	8–10
Yogurt	2 cups
Coriander leaves fresh chopped	2 Tbs
Buttermilk	1–2 cups
Or	
Sour cream	½ cup

Coconut Rice
Nariyal Chawal

A delicious, refreshing and crisp preparation of rice. Great for a meal as well as light lunch and a snack. It goes very well with meat curries and vegetable curries.

SERVES 8 – 10

Ingredients

Rice	2 cups
Water	4 cups
Fresh coconut grated (whole)	1
Or	
Coconut powder dry (from an Indian grocery store)	1 cup
Mustard seeds	1 tsp
Curry leaves	6
Red pepper dried	4
Urad dal	¼ cup
Asafoetida	¼ tsp
Green chilies chopped	2 tsp
Cashew nuts or peanuts raw chopped	⅓ cup
Green coriander fresh chopped	⅓ cup
Clarified butter or oil	4-6 Tbs
Onions to garnish light golden fried	1 cup
Salt	to taste

METHOD

1. Cook the rice in water part of which may be the water collected after breaking a coconut if available in case fresh coconut is used. (Follow instructions of collecting the coconut water after breaking it under 'Preparation of coconut milk' in the introduction). Follow the plain rice preparation recipe and cook the rice.

2. Now fry the onions in 2 Tbs of clarified butter until they are lightly brown and set them aside. Also fry the coconut in the same oil until it is light brown and set it aside.

3. Heat the remaining 2 Tbs of oil in a large heavy-bottom saucepan and add the mustard seeds, curry leaves, asafoetida, red pepper and *urad dal* and wait till the mustard seeds start popping and *urad dal* turns light brown.

4. In the same pan add the cashew nuts and the green chilies. Fry for few minutes until the nuts are light brown.

5. Stir in the cooked rice gently with the salt to taste and mix in ½ of the fried coconut and onion mixture.

6. Mix the coconut rice gently but thoroughly and serve topped with remaining fried onions and chopped coriander.

Tamarind Rice
Imli Chawal

A south Indian rice specialty that is made usually on festive occasions and for snack time.

SERVES 6 – 8

Ingredients

Basmati Rice	2 cups
Water	5 cups
Vegetable oil	¼ cup
Red chili (whole)	2
Mustard seeds	1½ tsp
Urad dal	1½ tsp
Peanuts or cashew nuts (broken)	¼ cup
Asafoetida powder	¼ tsp
Turmeric powder	½ tsp
Tamarind paste	2 tsp
Curry leaves	4
Salt	1 tsp
Red pepper to taste or	1 tsp
Yellow or dry green split peas	¼ cup
Coriander leaves chopped	1 tsp
Garam masala	½ tsp

METHOD

1. Cook the rice (refer to plain rice recipe) in 4 cups of water and set it aside.
2. Soak the dry split peas and the tamarind paste in 1 cup of water in a bowl and let these sit for at least an hour. Strain the split peas from the tamarind water and save the water in a bowl.
3. Heat the oil in a pan and sauté the peanuts on medium low heat. Remove from the oil and set them aside. Also fry the strained split peas in the same oil and set them aside.
4. In the same oil fry the whole red pepper, mustard seeds, asafoetida powder, and the *urad dal* until the *dal* is light brown.
5. Add the tamarind water and mix keeping the heat on medium low.
6. Add turmeric powder, red pepper, salt, fried split peas and *garam masala* and gently stir the mixture. Cook till the water is almost absorbed.
7. Add the cooked rice and gently blend the spice mixture in to the rice. Add the peanuts or the cashew nuts and mix them gently into the rice. Serve topped with chopped green coriander leaves and *garam masala*.

Lemon Rice
Nimbu Chawal

A splendid rice dish that can be an accompaniment to any meal. It is flavored with lemon juice, peanuts, *urad dal* and dried peas *dal*. It is crunchy and can also be served as a snack at teatime, coffeetime or lunchtime.

METHOD

1. Cook the rice following the plain rice recipe and set it aside.
2. Heat the oil and add to it the dry split peas. Brown them and remove them from oil and set them aside in a bowl. Add the cashew nuts or peanuts to the same oil and wait till they turn light brown. Remove them from oil and also set them aside in the same bowl.
3. In the same oil add the mustard seeds, red pepper, and curry leaves, and wait until the mustard seeds start popping. Add the *urad dal* and wait till it turns light brown.
4. Add the chopped green chilies, onions, ginger, and wait till onions are light brown. Add turmeric, asafoetida and salt also.
5. Remove from heat, gently add the cooked rice and softly fold into the rice all the contents very carefully so as not to crush the rice. Add the roasted split peas and cashew nuts and mix them in. Fold in the fresh lemon juice and stir the rice well.
6. Serve topped with fresh coriander leaves, *garam masala* and chopped green onions.

SERVES 8 – 10

Ingredients

Basmati Rice	2 cups
Green or yellow dry/split peas	½ cup
Lemon juice	¼ cup
Vegetable oil	2-4 Tbs
Turmeric	1 tsp
Mustard seeds	1 tsp
Urad dal	2 tsp
Curry leaves	10
Red pepper (dry)	3
Salt	to taste
Ginger chopped	1 tsp
Asafoetida	¼ tsp
Green chilies chopped	2 Tbs
Cashew nuts or peanuts finely chopped	¼ cup
Coriander leaves chopped	2 Tbs
Onions chopped	1 cup
Or	
Green fresh onions chopped to garnish	½ cup
Garam masala	1 tsp
Water (to make rice)	4 cups

Vegetable Masala Rice
Masala Chawal (Vaangi Bhaat)

MAHARASHTRA

Rice cooked with fried vegetables and their local *masala* is a delicacy of Maharashtra. It makes a complete meal in itself when served with your favorite *raita* or meat dish but it can be a part of a big meal on a festive occasion.

METHOD

1. Cook onions, ginger, garlic and green chilies in 2 Tbs of oil in heavy-bottom medium size cooking pan till the onions are starting to turn brown. Remove the onion mixture with slotted spoon and grind it in the blender with the help of some water and set it aside.

2. In the same pan add 2 more Tbs of oil and fry all the chopped vegetables until they turn light brown. Sprinkle them with *Goda masala* (refer to introduction section) and set them aside in a bowl. Fry the cashew nuts and then the coconut powder until slightly brown and set it aside.

3. In same pan add 2 Tbs of oil. Add some curry leaves, and cumin seeds. When seeds stop popping add the rice and stir-fry the rice for 2 minutes, so that the outside covering is hardened and rice does not stick once cooked. Add the ground onions mixture and stir well to mix.

4. Add the coconut milk and water. Stir to mix. Let it boil open for a few minutes. When there is no water left on the top, cover it with a lid and lower the heat. Let it cook in its own steam until all the water is absorbed. Take out the rice in a bowl and fluff it with a fork. Gently mix in the fried vegetables.

5. Serve it in a platter sprinkled with fried cashew, chopped coriander leaves and freshly grated and fried coconut.

Note: The chopped vegetables can be replaced by fried eggplant cubes to make the famous **Vaangi Bhaat** of Maharashtra.

SERVES 4 – 6

Ingredients

Basmati Rice	2 cups
Water	3½ cups
Coconut milk	½ cup
Onions chopped	2 cups
Ginger chopped	1 Tbs
Garlic chopped	1 Tbs
Green chilies chopped	1 Tbs
Cumin seeds	1 tsp
Vegetable oil	5–6 Tbs
Peas frozen	½ cup
Cauliflower florets small one inch	½ cup
Grated carrots	½ cup
Goda masala mix	2 Tbs
Cashew nuts fried	2 Tbs
Lemon juice	1 Tbs
Fresh coriander leaves chopped	2 Tbs
Curry leaves	4–6
Coconut powder	2 Tbs

HINT

If *Goda masala* is not available then use 1 tsp of *garam masala* and mix it with 1 tsp each of turmeric powder, red pepper, coriander powder and 1 Tbs each of ground roasted sesame seeds and coconut powder.

Shrimp Masala Rice
Konkani Rice

GOA

From the west coast of India comes this recipe of shrimp rice. There is clear cut mixing of several cultures in the cuisine of this region, Portuguese, Muslim, Hindu and Persian. The dish is quite spicy and delicious. A meal by itself.

METHOD:

1. Marinade the shrimp in a bowl by rubbing salt and lemon juice and set it aside.
2. Grind in a blender chopped green chilies, chopped coriander leaves, chopped spinach, mint leaves, garlic ginger, and onions with the help of little water. This is the onion *masala*.
3. Blend it smooth and set it aside.
4. Heat the oil in a large-thick bottom saucepan of medium size and add the cumin seeds and, when they stop popping, add the ground onions *masala*. Cook it slowly until the oil starts to separate from the mixture.
5. Add the shrimp and sauté for 2–3 minutes. As the shrimp starts to change the color add the *huliyana masala* in it. Add the washed rice and fry it in the green onion paste and spices for 2–3 minutes.
6. Add the coconut milk and water. Let it simmer to a boil for few minutes without cover. When water is almost gone from the top of the rice lower the heat and cover the pan. Let it simmer until the water dries up. Cover the pan with light lid.
7. Turn off the heat and let it cook in its own steam for a minute or two if needed. Serve sprinkled with freshly chopped coriander leaves, lemon juice and freshly grated coconut. Serve it with your favorite *raita* or meal.

SERVES 6 – 8

Ingredients

Rice	2 cups
Water	4 cups
Shrimp cleaned and deveined	1 lb
Lemon juice	1 tsp
Salt	1 tsp
Vegetable oil	¼ cup
Cumin seeds	1 tsp
Onions chopped	2 cups
Garlic chopped	1 Tbs
Ginger chopped	1 Tbs
Green chilies chopped	¼ cup
Green coriander chopped	¼ cup
Mint leaves chopped	1 Tbs
Spinach chopped	1 cup
Fresh coconut grated	1 cup
Huliyana masala mix	2 Tbs
Coconut milk	½ cup
Coriander leaves chopped (to sprinkle)	2 Tbs

Note: If *Huliyana masala* mix is not available then use as many of its ingredients as you can find. (See Introduction).

The Exquisite World of Indian Cuisine

Rice & Lentils with Vegetables
Khichdi/Bisi Bele Bhaat of Hyderabad

ANDHRA PRADESH

When rice, lentils and few chopped vegetables are mixed and cooked it really turns out to be a delicious and complete dish. It is then garnished with onions, and spices and served topped with a little clarified butter along with milk, yogurt or pickle. It is a quick fixing and a very light family pleaser. *Mung* beans are easily digestible, therefore this preparation is served even to people recovering from illness. Try it on a busy day and you will like it.

METHOD

1. Wash the rice and *dal* in a couple of changes of water and soak in about 2 cups of water and set them aside.
2. Boil 6 cups of water in a medium size thick-bottom saucepan and add the drained mixture of rice, *dal* and the chopped potatoes, 1 tsp of salt and ½ tsp of turmeric, cauliflower, frozen peas, and chopped spinach. Cook over medium heat until all the water is absorbed and all the grains of rice and *dal* are softened and the mixture is smooth but still a little grainy. Add more water if needed. Set aside.
3. In a small saucepan cook the onions, ginger, garlic and green chilies in 4 Tbs of oil until the mixture is lightly brown.
4. Move the onion mixture aside in the saucepan and add the cumin seeds and wait till they pop.
5. Add the coriander powder, red pepper, black pepper, dry fenugreek leaves, salt and mix into the onion mixture.
6. Transfer the spiced onion mixture into the rice and *dal* mixture and stir well. Move the saucepan back to the stove or cooking range on low heat and mix the spices and onion mixture well into the *khichdi*. Add more water, if needed.
7. Sprinkle with *garam masala* and chopped green coriander leaves and remove from heat. Mix and serve the *khichdi* topped with a dab of butter and with yogurt, pickle, or with a vegetable curry.

Note: *Khichdi* makes a great meal for toddlers and children as it is very easy to digest and light on stomach. Use only ¼ tsp of red pepper and ¼ tsp of *garam masala* and don't use green chilies when cooking for infants.

SERVES 4 – 6

Ingredients

Rice	1½ cup
Mung dal (split and washed)	½ cup
Water	6 cups
Onions chopped	1 cup
Ginger chopped	1 Tbs
Garlic chopped	1 Tbs
Green chilies chopped	1 Tbs
Salt	to taste
Red pepper (or to taste)	½–1 tsp
Black pepper	½ tsp
Vegetable oil or *ghee*	4 Tbs
Cumin seeds	1 tsp
Coriander powder	1 tsp
Garam masala	¾ tsp
Chopped small cubes of peeled potatoes	½ cup
Cauliflower florets or carrots chopped	½ cup
Peas frozen	2 Tbs
Coriander leaves freshly chopped	1 tsp
Spinach fresh or frozen chopped (optional)	½ cup
Fenugreek leaves (dry)	2 Tbs

HINT

To make the popular dish **Bisi Bele Bhaat** from Andhra Pradesh, use *toor dal* instead of *mung dal* and tamarind dissolved in a tsp of water. Add the tamarind water in step 6, along with onion mixture. Also add 1 tsp each of crushed mustard seeds and fennel seeds along with cumin seeds in step 4. Fry 1 tsp each of poppy seeds, fenugreek seeds and anise seeds in a pan, when light brown and aromatic, grind them and add in step 5. You can also add 2 Tbs of fried cashew nuts and coconut powder at the end.

CHAPTER 8

Breads

Breads are the staple food of millions of Indians. They eat them plain, stuffed, baked and fried by wrapping them around tender morsels of curried vegetables or creamy curried meats. Several different grain flours like wheat, barley, millet, sorghum, gram, corn, garbanzo, lentils and rice are used in making these breads. Flours from these grains are available at Indian grocery stores or are sometime freshly ground at home.

There are unleavened flat griddle breads, like *chappatis*, *roghini roti* and *paranthas*. Then there are deep fried breads like *bhaturas*, *kachauris*, *luchhis* and *pooris*. Both types of these breads are the staple food of north India. These are made with whole wheat flour and are quite nutritious. They taste best when served hot and people like to eat them fresh. Now-a-days you can find ready-to-eat griddle breads even in the freezer section of the Indian grocery stores. *Paranthas* are stuffed with grated or boiled vegetables, ground meats, cheese and lentils. Then there are rice and lentil flour griddle breads like *rava dosa, plain dosa, adais* and *appams*. These breads are the speciality of south India. They are normally served fresh with hot *sambhar* (a lentil preparation), chutney and potato stir-fry.

Then there are also clay oven (*tandoor*) baked leavened breads brought to India by the Mughals like plain *nan*, mint *nan*, or onion *nan* made from all purpose flour. These breads are usually served with meat and vegetable curries. Flours like chappati flour, rice flour, black beans (*urad dal*) flour, gram flour, *suji* (uncooked cream of wheat), sorghum flour, millet flour are only available at health food stores or your local Indian grocery store.

Griddle Flat Bread
Chappati

METHOD

1. Transfer 2 cups of flour to a deep mixing bowl and make a deep depression in the middle.
2. In the heap thus formed, pour water, mix it and knead it into soft dough.
3. Knead for a few minutes until the dough becomes smooth, sprinkle with 1–2 tsp of water and cover with a wet cloth and let it sit for about half an hour.
4. Butter your hands well and knead again for a few minutes and divide into 10 to 12 pieces and using a little dry flour shape them into smooth round patties. Place them on the floured board and roll out with a rolling pin into thin pancake like forms (*chappati*) about 5-6 inches diameter and couple of millimeters in thickness.
5. Heat the griddle (medium heat) and transfer the rolled *chappati* on to it. When one side dries up and tiny bubbles began to appear, turn it over and cook until brown spots form on the under side.
6. Remove the griddle from the fire, place the *chappati* on direct heat *(see caution), if it is a gas stove, wait till it swells up into a shape similar to that of two saucers inverted over each other [*see picture on next page*] (If you have an electric stove, cover the gauge with a small wire grill and place the *chappati* on the wire grill). Keep turning using tongs, until it is browned on both sides. Remove from the fire and apply a little *ghee,* if you like, over one side. Serve immediately.
7. If the *chappatis* are made in advance, they should be placed one above the other, wrapped in a napkin and stored in a *chappati* container or tortilla container (this can be purchased at an Indian grocery store). If the *chappatis* container is not available then cover them in wax paper or paper towel and wrap them in aluminium foil and store them in a warm oven until ready to eat. Preferably serve hot.

Note: To make the *chappati* softer and proteinaceous add ½ lb of drained tofu and knead it into the dough. *Chappati* dough can be made ahead of time and refrigerated for a couple of days. They taste best when served fresh. Freeze them separated by wax paper and they would still be good for a week or two.

SERVES 4 – 6

Ingredients

Whole wheat flour (*Chappati* flour from an Indian grocery store)	2 cups
Water	1 cup + 2 Tbs
Wheat flour for rolling	¼ cup
Ghee or oil for brushing the *chappatis*	¼ cup

Caution: **Tongs should be used to toss and turn *chappatis* on gas or electric stoves.**

Milk Kneaded Griddle Bread
Rogini Roti

KASHMIR

Chappati or *roti*, the staple bread of India, is sometimes made a little differently in Kashmir. Mughal kitchens made the bread dough by adding *ghee* (clarified butter) to the flour and knead it with milk instead of water.

METHOD

1. Sift the flour with sugar and salt. Make a well in the center and add 4 Tbs of *ghee* or butter. Start to mix it in the flour until the flour becomes crumbly. Add the milk gradually and knead to make a soft dough. Keep kneading until the dough comes clean out of the pan and becomes elastic and has the consistency of the play dough. Cover it with a wet paper towel and set it aside.

2. Break a piece of dough and make a ball as big as a lemon and dust it with flour. Roll it on a flat surface into a circle with 6–8 inch diameter and about 1–2 mm in thickness. Repeat the process with rest of the dough.

3. Heat an iron skillet or a *tawa* (Indian griddle). Turn the heat down once the pan is heated and transfer the rolled *roti* on to it and wait till the light brown spots start to appear on the under side of the *chappati* (30–40 seconds). Turn it over and cook the other side for (about 20 seconds). Put a little grill on top of the gas burner and transfer the bread using tongs on to the grill. The bread will puff up like an oval saucer. Once both sides are cooked (15–20 seconds) remove from the stove and smear with melted butter and serve with your favorite meal or cool them slightly and wrap them completely in foil lined with paper towel to eat later. They can stay in a zip lock bag for a day or two and can be reheated to use later but they are best when used fresh.

4. Serve them with vegetable curries, a meat preparation, dal and other accompaniments.

SERVES 4 – 6

Ingredients

Chappati flour	2 cups
Clarified butter or *ghee*	4 Tbs
Sugar	1 tsp
Salt	½ tsp
Milk	½–¾ cup
Dry flour for rolling the bread	6 Tbs

Note: The state of Kashmir is known for its various exotic breads. One of them is *Sheermal*, which is very similar to *Rogini Roti* except it is quite sweet and flavored with saffron. Increase the sugar to ¼ cup and add a pinch of saffron. You have your traditional bread of Kashmir. Nowadays restaurants make it like a *nan* and the bread looks like a Danish pastry especially when it is garnished with chopped nuts.

The Exquisite World of Indian Cuisine

Clay Oven Bread
Tandoori Nan

PUNJAB

Leavened bread of Punjab made with all purpose flour, yogurt, yeast and eggs. Extremely delicious and soft.

SERVES 4 – 6

Ingredients

All purpose flour	4 cups
Sugar	2 tsp
Ghee or oil	¼ cup
Yogurt	½–1 cup
Salt	½ tsp
Eggs (large)	2
Yeast dissolved (in ¼ cup of warm water)	2 tsp
Flour for kneading	1 cup
Baking powder	1 tsp

Ingredients for basting over the *Nan*:

Melted *ghee*	4 Tbs
Poppy seeds	2 tsp
Lemon seeds or *Kalonji*	2 tsp

METHOD

1. Beat the yogurt and stir in the eggs, and the melted *ghee*. Beat it with egg beater smoothly.

2. Sift the flour in a large deep mixing bowl with baking powder, salt and sugar and make a depression in the middle. Pour the yogurt mixture and knead and mix it in. Add the dissolved yeast and start to knead the dough. Knead it well and make it as pliable as possible. Cover with a wet muslin cloth or any wet thin cloth and set it aside.

3. Leave it in a warm place for at least 4–6 hours to rise until it is more than double its size. Pat it down and knead it smooth again. Divide the dough into plum-sized balls and with the help of *ghee* make them smooth and set aside to rise for at least 15 minutes. Press them smooth again. Roll them into flat oblongs with the help of dry flour on a flat surface about 6–8 inch long and about 4–5 inch wide. They should be about $\frac{1}{8}$ inch thick. Sprinkle with poppy seeds or *kalonji* (onion seeds). Set the oven at broil.

4. Transfer the *nan* on to a greased baking sheet and place the sheet under the broil. As the *nan* starts to cook and puff up, and shows brown spots, remove the tray from the oven, turn over the *nan* and cook again for half a minute under the broil. This side does not have to show brown spots. Remove it from the oven and brush it with butter. Keep them wrapped in foil and store them to keep warm.

5. *Nan* goes well with all meals but especially with meat curries, vegetable curries and vegetable stir-fries.

Note: The *Tandoor* (similar to *bhatti* in India), originated in Afghanistan and was introduced in India by the Mughals. A *tandoor* is fired by burning charcoal. It is an important fixture in Indian restaurants. It is more or less a shallow clay pit with fire at the bottom. Now there are *tandoors* that are transferable from one place to another and are heated by electricity. The temperature inside these ovens can reach upto 480°C or 900°F and it needs very specialized handling and care. The broil temperature of the conventional ovens works as well.

Mint Bread
Pudina Nan

You can smell the fragrance of this *tandoor* baked bread when you enter an Indian restaurant. The smell of this leavened bread flavored by chopped onions, fresh chopped mint and butter will get your appetite going right away. They are moist and tender. They are a great accompaniment to any meat and vegetable curry.

METHOD

1. Cook the onions in 2 Tbs of *ghee* and add the mint leaves. Cook for 2 minutes. Set them aside.
2. In a large bowl, beat together yogurt and egg, remaining butter or *ghee*, baking powder, sugar, salt, and mix well.
3. Add the flour, cooked onions, yeast dissolved in 2 tsp of warm water, cooked mint leaves, coriander leaves and mix. Knead the dough with your hands using oil to facilitate the process. Knead until smooth. Use a little flour or water, if necessary. Leave the dough in a warm place for at least for 4 hours to rise.
4. Heat the oven to broil. Punch down the dough and knead it smooth. Pinch a piece as big as a plum and roll it with a rolling pin into a 6–8 inch circle and about $1/8$ inch thick with help of a little flour and using your fingers to stretch and shape.
5. Arrange them onto a cookie sheet and bake them in the preheated oven set on broil on the top rack. As soon as they are slightly brown and puffy turn the *nan* with tongs and put them back on the top rack under the broil. They puff up right away in 15–20 seconds. This side does not have to turn brown but should look cooked. Remove and brush them with a little butter and sprinkle some *chaat masala* if you like and serve them hot with a meat dish, vegetable curry, *dal* and rice. It is delicious with either one of them. You can make them ahead of time. Cool them to room temperature and store them wrapped in aluminium foil and keep them warm by putting the wrapped nans back into the oven at warm temperature.

Note: *Nans* can be made in a regular *tandoor* or the kitchen gas *tandoor* available for use in Indian households. Your local Indian grocer may have it in store. Use 2 Tbs of minced garlic instead of chopped mint leaves to make garlic *nans*.

SERVES 6 – 8

Ingredients

All purpose flour	4 cups
Yogurt	½–1 cup
Eggs beaten (large)	1
Baking powder	2 tsp
Yeast (dissolved in 2 tsp of warm water)	2 tsp
Clarified butter or *ghee*	¼ cup
Salt	1 tsp
Onions chopped	2 Tbs
Mint leaves chopped	¼ cup
Coriander leaves (Cilantro) finely chopped	¼ cup
Sugar	1 Tbs
Ghee to brush the *nans*	¼ cup
Chaat masala to sprinkle	

The Exquisite World of Indian Cuisine

Onion Bread
Tandoori Onion Nan

Nans are very popular in restaurants and formal gatherings. There are many variations but onion *nans* are my favorites. They go very well with meat curries especially.

METHOD

1. In a large mixing bowl mix together all purpose flour, baking powder, salt, sugar, beaten egg, chopped onions, green chilies, green coriander leaves, clarified butter and knead the dough. Add the milk and the dissolved yeast while kneading it well to a pliable consistency (use regular flour for kneading, if needed). When the dough starts to separate from the bowl cover it with a wet cloth and set it aside to rise for at least 4–6 hours in a warm place.

2. Divide the dough into 8 parts and roll each piece on a smooth floured surface into a circle with at least 6–8 inch diameter and $\frac{1}{8}$ of a inch thick. They can be made oblong too.

3. Set the oven at broil and transfer the rolled *nan* onto a greased baking sheet and put the sheet in the oven under the broil.

4. *Nan* starts to cook and shows brown spots in about 45–55 seconds. Remove the tray from the oven and turn it over. Return it to oven and cook the other side for about half-a-minute.

5. Remove the *nan* from the oven with tongs and brush it with butter, Serve warm with your dinner.

Note: Onions can be substituted with 2 Tbs of *ajwain* or carom seeds to make *Ajwain Nan*. Their smell is so addictive that you will want to make them for every meal. Boiled mashed potatoes, spiced with a little salt, chopped coriander and pepper can be stuffed into the *nans* (just like stuffing *paranthas*) to make Potato *Nan*. *Paneer Nan* can also be made by stuffing the plain *nan* with crumbled cheese, spiced with salt and red pepper.

SERVES 4 – 6

Ingredients

All purpose flour	4 cups
Milk (warm)	½ cup
Or	
Yogurt	⅔ cup
Yeast (dissolved in warm water)	2 tsp
Baking powder	2 tsp
Sugar	1 Tbs
Egg beaten	2
Salt	1 tsp
Clarified butter or *ghee*	¼ cup
Onions finely chopped	1 cup
Green chilies finely chopped	2 Tbs
Fresh green coriander leaves	¼ cup

Unfermented Deep-Fried Bread
Luchhi

WEST BENGAL

This deep fried bread from Bengal is extremely soft. The dough is made with all purpose flour, little salt, *ghee* and water. They are soft and delicious with any vegetable curry and are great favorites with children who love to eat them just plain.

METHOD

1. Mix the flour, cream of wheat, salt, and pepper in a medium size mixing bowl. Make a well in the center of the flour. Add the butter and mix it in. Slowly start pouring the water and start to mix the water into the flour and knead the flour to make the dough. When the dough starts to leave the sides of the bowl and is quite pliable, is not sticky or dry, cover it and let it sit for ½ hour at least.

2. Break a piece of dough as big as a golf ball and start to roll it flat with the help of a rolling pin on a lightly floured flat surface or the Indian *chappati* maker (*chakla*). Roll flat discs of about 3–4 inch diameter or oblong.

3. Heat the oil in a heavy-bottom pan or a fryer and heat to 300°F–350°F. Transfer the discs gently into the oil and fry them with a slotted spoon. Submerge them into the oil and slowly they will puff up like round balls. If the temperature of the oil is not right (too hot or too cold) the *luchhis* are not going to puff up completely. Turn them over and cook until the outside surface is starting to turn a little brown. Remove the *luchhi* with a slotted spoon from the oil on to a plate lined with a paper towel. Let the oil drain. Serve them hot with a meat curry or a vegetable curry.

SERVES 2 – 4

Ingredients

All purpose flour	1½ cups
Cream of wheat	½ cup
Yogurt	½–¾ cup
Salt	½ tsp
Red pepper	½ tsp
Clarified butter or *ghee*	2 Tbs
Vegetable oil for frying	3–4 cups
Baking soda	a pinch
Water as needed	

Note: The *luchhis* are going to be crisp because of cream of wheat. If you want softer bread please omit cream of wheat. Add a little more salt and ½ tsp of red pepper if *luchhis* are to be used as a snack.

The Exquisite World of Indian Cuisine

Fermented Deep-Fried Bread
Bhatura

PUNJAB

Fried bread made with flour and yogurt is very soft and fluffy. They are served mostly with *chholey* (a spicy chick-pea preparation which is a speciality of Punjab) but you can serve them with any curry of your choice.

METHOD

1. Sift together flour, oil, salt and baking powder. Knead with yogurt and yeast dissolved in 2 Tbs of water and sugar. Add more water, if needed, to make a soft and pliable dough like a pizza dough.
2. Knead it smooth with the help of oil till it stops sticking to the sides of the pan.
3. Cover it with a wet cloth and let it rise in a warm place for a couple of hours. It will rise and double in size.
4. Press it down and take a piece of dough and shape it into a ball as big as a plum.
5. Using a little dry flour, roll the balls flat into rounds on a flat board or *chakla* (a round marble or stone pedestal for making *chappatis*) with a diameter of about 6–8 inches and about ½ of an inch thick.
6. Heat the oil at 350°F. Check the oil if it is ready for frying. (Drop a tiny ball of dough into the hot oil and if it rises to the surface immediately then the oil is ready for frying). Fry them till they are slightly brown and puffed up. Take them out of the hot oil with a slotted spatula and drain them on a plate lined with a paper towel.
7. This bread goes best when served with *chholey*, (Chick-peas curried, called *Khatta Kabuli Channa* in Punjab), make a complete meal with a little salad on the side.

SERVES 6 – 8

Ingredients

All purpose flour	4 cups
Yogurt beaten smooth	1¼ cups
Salt	1 tsp
Baking powder	2 tsp
Sugar	1 tsp
Yeast (dissolved in water)	2 tsp
Water enough to make the dough	
Vegetable oil or *ghee*	¼ cup
Low fat oil for frying	4 cups

Note: This bread can also be served with a potato curry or any other curry. For a quick recipe to make *bhaturas* omit yogurt, baking soda, salt, and use 2 tsp or 1 packet of yeast dissolved in water and enough club soda to make the dough.

Whole Wheat Fried Puffs
Poori

A light fried puffy bread used extensively at festive occasions and a popular bread all over India. It goes very well when served with potato curry and *raita*.

METHOD

1. Mix the flour and cream of wheat and knead it into a smooth dough with the help of water and set aside. (See pictures on facing page)
2. Heat the oil to 300°F–350°F in a fryer or thick bottom saucepan of a medium size or a wok. Check the oil, if it is ready for frying.
3. Pinch off a piece of dough as big as a walnut and roll it into a small ball. (See pix 2)
4. Flatten it and roll it with the help of some oil or dry flour into a small circle shape with a diameter of about 4 inches. (See pix 3 and 4)
5. Drop these flattened discs one at a time into the heated oil. As the *poori* starts to rise to the surface pat it very gently a couple of times with the edge of the spoon. This helps in swelling and puffing up the *poori*. (See pix 5 and 6)
6. Turn it over and after a couple of seconds turn it over again. (See pix 7)
7. Cook a few seconds, if you want a crisper *poori*. Take it out with a slotted spoon, and drain it on a paper towel before serving. Makes approximately 15–20 *pooris*.
8. Serve with a vegetable stir-fry or any other curry.

SERVES 4 – 6

Ingredient

Whole-wheat flour	1½ cup
Cream of wheat	½ cup
Water as needed or	1 cup
Oil (for frying)	2 cups

Utensils required
A shallow plate with a raised edge
A rolling pin
A wooden board to roll the dough
A long handled flat, slotted spoon
A heavy-bottom deep pan for frying, preferably a wok.

Note: Cream of wheat (*suji*) makes the *pooris* crisper. It can be bought at your local Indian grocery store. If it is not available use all purpose or regular *chappati* flour only.

BREADS

Griddle Fried Bread
Plain Parantha

Plain *Paranthas* are nothing but pan-fried *chappati*. They are leavened with a little butter before you roll them which makes them fluffier, crisper and crunchy. They go very well with a vegetable curry or a meat curry or even stir-fry vegetable of your choice.

METHOD

1. Transfer the flour into a deep mixing bowl and add a pinch of salt and red pepper to it. Make a well in the middle. Add the water and knead to make pliable dough similar to *chappati* dough. Add more water, if needed.

2. Take a piece of dough and make a ball as big as plum and roll each ball into a round, about 4 inches in diameter. Coat the top with a little butter or *ghee* and fold the edges of the round over into half a circle and fold it one more time to make a triangle. Roll it gently with the help of the dry flour on a flat board or *chakla* (Indian *chappati* making board made of marble or wood) into a larger triangle with at least 4 inch sides.

3. Heat a 12–14 inch skillet or *tawa* (an Indian iron griddle for making *chappati*) for a minute on medium heat and transfer the *parantha* on to it. Turn over the rolled dough (*parantha*) when the surface is showing some bumps. Turn it over, and the turned side will show some brown spots. Coat it with *ghee* or oil and turn and cover the other side too with oil. Fry till the *parantha* is brown on both sides and turns crisp. Serve immediately with your favorite vegetable or meat curry.

SERVES 6 – 8

Ingredients

Flour	2 cups
Salt	a pinch
Red pepper	to taste
Vegetable oil or *ghee* for frying	¼ cup
Water	1 cup +1oz

Note: Any leftover *dal* can be used to knead the flour into dough and *dal paranthas* can be made easily. No water or spices are needed to knead the dough as *dal* provides both to make pliable dough for making *paranthas*.

The Exquisite World of Indian Cuisine

Grilled Fried and Stuffed Onion Bread
Lachhedar Parantha

PUNJAB

In Punjab, *Lachhedar Paranthas* are very common for breakfast. In Rajasthan, they are called *Batia Roti*. Knead the dough with spices and chopped onions and make them nice and soft by coiling the dough and then rolling them into 6 inch circles. They are my favorites for breakfast.

SERVES 4 – 6

Ingredients

Whole wheat flour	2 cups
Vegetable oil or *ghee*	½ cup
Onions chopped	½ cup
Ajwain (carom seeds)	1 tsp
Salt	1 tsp
Red pepper	½ tsp
Garam masala	½ tsp
Green chilies chopped	2 Tbs
Water or milk (enough to make a pliable dough)	

METHOD

1. Transfer the flour to a deep mixing bowl and add chopped onions, green chilies, carom seeds, salt, red pepper, *garam masala* and 2 Tbs oil or *ghee*.
2. Add enough water and knead to make a pliable dough. Knead until it is smooth and leaves the sides of the bowl.
3. Cover with a slightly wet cloth and set aside.
4. Break a piece as big as a ball 2 inch in diameter and start to roll it on a floured surface with a rolling pin. Roll it into a 6 inch circle and brush it with oil or *ghee*. Lift dough from one side and roll up tightly into a tubular form. Change the tube into a coil. Roll the coil with a rolling pin into a 6 inch flat disc.
5. Heat *tawa* or non-stick frying pan on medium heat and transfer the rolled flat dough on to it.
6. Cook until brown spots start to appear on the under side. Turn over and brush the cooked side with the remaining *ghee* or oil and turn it over. Brush top with *ghee* or oil again and cook both sides until light brown. Repeat the same with other pieces of dough.
7. Serve them hot with tea at breakfast time or at teatime. They can also be served as a bread accompaniment with a stir-fry vegetable or a curry.
8. Wrap cooked bread in tin foil and store it in an oven at warm temperature, if it is going to be used later.

Griddle Fried Stuffed Potato Bread
Aalu ke Paranthe

A superb treat, stuffed potato *Paranthas* are mostly served for breakfast in northern India. These are really a complete meal by themselves. Several different stuffings can be used.

METHOD

1. Boil the potatoes, peel them, mash them and set them aside.
2. Follow the recipe for making the dough, similar to *chappati* dough.
3. To the mashed potatoes, add the onions, 1 Tbs of *ghee*, ginger, garlic, green chilies, cumin powder, coriander powder, fresh chopped coriander leaves, red pepper, *garam masala*, salt and lemon juice. Mix well and set aside the stuffing.
4. Take a piece of dough and make a ball of 2 inch diameter and roll each ball on a smooth flat surface using a rolling pin and dry flour. You can use a slab of marble, fine smooth wooden chopping board or a traditional *chappati* making circular slab. Dab the rolling surface first with dry flour and then roll the dough balls into rounds about 4 inches in diameter by using more dry flour.
5. Put about 2 Tbs of the stuffing in the center of the round and fold the edges of the round over the stuffing and pinch them together making sure stuffing is completely covered with the dough from all sides. It is now a round patty with a diameter of 2 to 3 inches. Roll it in gentle circular motion with the help of the dry flour into a round disc of about 6 to 7 inches diameter with the rolling pin or with your fingers, making sure no stuffing protrudes out of the *parantha*.
6. Heat a 12–14 inch skillet or *tawa* and transfer the *parantha* on to it. When the underside is a little crisp and shows some brown spots turn it over. Coat it with *ghee* or vegetable oil. Turn it over again and coat this side also with the *ghee* or oil. Keep turning and frying until golden brown.
7. Serve immediately with plain yogurt, *raita*, pickle, or butter of your choice.

See pictures on facing page for step-by-step method to make *potato parantha*.

SERVES 2 – 4

Ingredients

For the dough:

Wheat flour	2 cups
Salt	a pinch
Vegetable oil or *ghee*	1 Tbs
Water to knead the dough	1 cup +1 Tbs

For Potato stuffing:

Boiled and smoothly mashed potatoes	1 cup
Onions finely chopped	2 Tbs
Coriander leaves chopped	1 Tbs
Green chilies chopped	1 tsp
Salt	1 tsp
Dried coriander seeds crushed or powder	1 tsp
Cumin powder	½ tsp
Coriander powder	1 tsp
Garam masala	½ tsp
Lemon juice	1 Tbs
Red pepper	½ tsp
Ginger finely chopped	1 tsp
Garlic finely chopped	1 tsp
Ghee or oil for frying the *paranthas*	¼ cup

The Exquisite World of Indian Cuisine

Griddle Fried Fenugreek Bread
Methi ke Paranthe

PUNJAB

Fenugreek flavored *paranthas* are a favorite in Punjab. These *paranthas* are wholesome, delicious and very healthy as fenugreek leaves have many health benefits. Easy to make too.

SERVES 4 – 6

METHOD

1. Mix together the flour, chopped fenugreek leaves, coriander leaves, *garam masala*, onions, ginger, garlic, salt, red pepper, green chilies, and 2 Tbs of oil in a mixing bowl.
2. Add the water slowly and knead to make a smooth and pliable dough like the *chappati* dough.
3. Pinch off a piece of dough to make a ball of 1½ inch diameter.
4. Using dry *chappati* flour, roll the ball into 4 inch diameter disc and smear the center with a dab of butter and fold the disc into a half circle and fold it again into a triangle and roll it into a triangle with 3–4 inch sides.
5. Heat an iron skillet (*tawa*) or any other medium size thick bottom skillet for a minute and keep the heat on medium.
6. Transfer the rolled dough (*parantha*) onto it. Soon little bumps start to appear on the surface of the *parantha*. Turn it over and you will see some brown spots on the turned side. Smear its surface with ¼ tsp of oil or *ghee* and turn it over. Smear this side also with a little oil.
7. Keep turning and frying until both sides turn light brown.
8. Serve with *Boondi Raita* or any other *raita* of your choice or plain yogurt. Makes an excellent breakfast or lunch. This bread can be served just with one curry or a stir-fry vegetable or served as a bread with any regular meal.

See pictures on facing page for step-by-step method to make *methi parantha*.

Note: To make *Paneer* or Onion *Parantha*, fenugreek leaves can be substituted with ½ cup of ricotta cheese, or with just a cup of chopped onions with 1 tsp each of green chilies, ginger and garlic. Make the dough in the same fashion as above. Use 1 cup of gram flour and 2 cups of wheat flour for making the dough. The *paranthas* will be more crisp and tasty.

Ingredients

Chappati flour	3 cups
Fresh fenugreek leaves washed and finely chopped	1½ cup
Onions finely chopped	½ cup
Ginger finely chopped	1 Tbs
Garlic finely chopped	1 Tbs
Green chilies finely chopped	1 tsp
Water to make dough for making the *chappatis*	1½ cup
Garam masala	½ tsp
Coriander leaves chopped	2 Tbs
Vegetable oil or *ghee*	2 Tbs
Salt	¾ tsp
Red pepper	1 tsp
Oil or clarified butter (for frying the *paranthas*)	½ cup

The Exquisite World of Indian Cuisine

297

BREADS

Griddle Fried Daikon Stuffed Bread
Muli ke Paranthe

Stuffed Daikon *Paranthas* are mostly served for breakfast in India. These are delicious and really a complete meal by themselves. Several different stuffings can be used. These can be enjoyed for breakfast or lunch.

METHOD

1. Grate the daikon radish and add ginger, garlic, green chilies, all the spices and mix well. Squeeze well to take out all the juices and save in a bowl, this will be the water to knead the dough.

2. Follow the recipe for making the dough similar to *chappati* dough. Instead of water use the mixture of squeezed juices and water. Knead to make a pliable dough just like the *chappati* dough. Butter the dough, cover it and set it aside.

3. Take a piece of dough and make a ball as big as plum and roll each ball on a smooth flat surface using a rolling pin. You can use a slab of marble, fine smooth wooden chopping board or a traditional *chappati* making circular slab bought from an Indian grocery store. Dab the rolling surface first with dry flour and then roll the dough ball into a round, about 4 inches in diameter by using a rolling pin and applying more dry flour.

4. Put about 2 Tbs of the stuffing in the center of the round and fold the edges of the round over the stuffing and pinch them together making sure stuffing is completely covered with the dough from all sides. It is now a round patty with a diameter of 2–3 inches. Roll it gently with the help of the dry flour into a round disc of about 6–7 inches in diameter with gentle circular motion, using a rolling pin, making sure no stuffing protrudes out of the dough.

5. Heat a 12–14 inch skillet or *tawa* and transfer the dough on to it. When the underside is a little crisp and shows some brown spots turn it over. Coat it with oil or *ghee* or vegetable oil. Turn it over again and coat it with *ghee*. Keep turning and frying until both sides are crisp and light brown. Remove and serve with plain yogurt or a stir fry vegetable of your choice or pickle.

SERVES 4 – 6

Ingredients

Wheat flour	2 cups
Salt	a pinch
Vegetable oil or *ghee*	¼ cup
Water (and juices squeezed out of the vegetable stuffing) to make the dough	1 cup
Grated daikon radish	1 cup
Coriander leaves chopped	1 Tbs
Green chilies finely chopped	1 tsp
Ginger finely chopped	1 tsp
Garlic finely chopped	1 tsp
Carom seeds (*Ajwain*)	½ tsp
Salt	1 tsp
Coriander powder	1 tsp
Garam masala	½ tsp
Lemon juice (optional)	1 Tbs
Red pepper	½ tsp

The Exquisite World of Indian Cuisine

Griddle Fried Stuffed Cauliflower Bread
Gobhi ke Paranthe

PUNJAB

A complete meal in itself, cauliflower stuffed bread is served for breakfast in India. This is yet another yummy *parantha* from the state of Punjab.

SERVES 4 – 6

METHOD

1. Grate cauliflower and add onions, ginger, garlic, green chilies, green coriander and all the spices. Squeeze out all the juices and set it aside. The stuffing is ready.

2. Follow the recipe for making the dough similar to *chappati* dough. Instead of water use the mixture of squeezed juices and water. Knead to make a pliable dough. Cover and set it aside.

3. Take a piece of dough and make balls as big as a plum and roll each ball on a smooth flat surface using a rolling pin. You can use a slab of marble, fine smooth wooden chopping board or a traditional *chappati* making circular slab (available at an Indian grocery store). Dab the rolling surface first with dry flour and then roll the dough ball into a round, about 4 inches in diameter by using more dry flour.

4. Put about 2 Tbs of the stuffing in the center of the round – fold the edges of the round over the stuffing and pinch them together making sure stuffing is completely covered with the dough from all sides. It is now a round patty with a diameter of 2–3 inches. Roll it gently in circular motion with a rolling pin using dry flour, turning it into a round circle of about 6–7 inches. Ensure that no stuffing protrudes out of the rolled dough.

5. Heat a 12–14 inch skillet or *tawa* and transfer the stuffed rolled dough on to it. When the underside is a little crisp and shows some brown spots, turn it over. Coat it with *ghee* or vegetable oil. Turn it over again and coat this side also with the *ghee* or oil. Keep turning and frying until golden brown. Serve immediately with plain yogurt, *raita*, pickle or butter.

Ingredients

Flour	2 cups
Salt	a pinch
Vegetable oil or *ghee*	¼ cup
Use juices squeezed out of the vegetable stuffing+water for making the dough)	1 cup
Cauliflower florets grated	1 cup
Onions finely chopped	2 Tbs
Coriander leaves chopped	1 Tbs
Green chilies finely chopped	1 tsp
Salt	1 tsp
Coriander seeds crushed or powdered	1 tsp
Garam masala	½ tsp
Lemon juice (optional)	1 Tbs
Red pepper	½ tsp
Ginger finely chopped	1 tsp
Garlic finely chopped	1 tsp

Griddle Fried Tricolor Bread
Tiranga Parantha

A superb lunch time treat.

SERVES 4 – 6

METHOD

1. Grate the radishes and carrots, and mix the chopped fenugreek leaves. Add chopped onions, ginger, garlic, green chilies, green coriander leaves. (Squeeze all the juices out and save the juices in a bowl.) Add all the spices. Mix, and the stuffing is ready.
2. Follow the recipe for making the dough similar to *chappati* dough. Except for water use the mixture of squeezed juices plus water, knead to make a pliable dough. Butter the dough, cover it and set it aside.
3. Take pieces of dough and make balls as big as a plum and roll each ball on a smooth flat surface using a rolling pin. You can use a slab of marble, fine smooth wooden chopping board or a traditional *chappati* making circular slab (available at an Indian grocery store). Dab the rolling surface first with dry flour and then roll the dough ball into a round about 4 inches in diameter by using more dry flour.
4. Put about 2 Tbs of the stuffing in the center of the round and fold the edges of the round over the stuffing – pinch them together making sure stuffing is completely covered with the dough from all sides. It is now a round patty with a diameter of 2–3 inches. Roll it gently in circular motion with a rolling pin using dry flour, turning it into a round disc of about 6–7 inches. Ensure that no stuffing protrudes out of the rolled dough.
5. Heat a 12–14 inch skillet or *tawa* and transfer the rolled dough on to it. When the underside is a little crisp and shows some brown spots, turn it over. Coat it with *ghee* or vegetable oil. Turn it over again and coat this side also with the *ghee* or vegetable oil. Keep turning and frying until golden brown. Serve immediately with plain yogurt, *raita*, pickle or butter.

Ingredients

Flour	2 cups
Salt	a pinch
Vegetable oil or *ghee* for frying the *paranthas*	¼ cup
Water (juices squeezed out of the vegetable stuffing plus water) Or	1 cup
Combined grated radishes, carrots, and fenugreek leaves squeezed	1 cup
Onions finely chopped	2 Tbs
Ginger finely chopped	1 tsp
Garlic finely chopped	1 tsp
Green chilies finely chopped	1 tsp
Coriander leaves chopped	1 Tbs
Coriander seeds crushed or powdered	1 tsp
Garam masala	½ tsp
Lemon juice	1 Tbs
Red pepper	½ tsp

The Exquisite World of Indian Cuisine

Griddle Fried Stuffed Meat Bread
Shaphale (Meat Parantha)

TIBET

A superb lunch time treat, stuffed meat *parantha* is called *Sha* (bread) *phale* (filling) in Tibet. They are mostly served in Tibet by the roadside vendors and make a complete meal by themselves. Several different stuffings of ground beef, chicken, yak meat or pork can be used.

METHOD

1. Pan-fry the ground beef, drain the fat and set the beef aside.
2. Follow the recipe for making the dough similar to *chappati* dough. Butter the dough, cover it and set aside.
3. Cook the onions in one tablespoon of oil until light brown and add the ginger, garlic and green chilies. Stir and cook for 2 minutes. Add the coriander powder, fresh chopped coriander leaves, red pepper, *garam masala*, salt, and gram flour mixed in the lemon juice. Mix well and add the drained beef. Cook for 10 minutes on low heat stirring to prevent any sticking. Set it aside.
4. Take a piece of dough and make balls slightly bigger than a golf ball and roll each ball on a smooth flat surface using a rolling pin. You can use a slab of marble, fine smooth wooden chopping board or a traditional *chappati* making circular slab called *chakla* (available at an Indian grocery store). Dab the rolling surface first with dry flour and then roll the dough ball into a round about 4 inches in diameter by using more dry flour.
5. Put about 2-3 Tbs of the stuffing in the center of the round and fold the edges of the round over the stuffing and pinch them together making sure stuffing is completely covered with the dough from all sides. It is now a round patty with a diameter of 2–3 inches. Roll it gently in circular motion with a rolling pin using dry flour, making it into a round disc of about 6–7 inches. Ensure that no stuffing protrudes out of the rolled dough.
6. Heat a 12–4 inch skillet or *tawa* and transfer the rolled dough on to it. When the underside is a little crisp and shows some brown spots, turn it over. Coat it with *ghee* or vegetable oil. Turn it over again and coat this side also with the *ghee* or oil. Keep turning and frying until golden brown. Serve immediately with plain yogurt, *raita*, pickle or butter. *Paranthas* are a very popular breakfast item in Indian cuisine.

SERVES 4 – 6

Ingredients

Flour	2 cup
Salt	a pinch
Vegetable oil or *ghee*	1–2 Tbs
Water	1 cup
Lean ground beef*	½ lb
Onions finely chopped	¼ tsp
Green chilies finely chopped	1 tsp
Ginger finely chopped	1 Tbs
Garlic finely chopped	1 Tbs
Gram flour	1½ Tbs
Salt	1 tsp
Dried coriander seeds crushed or powder	1 tsp
Garam masala	1 tsp
Lemon juice	2 Tbs
Red pepper	1 tsp
Coriander leaves chopped	1 Tbs
Ghee or oil (for frying *paranthas*)	¼ cup

*Instead of the beef, minced chicken or turkey can also be used.

Griddle Fried Rice Flour & Coconut Crepes
Appam

KERALA

Another speciality from Kerala. These spongy pancakes are made with fermented rice flour and *urad dal* flour slightly sweetened with sugar and finely grated coconut and coconut milk. They are also called Hoppers. Serve with potato curry or other curries. They soak up gravies and sweetness of the coconut and the slightly sour taste of their curries make them very delicious and unique.

METHOD

1. Soak the *dal* overnight in a bowl full of water. Grind the coconut fine in a blender. Set it aside in the refrigerator.
2. Next morning drain the water from the soaked *dal* and grind it fine in a blender with salt and sugar. Mix with the rice flour and water to make a batter. Whisk well, cover it with a cloth and let it ferment. Leave it in a warm place. It usually takes about 8 hours to rise well.
3. Just before cooking add the ground coconut, coconut milk and stir well. If the batter is too thick, add some water to maintain a creamy consistency.
4. *Appam* is cooked in a wok-like pan in India which is deeper, and pointed in the center to give it a thicker center. But, *appam* can also be cooked in a 10–12 inch thick nonstick skillet.
5. Heat and oil the skillet and pour about $\frac{1}{3}$ cup of the thin batter over the skillet to form a pancake about 7–8 inches in diameter. Lift and tilt the pan so the batter spreads thin around the edges and kind of thick in the middle. No need to turn over and let it cook until the edges are light brown and the center is cooked.
6. Run the spatula around the edges to transfer the *appam* over to the serving dish and serve it with your favorite potato curry. It is really creamy, spongy and delicious.
7. Serve as a meal.

SERVES 4 – 6

Ingredients

Rice flour	1½ cups
Sugar	3 Tbs
Urad dal	½ cup
Fresh coconut finely grated	½ cup
Canned coconut milk	1½ cups
Salt	½ tsp
Water	3 cups
Oil (for making *appams*)	¼ cup

Note: A faster way to cook *appam*:
Cook ¼ cup of cream of rice in ¾ of water until it thickens. Combine this with 2 tsp of yeast dissolved in 1 Tbs of lukewarm water and mix. Use this mixture instead of ground *urad dal* in Step 2 (above), add the rice flour and use the remaining water to make the batter. Follow Steps 3–7 to make *appams*. These *appams* are crisper and as delicious.

The Exquisite World of Indian Cuisine

Cream of Wheat Crepes
Rava Dosa

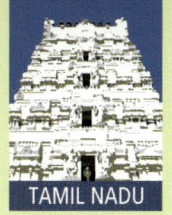
TAMIL NADU

These thin cream of wheat pancakes from south India are among my favorites. Garnished with fresh green peppers, onions, coriander leaves, *ghee*, fresh cumin, red pepper and salt, they really get the appetite going. The smell of fresh spices makes them a favorite of everyone and they are quick to fix too. Serve them with a *chutney* and *sambhar*. Taste best when made fresh.

SERVES 4 – 6

Ingredients

Cream of wheat (at the Indian grocer known as *Rava*)	1 1/3 cups
Rice flour (from local Indian grocer)	2–3 cup
All purpose flour	½ cup
Water	3 cups
Yogurt	1 cup
Cumin seeds	1½ tsp
Urad dal	1 Tbs
Asafoetida	1/8 tsp
Salt	to taste
Coriander powder	1 tsp
Red pepper	½ tsp
Green and red bell pepper finely chopped	1 cup
Green onions finely chopped	1 cup
Garlic chopped	1 tsp
Green chilies chopped	1 tsp
Green coriander finely chopped	1 Tbs
Vegetable oil or *ghee* (for making *dosa*)	4 Tbs

METHOD

1. Mix the cream of wheat, rice flour, and all-purpose flour in a deep mixing bowl and add the yogurt, 1 Tbs of the oil and water.

2. Beat as smooth as possible with a fork. Set it aside for the cream of wheat to soften.

3. Take a thick bottom skillet and add 3 Tbs of oil and heat it. Add the bell pepper, garlic, green chilies and green onions in to the oil, and fry them about 2–3 minutes. Move them to one side and add the cumin seeds, *urad dal* and wait till they pop. Then, add the red pepper, coriander powder, asafoetida, salt and cook the spices as they change color. Add the mixture to the cream of wheat batter and stir it in the batter evenly. Add the chopped green coriander and mix it in.

4. Wipe the skillet clean and heat it. Coat the surface with a thin film of oil and pour a ladle full of the batter and spread it evenly by tilting the skillet back and forth. Cook until the underside is light brown, adding more oil if needed (for about 2 minutes) and turn it over with a turner. Cook the other side also for as long as it takes to get it cooked. Remove with a turner from the skillet on to a plate and serve warm with coconut *chutney* or eggplant *chutney* or *channa dal chutney*, or plain yogurt.

5. Serve them warm, as they are cooking, for breakfast, lunch or dinner.

Ground Rice Crepes
Plain Dosa

South Indian crepes made from the fermented batter of rice and *urad dal*. They are mostly wrapped around potato stir-fry and served with coconut *chutney* and *sambhar*. Excellent for breakfast, lunch, afternoon snack or dinner.

METHOD

For the *Dosa* batter:
1. Soak the rice in 2 cups of water. Separately soak *urad dal* with fenugreek seeds in ¾ cup of water overnight. Grind the rice and the *dal* along with the soaked water into a smooth paste separately.
2. Mix them together, add the salt and sugar. Stir well and leave it to rise, covered in a warm place overnight.

For Stuffing:
1. Boil, peel and chop the potatoes and set them aside.
2. Heat the oil and add *urad dal*, *channa dal*, mustard seeds, cumin seeds, asafoetida and the curry leaves.
3. Add the onions, ginger, garlic, green chilies and fry till the onions, are light brown and then add the rest of the seasonings, salt, coconut powder, turmeric powder, red pepper, coriander powder and stir to mix.
4. Now, add the chopped potatoes, water and mix well. Let it simmer until the mixture is well blended. Set aside.

SERVES 4 – 6

Ingredients

For *dosa* batter:

Long grain rice	2 cup
Urad dal	1 cup
Fenugreek seeds	1 tsp
Salt	1 tsp
Sugar	½ tsp
Oil for cooking the *dosa*	¼ cup
Cream of wheat (optional)	1 Tbs
Channa dal	2 Tbs
Baking soda (optional)	a pinch

For the stuffing:

Potatoes (boiled chopped)	1½ lb
Onion	½ cup
Ginger	1 Tbs
Garlic	1 Tbs
Green chilies	1 tsp
Urad dal	1½ tsp
Asafoetida	⅛ tsp
Channa dal	1½ tsp
Red pepper	½ tsp
Cumin seeds	1 tsp

TAMIL NADU

Cooking *Dosa*:

1. Beat the *dosa* mixture with hand and add the cream of wheat and baking soda. If the mixture is thick add a little water – the mixture should be of pouring consistency. Keep a heavy large frying pan or *dosa* making skillet on moderate heat and wait till it is hot. Smear the pan with a little oil or *ghee* and pour a ladle full of the batter and spread it thin starting in a circular motion from center outwards and cover the pan. The spread should be very thin and of even consistency. The *dosa* can be made large 8–10 inch or small, 6–8 inch in diameter. Usually it is served in restaurants paper thin and of larger size. Cover the *dosa*, with a lid.

2. Remove the lid in two minutes and overturn the *dosa*. Cook for a few more minutes and remove from fire. In the center of the *dosa* put a couple of tablespoons of the potatoes mixture (depending on the size) and fold over.

3. Serve with *sambhar* and coconut *chutney*.

Vegetable oil	2-3 Tbs
Turmeric powder	¾ tsp
Coconut powder	½ cup
Mustard seeds	1 tsp
Curry leaves	2–3
Water	1 cup
Oil or *ghee* as needed	2–3 Tbs
Coriander powder	1 Tbs
Salt	1 tsp

HINT

Sometimes ½ cup of cooked rice is added while grinding the dough or batter to make better *dosa*. *Dosa* making skillet can be bought at your local Indian grocery store.

Note: Making *dosa* from fermented batter can be rather cumbersome and tricky. Here is an easy recipe for making *dosa* without any fermentation.

Rice flour	1 cup	All purpose flour	2 Tbs	Cream of wheat	½ cup
Yogurt	½ cup	Water	2 cups	Salt	1¼ tsp

Mix together rice flour, all purpose flour, cream of wheat, yogurt and 2 cups water to make a thin batter, add more water, if required. Let it sit for a couple of hours. Make *dosas* the same way as mentioned above. Enjoy them with *sambhar* and with potato.

Griddle Fried Cheese and Legume Stuffed Bread
Paneer aur Dal ke Paranthe

Cooked *dal* and crumbled *paneer* (or ricotta cheese – completely drained of water) flavored with spices, is used as a filling to stuff the regular *chappati* dough in making these *paranthas*. These are nutritious and wholesome and make a very good meal or a finger food for children.

METHOD

Make the flour dough as described in the recipe for *chappati*.

Filling:

1. Heat 2 cups of water in a pressure cooker and transfer the washed *dal* into it.
2. Add salt, turmeric powder, coriander powder, ginger, onion, black pepper, red pepper and *garam masala*.
3. Cook until all the water is absorbed. Cool and set it aside. Add more water to cook, if needed.
4. Add 2 Tbs oil to the *dal* and stir it well. Mix it into *paneer*, add the chopped coriander leaves and mix well. Set aside.

Rolling:

5. Roll a piece of dough as big as a plum on a floured rolling surface into a 3 inch diameter circle. Place 2 Tbs of the filling in the center of the rolled circle. Lift the edges of the circle and pinch them together to seal the filling inside the dough and make a ball. Lift the ball, flatten it a little and roll it on the floured board into a disc 5–6 inch in diameter and transfer it to the heated iron skillet (*tawa*) or a heavy-bottom non-stick pan. Keep the heat at medium-high.
6. Cook until the *parantha* is firm enough to turn. Once turned, smear it with ½ tsp of *ghee* or oil on the cooked side and turn it over. Do the same on the other side.
7. Cook both sides by turning the *parantha* till it turns light brown. Remove from the fry pan and serve hot.
8. Serve it with plain yogurt or *raita*. If you prefer, you can also serve it with a vegetable stir-fry of your choice.

*Omit red pepper if you are making this bread for children. Use ricotta cheese drained of water if *paneer* is not available.

SERVES 4 – 6

Ingredients

Dough:

Chappati flour (Indian grocer)	2 cups
Water to make the dough	1 cup + 1 Tbs

Filling:

Paneer (or ricotta cheese completely drained of water) crumbled	1 cup
Masoor or *toor dal* washed	¼ cup
Water	2 cups
Onions chopped	1 Tbs
Ginger chopped	1 tsp
Turmeric powder	½ tsp
Salt	½ tsp
Coriander powder	½ tsp
Black pepper	¼ tsp
Red pepper*	¼ tsp
Garam masala	½ tsp
Vegetable oil or *ghee*	¼ cup
Coriander freshly chopped	2 Tbs
Dry flour to roll the *parantha*	¼ cup

The Exquisite World of Indian Cuisine

Steamed Ground-Rice Cakes
Idli

KARNATAKA

These are tender steamed rice cakes that are served for breakfast, lunch or dinner and go best with coconut *chutney* and *sambhar*. This speciality from south India is popular everywhere in India and abroad.

SERVES 6 – 8

Ingredients

Rice long grain	4 cups
Urad dal	1 cup
Cooked rice	1 cup
Salt	4 tsp
Water as needed	
Vegetable oil or *ghee* as needed	

METHOD

1. Soak the rice and *urad dal* in separate containers for 6–8 hours.
2. Grind the rice by adding a little water in an electric blender and add the cooked rice while grinding to make a creamy but grainy batter. Set aside.
3. Grind the *urad dal* to a creamy mixture. Mix the two batters and add the salt and let it stand to ferment overnight in a warm place.
4. The following morning the batter would rise. Press down the dough with a spatula and beat it smooth with an eggbeater or your hand. It should have the consistency of a pancake batter.
5. Prepare the *idli* maker to make the *Idlis*. It is a special kind of steamer pot with inserts. Each of these inserts or plates has depressions to put *idli* batter. These plates get fitted into their respective slots in this pot, layered over one another, with enough room for the steam to go around them to cook the *idli*.
6. Remove the empty plates from the pot and pour water into the pot to fill only enough to stay 1 inch below the surface of the lowest plate. Grease the circles in the insert plates with oil and pour the batter into the circles making sure the circles are only two-third full. After filling the circles with the batter put the plate inserts back carefully into the steam pot layering them over one another. Cover the pot with the lid. Turn the heat on and start boiling the water. It takes about 8–10 minutes for the *idlis* to cook once the water starts to boil. Keep the heat low.
7. Remove the cover and check the *idlis*. Stick a toothpick in the middle of the *idli* and if it comes out clean that means it is done. Take the plate inserts out of the pot very carefully. Gently take out the *idlis* from the circles with a spatula. Serve them hot with *sambhar* and coconut *chutney, channa dal chutney* or peanut *chutney*.

HINT

Fresh *idli* batter and *Idli* mixes are also available at your local Indian grocery stores. They are a very good way to fix *Idlis* quickly. Follow the instructions on the package carefully and enjoy the *idlis*. If you want to save yourself a trip to the store and fix *idli* quickly at home here is a recipe: Cook 1 cup of cream of wheat in a Tbs of oil until light brown, cool and mix with ¼ tsp each of salt and baking soda and 1½ cup of yogurt and if the mixture is too thick, add 2–4 Tbs of water. Use this mix to make *idlis* in an *Idli* maker. This is an another way to cut down all the cumbersome work needed in preparing the batter by grinding and fermenting.

Rice and Lentils Crepes
Aadai

These rice pancakes are made with a batter of ground soaked lentils, rice and spices. A refreshing and nutritious pancake served with stir-fried potato curry, peanut or red pepper *chutney*. It can also be served for lunch with a little salad and pickles or *raita*.

METHOD

1. Wash and soak *toor dal*, *mung* beans, *urad dal*, split peas, rice, red peppers and cumin seeds in water for atleast 3–4 hours.
2. Drain the water and grind them in a blender coarsely to a consistency of pancake batter by adding 2 cups of water as needed and grind the batter to a desired consistency. Add more water, if necessary.
3. Add salt, fennel seeds, green chilies, ginger, garlic, grated coconut or dry coconut powder, asafoetida powder, fresh cilantro and onions, and mix well.
4. Heat a nonstick *tawa* (Indian skillet) or a thick bottom 12 inch skillet or a skillet to make *dosa* and cover it with 1 tsp of oil. Drain the excess oil and pour a ladle full of batter spreading thin by going in circular motion, starting from the center on the hot surface of the skillet. Spread about 6–8 inch in diameter or larger, keeping the heat on medium-low. As the batter is browning on one side brush the top side with cooking oil. It takes a couple of minutes. Cover and let it cook until the underside is light brown. Turn it and cook the other side until the batter is lightly brown and crisp.
5. Serve it hot with red pepper *chutney* or peanut *chutney* just like *dosa*. Boiled potatoes, onions stir-fry and *sambhar* can also be served along with the *chutney*.

SERVES 4 – 5

Ingredients

Urad dal	⅓ cup
Toor dal	⅓ cup
Mung beans split (washed or unwashed)	⅓ cup
Split peas yellow or green	⅓ cup
Basmati rice	⅔ cup
Red dried peppers broken in pieces	2
Cumin seeds	½ tsp
Green Serrano chilies finely chopped	½ tsp
Fresh cilantro chopped	⅓ cup
Shallots or yellow onions finely chopped	⅓ cup
Fresh ginger finely chopped	½ tsp
Oil as needed	
Water to grind the mixture of lentils and rice	2 cups
Fennel seeds (optional)	1 tsp
Fresh grated coconut	½ cup
Or	
Dry coconut powder	¼ cup
Salt	½ tsp
Asafoetida powder	⅓ tsp
Ginger chopped	1 Tbs
Garlic chopped	1 Tbs

The Exquisite World of Indian Cuisine

Crisp Fried Pastries
Khasta Kachauri

Deep-fried leavened bread stuffed with spiced ground lentils make a great snack and can also be served for breakfast. These go well with a potato curry or *raita*. They are delicious and crisp especially when served hot. An alltime favorite for breakfast mostly in the northern parts of India. Excellent snack any time.

METHOD

1. Make smooth and tight dough by kneading together flour, baking powder, *ghee*, salt and about ½ cup of water. Add more water, if necessary. Cover with wet cloth and set it aside.

Filling:

2. Heat the oil in a deep saucepan and add the ginger, chopped chilies and fry them. Then add the cumin seeds, fennel seeds, coriander seeds and coriander powder, and wail till they all crackle. Now add the asafoetida powder – wait till it sizzles and then add the ground *dal*, salt, red pepper, black pepper and gram flour. Mix and fry for few minutes until the flour and *dal* start turning slightly brown. Simmer with 1½ cups of water until the *dal* is softened but is not mushy (about 10–15 minutes) on medium heat. Add more water, if needed necessary. *Urad dal* will take a little longer to cook and may require more water to soften. Make sure that the water is completely gone and the *dal* is dry enough to be used as a filling. Set it aside.

3. Divide the dough into 16 equal parts and roll each into a 2½ inch disc. Put 1 tsp of the filling in the center and bring the sides of the circle over the filling and seal firm. Roll them a little with a rolling pin and set them aside covered with a wet paper towel.

4. Heat the oil at about 300°F in a deep wok. Keep the temperature steady ground 300°F only and fry them few at a time, making sure the seam side of the *kachauri* is down. Fry until golden brown. Slow frying is very necessary to make them crisp and cooked inside. It take a few minutes to get that result. Take them out with a slotted spoon and drain them on a paper towel. Serve them with potato curry or *raita*.

SERVES 4 – 6

Ingredients

All purpose flour	2 cups
Clarified butter to make the dough	2 Tbs
Water	½ cup
Salt	1 tsp
Baking powder	a pinch

Filling ingredients

Mung or *urad dal* soaked overnight and coarsely ground	½ cup
Oil for making the filling	2 Tbs
Cumin seeds	1 tsp
Asafoetida	¼ tsp
Ginger	1 tsp
Green chilies chopped	1 Tbs
Ajwain	½ tsp
Black pepper	½ tsp
Red pepper	1 tsp
Salt	1 tsp
Amchoor	1 Tbs
Fennel seeds crushed	½ tsp
Gram flour	2 Tbs
Water	½–1 cup
Coriander powder	1 tsp
Coriander seeds crushed	½ tsp
Oil for frying	

The national bird of India, the majestic and colorful peacock

Crisp Potato Pastries
Aalu ki Kachauri

Spiced potato filled deep fried pastries shaped like *pooris* are crisp and crunchy. They sometimes are served instead of a *poori* at a festive occasion with a meal. *Kachauris is* also make a popular breakfast accompaniment and a teatime snack in north India.

SERVES 4 – 6

METHOD

1. Mix together the flour, 1 tsp salt, baking powder and 3 Tbs of butter in a bowl and blend. Add water and knead to make smooth dough but not very soft and set it aside.
2. Cook the ginger and green chilies in 2 Tbs of oil for two minutes and add the cumin seeds and sauté till they start to pop.
3. Add turmeric powder, ground fennel seeds, salt, coriander powder, lemon juice, red pepper, *garam masala* and chopped green coriander.
4. Add the mashed potatoes and mix well. Remove from heat and cool.
5. Divide the dough into 18 equal parts and roll each piece into 3 inch rounds. Place about 1 Tbs of the filling in the center of each one of them and bring the sides up and seal the seams completely and roll them twice gently with a rolling pin. Cover the *kachauris* with a plastic wrap and set them aside.
6. Heat the oil in a wok to 300°F-350°F and fry the *kachauris,* few at a time until light golden and crisp. Do not overheat the oil because *kachauris* need slow browning and cooking.
7. Remove from oil and drain them on a paper towel. Serve them with mint or tamarind *chutney*. They make a great teatime snack. These can also be served as bread with a curry, rice and a salad.

Ingredients

Potatoes boiled, chopped and mashed	1½ cup
All purpose flour	2 cup
Salt	2 tsp
Ghee or clarified butter	5 Tbs
Baking powder	a pinch
Ginger chopped	1 Tbs
Green chilies chopped	1 Tbs
Red pepper	½ tsp
Coriander powder	1 tsp
Lemon juice	1 Tbs
Cumin seeds	1 tsp
Fennel seeds ground	1 tsp
Turmeric powder	½ tsp
Salt as needed	
Green coriander chopped	1 Tbs
Water	½ cup
Garam masala	1 tsp
Vegetable oil (for frying)	4 cups

Note: Boiled potatoes can be substituted by boiled peas.

Griddle Millet Flour Bread
Thepla

GUJARAT

Millet is very nutritious and one of the oldest grains known in India. It is widely used in northern India and Gujarat for making griddle breads. Below is a recipe of a pan-fried millet flour bread (*thepla*) from the state of Gujarat. They make a good snack too and can be served with any meat curry or a vegetable curry.

SERVES 4 – 6

Ingredients

Millet flour	1 cup
Wheat flour	1 cup
Yogurt	1 cup
Dry fenugreek leaves	2 Tbs
Or	
Fresh fenugreek leaves chopped	1 cup
Fresh or frozen Spinach leaves chopped	1 cup
Ginger chopped	1 tsp
Garlic chopped	1 tsp
Turmeric powder	½ tsp
Cumin and coriander powder	1 tsp
Sesame seeds	2 Tbs
Melted *ghee* or oil	4 Tbs
Salt	1 tsp
Green chilies chopped	1 tsp
Green coriander chopped	1 Tbs
Oil to fry the bread in the pan	¼ cup
Extra flour to roll the bread	

METHOD

1. Transfer the wheat and the millet flour into a large-deep bowl. Add chopped green chilies, chopped ginger, chopped garlic, salt, fenugreek (*methi*) leaves, chopped spinach leaves, *ghee*, turmeric, *dhania* (coriander) powder, sesame seeds, chopped green coriander leaves and mix well. Add yogurt and knead the flour into pliable dough. Add more yogurt, if needed, and slowly knead the dough until it starts to hold together and to separate itself from the sides of the pan.

2. Dust wheat flour lightly on any smooth surface used for rolling the bread and roll 5–6 inch diameter discs about 2–4 mm thick.

3. Heat a thick bottom skillet, at least 8–10 inches wide, or an Indian griddle (*tawa*) and transfer the rolled bread onto it. Cook until the underside shows light brown spots (about 1–2 minutes). Turn it over and apply the oil on the cooked side. Turn it over again and cook this side also with oil similarly. Keep turning until both sides get cooked and turn light brown. Remove from the skillet and serve them hot. They can be stored wrapped in tin foil airtight for a few hours at room temperature. Reheat them before serving.

The Exquisite World of Indian Cuisine

Griddle Sorghum Flour Bread
Jowar ki Roti

RAJASTHAN

Sorghum is widely grown in the U.S. but is not used for making any kind of bread. It is very nutritious. A very delicious griddle bread or *parantha* is prepared from it in the state of Rajasthan and is served with butter. The flour is available at your local Indian grocery store.

SERVES 4 – 6

Ingredients

Sorghum flour	2 cups
Salt	to taste
Onions chopped	2 Tbs
Ginger chopped	1 Tbs
Green chilies chopped	1 Tbs
Melted butter or *ghee* (optional) Or	1 Tbs
Vegetable oil	1 Tbs
Red pepper	½ tsp
Coriander leaves chopped	2 Tbs
Ghee or butter for brushing	⅓ cup
Water for kneading the bread	1 cup
Ghee or oil for brushing the bread, as needed	

METHOD

1. In a blender, blend together chopped onions, ginger, green chilies and coriander leaves, and set them aside.

2. Transfer flour, the above blended mixture, 1 Tbs of *ghee* or butter, salt, and red pepper in to a large bowl, and mix in the water. Knead the dough. Add more water, if needed, to make pliable dough until it starts to hold together and separates from the pan.

3. Break piece of dough as big as a plum. Due to the low protein content of the dough it is not easy to roll it into a flat bread because the dough does not hold together. Therefore pat the lemon size ball of dough between your hands in to about 3–4 inch discs. These should not be very thick. Roll them, if you can manage to roll on a floured board or rolling surface, and lift the bread from the surface with the help of a spatula.

4. Transfer the rolled or patted bread onto a hot iron skillet (*tawa*) or thick-bottom 8 inch non-stick pan. When brown spots start to appear on the underside turn it over. Cook the other side also. The bread can be fried like a *parantha* or can be cooked like a *chappati*. See recipe for *chappati*.

5. Serve it with your favorite vegetable curry or meat curry.

Colorfully decorated camels await tourists for a safari in the Thar desert at Jaisalmer, Rajasthan

Griddle Gram Flour Bread
Missi Roti

The most proteinaceous of breads. It is highly recommended for diabetic people. It is rich in essential proteins and nutrients. Serve it plain or flavor it with fenugreek leaves and spices and cook like *parantha*. Either way it is wholesome and good.

SERVES 4 – 6

Ingredients

Gram flour (available at your local Indian grocery store)	1 cup
Chappati flour	1 cup
Water	1 cup
Ghee or oil	1 Tbs
Salt	¾ tsp
Red pepper	½ tsp
Ghee or oil for brushing the bread as needed	

METHOD

1. Mix flours, salt, red pepper, and *ghee* together in a deep mixing bowl, and slowly pour water into the ingredients to mix and knead into a pliable dough. Add more than 1 cup water, if needed.

2. When the dough starts to hold together and separates from the pan then cover it and set it aside.

3. Break a piece of dough as large as a lemon and roll with a rolling pin on a floured smooth surface into 5–6 inch diameter discs, about 2–4 mm thick.

4. Transfer the discs one by one onto a hot iron skillet (*tawa*) or a heavy-bottom non-stick pan and follow the recipe for *chappati*. Brush with *ghee* or oil.

5. Serve it plain with just a *raita* and salad as a light lunch or as a bread with a regular meal.

Note: Follow the recipe for plain *paranthas* if you want to make *paranthas*.

Persian Bread
Taftan

This all purpose flour bread garnished with melon seeds, coriander leaves and butter, is delicious. Try it – you will relish it.

METHOD

1. Sift the flour into a deep bowl with the salt.
2. Heat the milk slightly and add the sugar and add yeast and saffron into it. Mix it and set aside. Make a well in the center of the flour and add the baking powder, milk mixture, *ghee* and yogurt into it. Mix together and start to knead the flour into a soft pliable dough with the help of more milk, if needed. Cover it and set it aside overnight or till the dough has doubled.
3. Dust lightly a rolling board. Make 6 pieces of the dough. Make the balls and let them rise again for another 15–20 minutes in a covered bowl. Roll each ball to 5–6 inches diameter and about ¼ inch in thickness. Sprinkle with coriander leaves and sesame seeds. Give it an oblong shape if you wish.
4. Heat the oven at broil and place a pizza stone on the top rack to heat. Once the stone is hot transfer the rolled bread on to it. The bread can be cooked on a greased cookie sheet also.
5. As soon as brown spots start to appear on the underside turn it over and bake for another minute or two till the bread is done. Remove from the oven with tongs and serve hot topped with melted butter. Goes well with any meat or vegetable curry.

SERVES 4 – 6

Ingredients

All purpose flour	2 cups
Salt	to taste
Sugar	1 Tbs
Yeast	1 tsp
Baking powder	1 tsp
Clarified butter or *ghee*	2 Tbs
Yogurt	¼ cup
Milk as needed or	¼ cup
Few sprigs of saffron dissolved in the milk	
Coriander leaves chopped	2 tsp
Sesame seeds or poppy seeds Or melon seeds (available only at your local Indian grocery)	1 Tbs

Note: Use a regular kitchen *tandoor* if you like. These *tandoors* are available in India in some appliance stores. In western countries your local Indian grocery store may carry them. Rice flour can also be used instead of all purpose flour, in which case increase the quantity of butter to 1 cup.

Griddle Fried Corn Flour Bread
Makki ki Roti

This bread goes specifically with mustard greens (*saag*) and is a popular bread of Punjab. Hot corn bread topped with butter is delicious with any curry.

SERVES 4 – 6

METHOD

1. Transfer the flour into a bowl. Make a depression in the middle and add 1-2 Tbs of *ghee* and water into it. Mix in the water with clean hands and knead to make a pliable dough so it can be rolled into *chappati* or Tortilla shapes.

2. Take pieces of dough slightly bigger than a plum and roll them into 3 inch diameter discs with a rolling pin on a flat rolling stone or a board (*chakla*) or any clean flat surface.

3. Heat a *tawa* or heavy-bottom iron skillet. Sometimes the bread starts to fall apart while transferring. In that case use a large spatula to transfer the rolled bread onto the *tawa* and cook on medium heat till light brown spots appear on the underside of the bread. Turn it over and cook for a few minutes until this side also has light brown spots. Remove the bread from the skillet or *tawa* and holding with tongs put it directly on the flame that is covered with a little grill or a frame to hold the pots and pans. Leave it on the flame for a few seconds till it gets lightly roasted on both sides. Serve it hot topped with butter or *ghee*. It is mostly served with mustard greens preparation but can be served with any other curry of your choice. It is very delicious.

Ingredients

- Fine ground corn tortillas flour — 2 cups
- warm water to make the dough
- Butter or melted *ghee* — ¼ cup
  (for brushing the bread before serving)
- Dry flour for rolling

Note: If corn meal is being used then mix 2 cups of it with ½ cup wheat flour and add boiling water to the mixture. Stir it with a large spoon and as soon as it is cool enough to handle, knead it into a dough. Wet your hands slightly and make 8–10 equal parts and pat each part into 4–5 inch diameter discs and lay them down on a piece of plastic wrap. Heat the griddle and transfer each disc onto the hot griddle and wait till brown spots start to appear on the underside. Turn it over the disc and cook until brown spots appear on this side too. Cook the disc on direct flame. Follow and refer to the recipe of *chappati* making for this particular step. Enjoy with a dab of butter with mustard greens (*saag*).

The Exquisite World of Indian Cuisine

Griddle Fried Gram Flour Pancakes
Besan ke Pudey (Cheela)

Gram flour pancakes are made with batter of gram flour flavored with *ajwain*, shallots, coriander leaves, ginger and green chilies. They are served with *raita* or pickle and usually go very well for lunch.

METHOD

1. Mix together gram flour and millet flour in a deep mixing bowl and add 2 Tbs of *ghee*.

2. Add the onion seeds, carom seeds, cumin seeds, salt, red pepper, onions, garlic, green chilies, chopped ginger, coriander powder, *garam masala*, fenugreek leaves and chopped coriander leaves to the flour and mix the ingredients well into the flour. Add the chopped tomatoes.

3. Add the water slowly to make a batter as thick as pancake batter. Heat a skillet or an iron skillet of at least 10–12 inch diameter and coat it with ½ tsp of oil or *ghee*. Lower the heat and pour a ladle full of batter and spread it thin (as thin as possible) with the help of spatula or your hand. Spread a thin film of *ghee* on top of the pancake. As soon as the underside of the pancake gets light brown (1–2 minutes) turn the pancake over and smear this side also with *ghee*. Cook for ½–1 minute until both sides are ready. Remove from the skillet and serve it hot with a pickle or *raita* of your choice.

4. Serve them for a light lunch or a snack at teatime.

SERVES 2 – 4

Ingredients

Gram flour	1 cup
Millet flour	½ cup
Vegetable oil or *ghee*	2 Tbs
Cumin seeds	1 tsp
Onion seeds	1 tsp
Carom seeds	1 tsp
Water	¾–1 cup
Salt	1 tsp
Red pepper	½ tsp
Fenugreek leaves freshly chopped	1 cup
Or fenugreek leaves (dry)	2 Tbs
Onions or shallots chopped	2 Tbs
Green chilies chopped	1 Tbs
Green coriander leaves chopped	2 Tbs
Garlic chopped	1 tsp
Ginger chopped	1 tsp
Garam masala	½ tsp
Coriander powder	1 tsp
Tomatoes finely chopped	½ cup
Ghee or oil (for frying)	½–1 cup

CHAPTER 9

Lamb, Beef and Pork

North India was greatly influenced in its cuisine by various invaders. Mughals, who were the connoisseurs of food influenced the meat cuisine tremendously. They made their homes in beautiful Kashmir, colorful Rajasthan, Lucknow, Hyderabad and Delhi and fabulous meat dishes originated in these states. *Tandoori* meats from Lucknow and Hyderabad and *kormas* of Kashmir are a few to be mentioned here. The Mughals brought the *tandoor* with them similar to *bhatti* (local name for a hot pit) to India. It is a clay oven and gets heated to about 400°C. Meats cooked in these ovens are tender and full of flavor. Before cooking, the meats are usually marinated in spices and yogurt and then *tandoor* baked.

Lamb and beef *kormas* are prepared by pan-frying the meat first and then curing them in a rich sauce of ground roasted spices, nuts, creams and tomatoes. In India mutton preparations are very elegant and are reminiscent of dishes prepared for the British aristocrats. *Rogan Josh* (pan roasted meat curried), lamb with spinach, lamb *kebab* curry are among the very popular dishes.

Being a predominately Hindu society Indians do not have meat as their staple food. It is not prepared on a regular basis in a household as is the case in western countries, but its meat dishes are amazingly delicious. Hindus, Buddhists, Sikhs and Jains consider cow as a sacred animal, therefore beef is not consider kosher. Hindus consider the cow sacred because she provides for the human race in innumerable ways. Indians consider it as the most valuable asset of a family and a family's wealth was measured by the number of cows they owned through history.

The Muslims and Jews do not consider pork kosher either. Beef and pork dishes in India are more prevalent in Goa and Kerala because these states have a good population of Christians. Pork *vindaloo*, Sorpotel of Goa, Beef curry and Beef *Korma* from Kerala are a few dishes worth mentioning. As you go through the recipes they tell you of their past with their Mughal, Portuguese, Persian and British influences and also speak of the influences of the climate and culture.

It is hard to forget the taste of tender and creamy curried meat pieces eaten with the famous *tandoor* baked bread called *nan*. *Kofta* (croquettes) curries made of ground meats in creamy sauces are also very delicious when served with rice *pulavs*.

The key point in cooking an Indian meat curry is choosing the right pan. Always use a thick-bottom, non-stick and kind of wide as well as deep metal pan. If the curries burn or stick to the pan due to overheating, then you have lost the flavor of the curry entirely. The use of the right kind of pan determines how good your curry is going to be.

Beef Curry with Nuts
Beef Korma

Beef *Korma*, cooked in a style reminiscent of south Indian cuisine, is rich in sauce prepared with coconut milk, poppy seeds, onions and spices. The recipe uses *baffad masala* that is pretty hot for the palate. Use less for milder curry.

METHOD

1. In large nonstick saucepan add a Tbs of oil and brown the beef cubes lightly. Drain the fat from the pan and remove the meat pieces in a bowl.
2. In a small skillet dry roast the poppy seeds until light brown.
3. Grind them in a coffee grinder coarsely. Set them aside.
4. To the same saucepan add 2 Tbs of oil and add the onions, ginger and garlic. Cook, until lightly brown. Add the curry leaves and cinnamon sticks.
5. Move the onion mixture to one side and add the asafoetida, and *baffad masala* and let the spices cook in the oil for ½ a minute. Add roasted ground poppy seeds, turmeric powder and salt, and stir well. Add the browned beef cubes and mix them in.
6. Add the coconut milk. Lower the heat, stir the beef curry and add the tomato sauce. Stir to mix and add 1–1½ cups of water and let it simmer for 25–30 minutes or until done. If the curry is too thick add more water and boil again.
7. Remove from heat and serve sprinkled with coriander leaves.

SERVES 4 – 6

Ingredients

Beef tenderloin cut into 1 inch cubes	2 lbs
Poppy seeds	2 Tbs
Vegetable oil	3 Tbs
Onions chopped	2 cups
Ginger chopped	1 Tbs
Garlic chopped	1 Tbs
Curry leaves	2 Tbs
Coriander leaves chopped	1 Tbs
Salt	1 tsp
Baffad masala	2 Tbs
Tomato sauce	1 cup
Turmeric powder	1 tsp
Asafoetida	¼ tsp
Whole stick of cinnamon (matchstick size)	1
Coconut milk	2 cups
Water	1–1½ cup

Lamb or Beef with Turnips
Shabdeg

KASHMIR

Mughal kings made Kashmir their summer home and this dish originated in their palace kitchens. Turnips grow there abundantly in the spring months. It is elegant and has a great appeal on the serving table. Baby turnips are sweet and have a juicy taste. Try them and you have a built-in vegetable dish with the main course.

SERVES 8 – 10

Ingredients

Vegetable oil	4 Tbs
Onions finely chopped	1 cup
Ginger finely chopped	1 Tbs
Garlic finely chopped	1 Tbs
Red Hot chilies finely chopped	1 Tbs
Turmeric powder	1 tsp
Red pepper	½ tsp
Coriander powder	1 Tbs
Cumin powder	½ tsp
Salt	to taste
Black pepper ground	1 tsp
Cumin seeds	1 tsp
Cinnamon stick 2 inch long	1
Cloves	½ tsp
Black pepper corns	½ tsp
Brown cardamoms spilt open	2
Yogurt beaten smooth	1 cup
Water	1 cup
Tomatoes medium finely chopped	2 cups
Small fresh turnips peeled and cut in halves if medium size	1 lb
Lean beef or leg of lamb cut into 2 inch cubes	2 lbs
Tomato sauce	1 cup
Garam masala	1 tsp
Green coriander finely chopped	¼ cup

METHOD

1. Fry the onions, ginger, garlic and chilies in 2 Tbs of oil in thick-bottom saucepan and wait till they turn light brown. Add the cumin seeds and wait till they pop and then add the cinnamon sticks, cloves, brown cardamoms, and black pepper corns, and cook for another minute.
2. Add the turmeric powder, red pepper, black pepper, coriander powder and cumin powder. Stir to mix and cook until the spices start to sizzle.
3. Add salt, tomatoes and stir well. Cook, stirring for 5 minutes. Clean the turnips of any leaves or tails and peel them. If the turnips are medium size cut them in half, otherwise use them whole, if small.
4. Add the turnips and stir well. Cook them in the sauce for 5 minutes and set the pan aside.
5. In a nonstick medium size skillet (*tawa*), fry the lamb on low heat until it turns white and some of the fat has come out. Drain the fat and transfer the lamb into the saucepan with turnips and stir to mix. Cook for 5 minutes and add the tomato sauce and yogurt and ½ cup of water. Stir and cover the pan. Lower the heat and simmer for 40 minutes on low heat. Keep adding water, if needed.
6. Stir occasionally to check if the meat is sticking to the bottom and if the turnips have softened and meat is done.
7. If the curry is too dry add another ½ cup of water and simmer for another 5–10 minutes
8. Add the *garam masala*, coriander leaves. Transfer the meat curry to a serving dish and serve.

The Exquisite World of Indian Cuisine

Bombay Lamb Curry

Lamb in a sauce of ground roasted peanuts, almonds and cashew, gram *dal*, sesame seeds, tamarind pulp, coconut and roasted spices. Serve topped with chopped coriander and mint leaves. The curry shows Mughal origin with the rich flavor of nuts, influences of local Gujarati cuisine in the use of peanuts and gram *dal*, and a Bombay flavor with the use of coconuts, tamarind and sesame seeds. Try it, you will like it.

METHOD

1. Fry the almonds, cashew, sesame seeds and peanuts in a small frying pan lightly browned and grind them with a pestle and mortar or in a coffee grinder coarsely and mix 1 Tbs of gram flour to it and set it aside.
2. In medium-size saucepan, fry the onions in a ¼ cup of oil and add the ginger, garlic, green chilies and the curry leaves, and fry them lightly.
3. Add the cumin seeds and wait till they start to pop and add the cinnamon sticks, cloves, cardamoms, dry red chilies and heat them through. Add the potatoes and fry them until they are lightly brown. Fry the meat pieces in a separate pan until they turn white. Drain the fat and add the meat to the above pan.
4. Add the turmeric, coriander powder, red pepper, and salt. Stir and cook for ½ a minute. Add 2 cups of water and cook the meat for about 30 minutes on low heat.
5. Add the groundnuts mixture, and coconut milk and stir to mix it well. Let the curry simmer on low heat for another 5 minutes and add the tamarind pulp dissolved in ½ cup of water. Mix well and cook for 5–10 more minutes or until the potatoes are done and the meat is tender.
6. Add the coriander leaves, *garam masala* and the mint leaves and heat through, If the curry is too thick, add ½ cup or more of water and simmer for another 5 minutes.
7. Serve topped with the chopped coriander leaves.

Note: Beef can be substituted for lamb in this recipe. *Tamarind pulp can be substituted by ½ cup of tomato sauce.

SERVES 4 – 6

Ingredients

Almonds chopped	1 Tbs
Cashew nuts	1 Tbs
Peanuts roasted	1 tsp
Sesame seeds	1 tsp
Onions chopped	1 cup
Potatoes peeled and cut in quarters,	2 large
Ginger chopped	1 Tbs
Garlic chopped	1 Tbs
Green chilies chopped	1 Tbs
Coriander powder	3 Tbs
Turmeric powder	1 tsp
Cumin seeds	1 tsp
Red pepper	1 tsp
Garam masala powder	1 tsp
Cinnamon stick 2 inch	2
Cloves	½ tsp
Brown cardamoms	2
Red dry chilies broken	2–3
Lean pieces of Lamb or Beef chopped	2 lbs
Vegetable oil	¼ cup
Curry leaves	8–10
Fresh coriander and mint leaves chopped	⅓ cup
Gram flour	1 Tbs
Coconut milk	½ cup
*Tamarind pulp dissolved in ½ cup water	1 tsp
Salt	to taste
Water	3 cups

Ground Meat Curried
Keema

This meat curry is a great addition to a dinner party and would go well with *Shahi Paneer*, vegetable stir-fry, *dal* and any bread.

METHOD

1. Cook the meat in a skillet until it is lightly browned and drain the fat.
2. In a Dutch oven or a heavy-bottom cooking pan cook the onions in 2 Tbs of oil and add the ginger, garlic, green chilies and wait till the onions are lightly browned. Add the cumin seeds and wait till they stop popping. Add the cinnamon sticks, cloves, cardamoms, whole red peppers and bay leaves. Fry for a few minutes.
3. Lower the heat and then add all the dry spices one by one, turmeric powder, red pepper, salt, and coriander powder. Add the tomatoes and the tomato sauce. Mix well. Cook till the tomatoes are completely dissolved and the oil separates from the sauce. Mix well.
4. Add the drained fried ground meat. Stir to mix.
5. Add the chopped potatoes, peas and simmer till the potatoes are tender (about 15–20 minutes or longer). Add water, if needed.
6. Add the heavy cream and stir to mix.
7. Mix well and cook for 2–3 minutes until the curry heats through.
8. Serve topped with chopped coriander leaves and sprinkle of *garam masala*.

SERVES 4 – 6

Ingredients

Lean ground lamb or beef	1½ lbs
Lean turkey or pork	½ lb
Vegetable oil	2 Tbs or more
Onions chopped	1 cup
Ginger chopped	1 Tbs
Garlic chopped	1 Tbs
Green chilies chopped	1 Tbs
Cumin seeds	1 tsp
Cinnamon sticks	2 small
Bay leaves	2–3
Cloves	½ tsp
Cardamoms brown whole broken	2
Red pepper whole	3
Turmeric powder	1 tsp
Red pepper ground	1 tsp
Salt to taste	1 tsp
Ground coriander powder	2 Tbs
Tomato sauce	1 cup
Tomatoes chopped	1 cup
Potatoes chopped	½ cup
Peas frozen or fresh	1 cup
Heavy cream (optional)	2 Tbs
Water	½ cup
Fresh coriander leaves chopped	2 Tbs
Garam masala	1 tsp

Note: Left over meat can be used to make sloppy joes (curried meat served on top of a bun). Whole spices can be used in a porous bag or *garni*.

Kashmiri Beef Curry

KASHMIR

Kashmir, the beautiful scenic mountain state of India, grows plentiful of nuts, fruits and spices and one can see that in its cuisine too. The Mughal chefs used these to come up with this rich curry sauce of yogurt, nuts and spices like cinnamon and cardamoms. The curry is garnished with saffron and chopped green coriander.

SERVES 4 – 6

Ingredients

Sirloin beef chopped into 1 Inch cubes	2 lbs
Ginger chopped	1 Tbs
Vegetable oil	¼ cup
Onions chopped	1 cup
Garlic chopped	1 Tbs
Cinnamon stick	1–2
Green chilies chopped	1 tsp
Cloves	½ tsp
Cashew nuts	2 Tbs
Brown cardamom broken slightly	3
Cumin seeds	1 tsp
Turmeric	1 tsp
Red pepper	1 tsp
Black pepper powder	1 tsp
Coriander powder	1 Tbs
Salt	to taste
Tomato sauce	2 cups
Yogurt beaten smooth	1 cup
Apricots dry chopped	½ cup
Water	2 cups
Fenugreek leaves dry (methi)	1 Tbs
Coriander leaves chopped	2 Tbs
Saffron (optional)	a pinch
Cream	1–2 Tbs
Garam masala	½ tsp

METHOD

1. Transfer the meat into a thick-bottom saucepan with 2 Tbs of the oil and fry until it changes color.
2. Drain the fat and save the meat in a bowl. In the same saucepan add 2 Tbs of oil and fry the cashew nuts until they turn light brown. Remove from oil and set them aside.
3. Soak the apricots in ½ cup of water and set them aside.
4. In the same saucepan add the onions, ginger and green chilies. Fry and wait until the onions turn light brown.
5. Add the cinnamon stick, cloves and the cardamoms, and stir-fry for a minute.
6. Add the cumin seeds and wait till they start to pop. Add the turmeric, red pepper, black pepper, coriander powder, dry fenugreek leaves, salt, and stir well to cook the spices for a minute.
7. Add the tomato sauce and stir to mix.
8. Add the meat and coat it well with spices. Add the yogurt and cook the meat by stirring on low heat for about 5 minutes. Add the cashew nuts and apricots with water and stir them in. Add 2 cups of water and cover it with a lid and let it cook, occasionally stirring to prevent sticking. Let it simmer until the meat is tender about 35–40 minutes. If the curry is too thick add more water during cooking. Add the cream, stir well and heat it through.
9. Serve sprinkled with chopped coriander leaves, *garam masala* and saffron. Serve with rice or *nan*.

'If there is a paradise on earth, it is here, it is here, it is here...' Dal Lake, Kashmir

Goa Beef Stir-Fried

GOA

Beef cooked with freshly ground spices, creamy gravy of coconut milk with sliced bell peppers and mushrooms. It is really flavorful.

METHOD

1. Fry the meat in a saucepan until slightly brown and drain the fat. Set aside.
2. Pan-roast the cardamom seeds, fenugreek seeds and fennel seeds. Grind them in a coffee grinder or with pestle and mortar and set them aside.
3. Fry the mushrooms and bell peppers in about 2 Tbs of oil in a thick-bottom large frying pan until they turn light brown (about 2 minutes). Remove them with a slotted spoon from the pan and set them aside in a mixing bowl.
4. Add another 2 Tbs of oil to the frying pan and fry the onions, ginger on medium-low heat until the onions turn light brown. Add the garlic. Cook for another 2 minutes.
5. Add the meat and fry. Add the cumin seeds and wait till they pop.
6. Add the turmeric, coriander powder, black pepper, red pepper, salt, cumin powder. Add the mixture of ground cardamoms, fennel seeds, and the fenugreek seeds. Mix everything well.
7. Add the coconut milk and let it simmer on low heat. Cover the pan and add a cup of water. Let the beef curry cook for about 30–40 minutes or until the beef is tender.
8. Add the cooked red bell pepper and mushrooms and the vinegar and cook for another 5–10 minutes. Try to keep the vegetables a little firm and not completely softened. Sprinkle coriander leaves, *garam masla* and serve with rice or pea *pulav*.

SERVES 4 – 6

Ingredients

Cardamom seeds	1 tsp
Fenugreek seeds	½ tsp
Fennel seeds	1 tsp
Mushrooms chopped	½ cup
Red bell pepper sliced	1
Beef sirloin cut into cubes	2 lbs
Vegetable oil	¼ cup
Vinegar	1 Tbs
Cumin seeds	1 tsp
Cumin powder	1 tsp
Coriander powder	1 Tbs
Turmeric powder	½ tsp
Black pepper	1 tsp
Salt	to taste
Red pepper	1 tsp
Onions chopped	1 cup
Ginger chopped	1 Tbs
Garlic chopped	1 Tbs
Coconut milk	1½ cup
Water	1 cup
Coriander leaves	1 Tbs
Garam masala	½ tsp

The Exquisite World of Indian Cuisine

Kerala Beef Curry

KERALA

Beef is fried over low heat with chopped ginger, garlic, green chilies and then mixed and fried with potatoes and peas. In Indian cuisine the concept of roasting (*bhoon-na*) is very commonly used to let the spices penetrate and flavor the main ingredient well. This stir fried dish from Kerala shows a regional influence in the use of soya sauce, lemon juice, and tomato sauce in its curry. Just serve your favorite bread or rice with an accompaniment and the dinner is complete.

METHOD

1. In a medium thick-bottom skillet, heat the oil and add the beef strips, ginger and fry for 2 minutes. Drain the fat.
2. Add 2 Tbs of oil to the same skillet and the add green chilies, onions and cubed potatoes and fry until the potatoes turn light brown.
3. Now, add the chopped garlic, black pepper, salt, curry leaves and fry for 2 more minutes and set this potatoes and beef mixture aside.
4. In large heavy-bottom saucepan, on low heat, mix together soya sauce, 1 cup of beef stock, red pepper, lemon juice, and tomato sauce and cook until the gravy gets thick (about 5 minutes) and the oil starts to separate from the sauce.
5. Add the tomatoes and peas. Cook for another 2–3 minutes and then transfer the potatoes, onions, and the beef strips mixture from the skillet into the saucepan and add the remaining beef stock and the curry leaves. Cook until the potatoes and meat get cooked (20–30 minutes). Add more beef stock, if needed.
6. Serve with rice or your favorite bread.

SERVES 4 – 6

Ingredients

Lean Beef sliced	2 lbs
Ginger chopped	1 Tbs
Garlic chopped	1 Tbs
Onions chopped sliced	1 cup
Green hot chili peppers chopped	1 Tbs
Vegetable oil	¼ cup
Potatoes white medium peeled and quartered	2
Peas frozen	½ cup
Tomatoes fresh chopped	2 cups
Soya sauce	2 Tbs
Beef stock	2 cups
Red pepper	1 tsp
Lemon juice	⅓ cup
Tomato sauce	1 cup
Black pepper	1 tsp
Salt	to taste
Curry leaves	5–6

Lamb Cooked with Spinach
Saag Gosht

PUNJAB

A rich and delicious preparation from the state of Punjab in India. It can be served with rice, *parantha* or *roti*.

METHOD

1. In a large bowl, whisk the yogurt and mix in it the chopped ginger, garlic, and the green chilies.

2. Add the lemon juice, 1 tsp of salt and 1 Tbs of oil. Marinate the lamb pieces in this mixture for at least an hour.

3. In the meantime cook the onions in the remaining oil and add the cinnamon stick, cloves, cardamoms, bay leaves and the cumin seeds.

4. Wait till the seeds start popping and then add the tomatoes, the tomato sauce, salt, turmeric, red pepper, coriander powder and the water, and cook until the mixture is smooth and sauce is thick, and the oil separates from the sauce.

5. Add the marinated meat along with the marinade and cook the mixture on low heat until the moisture is almost gone.

6. Add the chopped spinach and mix it well into the curry. Add a ½–1 cup of water and mix.

7. Cook for another 15–20 minutes. Add a little water if curry gets too thick and cook until the meat is tender. Add the cream, stir it in and heat it through.

8. Add the *garam masala* and the chopped green coriander leaves and heat it again.

9. Serve it with *paranthas*, *pulav*, *chappatis* or as a main dish in a meal.

SERVES 6 – 8

Ingredients

Yogurt	1 cup
Ginger chopped	1 Tbs
Garlic chopped	1 Tbs
Green chilies chopped	1 Tbs
Cumin seeds	1 tsp
Garam masala	1 tsp
Oil	3 Tbs
Onions chopped	2 cups
Cinnamon stick piece	1 inch
Cloves kernels	6
Cardamoms	2 large
Bay leaves	couple
Tomatoes chopped	2 cups
Salt	to taste
Tomato sauce	1 cup
Green coriander leaves chopped	¼ cup
Lemon juice	2 Tbs
Coriander powder	1 Tbs
Red pepper	1 tsp
Turmeric powder	1 tsp
Spinach frozen chopped (8 oz package)	1
Water	1 cup
Lamb lean chopped 1–2 inch pieces	2 lbs
Cream	2 Tbs

The Exquisite World of Indian Cuisine

Mughlai Lamb Curry
Roghan Josh

Lamb curry prepared as the Mughals served it to their kings in the sauce of ground onions, poppy seeds, coconut, almonds and the aromatic spices. An excellent dish for special occasion.

METHOD

1. Marinade the chopped lamb in ½ cup of yogurt, lemon juice, salt, 1 Tbs oil, ½ tsp of red pepper and turmeric for at least ½–1 hour. Fry the meat in a skillet till browned and set it aside in a bowl.
2. Roast coriander seeds, cumin seeds, almonds, coconut, cardamom seeds, peppercorns, and cloves and grind them with ginger, garlic, and the Kashmir chilies with ½ cup of water. Set aside this spice paste.
3. Heat 3 Tbs oil or *ghee* in a thick-bottom saucepan of medium size and add the chopped onions and fry till light brown and add the remaining turmeric powder, red pepper and salt, and cook on low heat for two minutes.
4. Add the tomatoes and the tomato sauce and mix the sauce until well blended. Cook the sauce until the fat separates from the sauce.
5. Add the browned lamb meat. Cook and simmer with the above sauce for 10–15 minutes on low heat, stirring to make sure it does not stick to the bottom.
6. Add a cup of water and the ground spice paste. Stir to mix. Cover and let it simmer on low heat for 30–35 minutes or until the meat is tender.
7. Sprinkle with *garam masala*, saffron and chopped coriander leaves.

SERVES 6 – 8

Ingredients

Ingredient	Amount
Coriander seeds	1 Tbs
Cumin seeds	1 tsp
Almonds	1 Tbs
Coconut dry unsweetened	2 Tbs
Brown cardamoms seeds	2
Pepper corns	½ tsp
Onions chopped	2 cups
Ginger chopped	1 Tbs
Garlic chopped	1 Tbs
Kashmir chilies broken	2
Water	1 cup
Vegetable oil or *ghee*	¼ cup
Cloves	½ tsp
Poppy seeds	1 tsp
Turmeric powder	1 tsp
Red pepper	1 tsp
Salt	2 tsp
Tomatoes chopped	1 cup
Garam masala	1 tsp
Lean lamb meat cut in cubes	2 lbs
Lemon juice	1 Tbs
Yogurt	1 cup
Tomato sauce	½ cup
Coriander leaves chopped	2 Tbs
Saffron	½ tsp

Lamb Tikka Masala
Kebab Curry

ANDHRA PRADESH

A special dish from the Mughal courts of Hyderabad uses lean mutton pieces marinated in a spicy yogurt, grilled on the skewers or oven roasted and then curried in the spicy onion sauce. This makes a very delightful dish not too rich but very flavorful. Serve it with a *pulav* or *nan*.

SERVES 6 – 8

Ingredients

For marinade:

Yogurt	½–1 cup
Salt	1 tsp
Turmeric powder	½ tsp
Ground poppy seeds	1 tsp
Ginger chopped	1 Tbs
Garlic chopped	1 tsp
Onions chopped	¼ cup
Red pepper	½ tsp
Ground coriander powder	1 Tbs
Salad oil	1 Tbs
Lemon juice	1 Tbs

For curry:

Marinated lean mutton pieces cut into 1 inch pieces	2 lbs
Vegetable oil or *ghee*	2 Tbs
Onions chopped	½ cup
Garlic and ginger finely chopped	1 Tbs
Cloves	½ tsp
Cinnamon stick	2 inch
Brown cardamoms whole	2
Cumin seeds	1 tsp
Small onions peeled washed	½ cup
Small mushrooms cleaned and washed	½ cup
Salt	½ tsp
Red pepper	1 tsp
Turmeric powder	1 tsp
Tomato sauce	2 cup
Dry coconut powder unsweetened	¼ cup
Water with ½ tsp of saffron	1 cup

To garnish:

Garam masala	½ tsp
Coriander leaves	1 Tbs
Green chilies chopped cut length wise	3 or 4 cup

METHOD

1. Prepare the marinade by mixing in the yogurt, salt, red pepper, coriander powder, turmeric powder and salad oil. Grind ginger, garlic, onions and poppy seeds, and add the lemon juice. Transfer this mixture into the yogurt mixture. This is the marinade.

2. Add the cleaned and washed lamb meat, small onions and mushrooms into the marinade and coat them well. Leave them in the marinade for at least 2–3 hours in the refrigerator. Start your grill and pack the marinated pieces of the lamb alternating with small onions and mushrooms onto the skewers. Cook them on the grill turning them to brown them evenly.

3. In a medium size heavy-bottom saucepan cook the onions in 2 Tbs oil and add the ginger, garlic, and cook until light brown. Move the onion mixture to one side and add the cumin seeds, and wait till they pop and then add the cinnamon stick, cardamoms and cloves. Cook for another half a minute and add the tomato sauce, turmeric, red pepper, dry coconut and salt. Mix and simmer on low heat stirring continuously until the oil separates from the mixture.

4. Add the cooked *kebabs*, onions, mushrooms and the leftover marinade and stir well. Keep on low heat and stir. Add 1 cup of saffron water.

5. Cook covered for 30 minutes or until the meat is done. If the curry looks too dry you can add another ¼ cup water and cook for another 5 minutes or until the curry has boiled through.

6. Remove from heat and transfer it to a serving dish. Sprinkle with *garam masala*, coriander leaves, chopped green chilies, and serve.

The Exquisite World of Indian Cuisine

Lamb Curry
Gosht Curry

PUNJAB

A stunningly delicious curry from north India. The flavor of this curry comes from the fact that the meat is cooked initially in its own juices with spices on low heat so that the flavors of the spices penetrate the meat well. It goes very well with *chappati*, *pulav*, plain rice, *nan* or *parantha*.

METHOD

1. In a deep 2–3 quart thick-bottom saucepan cook onions, garlic, ginger, and green chilies in the oil until the onions are light brown.
2. Add the cinnamon, bay leaves, pepper corns, cloves and the cardamoms, and cook on low heat until they begin to fry (about 2 minutes).
3. Add the cumin seeds and wait till they pop. Lower the heat and add the meat and fry the meat pieces with the spices until they start to turn brown.
4. Add the tomatoes and the powdered spices like coriander powder, turmeric, salt and the red pepper, and stir-fry for 5 minutes till the tomatoes are quite soft. Add half cup of water.
5. Stir-fry the meat in this spice mixture for at least 10 minutes so as to prevent any sticking to the bottom of the pan, and the oil separates from the meat. Add more water, if needed.
6. Turning the heat low, add the yogurt and mix well. Let it simmer for another 15–20 minutes until the meat is tender.
7. Add water according to the consistency of the curry required and simmer for 5 more minutes and add the *garam masala* and 1 Tbs of chopped coriander leaves. Mix and heat through.
8. Serve topped with the rest of the chopped coriander leaves, saffron and *garam masala* and serve it with your choice of bread, vegetable or rice.

SERVES 8 – 10

Ingredients

Onions chopped	1 cup
Garlic chopped	1 Tbs
Ginger chopped	1 Tbs
Green chilies chopped	1 tsp
Turmeric powder	1 tsp
Coriander powder	2 Tbs
Red pepper	1 tsp
Oil	¼ cup
Cinnamon stick piece	1 inch
Black pepper corns	10
Cloves	8
Bay leaves	3
Salt	to taste
Black cardamom	1
Cumin seeds	1 tsp
Lamb meat chopped into 1 inch pieces	2 lbs
Tomatoes chopped	2 cups
Yogurt	1 cup
Water	½ cup
Garam masala	1 tsp
Green coriander leaves chopped	2 Tbs
Saffron	½ tsp

HINT
Tender cuts of beef can easily be substituted for lamb in this recipe.

Marinated Leg of Lamb
Raan

Lamb Roast barbecued or oven baked in spicy, hot, sweet, and sour coating of yogurt and almond based marinade. It is an excellent dish to serve for an outdoor lunch or dinner barbecue. The meat is marinated ahead of time preferably overnight to get the full flavor of spices. It has a great presentation, having a dark glaze topped with fresh chopped coriander, lemon slices and served with vegetables like potatoes, carrots and beans grilled or baked with the meat or any easy to fix stir-fry vegetable. To complete the meal serve a pasta or a bean salad and rice or bread of your choice.

METHOD
Preparation of Marinade:

1. Grind the onions, ginger, garlic, almonds, cashew nuts, chilies, and the cardamom seeds along with lemon juice. Omit the nuts if the lamb is barbecued.
2. Add to the above salt, salad oil, brown sugar, yogurt, turmeric powder, coriander powder, red chili powder, cumin powder and 1 tsp *garam masala* and mix it well. This is the marinade.
3. Transfer the leg of lamb on to a large platter and prick it all over with a sharp knife or a fork. Pour the marinade over it and coat it well on both sides. Refrigerate for at least 4 hours or overnight, covered.
4. Bake it in the oven at 350°F covered for 1 hour turning it once or twice and pour the saffron water over the roast during this time.
5. Remove the cover and roast it for another 1 hour or until golden brown, occasionally basting it with *ghee*. If using a roasting pan then you can arrange peeled chopped potatoes, baby carrots, baby onions and fresh beans around the roast. Check the temperature of the roast meat thermometer for doneness (180°F).
6. If the roast is being grilled then transfer it over to the grill leaving some of the marinade in the pan and grill it covered for 30–40 minutes opening the lid of the grill to baste the steak with the left over marinade. Grill it open turning it occasionally to brown it even or until the steak is done.
7. Serve it topped with coriander leaves, *garam masala* and slices of lemon. Slice and serve the meat just like a roast and serve with vegetables, pasta or rice of your choice.

SERVES 8 – 10

Ingredients

Onions chopped	1 cup
Ginger chopped	2 Tbs
Garlic chopped	2 Tbs
Green chilies chopped	1 Tbs
Cardamom seeds	2 tsp
Lemon juice	¼ cup
Salt	2 tsp
Salad oil	¼ cup
Yogurt	2 cups
Turmeric powder	1 tsp
Coriander powder	2 Tbs
Red chili powder	1 tsp
Cumin powder	1 tsp
Garam masala	1½ tsp
Leg of lamb trimmed of fat or a lean beef roast	4–5 lbs
Brown sugar	2 Tbs
Saffron strands dissolved in warm water	½ tsp
Lemon slices	½ cup
Cilantro leaves	¼ cup
Almonds and cashew each	2 Tbs
Vegetable oil or *ghee*	⅓ cup

Note: If you are cooking the steaks in the oven then you can grind 1 Tbs each of almonds and cashew along with the onions, ginger, and garlic to make the marinade, but the nuts would have to be omitted if the meat is being barbecued. Beef can be substituted for lamb.

The Exquisite World of Indian Cuisine

Meat Croquettes Curry
Shahi Kofta Curry

A dish worth serving to the kings. Ground lamb or ground turkey balls are pan-fried or grilled and then curried in the creamy sauce of groundnuts and cream. It has a rich and flavorful taste and is usually served with pea *pulav*, *nan* and stir-fry vegetable of your taste. Perfect for a party.

METHOD

1. Cook and fry the ground meat in a heavy skillet until the meat changes color and the fat separates. Drain the fat and set the meat aside.

2. Mix the drained meat with chopped onions, ginger, garlic, green chilies, pureed peas, ground almonds, salt, lemon juice, coriander leaves, red pepper, coriander powder, beaten eggs, pieces of milk soaked and squeezed bread and *garam masala* in a mixing bowl. Form the mixture into balls of the size of a walnut. Heat ¼ cup oil in a skillet and fry the meatballs until light brown. Drain them on a paper towel and set them aside.

3. Fry the onions in a large deep thick-bottom saucepan in *ghee* or oil and add the cumin seeds and wait till they start popping. Add the cinnamon stick, whole dry red peppers, cardamoms, and wait till they start sizzling. Add the ground pistachio, ground almonds, chopped tomatoes and fry until they become soft. Lower the heat.

4. Add the turmeric, red pepper, coriander powder, salt, and tomato sauce. Stir the whole mixture.

5. Add 2 cups of water and simmer until it starts boiling. Cook for at least 10 minutes. Lower the heat and add the meatballs slowly and gently stir them into the curry. Add more water if the sauce is too thick. Simmer until the meatballs really become soft and spongy (5 minutes). Add the coconut milk and mix it into the sauce. Heat it through. Remove from heat and transfer them to a serving bowl.

6. Sprinkle them with *garam masala*, saffron and coriander leaves and serve.

7. Serves best with, *pulav* and bread. Can also be served as a main course in a meal.

Note: Ground meat can be used as is for the meatballs but, if you prefer to drain the excess fat then fry the meat in a skillet first and drain the excess fat out of it. ½ cup yogurt (smoothly beaten) or 2 Tbs of cream can be used instead of the coconut milk. Ground beef can be substituted for lamb meat.

SERVES 6 – 8

Ingredients

For the meatballs:

Ground turkey or lamb	2 lbs
Onion chopped	1 cup
Ginger chopped	1 Tbs
Garlic chopped	1 Tbs
Green chilies chopped	1 tsp
Oil	¼ cup
Dried yellow split peas boiled, drained, and pureed	½ cup
Almonds ground	2 Tbs
Salt	1 tsp
Red pepper	½ tsp
Coriander powder	1 tsp
Lemon juice	2 Tbs
Coriander leaves	2 Tbs
Eggs beaten	2
Slices of bread soaked in milk squeezed and crumbled	4
Garam masala	1 tsp

For sauce:

Canned Coconut milk	1 cup
Ghee or oil	2 Tbs
Onions chopped	1 cup
Cumin seeds	1 tsp
Cinnamon stick	1
Red pepper whole (dry) broken	2–3
Cardamoms whole half opened	2
Pistachio ground	1 Tbs
Almonds ground	1 Tbs
Tomatoes chopped	1 cup
Tomato sauce	1 cup
Turmeric powder	1 tsp
Red pepper	to taste
Salt	to taste
Coriander powder	1 tsp
Water	2 cups
Garam masala	1 tsp
Coriander leaves chopped	2 Tbs
Saffron	¼ tsp

Pork Curry

Pork curry is basically cooked like chicken curry. The meat is pan-fried and excess fat is drained from the pan. This meat is then curried. Only very lean and fresh pork is used.

METHOD

1. Fry the chopped pork cubes in thick-bottom skillet until these turn color. Drain the fat and set it aside.
2. Fry the onions, ginger, garlic, and green chilies in 2 Tbs of oil until light brown. Add the cumin seeds and when they pop, add the whole dry red pepper, curry leaves, cinnamon stick, black pepper corns, and the cardamoms.
3. Add turmeric powder, red pepper, coriander powder, salt, tomato sauce and the tomatoes, and fry until the tomatoes are soft.
4. Add the pork cubes and coat them with sauce by stirring gently. Add the water and simmer until the pork pieces are soft and curry is smooth (about 35–40 minutes). Lower the heat and add the heavy cream and mix well. Cook another 5 minutes and bring it to a boil.
5. Sprinkle with *garam masala* and fresh coriander. Serve with pea *pulav*, plain rice, *nan* and a vegetable.

SERVES 8 – 10

Ingredients

Lean pork cut up in cubes	2 lbs
Vegetable oil	2-4 Tbs
Onions chopped	1 cups
Ginger chopped	2 Tbs
Garlic chopped	2 Tbs
Green chilies chopped	1 Tbs
Cumin seeds	1 tsp
Whole red pepper broken	2–3
Cinnamon stick (small)	1
Bay leaves or curry leaves	4–5
Tomatoes chopped	1 cup
Tomato sauce	1 cup
Turmeric powder	1 tsp
Coriander powder	1 Tbs
Red pepper	1 tsp
Salt	to taste
Black pepper corns	½ tsp
Cardamoms (large)	2
Water	1½ cup
Heavy cream	2 Tbs
Garam masala	1 tsp
Green coriander leaves chopped	½ cup

Mediterranean Pork & Peas

GOA

Pork is not very popular in north India but in the southern states pork dishes are more common because Portuguese, Dutch and other seafarers influenced the cuisine. It is cooked with tamarind sauce, coconut milk, and other spices. It is really delectable.

SERVES 6 – 8

Ingredients

Ingredient	Amount
Lean pork cut in 1 inch cubes	2 lbs
Cashew nuts	¼ cup
Brown cardamoms	3
Cinnamon stick 2 inch	1
Cloves	½ tsp
Onions chopped	1 cup
Coriander leaves chopped	1 Tbs
Ginger chopped	1 Tbs
Garlic chopped	1 Tbs
Fresh or frozen peas	½ cup
Cumin seeds	1 tsp
Red dry chilies broken	2
Black pepper corns	1 tsp
Red pepper	1 Tbs
Salt	1 tsp
Sugar	1 Tbs
Tamarind pulp	1 tsp
Coconut milk	1 cup
Coconut vinegar or *feni*	2 Tbs
Oil	3 Tbs

METHOD

1. Lightly brown the pork in a heavy-bottom saucepan in a tablespoon of oil on low heat and drain the fat and set aside.

2. Grind the cashew nuts with cinnamon, black pepper corns, cloves, cumin seeds and dry red chilies together with 2 Tbs of coconut vinegar or *feni* and set it aside.

3. Transfer 2 Tbs of oil into the saucepan and add the onions. Fry until they become transparent (1–2 minutes). Add the ginger and garlic, and fry until light brown. Add the above ground *masala* and mix. Fry for a minute. Wait till it changes color and add the peas and stir to mix. Add the fried pork. Stir-fry for 2 minutes.

4. Add the red pepper, salt and sugar, and mix well.

5. Add the tamarind pulp dissolved in 1 cup of coconut milk. Mix the curry well and cover it with a lid to simmer for about 45–60 minutes on low heat or until the pork is tender. Add more water, if you feel the curry is too thick and cook for a while again. Sprinkle with coriander leaves.

6. Serve with rice or any other bread of your choice.

Note: This recipe is very similar to the famous sorpotel dish of Goa. It has a Portuguese origin. It is usually prepared at the time of Catholic festivals or other special occasions in the family. It uses not only the pork meat, but pork liver and heart. For the sauce, pork blood is mixed with the local coconut vinegar. But outside Goa, nobody likes to use pork blood and it is either substituted by coconut milk or water. The cooking time can be reduced if tamrind is added during last 10 minutes of cooking.

Pork Stir-Fried
(Southern style)

Pork is stir-fried in a mixture of ground mustard, spices and lemon juice. It is delicious and can be served as a main entry along with a rice dish, and a vegetable.

SERVES 6 – 8

METHOD

1. Heat a small nonstick skillet and fry the meat until it changes color. Drain the fat.
2. In a medium heavy-bottom saucepan transfer 3 Tbs of oil and add to it the onions, ginger, garlic, and the green chilies, and stir-fry them until the garlic turns light brown.
3. Add the meat and stir-fry it for few minutes or until it turns slightly brown (about 5 minutes). Add to the meat, dry fenugreek leaves, salt, cumin powder, turmeric powder, coriander powder and 2 Tbs of *huliyana masala*.
4. Coat the meat well while stirring for 2–3 minutes. Add the tomato sauce and mix it in.
5. While stirring add the water. Cover with a lid and turn heat to medium-low.
6. Add ½ tsp of black pepper, and stir to mix. Cook and simmer the pork for at least 1 hour or until the pork is done.
7. Serve after mixing and stirring in *garam masala*, lemon juice and the rest of the black pepper.
8. Serve preferably with plain rice only or along with a vegetable curry and *nan*.

Ingredients

Lean pork cut into 1 inch cubes	2 lbs
Vegetable oil	¼ cup
Onions chopped	1 cup
Fresh Ginger chopped	1 Tbs
Garlic chopped	1 Tbs
Green hot chili chopped	1 Tbs
Fenugreek leaves	2 Tbs
Turmeric powder	1 tsp
Coriander powder	1 Tbs
Huliyana masala	2 Tbs
Cumin powder	1 tsp
Garam masala	1 tsp
Salt	1 tsp
Water	½ cup
Black pepper	1 tsp
Lemon juice	3 Tbs
Tomato sauce	3–4 cups

The Exquisite World of Indian Cuisine

Inner view of Church of St. Cajetan, Goa

Pork Curry in Vinegar Sauce
Pork Vindaloo

GOA

Pork curry recipe originated in Goa, but is widely adapted in south India. In Goa, *'Vin'* means vinegar and *'aloo'* for *alho*, meaning garlic in Portuguese. In south India the pork and chicken *vindaloo* recipe uses tamarind instead of vinegar and a touch of coconut milk. Curry is deliciously tender, flavorful and very hot.

SERVES 6 – 8

Ingredients

Feni (a cashew drink) or Vinegar	¼ cup
Salt	to taste
Cumin powder	1 tsp
Coriander powder	3 tsp
Red pepper	2 tsp
Black pepper	½ tsp
Turmeric powder	1 tsp
Cardamom powder	2 tsp
Cinnamon powder	1 tsp
Cloves powder	½ tsp
Fenugreek leaves	½ tsp
Brown sugar	1 Tbs
Pork tenderloin cut in 1 inch cubes	2 lbs
Onions chopped	2 cups
Vegetable oil	¼ cup
Ginger chopped	l Tbs
Garlic chopped	1 Tbs
Green chilies chopped	1 tsp
Mustard seeds	1 tsp
Curry leaves	4-5
Coconut milk	½ cup
Garam masala	1 tsp
Green coriander leaves chopped	1 Tbs
Water	2 cups

METHOD

1. Marinate pork in a paste prepared by mixing 2 Tbs of feni or cashew vinegar, salt, coriander powder, red pepper, cardamom powder, cinnamon powder, cloves powder, crushed fenugreek seeds or fenugreek leaves dry, brown sugar, cumin powder, black pepper and turmeric for at least an hour.
2. In a deep thick-bottom saucepan, fry the onions, ginger, garlic and green chilies in the oil until the onions are light brown.
3. Add the mustard seeds and wait till they start popping. Add the curry leaves.
4. Now add the marinated pork meat along with the marinade and stir-fry for a few more minutes.
5. Add the remaining *feni* and fry for few minutes and then add 2 cups of water and mix well.
6. Simmer for 30 minutes on low heat and add ½ cup of coconut milk and cook till the meat is tender.
7. Serve garnished with *garam masala* and green coriander. Serve

Feni: *Feni* of Goa is a drink as synonymous as scotch is to a Scot and tequila is to a Mexican and champagne is to the French. There are two types of *fenis*, one is made from the toddy collected from a coconut palm and the other is a cashew apple *feni* made by distilling the juices of cashew apple fruit. Cashew are everywhere in Goa. In early spring the yellowish orange fruit is picked from the tree crushed and its juices are collected in large vessels. The fresh juice is sweet and refreshing but starts to ferment very quickly. It is distilled twice to produce a drink that is 30–35% proof. Its aroma is unique and it is basically used as a base for many cocktails. It is also used for aroma in cooking in the local curries.

The Exquisite World of Indian Cuisine

Pork with Potatoes & Peppers

This is a great way to serve pork as a complete dish with vegetables. It is delicious. Just serve with the bread of your choice and the meal is complete.

METHOD

1. Fry the meat on low heat in a thick-bottom skillet with one Tbs of oil until light brown. Drain the fat and set it aside.
2. Add 2 Tbs of oil to the skillet and fry the potatoes until light brown and add the bell peppers and fry for another 5 minutes and set the potatoes and peppers aside in a bowl.
3. In a medium size saucepan add the rest of the oil and add the onion, ginger, garlic and green chilies, and fry until the onions are light brown.
4. Move aside all the contents in the pan so the oil is visible and add the cumin seeds, mustard seeds, whole red peppers and curry leaves into the oil and wait till the cumin seeds and mustard seeds start popping.
5. Add the chopped tomatoes and cook till they become soft. Add the turmeric, salt, coconut powder, red pepper, black pepper, coriander powder and stir to mix well and keep cooking on low heat while stirring for another two minutes.
6. Add the fried meat and stir well and add the tomato sauce. Mix it in. Add 2 cups of water.
7. Cover the pan and let it simmer for another 30 minutes.
8. Add the potatoes and the remaining water and cook for 10-15 minutes or until the potatoes are tender and meat is done. Add the bell peppers and mix. Cook for another 5 minutes. Add the cream and stir to mix it well.
9. Add the *garam masala*, and chopped green coriander and stir the ingredients. Simmer for 2–3 minutes longer and remove from heat.
10. Serve with rice, vegetable stir-fry and your favorite bread like *nan*, *parantha*, or *chappati*.

- SERVES 8 – 10

Ingredients

Pork lean cut into 1 inch cubes	2 lbs
Potatoes preferably white medium peeled and quartered	4
Bell peppers chopped (green and red)	1 cup
Onions chopped	2 cups
Ginger chopped	1 Tbs
Garlic chopped	1 Tbs
Green chilies chopped	1 Tbs
Tomato sauce	1 cup
Tomatoes chopped	1 cup
Oil	¼ cup
Red pepper whole dry broken	3
Cumin seeds	1 tsp
Mustard seeds	1 tsp
Curry leaves	4-5
Turmeric powder	1 tsp
Coconut powder	1 Tbs
Salt	2 tsp
Red pepper	1 tsp
Black pepper	1 tsp
Coriander powder	1 Tbs
Water	2–2½ cups
Cream	2 Tbs
Garam masala	1 tsp
Coriander leaves chopped	2 Tbs

CHAPTER 10

Desserts

Indian cuisine sweets (*mithai*) are not only enjoyed as dessert but as snacks too. Boxes of sweet are offered as gifts on festivals like *Diwali* (Festival of Lights), *Raksha Bandhan* (a festival when sisters tie a holy-thread round the wrist of their brothers), *Holi* (Festival of Colors) and also during weddings or other family occasions.

Most of the sweets are milk based and are prepared mixed with nuts, coconut, *ghee* and sugar. They are often falovored with cardamom, rose water, *kevra* essence and sometimes decorated with ultra thin gold or silver leaf (*varq*). One of most loved desserts is the milk fudge called *Burfi*. It is prepared with dried milk (*khoa*) and sugar, and flavored with ground cardamom and saffron. It has several versions and is also made from nuts like cashew nuts, pistachios, coconut and almonds. These variations are respectively called Cashew *Burfi*, Pistachio *Burfi*, Coconut *Burfi* and Almond *Burfi*. Sweets are also served at teatime and as snacks during weddings, engagements and birthday parties.

Some Indian sweets are only prepared during specific festivals. *Pongal* in Tamil Nadu would not be complete without the famous *kheer* called *Payasam*. Similarly, *Ganesh Chaturthi* (a festival when Lord Ganesha, the son of Shiva and Parvati, is believed to bestow his presence on earth for all his devotees) in Maharashtra would be incomplete without *Rava Ladoo* (*Modak*). Muslims celebrate *Eid-ul-Fitr* (a festival that marks the end of *Ramzan*, the Islamic holy month of fasting) with *Savein Kheer*. Sweets are normally distributed among family and friends, to celebrate a happy occasion, like the arrival of a new baby, a wedding, an engagement, on moving into a new house and virtually any celebration. Therefore, some sweets are made specifically for a occasion or a celebration.

There are sweets that are *paneer* or cheese based like *Rasgullas, Sandesh, Chumchum, Rasmalai* and *Gulabjaman*. During festival times Indian markets are flooded with vendors selling beautifully decorated and gift-wrapped sweet boxes filled with *Burfi, Gulabjaman, Gajar ka Halwa, Jalebi, Imarti* and many assorted fudges. People buy sweets to perform *Lakshmi Puja* (prayer to Goddess of Wealth) at their house in the company of their dear ones on *Diwali*. The whole city twinkles with lights like a firefly, crackers and fireworks fill the skies at night. Every city in India has dozens of sweet shops managed as family business. The *halwai* (the sweet-meat maker), who crafts these sweets is normally very possessive about his own – often inherited – recipes and there is a lot of scope for innovation or fusion in the making of even more improved varieties of sweets. These shops are conspicuous by their smoke blackened big vats of milk sitting on large open coal stoves. But for a few desserts, normally sweets are not prepared at Indian homes and are bought from the traditional sweet shops found in almost all markets.

Cakes and pastries are also popular in India indicating clearly the merging of western and eastern cuisines. Still, local sweets are preferred by a very large section of the society. Nowadays mango and pistachio ice cream, mango mousse and pudding are also very popular in India. A delicious preparation close to the ice cream is the Indian *kulfi* which is now being served by some restaurants in the US too. It is flavored with cardamom, saffron and grated nuts, and is served with noodles like corn flour vermicelli called *Faluda*.

Cream of Wheat Pudding
Suji Halwa

This cream of wheat pudding is one of the very quick and easy desserts to fix for any occasion. It is delicious and very nutritious. It is usually served at a religious gathering but is a versatile dessert and can be served anytime. In Egyptian culture, there are 101 variations of this dish.

SERVES 10 – 12

Ingredients

*Cream of wheat (instant) see Note below	2 cups
Clarified butter or *ghee*	½ cup–1½ cup
Almonds grated or slivered	2 Tbs
Raisins (optional)	2 Tbs
Water	4–5 cups
Sugar	1½ cup
Cardamom seeds crushed	½ tsp
Saffron	a pinch

METHOD

1. Cook the instant cream of wheat on medium-low heat in the clarified butter or *ghee* for a few minutes until the cream of wheat turns light brown (about 5–7 minutes).

2. Add the raisins or the almonds or both and cook for a few more minutes and then add the water. The amount of water can vary from place to place. Lower the heat.

3. While mixing and stirring, add the sugar. Stir until the water dries up and the butter or *ghee* starts to separate from the *halwa*. It takes about 10 minutes of stirring patiently.

4. Sprinkle with the crushed cardamom seeds, saffron and serve.

HINT

Use any Instant brand of cream of wheat with 1 minute or 5 minute cooking time.

Apple *Halwa* can be made similarly. Sprinkle some lemon juice and sugar over 2 cups of peeled, chopped and grated green apples. Set it aside. In a heavy bottom saucepan, heat ¼ cup of *ghee* and fry the grated apples (10 minutes). Add sweetened condensed milk (¼ cup flavored with ½ tsp of saffron, 1 Tbs of slivered almonds and raisins. Pour it over the fried *halwa*. Stir well. Cook until it stops sticking to the pan. Serve garnished with almonds, pistachio and cardamom powder.

Note: If *suji* (the uncooked cream of wheat available at an Indian grocery store) is used then frying time will be double and the water used will be almost 3 times as much. Traditionally the quantity of *ghee* and sugar added to the *halwa* is equal to the quantity of cream of wheat used but I have reduced the amount to cut down on calories. The *halwa* is equally delicious with these reduced amounts in the above recipe but if you wish you can make it in the traditional way.

Rice Pudding
Kheer

This is made by boiling rice in milk on slow heat and then sweetening with sugar. It is served flavored with rose or *kevra* essence, ground cardamoms, almonds, pistachio or coconut. It is one of the most commonly served and very well liked desserts of Indian cuisine.

SERVES 6 – 8

Ingredients

Milk 2% fat	2 quart
Whipping cream	1 cup
Basmati rice	3 Tbs
Cardamom pods	2–4 pods
Sugar	½ cup
Almonds	1 Tbs
Raisins	1 Tbs
Kevra essence	4 drops
Pistachio	1 Tbs
Powdered coconut	1 Tbs

METHOD

1. In a Dutch oven (heavy bottom cooking pan) pour the milk, washed and drained rice and cardamoms and cook over low heat until milk is reduced to half (see Note below). Add a cup of whipping cream.

2. Keep stirring diligently because milk tends to stick to the bottom if you stop stirring. Cook until the consistency is somewhat like pudding but bit thinner.

3. Remove from heat. Add the sugar and nuts and mix well.

4. Cook over very low heat for 2–4 minutes until the sugar is well dissolved. Add a few drops of *kevra* essence and stir. Cook for a few more minutes.

5. Leave it to cool. Serve garnished with chopped nuts, raisins and coconut. It can be made couple of days ahead and refrigerated and can be reheated when needed or can be served cold.

6. Serve after a meal.

Note: The time of preparation of this dessert can be cut by half, using the method below:

Add 6 Tbs of boiled rice to a quart of milk, stir and cook for 10 minutes and add 1 cup of dry milk powder. Cook until thickened (about 10 minutes) and serve with the same garnishing as above.

Facing page:

Appliqué work - a traditional craft from Orissa

The Exquisite World of Indian Cuisine

Dried Carrot Pudding or Fudge
Gajar Halwa or Burfi

This is one of the most popular Indian desserts. It is served as a pudding as well as cut into delicious bars. It may be considered as the eggless carrot cake of Indian cooking.

METHOD

1. Wash, peel and grate the carrots finely.
2. Heat the *ghee*, add the carrots and the crushed cardamom seeds and fry for 5 minutes.
3. Add the water, cover the pan and simmer till the carrots are tender or pressure cook for 10 minutes.
4. Again fry the carrots until the water dries up. Add more *ghee* if needed.
5. Add the sugar and continue stirring till sugar is completely mixed and the carrots have no more water.
6. Add the dry milk powder, stir well to mix. Add a little *ghee* and keep frying until carrots stop sticking to the pan and *ghee* starts to separate from the fudge.
7. Add the *kevra* essence as soon as it cools.
8. Grease an 8x10 inch pan and spread the mixture evenly. Decorate with silver leaves, remaining almonds, pistachios and allow it to set and then cut into neat squares and serve.
9. Makes a great dessert to serve after dinner or on a special occasion.

SERVES 10 – 12

Ingredients

Carrots	2 lbs
Ghee or clarified butter	1 cup
Green cardamoms seeds crushed	8
Water	1 cup
Sugar	1¼ cup
Dried whole milk	2 cupa
Kevra essence	4 drops
Silver leaves (*varq*)	4

The Exquisite World of Indian Cuisine

Golden Cream Cheese Balls in Syrup
Gulabjaman

The word "*Gulab*" means rose and "*Jaman*" is a delicious purple Indian berry which grows during the monsoon season in India. These rose colored *Jamans* (favorite of the Mughal queen *Noorjahan*) will really steal your heart.

METHOD

1. Combine the sugar and water in a pan. With a sharp knife, make a slit in the ends of each cardamom pod and drop the seeds into the sugar mixture alongwith cinnamon sticks.
2. Bring to a boil, stirring until sugar is dissolved, and boil until reduced by about half. Turn the heat to low and set it aside to be used later.
3. Combine the dry milk powder, bisquick mix and baking soda, and add the softened butter. Mix until well distributed.
4. Stir in the milk and then turn out on a lightly floured board and knead well for 10–15 minutes or more until the dough is smooth and elastic.
5. Break off pieces of dough, roll into balls about the size of cherries.
6. Roll in a piece of almond inside each, if you wish.
7. Drop the balls, few at a time, into the oil heated to 340–350°F. Slow browning is very important in cooking the *Gulabjamans*. The oil should not be very hot. It should take 2–3 minutes in browning them.
8. Remove from fat with a slotted spoon and drop them into the hot syrup.
9. You can cook the balls ahead of time and let the cooked balls sit in a bowl at room temperature. Add them to the warm syrup for a few minutes before serving. The cooked balls can be refrigerated in a ziplock bag to be used later. Just make fresh syrup and add the frozen balls to the hot syrup and heat them on slow heat until they become plump with sugar syrup, and serve.

SERVES 8

Ingredients

Sugar	2 cups
Water	4 cups
Cardamoms	4 pods
Cinnamon	4 sticks
Bisquick or pancake mix*	$2/3$ cup
Dry milk powder	1 cup
Baking soda	$1/8$ tsp
Butter softened	3 Tbs
Whole Milk	½ cup
Almonds sliced	¼ cup
Shortening or oil or as needed for frying	2 cups

*Bisquick is available in western countries at local grocery store. Ready to make *gulabjaman* mixes are available at Indian grocery stores. If Bisquick is not available the *gulabjaman* dough can be made with 2½ cups of *mawa* flour mixed with ½ cup of all purpose flour, ¼ cup of any shortening or crisco and a pinch of soda. Knead this mixture with heavy cream and make a smooth dough. Then follow step 5 onwards. Makes excellent *gulabjaman*.

Cheese Balls in Sweet Syrup
Rasgulla

WEST BENGAL

A sweet for all seasons and all occasions that originated in Bengal in the 1830s, but are prepared and consumed all over India. These are spongy cheese balls made of *paneer* or homemade cheese. These white balls, the size of golf balls, are cooked in plain, rose flavored or cardamom flavored sugar syrup and are always served chilled.

METHOD

1. Rub together cheese (see note below) and a pinch of baking powder, all purpose flour and cream of wheat into a smooth and creamy dough. Use blender to blend it for 30 seconds. Divide into 16 equal parts.
2. Insert a raisin in the center of each one of them and form them into small cherry size smooth round balls.
3. Mix 2 cups of sugar with 6 cups of water in a large deep pan and boil it for 3–5 minutes. Add the cardamom powder.
4. Add the cheese balls one by one into the hot syrup. *Rasgullas* puff up a lot in size, so add a few at a time. Cook for about 5 minutes in the open pan.
5. Lower the heat and cover the pan. *Cook for another 10–15 minutes. The *rasgullas* should puff up and become spongy. Keep adding a little water to keep the syrup thin (1 Tbs every 2–3 minutes).
6. In another pan boil the rest of the sugar in two cups of water to make thick syrup. Set it aside. Transfer the cooked *rasgullas* from the thin syrup to this thick syrup and flavor them with rose water before serving.

SERVES 6 – 8

Ingredients

Homemade *paneer* or well-drained Ricotta cheese	1 lb
Cream of wheat and all purpose flour (each)	1 Tbs
Baking powder	a pinch
Raisins	1 Tbs
Sugar	2 cups
Water	4 cups
Cardamom powder	½ tsp
Rose water	1½ tsp

Note:
1. Washing of *paneer* or *chhenna* (as soon as you make it) with clean water to remove all traces of vinegar or lemon juice is very important for making good *rasgullas*. Draining of water from the *paneer* or *chhenna* is also very important.
2. You can pressure cook them for 6 minutes (or longer if need be) instead of cooking in the syrup.

The Exquisite World of Indian Cuisine

Sweet Cheese Patties in Cream
Rasmalai

Sweet patties of *paneer* cooked in flavored heavy cream are a very popular dessert for festive occasions. These are prepared the same way as the *rasgullas* but are served in heavy cream instead of sugar syrup.

METHOD

1. Rub the (see notes 1 and 2 below) homemade *paneer* or cheese together with all purpose flour and baking powder until it is smooth. Divide the cheese into 24 equal parts and roll each into smooth round balls.
2. Flatten the cheese balls into about 2 inch diameter flat patties.
3. Heat the heavy cream and the condensed milk together in a deep fairly large saucepan and add the sugar as needed. Cook for 5–10 minutes. Set it aside.
4. Prepare the syrup by boiling 4 cups of sugar in 3 cups of water in a large heavy-bottom saucepan and boil for 2 minutes. Add the flat patties of cheese and cook for 10 minutes. Add a few at a time.
5. Lower the heat and cover the pan and cook for another 5 minutes. As the patties get cooked they should puff up and float on top of the syrup.
6. Add the cooked *rasmalai* by taking them out of the hot syrup with a slotted spoon and squeeze out the syrup a little and transfer them into the heavy cream mixture. Let them simmer on low heat for 10 minutes.
7. Cool in the refrigerator and serve in a serving bowl topped with chopped slivered almonds and chopped pistachio and add the rose water and saffron before serving. It is a delicious and refreshing dessert, especially during summer months.

SERVES 10 – 12

Ingredients

Homemade cheese or *paneer* completely drained ricotta cheese	2 lbs
All purpose flour	2 Tbs
Baking powder	a pinch
Heavy cream	1 cup
Condensed sweetened milk	2 cups
Pistachio chopped	1 Tbs
Almonds slivered chopped	1 Tbs
Cardamoms crushed	½ tsp
Sugar	4 cups
Water	3 cups
Rose water	1 tsp
Saffron	1 tsp

Note 1: To make *Rasmalai* from ricotta cheese follow the procedure below : Blend together 15oz pkg of ricotta cheese with ¼ cup of sugar. Transfer 1 Tbs of this mixture to each cup of a muffin pan. Bake at 350°F for 35–40 minutes covered with tin foil. Cool and remove these and transfer them to the heavy cream mixture and serve.
Note 2: Prepare the Homemade cheese or *paneer* as mentioned in the recipe for *rasgullas* and follow the notes 1 and 2 under that recipe.

Sweet Cheese Cakes
Chumchum

These cheese cakes are cooked a little longer in syrup, then the *rasgullas*, until they are firm. These are served without the syrup and flavored the same way as the *rasgullas* with rose essence or *kevra*. Topped with grated nuts like almonds, pistachio and silver leaves these make an elegant presentation.

METHOD

1. Cream the cheese* with your fingers and baking powder and all purpose flour until creamy. Divide the dough into 3 parts. Add different food color to each part.
2. Divide each part of the cheese into 10–15 equal parts and give them 2 inch long oval or finger shapes.
3. Boil the sugar in about 4 cups of water for at least 5–10 minutes.
4. Drop the cheese balls into the above syrup and continue to cook them in this syrup until the *chumchum* are floating on top of the syrup. Add few at a time. Leave these in the syrup for at least 10 minutes.
5. Remove from the fire. Cool.
6. Take the *chumchum* out of the syrup with a slotted spoon and squeeze out the syrup a little and arrange them one at a time on a platter.
7. Top each one of them with a gold or silver leaf and grated nuts or roll them into grated unsweetened coconut and serve.
8. This dessert is usually served at festive occasions and the different colors make it very appealing.

SERVES 8 – 10

Ingredients

Homemade cheese (*paneer*)	2 lbs
All purpose flour or fine cream of wheat from Indian grocer	1½ Tbs
Baking powder	⅛ tsp
Sugar	4 cups
Water	4 cups
Different food colors	
Kevra extract	a drop or two
Or	
Rose water	1 tsp
Almonds grated	1 Tbs
Pistachio grated	1 Tbs
Or	
Coconut grated	1 cup

Note: *Prepare the cheese in a manner as descibed in the similar *rasgullas* recipe (follow the notes).

Sweet Cheese Balls
Kamal Bhog

These spongy cheese balls are much like *rasgullas,* but less syrupy and a lot firmer with an orange flavored inner filling.

SERVES 10 – 12

METHOD

1. Prepare the cheese following the notes under *Rasgulla* recipe.
2. Knead the homemade cheese or *paneer* smooth with 2 Tbs of all purpose flour in a bowl with 1 Tbs of the orange (drink) powder.
3. With two-third portion of this cheese make 15 gold size balls and refrigerate.
3. In the remaining cheese add the rest of saffron and orange (drink) powder, and knead it smooth.
4. Make another 15 smaller balls as big as a cherry with this cheese and set these aside.
6. Take out the larger balls from the refrigerator and make dents in them and insert the smaller balls into these and close the balls smooth and round again. Set them aside.
7. Boil the water in a large saucepan and add the cardamom powder and sugar. Bring to boil for a few minutes.
8. Add the balls to the syrup and cover with a lid. Continue cooking in the syrup for another 10–15 minutes. Keep adding a Tbs of water every few minutes so that the syrup does not become very thick. Lower the heat and add the *kevra* essence. Cook until the balls get firmer and these float on the top of the syrup. Remove from heat with a slotted spoon and squeeze out the syrup a little.
9. Arrange the balls onto a platter and sprinkle with confectioner's sugar or sweetened coconut flakes. Serve after dinner as a dessert or as a tea snack. The dessert is moderately sweet and the orange flavor makes it very refreshing.

Ingredients

Homemade *paneer*	2 lbs
All purpose flour	1 tsp
Baking powder	1/8 tsp
Sugar	4 cups
Water	4 cups
Orange (drink) powder	2 Tbs
Confectioner's sugar	1 cup
Sweetened coconut powder	1 cup
Saffron	1 tsp
Cardamom powder	½ tsp
Kevra essence	a drop

Sweet Pieces of Cheese
Sandesh

WEST BENGAL

Baked sweet pieces of *paneer* sprinkled with grated almonds, pistachio, powdered cardamoms, and flavored with rose water or *kevra*. A light and delicious dessert from West Bengal.

SERVES 6 – 8

Ingredients

Paneer or cheese	1 lb
Sugar powder	¾ cup
Nuts of your choice chopped	¼ cup
Food color of your choice (optional)	
Silver leaves	2–3
Saffron dissolved in 1 tsp of warm milk	½ tsp
Cardamom powder	½ tsp

METHOD

1. Knead the cheese with your palms with powdered sugar and cardamom powder. Fry on low heat for 5–7 minutes in a saucepan.

2. Grease an 8 inch square pan and spread the mixture evenly on the bottom of the pan.

3. At this point divide the cheese into two halves. Color each half in different color and spread one half at the bottom of the pan. Spread half the nuts and saffron. Spread the other half of the cheese on top of the first half and then top it off with the remaining nuts and saffron. Cut these into 1 inch squares and serve. *Sandesh* has a short shelf life and should be used preferably the same day.

SHRIKHAND
Another fast fixing desert is *Shrikhand*. Mix 1 cup of confectioners sugar into 16 oz. carton of sour cream. Mix ¼ tsp of cardmon powder and 1 tsp of saffron threads. Mix well. Add ½ cup of mango pulp. Stir well and serve in serving dishes sprinkled with chopped almonds and pistachios. Excellent dessert to serve after dinner.

Gram Flour Sweet Balls/Lentil Balls
Besan Laddoo / Dal Pinni

PUNJAB

These sweet round balls are made of pan-fried gram flour (*Besan*) or ground *urad* or *mung dal* flour in clarified butter or *ghee* and dry milk powder, sugar and chopped nuts. A very delicious dessert from the state of Punjab. The round balls made of ground lentils flour are called *pinnis*. *Pinnis* are supposed to be very nutritious as these are made with proteinaceous lentils flour. These melt in your mouth.

SERVES 10 – 12

Ingredients

Gram flour *(Besan)*	2 cups
Or	
Urad or *mung dal* flour	1½ cups
Suji (cream of flour)	½ cup

METHOD

1. Fry the gram flour (*Besan*), *mung* or *urad dal* flour in a deep thick-bottom pan in ½ cup of *ghee* until light brown. In another pan, fry the *suji* in ¼ cup of *ghee* until brown and mix these together.
2. Add 1 Tbs each of the nuts and grated fresh or dry coconut and continue frying for a few more minutes. Add the dry milk powder and continue frying until well blended.
3. Cook the sugar* with 1 cup of water in a saucepan and stir until the sugar is well dissolved. Cook till a drop of syrup when pulled between two fingers forms a string. Cool it. Pour it over the cooked gram flour (*Besan*) or *mung* or *urad dal* and mix well.
4. Cool enough to form round balls each of about 2 Tbs of the mixture and arrange these on a serving platter.
5. Serve these topped with the remainder of the grated nuts and coconut and the silver leaves.
6. *Laddoos* and *pinnis* are mostly served on festive occasions and are among of the most liked desserts.
7. They also make favorite teatime snacks.

Ghee	¾ cup
Sugar	¾ cup
Almond and walnuts chopped each	2 Tbs
Coconut grated	2 Tbs
Dry milk powder (optional)	1½ cup
Milk (whole of 2% fat)	2 Tbs
Silver leaves	3–4

Note: *Instead of making sugar syrup, powdered sugar can be used. Add the powdered sugar to the roasted besan or dal flour while it is still warm. Knead these into *laddoos/pinnis*, when the mixture is cool enough to handle.

Sweet Balls of Cream of Wheat
Rava Laddoo / Modak

This yummy dessert can be made quickly.

METHOD

1. Fry the cream of wheat (*rava*) in the clarified butter in a thick-bottom saucepan until light brown. Add coconut powder and keep frying for 2 more minutes.
2. Add the chopped cashew and raisins and fry for another 3–5 minutes. Set it aside.
3. Cook the sugar, cardamom powder and the milk in another saucepan on low heat and keep cooking and stirring until a little sticky (about 8–10 minutes) and stringy. (When a drop of syrup is pulled between two fingers, it forms a string).
4. Add the cooked cream of wheat to the syrup and mix it well.
5. Cool and gather the cooked dough in your hands enough to make into balls the size of golf balls and arrange them on a platter.
6. Decorate the balls with one raisin each on top, pushed in with slight pressure.
7. Serve these with tea or as after dinner dessert. These are made especially for *Ganesh Chaturthi* (a festival when Lord Ganesha, the son of Shiva and Parvati, is believed to bestow his presence on earth for all his devotees).

SERVES 4 – 6

Ingredients

Cream of wheat or *Rava*	1 cup
Sugar	1 cup
Clarified butter or *ghee*	¼ cup
Milk (2% fat)	1 cup
Cashew nuts chopped (raw)	1 Tbs
Coconut grated dry	¾ cup
Raisins	1 Tbs
Cardamom powder	½ tsp

The Exquisite World of Indian Cuisine

Modak or Modkam is a favorite sweet of Lord Ganesha (God with an elephant tusk), who, when happy, removes all obstacles and showers wealth and prosperity. Back home, when we were growing up, this festival used to be very exciting. With great faith and reverence my mother would make modaks on **Ganesh Chaturthi** to welcome Lord Ganesha, into our home. It is believed that he stays only for a few days and promises to come back again the following year. In a great procession with the beating of the drums the idols of Lord Ganesha are taken for immersion in an ocean or a river with devotees singing, dancing and chanting Ganpati Bapa Morya... all through the way. In Indian culture there are quite a few such festivals which reaffirm people's faith in God.

Sugar Coated Doughnuts
Balushahi

Delicious sugar coated doughnut without using egg. *Balushahi* is so tempting that you just cannot resist it. These are light, sweet and delicious; simply the best dessert, comparable to doughnut of the western countries.

METHOD

1. Sift flour and baking soda together and rub it with the *ghee* and add warm yogurt and knead with the help of warm water into a soft dough. Let the dough rise for at least 2 hours in a warm place. Divide the dough into 12 equal parts and shape them into balls. Make a hole in the center, flatten and set aside.
2. Heat the oil, in a deep heavy pan or wok, to 300°F–340°F.
3. Add the flattened doughnuts and fry them on a very low heat. Cook until they puff up and are light brown in color; slow browning is needed. Take them out of the oil with a slotted spoon and drain them in a large strainer.
4. Prepare the syrup by mixing sugar and water in a deep saucepan and cook till the syrup has become very sticky and stringy (2–3 strings consistency). Add the *kevra* essence. Arrange the *balushahi* in a deep 8-10 inches pan and pour the syrup over these. Sprinkle these immediately with chopped nuts and the silver leaves and serve.

SERVES 6 – 8

Ingredients

All purpose flour	2 cups
Yogurt	¾ cup
Warm water	2 Tbs
Almonds chopped	2 Tbs
Ghee	½ cup
Baking soda	½ tsp
Kevra essence drops	2–3
Sugar	2 cups
Water	2 cups
Pistachio	2 Tbs
Vegetable oil (for frying)	4 cups
Silver leaves (optional)	3–4

HINT

A very famous dessert **Shahi Tukra** can also be made quickly similarly. Fry a couple of bread slices (remove their crust and cut across diagonally). Heat contents in ¼ cup of *ghee* until dark brown. Add the sweetened condensed milk flavored with ½ tsp of saffron, 1 Tbs each of almonds, pistachios and raisins. Pour it over the toasts and serve. Makes a delicious las minute dessert. Decorate with few pieces of nuts.

The Exquisite World of Indian Cuisine

Cookies without Eggs
Khatai

Delicious vegetarian cookies that are favorites since my childhood. These are flavored with yogurt and do not take long to make.

SERVES 4 – 6

Ingredients

All purpose flour	2½ cup
Ghee	½ cup
Baking powder	2½ tsp
Almonds grated	2 Tbs
Pistachio	2 Tbs
Powdered sugar	1½ cup
Yogurt	½ cup
Almond extract	½ tsp
Salt	a pinch

METHOD

1. Beat the *ghee* with a fork until it is white and fluffy and add sugar and continue beating until creamy. Add baking powder, salt and yogurt and continue beating till quite light and fluffy.
2. Fold in the flour, almond essence, and half of the grated almonds and pistachio. Shape the dough into a long roll and slice off cookies about 1 inch thick with a sharp knife.
3. Sprinkle these each with the grated almonds and pistachio and arrange these on a cookie sheet.
4. Bake at 350°F for 8–10 minutes. Remove them from the oven and cool. Roll these in powdered sugar, if you wish before serving.
5. Store in an air tight container.

Apple or Zucchini Pudding
Seb Kheer / Ghia Kheer

Grated apples or zucchini make a great substitute for rice in this *kheer* and its cooking time is less than half. It is a perfect idea for a last minute dessert.

METHOD

1. Mix and stir the condensed milk and the regular milk in a thick bottom medium size cooking pan. Bring it to full boil and cook for 2 minutes while stirring on medium low heat. Set it aside.
2. Fry the grated apples or zucchini in 1 Tbs of *ghee* in a cooking pan until it is dry and brown. Add boiled milk and keep mixing and stirring until it starts to boil again. Cook for few minutes until the *kheer* is thick and smooth.
3. Remove from heat and add the cardamoms, almonds, pistachio and stir. Heat it again. Cook for few minutes while stirring and serve.
4. Makes a very nice dessert for a last minute dinner idea. Serve it sprinkled with few strands of saffron.

SERVES 4 – 6

Ingredients

Sweet and sour apple grated	1 cup
Or	
Zucchini grated	1 cup
Sweetened condensed milk	½ cup
Milk (2% fat)	2 cups
Cardamom powder crushed	½ tsp
Almonds	2 Tbs
Ghee	1 Tbs
Saffron (optional)	few strands

Sweet Vermicelli Pudding
Sevian Kheer

A sweet thin vermicelli pudding with nuts and flavoring. A perfect light dessert after dinner.

METHOD

1. Fry the *sevian* in *ghee* in heavy-bottom medium size saucepan until light brown.
2. Add the milk and cook on low heat until the milk thickens and the *sevian* are soft.
3. Add the ground nuts and continue cooking until the mixture thickens and is still of even pouring consistency.
4. Add the *kevra* extract and cardamom powder.
5. Stir well and cook for few more minutes on very low heat. While stirring, add the sugar. Stir it.
6. Cool and top it with silver leaves and grated nuts and serve.
7. Another dessert which you can fix for a weekend company in a rush.

SERVES 6 – 8

Ingredients

Milk (2% fat)	3 cups
Vermicelli (*Savien*)	1 cup
Sugar	¾ cup
Cardamom powder	½ tsp
Almonds ground	2 Tbs
Almonds grated	1 Tbs
Pistachio grated	1 Tbs
Kevra extract drops	2–3
Silver leaves small	6
Ghee	2 Tbs

Note: Significantly made on *Eid* - a festival celebrated by the Muslim community. *Eid-ul-Fitr* is the end of one month long fasting called *Ramadan*. The end of this fasting is celebrated with great religious fervor and bonhomie.

HINT

Milk can be substituted with water to make real *sevian* that are made on *Eid-ul-Fitr*

Ground Rice Pudding
Phirni

Rice pudding made with rice flour is smooth and has a very creamy taste. It is very quick to make and when flavored with *kevra* extract or rose extract, ground almonds and pistachio, it is very appealing to the palate.

METHOD

1. Heat the milk to a full boil. Lower the heat.
2. Mix the rice flour into a couple of teaspoons of milk separately and then mix it into the boiled milk.
3. Cook on low heat and keep cooking until the mixture thickens to a consistency of a pudding.
4. Add the sugar, ¾ Tbs each of grated pistachio and the rose extract and stir to mix well.
5. Cook until sugar is well dissolved.
6. Cool and pour in pretty pudding cups or ice cream cups for individual serving or pour in one serving bowl. Refrigerate until set.
7. Serve it topped with remaining almonds and pistachio and silver leaves, or freshly sliced small pieces of strawberry or kiwi fruit.

SERVES 6 – 8

Ingredients

Milk (2% fat)	4 cups
Rice flour	4 Tbs
Sugar to taste or	½ cup
Blanched slivered almonds	1 Tbs
Rose extract drops	1–2
Silver leaves	3–4
Pistachio grated	1 Tbs
Fresh strawberries chopped Or kiwi fruit slices	½ cup

The Exquisite World of Indian Cuisine

Sweet Rice
Meethey Chawal

Sweet rice *pulav* is a welcome sight at almost every auspicious occasion in northern India. Whether it is the birth of a new baby, birthday or a wedding anniversary, Sweet Rice is a part of all celebrations. Its sweet and delicious aroma is enticing.

METHOD

1. Wash and drain the rice and set it aside.
2. Heat the *ghee* and add the cloves, turmeric powder, cardamoms, and fry for 5 minutes on slow heat.
3. Add the rice and fry in the *ghee* for 2–3 minutes. Add 2 cups of water. When water dries up add 2 cups of milk with sugar dissolved in it.
4. Add the dissolved saffron, 2 Tbs of almonds, pistachio and all the raisins and stir the rice gently.
5. Cover with a lid and cook for another 10–15 minutes on very low heat until there is no moisture floating on the top. Lower the heat to minimum and cook till rice is tender.
6. Add the *kevra* essence and serve sprinkled with the rest of the almonds, pistachio and decorate with silver leaves.

SERVES 4 – 6

Ingredients

Rice	2 cups
Ghee	½ cup
Cloves	6
Raisins soaked in sugar water	¼ cup
Pistachio nuts	¼ cup
Water	2 cups
Milk (2% fat)	2 cups
Cardamoms green	8
Turmeric powder	½ tsp
Sugar	1¾ cup
Almonds chopped	¼ cup
Saffron (dissolved in a 2 tsp of water)	¼ tsp
Silver leaves	3–4
Extract of *kevra* drops	5–6

Note: Saffron has been grown in India since ancient times. It became popular during Mughal times when they started to adorn their sweet dishes as well as meat dishes with saffron for its beautiful aroma and color. It is an essential ingredient of Spanish paellas, Indian *biryanis*, desserts and *pulavs*.

Mango Pie

Made with mango pulp, sour cream and gelatin, it is a dessert that can be quickly fixed for your guests and still remain very unique and delicious. It is quite refreshing for a summer informal party. Children love it.

METHOD

1. Dissolve 3 packages of gelatin in 3 cups of boiling water. Cool it and blend in the cream cheese, sugar and the sour cream. Use a hand held mixer if possible.
2. Add the mango pulp and mix. Make it smooth and set it aside.
3. Mix the gram cracker crumbs with butter, knead into a paste and layer evenly on the surface of a 13x9x2 inches pan. Refrigerate for a couple of hours until set.
4. Remove the pan from the refrigerator and pour the mixture of gelatin and mango pulp over the layer of bread crumbs. Cover it and place the pan back into the refrigerator for another 3–4 hours or until the mango pie is set.
5. Cut into squares and serve, sprinkling each square with a mint leaf and couple of saffron threads and some pieces of fresh mango.

SERVES 10 – 12

Ingredients

Mango pulp from a can	3 cups
Sour cream	2 cups
Gelatin (unflavored)	3 pkgs
Cream cheese	1 cup
Boiling water	3 cups
Sugar	1 cup
Gram cracker crumbs	¾ cup
Butter	4 Tbs
Mint leaves	2 Tbs
Saffron threads	1 tsp
Fresh mango or nuts to decorate	

Note: You can set the pie in small decorative individual dessert dishes also without the gram cracker layer at the bottom.

The Exquisite World of Indian Cuisine

Mango Mousse
Aam ki Phirni

A lighter and creamier dessert made up of mango pulp, gelatin, a little heavy cream and very little sugar but using the sweetness of mango pulp and sourness of lime juice. It is quite refreshing and delicious.

SERVES 6 – 8

Ingredients

Mango pulp	1¾ cup
Cardamom powder	½ tsp
Heavy cream	8 ozs
Unflavored gelatin	1 pkg
Boiled water	¼ cup
Eggs separated	2
Sugar powder	1½ tsp
Lime juice	1 Tbs
Saffron threads	½ tsp
Fresh tangerine fingers (optional)	few slices
Strawberry (optional)	few slices
Mint leaves for serving	

METHOD

1. Add the cardamom powder to the mango pulp and beat it with the electric beater. Set it aside.
2. In a large bowl beat the heavy cream until it is light and fluffy. Set it aside.
3. Whisk the egg whites separately until these are frothy and hold peak. Set aside.
4. Dissolve the gelatin in ¼ cup of boiling water in a saucepan and cool it. Beat it into the mango pulp, add lime juice, beaten egg whites and whipped cream. Mix gently until well blended.
5. Transfer the mango mixture into 8 serving bowls or into a small baking dish, about 8–11 inch in diameter and about 2 inch deep. Leave it in the refrigerator for at least 3 hours to set. Serve it decorated with a couple of saffron threads, mint leaves and powdered sugar, or fresh sliced pieces of tangerine fingers or sliced strawberry.

Fried Spiral Sweet Rings
Jalebi

These spiral, juicy rings are a very desirable dessert. Almost everybody loves these. They are always served at a wedding or at a big festive occasion. Made with fermented flour, deep-fried and soaked in the sugar syrup these are crunchy and a bit sweet and sour. You have to eat one to admire.

SERVES 8 – 10

Ingredients

All purpose flour	2 cups
Rice flour	¼ cup
Yogurt	½ cup
Baking powder	½ tsp
Water	5½ cup
Sugar	4 cups
Cardamom powder	½ tsp
Saffron (dissolved in 1 tsp of water)	½ tsp
Oil for frying	4 cups
Yellow food color	¼ tsp
Kevra essence	2 drops

METHOD

1. Combine all purpose flour, baking powder, rice flour and yogurt in a bowl, and add 1½ cup water, saffron water, cardamom powder, and yellow food color. Whisk it well.
3. Cover it with a cloth and set it aside at a warm place for two hours.
4. Mix 4 cups of water and remaining 4 cups of sugar and a drop of yellow food color in a deep saucepan and boil. Wait until the sugar syrup is starting to make a string when pulled between fingers. Add the *kevra* essence to it and stir to mix.
5. Beat the flour batter again and pour it into a pastry bag.
6. Heat oil in a large wok or a large thick-bottom saucepan to 300°F–340°F. Squeeze the batter into the hot oil from the batter filled pastry bag going round and round making a string of circles starting from outside ending inside. Each disc of string of circles should not be more than 4 inches in diameter. Several such discs of strings can be fried at the same time. Fry until golden brown. Remove from the oil with a slotted spoon or tongs and transfer into the hot sugar syrup.
7. Leave these in the syrup for at least 10–15 minutes and then remove with tongs from the sugar syrup into a serving platter.
8. Serve hot or cold. They are delicious when eaten dipped in hot milk.

The Exquisite World of Indian Cuisine

Crunchy Lentil Sweet Rings
Imerti

Crisp, spiral and crunchy, these rings are definitely anybody's favourite dessert.

METHOD

1. Wash and soak *dal* overnight in 3 cups of water and grind it in a blender in the same water to a smooth paste. Pour the creamy paste into a large stainless steel bowl. Cover it with a lid and let the batter rise in a warm place for at least 2–4 hours. Add a pinch of baking soda and mix.

2. Add ½ tsp of saffron to the dough and beat it smooth and fluffy.

3. Prepare the syrup by boiling the sugar and remaining water in large saucepan until the syrup becomes very sticky. Add a drop of yellow food color and ½ tsp of cardamom powder to it. The syrup can be tested by lightly touching the cooled syrup with a finger and again touching this finger with your other finger and pulling this finger away. If you see a string between the 2 fingers then the syrup is done. Turn the heat to warm and set the syrup aside.

4. Heat the oil to about 300°F–340°F in a medium size wok.

5. Pour the batter in a small pastry bag or a small nozzle funnel plugging the hole with your finger and then pour the batter in circular motion into the oil by opening the hole. Form a small circle and keep rotating to make coils around the circles about the size of a doughnut. Lower the heat a little. Cook by turning them over once or twice and when the *Imerti* is crisp and golden brown remove from the oil and drain on a paper towel.

6. Drop these into the warm syrup for 2 minutes. Remove these from the syrup and they should still be crisp and firm but will be full of syrup. Serve on a platter by lining them in a circle. Sprinkle with saffron threads, almonds, cardamom powder, and chopped pistachio and serve.

SERVES 10 – 12

Ingredients

Urad dal spilt	2 cups
Water	7 cups
Baking soda	a pinch
Yellow food color	a pinch
Oil for frying	4 cups
Sugar	2 cups
Saffron	½ tsp
Cardamom powder	1 tsp
Pistachio grated	2 Tbs
Almonds grated	1 tsp

*Makes about 20 *imertis*.

Cashew Fudge
Kaju Burfi

Made by mixing ground cashew nuts, *ghee*, *paneer* or ricotta cheese and sugar, Cashew Fudge (*Kaju burfi*) is flavored with *kevra* extract and decorated with silver leaves. This is one of those special desserts which is made on weddings and other important events.

METHOD

1. Grind the cashews (rather coarse) by grinding and by adding a little milk and cook on low heat in a thick-bottom pan in ¼ cup of the *ghee*. Fry the ground cashews until lightly roasted and till the *ghee* separates from the dough. Mix the dry milk powder at this point to increase the bulk of the *burfi*. This is optional.
2. Boil the sugar in 2 cups of water until thick and has one string consistency and mix it with the cooked cashew dough.
3. Cool and add the *kevra* essence. Grease a shallow large baking pan and spread the mixture ½ inch thick evenly using spatula or your hand and decorate it with the silver leaves. When it cools down cut in diamond shapes and refrigerate. It can stay in the refrigerator in an air tight container for 4–6 weeks and makes a very delightful dessert.
4. Use it as a teatime snack or a dessert after dinner.

SERVES 10 – 12

Ingredients

Cashew nuts unsalted soaked (2–4 hours) and ground	1 lbs
Milk as needed (2% fat)	½–1 cup
Ghee	4–6 Tbs
Sugar to taste or	8 ozs
Dry milk powder (optional)	1 cup
Kevra essence	1 drop
Silver leaves	5–6
Cardamom powder	1 tsp
Saffron dissolved in 1 tsp of water	1 tsp
Water	2 cups

Note: Silver leaves and gold leaves were introduced to Indian cuisine primarily by the Mughals. They decorated their dishes for their royal guests with the gold or silver leaves (*varq*). Tradition trickled to all the other desserts and today all the desserts get decorated by these shiny (*varq*) leaves and make the desserts look so appealing and ethnic.

The Exquisite World of Indian Cuisine

Milk Fudge
Burfi

This *paneer* or ricotta cheese preparation with dry milk powder, *ghee* and sugar is one of the most popular sweets of India. Ricotta cheese here is being substituted for the traditional milk solids like *khoa*.

METHOD

1. In a deep thick-bottom saucepan cook the cheese with ¼ cup of *ghee*, sugar and water. Fry until it starts to leave the sides of the pan or till the water dries up.
2. Remove from heat and add the powdered milk one cup at a time. Stir well and add the remainder of the *ghee* and fry the mixture for a few minutes until you see the fudge is no longer sticking to the sides of the pan.
3. Add the almonds and saffron dissolved in water and mix well. Grease a rectangular cake pan and spread the mixture evenly, 1 inch thick. Sprinkle with ground cardamoms and layer the top with gold or silver leaf.
4. Chill and cut preferably in square or diamond shapes. Serve as a dessert after dinner or as a snack at teatime or a coffee break.

SERVES 10 – 12

Ingredients

Ricotta cheese or *paneer* or *khoa*	2 lbs
Clarified butter (*ghee*)	½ cup
Sugar	1½ cup
Gold or silver leaves (*varq*)	2
Water	½ cup
Almonds crushed	½ cup
Dry milk powder	3–4 cups
Saffron sprigs dissolved in water	¼ tsp
Green cardamom seds crushed	1 Tbs

If anything catches the eye of a foreigner in India it is the **Snake Charmer**. Their importance in culture is demonstrated by doing certain rituals and celebrations. Serpents live in the farms and fields of India and they help the farmers tremendously by feeding on the rodents that damage and destroy their harvest. Therefore on *Nag panchami* (Worship day for snakes) the farmers catch these slithery animals gently in their baskets and bring them to the village temple courtyard. The women of the village bathe and fast this day and they come to the temple with sweet milk, ghee and sweets (*jalebi*, and *burfi*). The snake charmers bring their catches to the courtyard and start playing these enchanting tunes with their beautiful flutes for the snakes. The cobras the most venomous snake in the world really gets charmed by the music and gently comes out of the basket. The ladies then offer them the sweets and milk and ask for their blessings not to harm their farmer husbands and their families while they work and toil in the farm fields. It is known that the snakes indeed never harm them. This practice results from the desire of Indian people to keep harmony between man and nature.

Pistachio Fudge
Pista Burfi

This delicious dessert made of ground pistachio, *ghee*, sugar and *paneer* or ricotta cheese simply dissolves in the mouth. It is decorative and colorful and its presence makes any occasion special. It is flavored with ground cardamoms and *kevra* extract and decorated with silver leaves before serving.

SERVES 10 – 12

Ingredients

Fresh unsalted Pistachio soaked overnight and shelled	1 lb
Milk (2% fat)	½ –1 cup
Sugar to taste or	1½ cups
Ghee	4- 6 Tbs
Cardamoms ground	½ tsp
Kevra essence	2 drops
Silver leaves	4
Saffron	½ tsp
Pistachio to decorate	1 tsp
Dry milk powder	1 cup

METHOD

1. Drain the soaked pistachio and shell them by rubbing on paper towel.

2. Grind them in a blender fine by adding as little milk as possible. Transfer to a deep heavy-bottom pan and add 4 Tbs of the *ghee*. Add 1 cup of milk powder and stir to mix. Cook on low heat until the mixture turns into a dough and leaves the side of the pan (the *ghee* separates from the pistachio mix).

3. Boil 1½ cups of sugar in 2 cups of water, until the syrup forms a string when a drop of it is pulled between 2 fingers. Cool and add ground cardamoms, and the *kevra* essence and mix. Add the cooked dough and mix well. Cool a little.

4. Grease a shallow large baking pan and spread the mixture evenly about ½ inch thick. Cool. When firm, decorate with the silver leaves and cut into diamond shapes with a sharp knife.

5. Take them out of the pan with the help of a spatula and decorate them in a nice serving plate. Makes a festive dessert for all occasions.

6. Keeps well in the refrigerator for couple of weeks.

Note: The quantity of *ghee* is reduced to cut down the calories. Traditionally, lot more *ghee* is used in these preparations. Either way the fudge is quite delicious and unique. If dry pistachio powder is available then do not add milk powder but just fry the powder in *ghee* until slightly brown, add the hot sugar syrup and set the *burfi*.

The Exquisite World of Indian Cuisine

Almond Fudge
Badam Burfi

Ground almonds fudge is very well liked. It is made by mixing *paneer* or ricotta cheese, ground almonds, powdered sugar, and flavored with ground cardamoms and *kevra* essence and decorated with silver leaves. It makes a very elegant and nutritious dessert for a dinner party or any festive occasion.

SERVES 10 – 12

Ingredients

Slivered almonds soaked overnight	1 lb
Milk as needed (2% fat)	1–2 cups
Ghee	4–8 Tbs
Sugar to taste or	1½ cups
Kevra essence drops	1–2
Cardamoms crushed	1 tsp
Silver leaves	5–6
Water	2 cups
Saffron	½ tsp
Dry milk powder (optional)	1 cup
Almonds crushed (for decoration)	1 tsp

METHOD

1. Grind the soaked almonds fine in a blender with help of milk. (Use as little as possible). Transfer them to a thick-bottom medium size pan and add ¼ cup of *ghee*. Cook on medium low heat until they become thick and doughy. Add the dry milk powder and 4 or more Tbs of *ghee*. Continue stirring and mixing until it starts to separate from the pan.

2. Boil the sugar in 2 cups of water until thick and one string consistency and mix it with the cooked almond dough. Mix well and cool.

3. Add the *kevra* essence, saffron and the crushed cardamoms. Stir well and spread it evenly in a well-greased shallow-large baking dish, at least ½ inch deep.

4. Cover with plastic wrap and refrigerate. Once cool and set, decorate it with silver leaves and cut it into diamond shapes with a sharp knife and take the pieces out in a nice decorative plate and serve.

Note: The quantity of *ghee* can be varied as desired. If using almond powder to make this burfi, then fry the ground powder in ¼ Tbs of *ghee* until light brown and add it to the prepared sugar syrup. Slightly cool and set it in the desired pan and decorate.

Overleaf:

Exquisite Rabari textiles and home furnishings from Kutch region of Gujarat

Photo: ©Idea pix

Coconut Fudge
Nariyal Burfi

Coconut with dry milk powder, sugar and *ghee* makes an excellent coconut fudge or *burfi*. Flavored with ground cardamoms and *kevra* essence it has a great aroma to it. Try it as a snack, any time of the day.

METHOD

1. Cook the grated coconut or dry coconut powder in ½ cup of *ghee*. Keep the heat low. Add the dry milk powder and milk and cook till the fat starts to separate and the mixture becomes doughy and aromatic.
2. Add the crushed cardamoms and *kevra* essence and stir well.
3. Cook sugar and water together in a pan until the syrup is stringy. Add the hot syrup to the dough, cool a little.
4. Grease an 8x10 inch baking dish and sprinkle the grated nut mixture. Pour and spread the coconut *burfi* over it in a ½ inch thick layer and spread the silver leaves on the top of the *burfi*.
5. Let it cool and then cut it in 2 inch diamond shaped pieces and serve. It can be refrigerated easily for a few weeks.

SERVES 10 – 12

Ingredients

Coconut fresh grated	1
or dry coconut powder	3 cups
Ghee	½ cup
*Milk (2% fat)	¼ cup
*Dry milk powder (optional)	2 cups
Cardamoms crushed	1 tsp
Silver leaves	4
Kevra essence	4 drops
Sugar	1 cup
Almonds and pistachio grated	1 Tbs
Water	½ cup
A few drops of food coloring (optional)	

*They are used together and are optional.

Facing page:
The world heritage site of erotic temple carvings at Khajuraho, Madhya Pradesh

Note: Coconut *burfi* can be prepared quickly from the coconut powder available at your local grocery store. Fry the coconut powder (3 cups) on medium heat in one-third cup of *ghee* until light brown and starts to separate from the pan. Add a 14oz can of sweetened condensed milk to it. Stir till it is doughy and thick. Cool it and transfer the contents to ½–1 inch deep small baking pan and spread it evenly. Decorate the burfi by spreading grated nuts over it and cut in diamond shapes. It is ready to serve.

The Exquisite World of Indian Cuisine

Cheese Fudge
Kalakand

Kalakand is a very traditional Indian dessert and has been a part of Indian weddings and festivities from a long time. It used to take lots of time and effort to prepare it from *khoa*. Here is a quick fixing recipe which will surprise you.

METHOD

1. In a thick-bottom pan mix all the ingredients.
2. Cook the mixture on low heat while stirring constantly but gently till it is thick and browned. Leave it on a very low heat until the sugar gets caramelized. Spread it in the 1½ inch deep baking dish. Sprinkle almonds over the layer.
3. Cool it for a few minutes and cut into 1 inch squares.
4. Serve as a dessert after dinner or as a snack with tea or coffee.

SERVES 10 – 12

Ingredients

Low fat cottage cheese unsalted or ricotta cheese or *paneer*	2 cups
Sugar	1 cup
Or	
Sugar substitute (1 gm pkg) (Equal or Splenda)	4
Heavy cream or Half-and-Half	1 cup
Dry milk powder	1 cup
Green cardamom seeds crushed	1 tsp
Almonds crushed	1 Tbs

The Exquisite World of Indian Cuisine

Indian Ice Cream
Kulfi Faluda

Indigenous ice cream preparation of India with finely chopped almonds and pistachio with *faluda* (arrowroot flour vermicelli). Till a few years back, it was made by a hand-churning machine. In spite of its being rich, it is still very popular especially when served with the calorie less *faluda*. Traditional small aluminum moulds give it a conical shape and it is a great dessert on a summer night.

SERVES 8 – 10

Ingredients

Milk (whole)	2 cups
Arrow-root powder dissolved in water	2 Tbs
Dry milk powder (Pkg to make quart)	1 cup
Heavy cream	2 cups
Mango pieces small (optional)	½ cup
Sugar	¾ cup
Almonds shredded	1 Tbs
Pistachio shredded	1 Tbs
Kevra essence drops (optional)	2–3
Faluda* (corn flour vermicelli) as needed	

METHODS

1. Boil the milk in a thick-bottom saucepan for a few minutes and add it to the dissolved arrow-root flour and stir well to blend it. Cook for 2 minutes. Add the heavy cream and stir to mix.

2. Add the sugar and the dry milk powder. Stir and remove from heat. Cool.

3. Add the shredded almonds, shredded pistachio and the *kevra* essence. Add the mango pieces, if you wish.

4. Blend everything well and pour it into moulds.

5. Tightly close the moulds and lay them all side-by-side in a box and put them in a freezer. Takes about 3–4 hours to set.

6. Serve the *kulfi* with *faluda* or plain.

*Faluda is available at your local Indian grocery store. Follow cooking instructions on the package. *Kulfi* has lately become very popular in north America and is being served in the most elite restaurants. Highlight the presentation by coloring the *faluda* in different food colors.

Note: *Holi*, the festival of colors, celebrates the triumph of good over evil and conquest of sensual values over the spiritual. The splurge of colors enriches the freshness of spring with an aura of togetherness. On *Holi*, people are caught unawares with colours being poured on them from top of houses, bursting water balloons or long pistons squirting coloured water (*pichkari*). People in small groups sing, dance and throw color on each other wishing their family, friends and neighbours **Happy Holi**. This colorful festival aims to bridge the social gap and tells us to forget our mutual differences.

Crisp Stuffed Pastry
Gujjia

Holi, the festival of colours, is celebrated all over India and is observed as a holiday. This dessert is traditionally made around this festival. *Gujjia* has a crisp pastry shell that is filled with cardamom, nutmeg, coconut and *khoa*.

SERVES 4 – 6

Ingredients

For Pastry:

Baking soda	⅛ tsp
All purpose flour	2 cups
Ghee	6 Tbs
Water as needed	

For Filling:

Dry milk powder	2 cups
Ghee	6 Tbs
Milk (2% fat)	¼ cup
Pistachio crushed	1 Tbs
Coconut powder	1 cup
Sugar	1 cup
Cinnamon powder	1 tsp
Cardamom powder (Brown *Illaichi*)	½ tsp
Nutmeg	a pinch
Oil for frying	4 cups
Silver or gold leaves and crushed	2–3
Pistachio to decorate	1 Tbs
Almonds crushed to decorate	1 Tbs

METHOD

Filling:

1. Heat the *ghee* in a heavy-bottom pan and add the crushed pistachio. Fry them till they are slightly brown.
2. Add the ground coconut powder and brown it a bit. Remove from heat. Add the dry milk powder and half cup of milk. Mix it together, cool it and add, cinnamon, sugar, nutmeg and cardamom powder. Mix well and set aside.

Pastry:

3. Mix together flour, baking soda with 6 Tbs of *ghee* and knead with water to make a pliable dough.
4. Make small balls from the dough and roll them about 4–6 inches in diameter and about 2 mm in thickness. Fill with the filling and fold over and twist the edges, make a crescent shape and fry in oil heated at 300°F–340°F or so until (slowly) golden brown. Slow cooking is required.
5. Serve these layered with silver leaves, crushed almonds and pistachio.

Gram Flour Fudge
Besan ki Burfi / Mohan Thaal

RAJASTHAN

Gram flour fudge is enjoyed all over India. It has different names in different parts of the country. It is called *Besan ki Burfi* in northern states whereas in Gujarat it is called *Mohan Thaal*. It is very delicious and is prepared with proteinaceous gram flour.

SERVES 6 – 8

Ingredients

Gram flour	2 cups
Milk (2% fat)	2 Tbs
Clarified butter or *ghee*	$2/3$ cup
Sugar	1½ cups
Water	1½ cups
Cardamom powder	½ tsp
Dry milk powder (optional)	1 cup
Saffron	¼ tsp
Almonds crushed	1 Tbs
Pistachio crushed	1 Tbs
Silver or gold leaf *(varq)*	as needed

METHOD

1. Mix the milk into the dry *besan* flour in a medium size bowl and rub it through the fine sieve into powder and set it aside.
2. In a large heavy-bottom frying pan fry the *besan* with the clarified butter until light brown and as soon as you smell the aroma add the crushed nuts. Fry a little and remove from fire and set it aside.
3. In a medium size pan transfer the sugar with water and bring it to a boil. Cook till the syrup is stringy (when the syrup is dropped slowly from the spoon it shows a stringy consistency) about 20–30 minutes.
4. Add a cup of dry milk powder to the cooked *besan* flour and stir to mix well (about 3–4 minutes on low heat). Add the cardamom powder and stir to mix.
5. Add the warm syrup to the cooked *besan* flour and stir and mix well for 2 minutes.
6. Pour the mixture into a 8-10 inches baking pan that is about 2 inches deep. Let it cool and spread a gold or silver leaf *(varq)* if you wish (available at your local Indian grocer).
7. Sprinkle the saffron powder, crushed pistachio and almonds on top and cut into 1 inch squares or into diamond shapes.
8. Serve as a snack or as a dessert after dinner.

The Exquisite World of Indian Cuisine

Sweet Pancakes
Maalpua

Maalpua or Sweet Pancakes as they are commonly known in northern India, are made on festive occasions as well as for a snack and are also occasionally served for breakfast. In the southern states these are flavored with mashed fruits of the season like banana, guava and mango, and most of the time, regular milk is substituted by coconut milk. In Bengal the regular milk is substituted by buttermilk and here they are served with sugar syrup. In Tamil Nadu, the milk is replaced by palm sap or *taadi* that also acts as a fermenter.

METHOD

1. Mix the flour, cream of wheat, and baking powder in a bowl and add any kind of milk you have available like regular whole milk, buttermilk, coconut milk or palm sap and sugar.
2. Beat the batter smooth and add the crushed cardamoms and the fennel seeds and mix them well. Add any of the mashed fruit you want to flavor with.
3. In a thick-bottom skillet heat one Tbs of oil or *ghee* for a minute and add 2 Tbs of the batter and by tilting the skillet back and forth spread the batter thin. Let the underside turn golden brown. Turn it with a spatula and add a little more oil or *ghee,* if needed. When this side also turns brown remove from the skillet and transfer it to the serving plate and serve sprinkled with powdered sugar, crushed almonds and pistachio.
4. Serve with hot milk or tea. It is a delicious breakfast. If you want to serve with sugar syrup follow Step 5. Serve with fresh fruits, if you wish.
5. Boil sugar and water for 15 minutes and add rose water, reduce the heat to low and keep warm. Pour it over the hot pancakes and serve.

SERVES 6 – 8

Ingredients

For the Batter:

All purpose flour	1 cup
Suji* or *Rava* or plain all purpose flour	1 cup
Milk (whole or 2% fat)	2–3 cup
Sugar	2–4 Tbs
Crushed cardamoms	1 tsp
Baking powder**	1 tsp
Butter or *ghee* or oil (for frying)	2 Tbs
Fennel seeds	1 tsp
Mashed bananas, mangoes, guavas, or jackfruit (optional)	1 cup

For the Syrup:

Sugar	1½ cup
Water	2½ cups
Rose water (optional)	1¼ tsp
Almonds crushed shelled	2 Tbs
Pistachio crushed shelled	2 Tbs

Here is a simpler way of making *Maalpua*:

Milk (whole or or heavy cream and milk	4 cups	Riceflour (Mixture of ¼ cup *maida* and ¼ cup *suji*)	½ cup
Sugar	2 Tbs	Ghee	1 cup
Water	½ cup	Cardamom powder	½ tsp

1. Cook the milk, until it is reduced to half. Add the rice flour, stir and cook it for 2 minutes. Remove from fire, add the cardamom powder and mix.
2. Prepare the syrup by boiling the sugar in water till it is little thick.
3. Smear a frying pan with ½ tsp of *ghee* and pour the batter into a pan, cook it.
4. Serve with sugar syrup over it.

Note:
*Suji or *Rava* is the Indian cream of wheat available only at Indian grocery stores.

**Baking powder can be omitted by adding a cup of yogurt and reduce the amount of milk accordingly.

CHAPTER 11

Condiments, Pickles and Dips

A dab of *chutney* or pickle makes the food go down in the most delightful way. These condiments are not only full of zest and taste but are also a powerhouse of health benefits. They provide a full spectrum of all six tastes which form a complete Indian meal according to the ancient *Vedas*. They provide digestive ingredients to reduce high blood pressure and have antibacterial properties. Fresh *chutneys* and pickles have been a part of the Indian meal from ancient times. They are a powerhouse of antioxidants. Some *chutneys* preserve very well and can be bottled and enjoyed over a period of time.

Back home whenever we complained of food being dull and drab our mother would tell us to take a little *chutney* or pickle which made all the difference to taste and the palate.

Chutneys are usually served with snacks. *Coconut Chutney, Eggplant Chutney, Channa Dal Chutney* and Peanut *Chutney* are very popular in south India. They are served with snacks like *Dosa, Idli* and *Vada*. Fresh herbal and fruit *chutneys* like Mint *Chutney, Coriander Chutney, Tamarind Chutney, Zucchini Chutney* and *Red Pepper Chutney* are from north India and are served with regular meals as well as snacks like *Pakoras. Samosas, Dahi Vada* and *Chaat* etc. Fruit *chutney*s like *Mango Chutney, Pineapple Chutney, Cranberry Chutney, Apple* and *Ripe Mango Chutney* are famous all over the world.

Use of *chutneys* and pickles is rather essential in the tropical weather because in the hot summer months the body tends to get sluggish in producing digestive juices and physical activity slows down. Pickles and *chutneys* stimulate the appetite and enhance digestion.

Pickles are also similar to *chutneys* except that these are made in a more sterilized manner and are prepared with pungent mustard oil so as to give them a longer shelf life. The contents are very well heated and all the moisture is removed so that the pickle can stay fresh in a bottle even without an airtight cap at room temperature. These are used as accompaniment to a meal that can do with little extra spicing.

Pickles also act as digestives (*Lemon Pickle*) and balance different tastes of the food. Pickles go very well with *Paranthas, Kichadi, Rava Dosa* and *Gram Flour Pancakes*. Carrot and Radish pickles are made fresh to go with daily meals. These do not stay fresh for more than a couple of days.

Condiments are nothing but smoothly beaten yogurt flavored with freshly chopped vegetables or fruits garnished by ground roasted cumin, salt, red and black pepper. Sometimes a little sugar is also added. The *Raitas* are known as *pachadi* in south India.

There are fresh vegetables *Raitas* like Spinach *Raita,* Eggplant *Raita,* Cucumber *Raita,* Banana-Raisins *Raita,* and Mint *Raita.* You will come across many more kind of *Raitas* in this book and they are as delicious as the ones mentioned above and are equally complimentary and interesting. It is not unusual to see both the side accompaniments, *Raita* and salad, in a meal depending on how spicy the food is.

Bananas & Raisins Condiment
Kele aur Kishmish ka Raita

Banana is one of the oldest and ancient fruits of India and is held in great reverence by the Indian people. Banana Condiment has a special significance and is usually made on an auspicious or a religious occasion and has a sweet taste. It also makes a great accompaniment to a hot and spicy meal.

METHOD

1. Whip the yogurt and add salt, red pepper and black pepper. Mix well.
2. Add the sugar and stir to mix.
3. Add the chopped bananas, raisins and chopped walnuts. Stir well to mix.
4. Serve topped with ground roasted cumin seeds and *garam masala*.
5. Makes a great side dish with a hot and spicy meal.

SERVES 6 – 8

Ingredients

Yogurt	2 cups
Salt to taste or	½ tsp
Sugar to taste or	1–2 Tbs
Red pepper	1 tsp
Black pepper	½ tsp
Bananas cut into ½ inch pieces (depending on the size)	1–2
Raisins washed and soaked and drained	2 Tbs
Walnuts finely chopped (optional) Or	2 Tbs
Coconut fresh grated Or	2 Tbs
Dried dates soaked and grated	2 Tbs
Cumin seeds roasted and ground	1 tsp
Garam masala	½ tsp

Mint Condiment
Pudina Raita

Yogurt mixed with ground mint and the spices makes a refreshing accompaniment to any meal.

METHOD

1. Grind or blend in the blender, mint, cilantro, green chilies and whipped yogurt, and transfer to a serving bowl.
2. Add boiled chopped potatoes*, salt and black pepper to this and mix well.
3. Garnish with finely chopped onions, red pepper, ground roasted cumin seeds and *garam masala*. Serve.

*Freshly chopped potato can be substituted by one finely chopped yellow or white onion.

SERVES 8 – 10

Ingredients

Mint leaves fresh washed	2 Tbs
Coriander leaves green	2 Tbs
Green chillies chopped (mild)	1 Tbs
Yogurt	2 cups
Freshly boiled chopped potatoes (optional)	1 cup
Salt	1 tsp
Black pepper	½ tsp

To garnish:

Green onions chopped to garnish	1 Tbs
Red pepper	½ tsp
Cumin seeds ground, roasted	1 tsp
Garam masala	½ tsp

Spinach Condiment
Palak Raita

Yogurt flavored with cooked spinach and garnished with roasted ground cumin seeds, *garam masala*, red pepper, salt and chopped coriander leaves makes a pleasant and appetizing accompaniment to any meal.

METHOD

1. Chop the spinach very fine and cook in water for 10 minutes and drain.
2. Heat vegetable oil in a skillet and add the fenugreek seeds. As soon as they start turning color add the spinach, salt, red pepper, and stir well and make it a little dry. Remove from heat and cool.
3. Mix the whipped yogurt with lemon juice in a bowl and add the cooked spinach.
4. Top it with roasted ground cumin powder, *garam masala*, paprika, and chopped coriander leaves and serve.

SERVES 8

Ingredients

Spinach fresh chopped or frozen 10 oz pkg	1
Vegetable oil	1 Tbs
Fenugreek seeds	½ tsp
Salt	½ tsp
Red (Cayenne) pepper	½ tsp
Yogurt (whipped)	2 cups
Lemon juice	1 Tbs
Cumin powder roasted	1 tsp
Garam masala	1 tsp
Paprika	½ tsp
Coriander leaves chopped	1 Tbs

Cucumber Condiment
Kheere ka Raita

Yogurt with grated cucumber and sprinkled with spices makes a very cool and refreshing accompaniment to any meal and is very easy to prepare.

METHOD

1. Beat two cups of yogurt with an eggbeater until smooth in a deep serving dish.
2. Grate the cucumber and squeeze its juices. Save the squeezed juice and set it aside. Add the squeezed cucumber to the yogurt and stir to mix. Use the squeezed juice to thin the *raita* to desired consistency and mix well.
3. Serve sprinkled with salt, red pepper, roasted ground cumin powder, black pepper and *garam masala* and garnish with chopped coriander leaves. Serve.

SERVES 8 – 10

Ingredients

Yogurt	2 cups
Cucumber grated	1
Salt	½ tsp
Red pepper	½ tsp
Black pepper	¼ tsp
Cumin seeds ground, roasted	¼ tsp
Garam masala	¼ tsp
Coriander leaves chopped	1 Tbs

The Exquisite World of Indian Cuisine

Gram Flour Balls Condiment
Boondi Raita

Yogurt dish made with the tiny fried gram flour balls called *Boondi*. This can be made by pressing a rather thick gram flour batter through a fine sieve into the hot oil or ready to use *boondi* can be bought from your local Indian grocers. Add *boondi* to the plain smooth yogurt and sprinkle with spices. This is one of the very popular yogurt condiments in a north Indian meal.

METHOD

1. Soak the *boondi* in medium size bowl in hot water and set aside for 10 minutes.
2. Whip the yogurt with a whisk and set it aside.
3. Add cold water to the bowl with soaked *boondi* and squeeze out the water. Transfer the *boondi* into the whipped yogurt. Mix the yogurt gently and add the salt, red pepper, ground roasted cumin, black pepper and *garam masala*.
4. Mix well. Serve sprinkled with chopped coriander leaves.
5. If the *raita* looks too thick add a couple of tablespoons of milk or buttermilk and stir it well. Makes a delicious accompaniment to any meal.
6. Serve with any curry, *pulav* and bread of your choice.

SERVES 6 – 8

Ingredients

Boondi	½ cup
Yogurt	2 cups
Hot water	3 cups
Salt	1 tsp
Red pepper	½–1 tsp
Cumin ground, roasted	1 tsp
Black pepper	½ tsp
Garam masala	½–1 tsp
Coriander leaves chopped	1 Tbs

Note: Homemade *boondi* can be added directly to the whipped yogurt (keep it little thin in consistency). Stir and garnish it as usual and serve.

Fresh Vegetable Condiment
Vegetable Raita

This refreshing yogurt preparation with chopped up salad vegetables and topped with ground roasted cumin powder, salt, red pepper, *garam masala* and chopped coriander leaves is very well liked with any curry. Try it.

SERVES 8

Ingredients

Yogurt	2 cups
Cucumbers peeled and chopped in small cubes	½ cup
Radish fresh finely chopped	½ cup
Tomatoes fresh finely chopped	½ cup
Carrots grated	2 Tbs
Green onions chopped	¼ cup
Green hot peppers chopped	1 Tbs
Bell peppers finely chopped	2 Tbs
Salt	to taste
Black pepper	½ tsp
Cumin powder roasted ground	1 tsp
Red pepper	1 tsp
Garam masala	1 tsp
Green coriander leaves chopped	1 Tbs

METHOD

1. Whip the yogurt smooth with a whisk and add all the chopped vegetables. Mix well and refrigerate.

2. Just before serving, top it with salt, black pepper, ground roasted cumin powder, red pepper, *garam masala*, and the chopped green coriander leaves. Makes a very appetizing and elegant presentation.

Note: Fresh vegetable *raita* soothes the palate while taking spicy food and also provides a salad to complete a meal.

Baked Eggplant Condiment
Baingan ka Raita

An appetizing accompaniment to any meal or can be used as a dip with your favorite teatime bread.

METHOD

1. Wash and cut the eggplant in half and lay it down in a nonstick roasting pan lined with a tin foil.
2. Brush the halves with a little oil, ½ tsp of salt, red pepper and turmeric and roast the eggplant in the oven at broil until the eggplant is very soft.
3. Take the eggplant out of the oven and scoop the pulp into a bowl leaving the skin behind. Mash it smoothly.
4. In a heavy-bottom skillet, heat 2 Tbs of oil and fry chopped onions, ginger and hot chillies till light brown. Add chopped tomatoes, remaining salt, red pepper, black pepper, *garam masala* and stir to mix. Add the cooked eggplant, cook for a while, mix everything well and add the chopped coriander leaves and mix them in.
5. Add the cooked eggplant to the yogurt and mix it well.
6. Transfer to a serving dish and serve topped with a sprinkle of cilantro and a pinch of *garam masala* as a dip or as a *raita*.

SERVES 6 – 8

Ingredients

Eggplant medium	1
Oil	2 Tbs
Turmeric powder	½ tsp
Onions chopped	½ cup
Ginger	1 Tbs
Red hot chillies chopped	2 Tbs
Tomatoes chopped small	½ cup
Salt	1 tsp
Red pepper	½ tsp
Cilantro chopped	½ cup
Black pepper	to taste
Cumin powder ground roasted	½ tsp
Garam masala	½ tsp
Yogurt beaten smooth	3 cups

Mango Condiment
Aam ka Raita

Mango condiment is the most delicious of all the *raitas* especially if right ingredients are used. It is important that we use fibreless and firm ripe mangoes. Flavored with ground roasted cumin, lemon juice and curry leaves, this *raita* is appetizing with any meal. Mango is one of the very ancient fruits of India and is greatly revered. Mango leaves are also used to decorate the canopy under which weddings and other auspicious events take place.

METHOD

1. Whip the yogurt and add the salt, red pepper, black pepper, ground roasted cumin seeds, *garam masala*, lemon juice and chopped *karhi* leaves and stir and mix the ingredients well.
2. Add the chopped mangoes and gently mix and coat them well with the spiced yogurt.
3. Chill a little and serve with any meal.

SERVES 6 – 8

Ingredients

Yogurt	2 cups
Salt	¾ tsp
Red pepper	1 tsp
Black pepper	1 tsp
Cumin seeds ground, roasted	1 tsp
Garam masala	1 tsp
Lemon juice	1 tsp
Karhi leaves chopped	½ tsp
Mangoes ripe and non-fibrous kind chopped	1½ cup

Mint Dip
Pudina Chutney (Sweet and Sour)

A refreshing herbaceous accompaniment for *pakoras, samosas* and a real meal. It is one of the most commonly used *chutneys* in Indian cuisine. It has many health benefits. It is packed with antioxidants and acts as an excellent digestant.

METHOD
1. Put all the ingredients in the blender and add as little water as possible to grind to a smooth paste to a consistency of a vegetable dip. Taste and adjust seasoning.
2. Chill till ready to serve.

SERVES 10 – 20

Ingredients

Fresh mint leaves washed	1 cup
Fresh coriander	2 cups
Green chilies chopped	2 Tbs
Lime juice	2 Tbs
Or	
Tamarind paste dissolved in 2 Tbs of water	1 Tbs
Sugar	to taste
Salt	to taste
Red pepper	½ tsp
Ginger chopped	1 Tbs
Green mangoes chopped (if available)	2 Tbs
Onion chopped	1 cup
Water needed to make smooth *chutney*	

Note: Mint *chutney* is served both ways, sweet and sour or only salty and tangy. Sweet and sour is more common. *Tamarind turns the *chutney* to a darker shade of green, and that is why lemon or lime juice is preferred. Omit sugar if you want salty and tangy *chutney*.

Note: Mix 2 Tbs of mint *chutney* into 1 cup of plain yogurt to make mint *raita*.

Coconut Dip
Nariyal Chutney

A wonderful accompaniment for *dosa, idli* and various appetizers. It is mostly served in the south-western parts of India.

METHOD

1. Heat 2 Tbs of oil in a skillet and fry the split gram until light brown. Remove from oil and set aside.
2. Remove the flesh of a fresh coconut *(see introduction)* and chop the pieces coarsely. Transfer them to blender and add ginger, green chilies, onions, coriander leaves, roasted split gram, yogurt, lemon juice or tamarind paste and grind them into a paste by adding as much cold water as needed to make a smooth and thick paste as a regular vegetable dip.
3. Add the salt to taste and set aside.
4. Heat the same oil in the skillet used for frying the split gram and add the mustard seeds, dry whole red peppers, curry leaves, *urad dal*, and asafoetida powder.
5. Cook until the mustard seeds start to pop and *urad dal* is light brown.
6. Add the ground coconut mixture to this skillet and stir the mixture for 10–20 seconds on the heat.
7. Remove from heat and transfer the *chutney* to a serving bowl.
8. Ready to be served with appetizers, *dosas* or *idlis*.

SERVES 15 – 20

Ingredients

Vegetable oil	4 Tbs
Coconut flesh fresh cut in small pieces	1
Or	
Dry unsweetened coconut	½ cup
Ginger chopped	2 tsp
Green chilies chopped	3 Tbs
Onion chopped	½ cup
Green coriander leaves	1 cup
Urad dal	1 tsp
Red peppers dry, whole to taste or	3–4
Split Gram (*Channa dal*) pan roasted	¼ cup
Yogurt	¼ cup
Tamarind paste	½ tsp
Or	
Lemon juice	1 Tbs
Salt	2–3 tsp
Mustard seeds	1 tsp
Curry leaves	¼ cup
Asafoetida powder	½ tsp
Water or fresh coconut powder as needed	

The Exquisite World of Indian Cuisine

Tomato Dip
Tamatar ki Chutney

Excellent accompaniment with a meal or an appetizer.

SERVES 6 – 8

Ingredients

Tomatoes chopped (ripe)	4 cups
Prunes or dry apricots soaked in ½ cup of warm water, chopped	¼ cup
Onion chopped	1 cup
Ginger chopped	1 Tbs
Garlic chopped	1 Tbs
Green chilies chopped	2
Cumin seeds	1 tsp
Mustard seeds	1 tsp
Salt	to taste
Turmeric powder	¾ tsp
Vegetable oil	3 Tbs
Sugar	to taste
Raisins	2 Tbs
Red pepper ground	1 tsp
Lemon juice	1 Tbs
Garam masala	1 tsp
Cilantro fresh chopped	2 Tbs

METHOD

1. Heat the oil. Add cumin seeds and mustard seeds. Wait till they start popping and then add chopped onions, ginger, garlic and green chilies. Fry the onions in oil till they turn light brown and then add the chopped tomatoes, prunes or apricots, raisins, salt and turmeric powder. Cook on low heat for about half an hour or till the oil separates from the mixture and tomatoes are puréed.
2. If you prefer smooth *chutney*, put the mixture in a blender and blend it smoothly, otherwise go to step 3.
3. Add sugar, lemon juice, red pepper and *garam masala* and stir.
4. Cook on low heat till it is of creamy consistency. Top it with fresh coriander and serve with appetizers or with a regular meal.

Note: Chopped green mangoes can be used instead of apricots or prunes. It will keep the original flavor of the *chutney*.

The Exquisite World of Indian Cuisine

Tamarind Dip
Imli ki Chutney

Tamarind Dip is also one of the most popular *chutneys* of India and can be served with almost all snacks. It is commonly served with *golgappa, papri, chaat, samosa, pakora, bhelpuri* and many other snacks. It can easily be compared with ketchup of the west.

METHOD

1. Mix and stir ¼ cup of ready to use tamarind pulp into 2 cups of water. Cook on slow heat till it gets thick and saucy. Set it aside.

To make fresh tamarind paste from deseeded tamarind:

2. If you are using solid deseeded dry flesh of tamarind then soak it in 2 cups of water overnight. The pulp will become soft.
3. Push the pulp through the strainer. Add more water to the pulp to have the consistency of a sauce.
4. Put it on fire and cook on low heat till it becomes thick like custard. This will take about 10 minutes. Set it aside.
5. Either one of the above tamarind sauces can be used.
6. Heat 2 Tbs oil and add the asafoetida, cloves, black pepper corns and cardamom seed. Wait till they sizzle. Add ginger, salt, red pepper and cook for few minutes until ginger browns. Add prepared tamarind sauce. Stir to mix. Transfer the mixed *chutney* to a blender and blend it smooth. Pour it into a little cooking pan.
7. Add sugar, ground roasted cumin powder, *garam masala*, raisins or dried dates and apple sauce. Stir to mix and cook until the *chutney* is of the consistency of a thick sauce. Add more sugar, if needed.
8. Simmer a little on low heat. Transfer it to a serving bowl. Chill till ready to serve.

SERVES 15 – 20

Ingredients

Tamarind de-seeded	1 cup
Tamarind pulp	¼ cup
Water	2 cups
Oil	2 Tbs
Asafoetida	a pinch
Black pepper whole	1 tsp
Cloves whole	4
Cardamoms seeds	½ tsp
Ginger chopped	2 Tbs
Salt to taste or	1½ tsp
Red pepper	1 tsp
Cumin powder roasted	1 Tbs
Sugar to taste or	¼ cup
Garam masala	1 tsp
Raisins or dried dates finely chopped	1 Tbs
Apple sauce	½ cup

A roadside golgappa seller

Eggplant Dip
Baingan ki Chutney

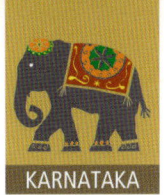
KARNATAKA

Eggplant, onions, ginger, garlic, green chilies, fresh coconut, tomatoes are fried with spices and fresh herbs. They are then ground to make a very delicious *chutney*. It is a great specialty of south India.

SERVES 10 – 15

Ingredients

Japanese eggplant 6 inches, chopped into thin strips	4
Vegetable oil	¼ cup
Urad dal	1 Tbs
Asafoetida	½ tsp
Green chilies chopped	1 Tbs
Red peppers whole broken	2
Tomatoes chopped	1 cup
Fresh coconut grated	¼ cup
Or	
Dry coconut (from your local Indian grocer)	2 Tbs
Tamarind paste	¼ tsp
Water as needed or	1–2 cups
Yogurt	¾ cup
Salt	1 tsp
Green coriander leaves chopped	1 Tbs
Mustard seeds	1 tsp
Cumin seeds	1 tsp
Onions chopped	¾ cup
Ginger chopped	1 Tbs
Garlic chopped	1 Tbs
Coriander seeds	1 tsp

METHOD

1. Fry the sliced eggplant in oil and set it aside.
2. In the same oil cook the mustard seeds, cumin seeds, coriander seeds, asafoetida and *urad dal* and wait till the mustard seeds start popping and *urad dal* is light brown.
3. Add the onions, ginger, garlic, and green chilies in the same pan and cook until the onions are transparent. Add the whole dry red peppers and cook a minute longer.
4. Now add the tomatoes and the grated coconut or dry coconut powder.
5. Cook on low heat for 2 minutes. Transfer the ingredients from the skillet to the blender and add the tamarind.
6. Blend the contents with the help of water and yogurt and add the fried eggplant and the salt.
7. Make sure you add only enough water to make a paste of the consistency of *chutney*. Serve with *vadas, idlis* or any meal and top it off with chopped green coriander leaves.
8. A very delicious and nutritious addition to the meal.

Coriander Dip
Dhaniye ki Chutney

This is another very popular *chutney* to go with meals and snacks, all over the country. This refreshing *chutney* of green coriander leaves, onions, green mango or lime juice and green chilies is very healthy and delicious. It goes very well with *pakoras, samosas, vada,* or *bondas* and can be served with any meal.

METHOD

1. Put all the ingredients in a blender and blend with the help of little water to a smooth paste.
2. Add salt to taste, store in the refrigerator and serve chilled.

SERVES 20 – 25

Ingredients

Coriander leaves green	2 cups
Green chilies (mild) chopped	½ cup
Onions chopped	¾ cup
Salt	to taste
Red pepper (optional)	1 tsp
Ginger chopped	1 Tbs
Lime juice or green mango	2 lbs
Or	
Tamarind paste	½ tsp
Water as needed or	1½ cup

HINT

Grind ½ cup of cooked chick-peas (from a can) and 2 Tbs of chopped coconut with the above ingredients to give it a south Indian touch.

Apple Dip
Seb ki Chutney

Apples are delicious, when fresh, but in the Indian Himalayan states where apples grow in abundance they are cooked with sugar, spices, lemon, raisins and nuts to make very delectable *chutney*. This can be served with regular meals but goes especially well with *tandoori nan* and a meat curry.

METHOD

1. In a saucepan combine the vinegar with brown sugar and cook on low heat until the syrup is thick and sticks to the side of the pan (about 8–10 minutes). Remove from heat.
2. Add the ground roasted cumin powder, crushed fennel seeds, chopped ginger, dry mustard powder, dry red chilies broken, *garam masala* and freshly ground black pepper, salt and lemon juice. Mix the spices well into the syrup.
3. Add the chopped apples and plums, and continue cooking until the fruits are soft (about 15 minutes).
4. Remove from heat and stir in the walnuts and raisins.
5. Cook for 2 more minutes and cool the *chutney* to serve.

SERVES 15 – 20

Ingredients

Vinegar	¼ cup
Brown sugar	1½ cup
Cumin powder roasted ground	1½ tsp
Fennel seeds crushed	1 tsp
Fresh ginger finely chopped	1 Tbs
Mustard powder	1 tsp
Red chilies dry broken	2
Garam masala	½ tsp
Black pepper freshly grated	1 tsp
Salt	1 tsp
Lemon juice	¼ cup
Apples washed, peeled and chopped	2 cups
Plums washed, peeled and chopped	2 cups
Walnuts chopped	½ cup
Raisins	¼ cup

Note: Serve *chutney* with all the meat curries and especially with the grilled and the *tandoor* baked meat dishes. It also goes very well with regular meals and sandwitches.

Cranberry Dip
Karonde ki Chutney

Cranberry (*Karonda*) taste very much like a berry in India called *phalsa* and is prepared here very much like the *phalsa chutney*. *Phalsa* berry is a regional fruit and grows only in India and south-east Asia. It has a unique sweet and sour taste. Cranberries cannot do full justice to their taste but they are the closest to *phalsa*. When it is flavored with lemon, sugar and raisins, the *chutney* is really delicious. It can be served with *dosas, paranthas*, or with regular meals. to give that special sweet and sour taste which makes the curries taste even better.

METHOD

1. Mix sugar and vinegar and bring to a boil. Add the black pepper, cardamoms, cloves and the cinnamon, and cook on low heat till it is sticky (about 10 minutes). Set it aside.
2. In a separate pan, heat the oil and add the mustard seeds till they start to splatter. Add curry leaves, ginger, serrano peppers, salt, red pepper, cranberries, raisins, and stir to mix and cook for 2 minutes.
3. Add the cranberries mixture to the syrup and mix thoroughly. Cook on low heat until it starts to sizzle and the cranberries are soft (about 8–10 minutes).
4. Remove from the heat and cool.

SERVES 15 – 20

Ingredients

Sugar	1 cup
Vinegar	2 Tbs
Black pepper corns	1 tsp
Cardamoms (large)	2
Cloves	1 tsp
Cinnamon sticks (small)	2
Oil	2 Tbs
Mustard seeds	1 tsp
Curry leaves	8–10
Salt	1 tsp
Ginger chopped	1 Tbs
Serrano chilies chopped	1 Tbs
Red pepper	1 tsp
Cranberries	1 lb
Raisins	1 Tbs

Note: Use 1 lb of cranberry sauce instead of fresh cranberries to make this *chutney*. Skip step 1 and start with step 2. Add 1 tsp of *garam masala* at the end of step 2 and cook for another 8–10 minutes. Remove from heat and serve. Omit step 3 also.

The Exquisite World of Indian Cuisine

Ripe Mango Dip
Aam ki Chutney

Mangoes grow in abundance in India and in the growing season even ripe mangoes are flavored with sugar, spices and lemon to make *chutney*. The sweet and tart taste of mangoes is just perfect for a *chutney*. Any meal will seem appetizing with it.

METHOD

1. Heat the oil in a deep saucepan and add the cumin seeds. Wait till they start popping.
2. Add the ginger, green chilies and fry till they are light brown.
3. Add the sliced mangoes, salt, red pepper, soaked and drained raisins and stir to mix. Turn the heat on low.
4. Add the lemon juice, sugar and *garam masala* and cook on low heat till the mangoes are tender (about 5–10 minutes).
5. Serve with rice *pulav* or any meal. The *chutney* can be stored in the refrigerator for several days.

SERVES 15 – 20

Ingredients

Oil	1 Tbs
Cumin seeds	1 tsp
Ginger	1 Tbs
Green chilies chopped	1 Tbs
Mangoes (ripe but firm), peeled and chopped	2 lbs
Salt	1 tsp
Red pepper	1 tsp
Raisins soaked in ¼ cup water	1 Tbs
Lemon juice	2 Tbs
Sugar	½ cup
Garam masala	1 tsp

Red Pepper Dip
Lal Mirch ki Chutney

This is a bright red *chutney* with a crunchy taste south Indian style. It goes with any meal or with an appetizer. Prepare it ahead of time because it can be stored in the refrigerator for several days.

METHOD

1. In a non-stick skillet add 3 Tbs of oil and fry the chopped red bell pepper till they start turning brown, then add the chopped tomato. Cook for few more minutes until they turn brown. Remove them from the oil and set them aside.
2. In the same oil fry onions, ginger, garlic and green chilies, and cook until the onions turn brown. Add the cumin seeds, asafoetida, and wait till the cumin start popping and then add the whole red dry pepper and cook for a few more minutes. Cool and transfer the contents into a blender.
3. Add the browned bell peppers, yogurt and tomatoes also to the blender along with the tamarind paste, red chili powder, salt and blend it all together. Add more water, if needed to blend. The *chutney* should have the fine consistency of a vegetable dip. Transfer the *chutney* to a mixing bowl and set it aside.
4. Heat 1 Tbs of oil in a skillet and add 1 tsp of mustard seeds, curry leaves, *urad dal*, and fry until the *dal* is brown and the mustard seeds start popping. Pour the tempering over the *chutney* in the mixing bowl and mix it well.
5. Mix and garnish the *chutney* with chopped coriander leaves and serve with your favourite bread, like *idli, dosa* or *parantha*.

SERVES 8 – 10

Ingredients

Red bell pepper seeded and finely chopped	1 large
Onion chopped	1 large
Yogurt	1 tsp
Garlic chopped	1 tsp
Green chilies chopped	1 tsp
Ginger chopped	1 tsp
Red hot chili powder	1 tsp
Tamarind paste	1 tsp
Tomato chopped	1
Coriander leaves chopped	2 Tbs
Salt	1 tsp
Mustard seeds	1 tsp
Whole red dry peppers	3–4
Asafoetida powder	½ tsp
Cumin seeds	1 tsp
Curry leaves	4–6
Urad dal	1 Tbs
Oil	¼ cup
Water as needed	

Zucchini Dip
Tori ki Chutney

MAHARASHTRA

Tori ki Chutney is very common in the western parts of India.

SERVES 10–15

Ingredients

Oil	2 Tbs
Onions chopped	½ cup
Green hot chilies	2 Tbs
Zucchini peeled and chopped into very small pieces	2 cups
Cilantro leaves chopped	½ cup
Almonds slivered and chopped	2 Tbs
Lemon Juice	1½ Tbs
Salt	1 tsp
Cumin ground roasted	1 tsp
Black pepper	½ tsp

METHOD

1. Heat the oil. Add the onions, chilies and cook until transparent and add the chopped zucchini. Stir to mix and cook on low heat till the zucchini is tender. Add the almonds. Cook for few minutes and set it aside.

2. Blend the coriander leaves in a coffee grinder with the lemon juice, salt, ground roasted cumin and black pepper and transfer it to a serving bowl. Mix the cooked zucchini mixture into it.

3. Serve with your favorite bread or a meal.

Note: The amount of green chilies used can vary according to taste. This *chutney* can easily be converted into most delicious salsa (Mexican dip) by adding ½ cup of finely chopped fresh tomatoes and avocado.

Peanut Dip
Mungphali ki Chutney

GUJARAT

Another delicious *chutney* from south India. Made with roasted peanuts mixed with yogurt, onions and red pepper is usually served with *idli*s, and *dosa*s. It has a unique creamy and spicy taste that makes it one of the most delicious and appetizing *chutneys*.

SERVES 10–12

METHOD

1. Heat the oil in a skillet and add the peanuts to roast them light brown (if they are not roasted). Take them out of the oil with a slotted spoon and set them aside. Add the chopped onions to the same oil and fry them golden brown. Remove onions too from the oil and set them aside.
2. Add the green chilies, chopped ginger and the red peppers to the oil and roast them until brown and transfer them to the same bowl with onions. Dissolve tamarind pulp in a cup of water and set it aside.
3. Cool and grind the onions, green chillies, ginger, red peppers and peanuts in an electric blender to a smooth purée with the help of tamarind water. Set aside the *chutney* in a medium size bowl. Add salt and sugar, and mix it well.
4. Heat the same oil used for frying onions and add the mustard seeds and wait till they pop and then add *channa dal* and fry till it turns golden brown. Add the asafoetida and curry leaves and fry for a minute or two.
5. Add the above tempering to the *chutney* in a bowl. Add red pepper, salt and stir to mix it well with a salad spoon and serve sprinkled with coriander leaves. Adjust seasonings.

Ingredients

Oil	3 Tbs
Peanuts roasted	1 cup
Tamarind pulp	1 tsp
Onions chopped and fried	1 cup
Red peppers whole, dry, broken	4
Green chilies	2
Ginger chopped	1 tsp
Garlic chopped	1 tsp
Mustard seeds	1 tsp
Cumin seeds	½ tsp
Channa dal	1 tsp
Curry leaves	4–6
Asafoetida powder	a pinch
Red pepper	1 tsp
Salt to taste or	1 tsp
Brown sugar to taste or	1 tsp
Coriander leaves chopped	1 Tbs
Water	1 cup

Note: Yogurt can be substituted with tamarind water.

The Exquisite World of Indian Cuisine

Pineapple Dip
Ananaas ki Chutney

This sweet and sour *chutney* makes a nice accompaniment with any meal.

SERVES 8 – 10

Ingredients

Vegetable oil	2 Tbs
Mustard seeds	1 tsp
Red hot chili finely chopped, medium	1 tsp
Ginger sliced in thin strips	1 tsp
Garlic finely chopped	1 tsp
Onions chopped sliced thin	¼ cup
Raisins	2 Tbs
Sugar	1 Tbs
Salt	1 tsp
Tamarind pulp	1 tsp
Crushed pineapple (1 can)	15 Ozs
Cumin roasted, ground	1 tsp
All purpose flour	1 tsp
Lemon juice	2 Tbs
Black pepper	½ tsp
Water to mix flour	2 Tbs

METHOD

1. Heat 2 Tbs of vegetable oil and add the mustard seeds, wait till they pop and then add the chopped chili pepper, ginger, garlic, onions and stir-fry until the onions are slightly brown.
2. Add the raisins and cook another minute. Add the salt, tamarind dissolved in 2 Tbs of pineapple juice (crushed pineapple with its juices, from the can) lemon juice and cook for 2 minutes on low heat. Add the sugar and stir to mix.
3. Add the all purpose flour mixed in water to the *chutney* and mix in well. Cook for another 2 minutes.
4. Remove from heat and add the roasted ground cumin powder and black pepper to taste and chill to serve.
5. It can be stored for several weeks in the refrigerator.

Gram Legume Dip
Channa Dal Chutney

This roasted *channa dal* dip is delicious and can be served not only with *dosas, idlis* and *vadas* but you can also serve it with any of your favorite crunchies and breads.

METHOD

1. Drain the water from the soaked gram legume.
2. Heat the oil in a skillet and fry the *dal* until dry and light brown. Remove the *dal* with a slotted spoon into a bowl lined with paper towel, and set aside.
3. In the same oil fry the onions, green chilies, whole red peppers and ginger, until the onions are brown. Transfer the contents to an electric blender and grind the fried *dal*, onions, green chilies, ginger, whole dry red peppers with yogurt, red pepper powder and salt to a rather coarsely smooth paste by adding a cup of water slowly. Add more water, if needed. Set it aside in a serving bowl.
4. Heat the same oil in the skillet and add the cumin seeds, mustard seeds and wait until they pop and add the *urad dal*. As soon as it turns brown add the curry leaves and asafoetida powder. Stir for half a minute and add this seasoning to the ground *chutney* in the bowl and mix. Add the chopped coriander to the *chutney*. Stir well and serve.

SERVES 15 – 20

Ingredients

Channa dal washed and soaked in 2 cups of water overnight	1 cup
Oil	¼ cup
Onions	1 cup
Green chilies	1 Tbs
Whole red peppers	2–3
Ginger	1 Tbs
Yogurt	1 cup
Cumin seeds	1 tsp
Red pepper	1 tsp
Salt	1 tsp
Mustard seeds	1 tsp
Water as needed or	1 cup
Urad dal	1 tsp
Curry leaves	4–5
Asafoetida powder	¼ tsp
Coriander leaves chopped	2 Tbs

Note: Yogurt can be substituted by 1 tsp of tamarind pulp.

Sweet Mango Dip
Aam ki Meethi Chutney

Mango Dip is one of the most popular *chutneys* in Indian cuisine. It is sold in jars in almost every part of the world and is very well liked by everyone. Its sweet, sour and tangy taste is unique and delightful. Tastes best with any regular meal, especially with *paranthas* or *pooris*.

METHOD

1. Wash and peel the mangoes and ginger and grate them fine.
2. Boil them in ½ cup of water on low heat with bay leaves and salt stirring regularly to avoid sticking. On low heat, cover and simmer until they are tender and soft.
3. Pour the vinegar in a heavy bottom sauce pan or wok and cook the grated dates. As soon as they are cooked remove them from the vinegar with a slotted spoon and set them aside. Mix the sugar with the vinegar in the pan and cook the syrup (a drop should make a string when pulled between two fingers) and add the cooked shredded mangoes and ginger, cooked grated dates, red pepper, black pepper, ground roasted cumin powder, cinnamon, cloves, nutmeg, mace and cardamoms, and cook till the mixture looks like a sauce.
4. Add the sliced almonds, pistachios, raisins, and lime juice.
5. Simmer till the sauce is thick.
6. Remove from heat, cool it and store or can the *chutney* in sterilized containers.

SERVES 20 OR MORE

Ingredients

Raw mangoes grated	1 lb
Ginger 2-inch piece grated	1
Water	½ cup
Bay leaves	4
Salt	5 tsp
Vinegar	½ cup
Sugar	1 lb
Red pepper	1 Tbs
Black pepper corns crushed	¼ tsp
Dates dried grated	¼ cup
Cinnamon ground	1 tsp
Cloves ground	1 tsp
Cardamoms seeds crushed	½ tsp
Nutmeg or mace ground	½ tsp
Cumin roasted powder	1 Tbs
Almonds toasted, chopped	¼ cup
Pistachio nuts chopped	1 Tbs
Raisins	¼ cup
Lime juice fresh	1 Tbs

Onion & Coconut Dip with Fish Flavor

Seeni Sambol

SRI LANKA

Sambols are the *chutneys* or condiments from south India where they are very particular about dry roasting and cooking their herbs and spices before they grind them into *chutney*. The dry roasting gives this *chutney* a very unique taste quite different from the fresh *chutneys* like coriander or mint in north India. They go well with grilled meats, *kebabs*, tortilla chips or any *paranthas*. Use it with grilled meats or as mustard on a hot dog bun or a hamburger bun or a sandwich. It may also be used as dip with your favorite bread or chips.

SERVES 20 OR MORE

Ingredients

Coconut oil	3 Tbs
Onions fresh chopped	2 cups
Green chillies chopped	2 Tbs
Ginger and garlic chopped (each)	2 Tbs
Garam masala	1 ½ tsp
Fresh coconut grated	½ cup
Or	
Dry coconut unsweetened powder	2 Tbs
Black pepper ground	1 tsp
Dry red chillies whole	4–6
Tuna fish fresh or dry	1 tsp
Curry leaves chopped	6–8
Coconut milk needed to grind the *chutney*	½–¾ cup
Salt	½ tsp
Sugar	1 tsp
Lemon juice	2 Tbs

METHOD

1. Heat coconut oil in a wok or heavy-bottom saucepan and add the onions, chopped green chillies, ginger, garlic and fry till the onions start turning brown.

2. Add the *garam masala*, black pepper, dry red chillies, fry them a minute and add fish wet or dry, curry leaves and the freshly grated coconut. Cook for 2 minutes and add coconut milk. Cook the sauce for 10 minutes stirring occasionally to prevent sticking.

3. Cool and transfer the sauce to blender and add the salt, sugar, and lemon juice. Blend it again for half a minute and pour it into a serving bowl. This *chutney* can be stored in the refrigerator for a couple of days.

The Exquisite World of Indian Cuisine

Carrots Pickle
Gajar ka Achaar

Here is a fresh pickle of carrots smothered in a little mustard oil with crushed mustard seeds, red pepper, grated ginger, green pepper and lemon juice to serve in a buffet lunch or on a festive occasion. It is a quick fixing crunchy and quite appetizing. It makes a great salad substitute.

METHOD

1. Wash and slice the carrots, ginger, garlic and green pepper and set them aside.
2. In a large bowl heat 2 Tbs of mustard oil and add crushed mustard seeds, fenugreek seeds crushed, nigella seeds, cayenne pepper or red pepper and salt. Add the grated ginger, chopped garlic and green chillies. Stir to cook for few minutes on low heat and add the chopped carrots. Cook for 3–5 minutes and add the sugar and lemon juice. Stir and cook for another 2–3 minutes on low heat until all the sugar is dissolved and the pickle is heated through.
3. Toss and coat the vegetables well with spices, cool and serve.
4. It can store well in the refrigerator for a couple of weeks.

SERVES 20 OR MORE

Ingredients

Carrots chopped and sliced small into matchsticks	1 lb
Ginger chopped	¼ cup
Garlic finely chopped	1 tsp
Fenugreek seeds crushed	1 Tbs
Mustard oil	2 Tbs
Crushed mustard seeds	¼ cup
Nigella seeds	1 tsp
Red cayenne pepper	1 Tbs
Salt	1 Tbs
Green chilies chopped	¼ cup
Lemon juice	2 Tbs
Brown sugar	1 Tbs

Radish Pickle
Mooli ka Achaar

ORISSA

Radishes are pickled rarely but this Oriya style pickle is worth mentioning. It is easy and makes a good and quick accompaniment to any meal.

METHOD

1. Mix and coat the chopped radishes cut in quarters with green chilies, ginger, turmeric powder, red pepper, salt, and set them aside.
2. In a small saucepan heat the mustard oil and when it is smoking remove from heat. When the smoke is gone place the pan again on the heat and add the *panchphoran masala*. Let the seeds pop and as soon as the popping stops add the radishes mix coated with spices and cook and stir about 2–3 minutes to heat through.
3. Transfer to a bowl and cool. Add the lemon juice and chopped ginger and stir to mix.
4. It can be refrigerated for several days.

SERVES 4 – 6

Ingredients

Daikon radishes or regular small radishes	1 cup
Turmeric powder	½ tsp
Red pepper	½ tsp
Salt	½ tsp
Mustard oil	1 Tbs
Panchphoran masala	1 Tbs
Lemon juice	1 Tbs
Green chilies chopped	1 Tbs
Ginger chopped	1 Tbs

The Exquisite World of Indian Cuisine

Sweet & Sour Lemon Pickle
Khatta-Meetha Nimbu ka Achaar

METHOD

1. Cut the lemons in quarters and squeeze the juice out of the lemons and set them aside.
2. Remove the fibrous part from the lemon quarters and discard it. Transfer the shell of the lemons to a medium size saucepan and also add to the pan the squeezed lemon juice, salt, cloves, black pepper corns, crushed cardamom seeds, *garam masala*, pinch of asafoetida, black pepper powder, red pepper powder and cook on low heat until the lemons get a little tender.
3. Add the sugar and keep cooking on low heat until the syrup is reduced to half. Cool and store it in sterilized jars with an airtight lid. Serve with *paranthas* or any meal.

MAKES COUPLE OF JARS

Ingredients

Lemons fresh	1 lb
Salt	2 Tbs
Cloves	½ tsp
Black pepper corns	½ tsp
Asafoetida	a pinch
Cardamom seeds of brown cardamoms crushed	½ tsp
Garam masala	1 tsp
Black pepper ground	1 Tbs
Red pepper	1 Tbs
Sugar	¼ cup

Green Chilies, Onions and Ginger in Vinegar
Sirkey-wali Hari Mirch, Pyaz aur Adrak

Fresh green chilies, ginger, and onions are pickled in vinegar and spices. They are very commonly served with everyday meals in north India. It is easy to prepare and enhances the taste of the meal considerably.

METHOD

1. Add the chopped chilies, ginger and onions to the vinegar in a glass jar.
2. Add the salt, pepper, lemon juice and sugar.
3. Shake it well and leave it tightly closed.
4. Leave them to marinate for a couple of days in the vinegar.
5. The pickle is ready for use in a few days.
6. Serve with any meal.

MAKES ONE JAR

Ingredients

Green chilies, chopped	½ cup
Ginger shredded	½ cup
Onions chopped	½ cup
Vinegar	1 cup
Salt	1½ tsp
Red pepper	1 tsp
Lemon juice	¼ cup
Sugar	1 Tbs

Green Chilies Pickle
Hari Mirch ka Achaar

Another great spicy pickle to go with a plain and bland meal like *khichadi*, rice and *dal* or a stuffed *parantha*. It can really add a lot of taste and zing to any simple and quick meal.

MAKES 2 – 3 JARS

Ingredients

Green chilies	1 lb
Ginger grated	2 Tbs
Mustard oil	¼ cup
Crushed mustard seeds	¼ cup
Fenugreek seeds crushed	2 Tbs
Anise seeds crushed	1 Tbs
Asafoetida	a pinch
Red pepper	1 Tbs
Black pepper	1 Tbs
Turmeric powder	1 tsp
Salt	1 Tbs

METHOD

1. Wash and cut the green chilies in halves and grate the ginger and set it aside.
2. Crush the mustard seeds, fenugreek and anise seeds.
3. Heat the oil and add the asafoetida and let it cook for a minute until it swells up and immediately add the red pepper, black pepper, turmeric, crushed anise seeds, mustard seeds and fenugreek seeds, and stir the mixture.
4. Add the green chilies and grated ginger and coat them well with all the spices and add the salt.
5. Stir well and heat through about 3–5 minutes on low heat. Transfer it to sterilized jars with airtight lids.

Papaya and Mango Pickle
Papeetey aur Aam ka Achaar

A typical tropical preparation from south India where papaya and mango grow in abundance. It is pickled with mustard seeds, red pepper and curry leaves. Makes a rather pleasing accompaniment to a leg of lamb or chicken *tandoori*.

METHOD

1. Chop the papaya, and grate the mangoes. Add the chopped green serrano (hot) chilies to the mixture and set them aside in a large bowl.
2. Grind coarsely in a coffee grinder or blender, the dry red chilies, onions, ginger, garlic, mustard seeds, fennel seeds and fenugreek seeds in half a cup of vinegar.
3. Heat the oil in a saucepan and add the ground spices and cook. Add the remaining vinegar also and cook till it has reduced and is giving out a fragrant aroma.
4. Add the chopped papaya, mango and chopped chilies mixture to the cooking vinegar. Add sugar, salt and turmeric powder, and simmer for another 5 minutes. Cool.
5. Transfer the pickle to sterilized pickling jars or bottles and store.

MAKES COUPLE OF JARS

Ingredients

Raw papaya peeled and chopped in ½ Inch cubes	2 cups
Raw mango peeled and grated	½ cup
Green serrano peppers chopped	1 Tbs
Dry red peppers	6
Onions chopped	½ cup
Mustard seeds	1 tsp
Fennel seeds	1 tsp
Fenugreek seeds	1 tsp
Vinegar	2 cups
Oil	2 Tbs
Ginger grated	1 Tbs
Garlic chopped	1 tsp
Sugar	1 cup
Salt	½ tsp
Turmeric powder	1 tsp

Lemon Pickle
Nimbu ka Achaar

A spicy and digestive accompaniment to snacks and meals. It is a good substitute for *chutney* and a quick folktale remedy for indigestion or stomach ache.

METHOD

1. Wash and dry the lemons and cut them in quarters and put them in a bottle or a plastic container.
2. Add salt and let them sit by a sunny window for 2–3 weeks, occasionally shaking them.
3. Roast the fenugreek seeds on a hot skillet but not burn and grind them and set them aside.
4. Heat the mustard oil in a large wok to 320°F. Remove from heat and after 2–3 minutes, add the mustard seeds and the whole red peppers. Wait till the mustard seeds start to pop.
5. Add the asafoetida, wait till it starts to swell up and then add the red pepper, black pepper, and cook but not burn.
6. Add the ginger, green hot chilies, sugar and stored and chopped lemons and stir to mix.
7. Cook till the lemons and ginger are a little soft and tender (about 10 minutes) on low heat
8. Squeeze the lemon juice of 6–8 fresh lemons and add to the pickle and boil through for 2–3 minutes.
9. Cool and store in a sterilized jar with a tight lid.

MAKES FEW JARS

Ingredients

Fresh lemons cut in quarters	1 lbs
Table salt	¾ cup
Fenugreek seeds roasted, ground	1 Tbs
Mustard oil	1 cup
Mustard seeds ground	1 Tbs
Red dry chilies whole	1 Tbs
Asafoetida powder	1 tsp
Red pepper	2 Tbs
Black pepper	1 Tbs
Fresh ginger sliced	1 cup
Green serrano chilies	2 Tbs
Sugar	½ cup
Lemon juice squeezed from lemons	12

The Exquisite World of Indian Cuisine

Mango Pickle
Aam ka Achaar

Indians try to pickle many vegetables and raw fruits but raw mango is one of their most favorite. It is pickled in many different ways. Sometimes in combination with other vegetables, sometimes with hot green chilies, ginger and spices. Whatever the preparation, it is always delicious and unique, and can be served with any meal of your choice.

METHOD

1. Wash and cut the mangoes in small slices. After washing and drying grate the ginger and carrots. Wash and dry the gooseberries, button onions. Chop the green chilies in halves. Set them aside.
2. Heat the oil to 320°F and remove from heat. Cool a little and then add the asafoetida. When it is cooked add the whole red pepper, turmeric, powdered red pepper, crushed fennel seeds, nigella seeds, and the fenugreek seeds.
3. Stir and add the mango slices, grated ginger, gooseberries, button onions, green chillies, grated carrots, and stir to mix.
4. Add the crushed peppercorns, crushed brown cardamom seeds and salt and mix well. Cook through for a few minutes.
5. Pour the pickle into sterilized glass jars with tight lids and store.

MAKES FEW JARS

Ingredients

Washed and dried raw mangoes sliced into pieces	1 lb
Ginger fresh sliced	½ cup
Carrots finely chopped	¼ cup
Gooseberries	¼ cup
Drained can of small button onions or fresh onions	¼ cup
Hot green chilies cut in half	¼ cup
Mustard oil	2 cups
Asafoetida	½ tsp
Turmeric powder	2 tsp
Red pepper powder	1 ½ tsp
Nigella seeds crushed	1 Tbs
Fennel seeds crushed	1 Tbs
Whole red pepper	1 Tbs
Fenugreek seeds crushed	1 Tbs
Peppercorns crushed	1 tsp
Brown cardamom seeds crushed	1 tsp
Salt	½ cup

Avakai Mango Pickle
South Indian Mango Achaar

South Indians love hot pickles and their meal is never complete without them. Mangoes grow abundantly in south India and are pickled very frequently. Only certain varieties of raw mangoes with a very firm non-fibrous flesh are used in this pickle. It is considerably hot and made in peanut oil with abundant amount of red hot pepper and ground mustard. Serve with your favourite meal or a snack.

MAKES 6 – 8 JARS

Ingredients

Raw mangoes peeled and chopped in ½ inch pieces	6 cups
Peanut oil or *Til* oil	2½ cups
Crushed mustard seeds	1 cup
Red pepper	1½ cup
Salt	1½ cup
Turmeric powder	2 Tbs
Fenugreek seeds crushed	4 Tbs

METHOD

1. Cut mangoes into small pieces and dry them in the oven at 250°F until they completely dry. Heat the oil to smoking and cool it. Set it aside.
2. Mix the chopped dried mango pieces with the dry ingredients and add the oil into it. Mix the ingredients well with your clean hands or large serving spoons.
3. Transfer the mixed pickle to a large glass jar and let it marinate for at least 7–10 days in the sun.
4. When the pickle is ready, transfer it to small jars and store.

Classic Sweet & Sour Pickle
Khatta-Meetha Achaar

This sweet and sour mixed vegetable pickle is tangy but very appetizing and delicious. It can be served with any meal.

METHOD

1. Wash and chop turnips, carrots, cauliflower and daikon radishes.
2. Boil the 4 cups of water in a deep, medium-size saucepan and add ½ cup of salt and the mixture of all the chopped vegetables. Boil them for a minute. Remove the pan from fire and drain the water in the colander.
3. Transfer the vegetables to a paper towel lined basket and dry them for at least 6 hours or dry them in the sun.
4. Heat the oil to smoking 320°F and cool it.
5. Heat the 4 cups of oil again to fry the ginger, garlic, and green chilies and the onions. Add the cinnamon, cardamoms, cloves, black pepper and whole red peppers and fry until the peppers start to change color. Lower the heat, add the dry fenugreek leaves, dry mustard, red pepper, *garam masala* and the rest of the salt. Mix well. Add the dry vegetables, stir the mixture to coat the vegetables with spices for a couple of minutes. Set it aside.
6. In a separate pan heat the vinegar and add the crude sugar (*Gur*) or brown sugar and stir until it dissolves. Cool it. Transfer the sweetened vinegar to the vegetables mixture. Cook on low heat until the oil separates from the vegetables. Cool the pickle. Transfer the pickle in canning jars. Leave the jars out in the sun for a couple of days. They are then ready to serve.

MAKES 12 – 14 ONE lb JARS

Ingredients

Turnips, carrots, cauliflower, daikon radish washed and chopped	10 lbs
Water	4½ cups

Salt	1 cup
Mustard oil	4 cups
Ginger chopped	½ cup
Garlic chopped	½ cup
Green chilies chopped	¼ cup
Onions chopped	1 cup
Red pepper whole (dry)	½ cup
Dry fenugreek leaves	¼ cup
Cinnamom large pieces	6 or 7
Cardamoms whole black	¼ cup
Cloves whole	2 tsp
Black pepper corns	2 tsp
Mustard ground	1½ cup
Red pepper	2 Tbs
Garam masala	⅔ cup
Vinegar	1 cup
Brown sugar or jaggery (*gur*)	1 lb

CHAPTER 12

Salads

Simple salads are a regular part of an Indian meal. They are a welcome accompaniment at the table as they not only lessen the fiery taste of hot spices but are nutritive and add color and a refreshing look to the meal. The fresh vegetable and fruit salads provide three out of the six important tastes important to an Indian meal. These three tastes are sour, salty and astringent – all found in salads and relishes. For centuries cooks have kept salads away from the main course and were more keen on making the creamy and rich curries. They had forgotten the healthy side dishes of a complete meal. Finely sliced salad (*Kachumber*) is the most common of Indian salads. It is made by mixing finely chopped fresh vegetables sprinkled with lemon juice, salt and pepper. It is popular all over the country.

The southern parts of the country have some gorgeous salads. For example, the *Kosambari Salad* of chopped vegetables and boiled lentils goes very well with the grilled *tandoori* meats. From western states comes the Onion Salad, Beetroot Salad, Tomato Salad, Mango Salad and Mango Salsa.

Around the world, today fancy salads have crept up on tables serving Indian food. Green leaf salad is being offered with dressings, nuts, chicken pieces and croutons just like in the western world and this has now acquired an elegant and appropriate place in modern Indian cooking.

Mixed Vegetable Salad

PUNJAB

A typical salad of Indian cuisine. It has chopped green vegetables tossed in lemon juice, salt, black pepper or red pepper. It is either arranged on a platter or it is tossed in a salad bowl.

SERVES 8 – 10

Ingredients

Cucumber green, peeled and chopped	1
Tomatoes chopped	2
Radish red small Or	
Radish white chopped	10
Bell pepper finely chopped	½
Onions medium chopped	1
Baby carrots, tender, little	1 cup
Green chilies chopped	4
Lemon juice	2 Tbs
Salt	1 tsp
Black pepper	1 tsp
Red pepper	½ tsp
Garam masala (optional)	1 tsp
Cumin powder ground, roasted	1 tsp
Apple green, firm, chopped*	½
Pear firm, chopped*	½
Plum firm, chopped*	1

METHOD

1. Mix all the chopped vegetables in a salad bowl and arrange in a fancy colourful pattern on a platter.
2. Add fresh or bottled lemon juice, salt and pepper into the salad bowl. With a mixing spoon, mix and coat the salad with the lemon juice and spices. However, if the salad is arranged on a platter, just sprinkle the lemon juice and the spices on top of the salad.
3. Add small pieces of green apples, pears and plums to the salad. The sweet and sour taste of fruits encourages young children into the habit of eating salad.
4. Serve it with meals or with lunch or with a soup and bread.

Note: For presentation, layer the salad platter – first arrange large salad leaves, then large size vegetable pieces on top of salad leaves and then smaller pieces along with fruits at the top layer.

*Fruits are optional

Cooked Beans Salad
Channe aur Rajmah ka Salad

TAMIL NADU

A refreshing bean salad of cooked chick-peas, red kidney beans and black-eyed beans garnished with lemon juice, freshly ground roasted cumin powder and other spices. It makes a very appetizing salad for a lunch buffet and also with barbecued fish, chicken or hamburgers.

SERVES 6 – 8

Ingredients

Chick-peas (cooked)	1 cup
Kidney beans (cooked)	1 cup
Black-eyed beans (cooked)	1 cup
Shallots	½ cup
Or	
Onions fresh green chopped	½ cup
Red bell pepper finely chopped	¼ cup
Green chilies chopped (mild)	1 Tbs
Salt	to taste
Black pepper ground	1 tsp
Cilantro leaves finely chopped	½ cup
Coconut fresh grated	1 cup
Or	
Dry coconut powder	2 Tbs
Olive oil	2 Tbs
Garlic cloves	2
Lemon juice	2 Tbs
Ginger finely chopped	½ tsp
Cumin powder ground, roasted	1 Tbs
Red pepper	1 tsp
Garam masala	1 tsp

METHOD

1. Transfer the cooked beans from the cans into a colander and wash them under running water. If the beans are boiled, then drain the water.
2. Combine the chick-peas, red kidney beans, and black-eyed beans in a large salad bowl. Add the chopped shallot or green onions, bell pepper, chopped ginger, hot green pepper, salt, black pepper and cilantro leaves, and mix them together.
3. Heat the olive oil in a small skillet and add the chopped garlic. Cook the garlic in the oil until it turns light brown. Cool it.
4. Add the oil to the salad holding the garlic pieces back in the skillet.
5. Add the ground roasted cumin powder, red pepper, fresh coconut or dry coconut powder, *garam masala* and lemon juice, and mix the salad well. Mix the beans and the vegetables well with salad fork and spoon and chill it in the refrigerator before serving. Taste and adjust the seasoning according to your liking.
6. A great accompaniment to any meal.

*All beans can either be boiled and cooked fresh or you can buy ready to use cans.

The Exquisite World of Indian Cuisine

Mango Salad
Aam ka Salad

TAMIL NADU

Ripe mangoes chopped firmly in a gravy of ground coconut, brown sugar and chilies make a very delicious salad. Another speciality from south India where you find coconuts and mangoes in abundance. Serve this salad for a lunch with a sandwich or with a meal, especially when the food is too spicy.

METHOD

1. Grind the coconut with brown sugar and whole red pepper into a paste with the help of little water and set it aside.
2. In a large salad bowl, transfer the chopped mangoes and pour coconut paste over it. Add the salt and black pepper to taste and stir well to coat the mangoes.
3. In a small saucepan heat the oil and add mustard seeds and crushed coriander seeds and wait till they pop. Later, add curry leaves.
4. Remove from fire and pour the contents over the salad and stir well. Sprinkle with ground roasted cumin powder and chopped coriander leaves.

SERVES 8 – 10

Ingredients

Coconut fresh grated	2½ cups
Brown sugar	2 Tbs
Red pepper dried, broken	2
Mangoes firm ripe, peeled and chopped	2 cups
Salt	1 tsp
Black pepper	1 tsp
Vegetable oil	1 Tbs
Mustard seeds	1 tsp
Coriander seeds crushed	1 tsp
Curry leaves	6–8
Coriander leaves chopped	1 Tbs
Cumin powder ground roasted	1 tsp

Exquisitely carved window panels at the Udaipur Palace, Rajasthan

'Puppets on a string.' Internationally famous string puppets from Rajasthan

Radish Salad
Gajar ya Mooli ka Salad

GUJARAT

A very easy way to serve fresh radishes with crushed roasted peanuts, chopped green chilies and lemon juice. A crunchy salad that can be served with any meal.

SERVES 8 – 10

Ingredients

Small red radish chopped cross wise and grated	2 cups
Or	
White daikon radish peeled and grated	2 cups
Ginger grated	1 Tbs
Green chilies finely chopped	1 Tbs
Lemon juice	2 Tbs
Salt	¼ tsp
Red pepper	¼ tsp
Black pepper	¼ tsp
Vegetable oil	1 Tbs
Mustard seeds	½ tsp
Turmeric powder	¼ tsp
Peanuts roasted crushed	2 Tbs
Asafoetida	a pinch
Coriander green, finely chopped	1 Tbs

METHOD

1. Grate radishes in a salad bowl and add grated ginger and the green chilies to it. Set it aside.
2. Add the lemon juice, salt, peppers and mix the salad well with salad fork and spoon.
3. Heat the vegetable oil in a small skillet and add the mustard seeds and let them pop.
4. Add the turmeric powder and the asafoetida. Remove from heat and add the seasonings to the salad.
5. Stir the seasonings well into the salad and add the roasted and crushed peanuts. Mix them well. Sprinkle chopped coriander leaves.
6. Cover and refrigerate before serving.

The Exquisite World of Indian Cuisine

Kosambri Salad
Mung ki Dal ka Salad

KERALA

Carrots, radishes and partially cooked *dal* salad. This crunchy salad, a speciality from south India, is refreshing and can be prepared in many different combinations. The boiled lentils along with grated coconut and other grated vegetables make it rather unique and very appetizing.

SERVES 8 – 10

Ingredients

Mung dal soaked in boiling water (split without skin)	½ cup
Radishes white or small red washed and grated	½ cup
Garbanzo beans boiled and cooked	½ cup
Tomatoes finely chopped in small cubes	½ cup
Bell pepper green, grated	⅓ cup
Cilantro leaves fresh, chopped	½ cup
Carrots washed peeled and grated	½ cup
Coconut fresh, grated	½ cup
Or dry powdered coconut	2 Tbs
Vegetable oil	1 tsp
Dry red chilies or pepper crushed (optional)	2
Mustard seeds	1 tsp
Red pepper powder	1 tsp
Salt	1 tsp
Black pepper powder	1 tsp
Lemon juice	3 Tbs

METHOD

1. Soak the *Mung dal* in 8 cups of boiling water for 3 hours and then drain the water. Cool it and set it aside.
2. Mix grated radishes, carrots, cooked garbanzo beans (or from a can), tomatoes and bell pepper in a salad bowl and add to it the cilantro leaves, coconut and drained *dal*. Toss them well.
3. Heat the oil in a small saucepan and add the mustard seeds. Wait till they pop and add the dry red pepper and cook for half a minute.
4. Remove the saucepan from the fire. Cool and garnish the salad by pouring the oil over it. Hold the peppers back.
5. Add the salt, red pepper, black pepper powder and lemon juice and stir with salad spoon to mix it well.
6. Serve with any meal. It goes very well with barbecued meat dishes.

Onion, Beetroot and Tomato Salad

Pyaz, Chukandar aur Tamatar ka Salad

Beetroots make a very good salad with onions and tomatoes. Beetroot is colorful and nutritious and therefore makes a very welcome accompaniment to any meal.

METHOD

1. Slice onions in thin circles, chop beetroot in long 2 inch by 1 inch wide strips and the tomatoes in small cubes. Chop 1 long-tender carrot into 2-inch long thin match sticks.
2. Transfer them to a salad bowl and set aside.
3. In a small skillet heat the olive oil and add the mustard seeds, cumin seeds, and let them pop.
4. Add the seasoning to the salad and add salt, red pepper, green chilies and ginger.
5. Stir to mix and add the lemon juice. Toss the salad well and refrigerate before serving.
6. Top it all with chopped coriander and a sprinkle of *garam masala*. Serve with your favorite barbecue or a meal preferably with a meat curry.

SERVES 8 – 10

Ingredients

Onions chopped in thin circles	2 cups
Beet root chopped in long 2x1 inch strips	½ cup
Carrot (long) chopped in thin long strips	1
Tomatoes chopped in cubes	½ cup
Olive oil	1 Tbs
Mustard seeds	1 tsp
Cumin seeds	1 tsp
Salt	1 tsp
Red pepper powder	½ tsp
Ginger chopped in thin long strips	2 Tbs
Green chilies finely chopped	1 Tbs
Lemon juice	2–3 Tbs
Coriander chopped	½ cup
Garam masala (optional)	½ tsp

Note: Beetroot can be boiled for 10 minutes, before use in order to soften it a little.

The Exquisite World of Indian Cuisine

Green Mango Salsa
Aam ka Salsa

Mangoes and coconuts grow in abundance in many parts of south India, and raw mangoes are used here not only in cooking but also in condiments in innumerable ways. This preparation is very easy to make and is very appetizing too. Use mangoes that are still ripening. It is very refreshing on a hot summer day with *kebabs*, grilled meats and bread.

SERVES 4 – 6

Ingredients

Raw mango peeled and chopped in small pieces	2 cups
Ginger chopped	1 tsp
Green chillies hot chopped	2
Coriander leaves picked and washed	½ cup
Mint leaves cleaned and picked	½ cup
Toasted coriander seeds and cumin seeds (each)	1 tsp
Gur or brown sugar	2 Tbs
Lemon juice	2 Tbs
Salt	to taste
Sumac*	1 tsp

METHOD

1. Mix chopped mango, ginger, green chillies, coriander leaves, mint leaves, toasted cumin and coriander seeds in a mixing bowl and transfer them to a food chopper and chop them fine.
2. Add the lemon juice, brown sugar and salt to taste.
3. Transfer the salsa to serving bowl and serve with sprigs of mint leaves and a sprinkle of sumac.
4. Serve the salsa with grilled meats and tortilla chips.

*****Sumac** is a mid-eastern red berry that has an intense sour fruity flavor that cuts through strongly flavored meats. Its powder, that is bright red in color, is used instead of lemon or vinegar to garnish rice, salads *kebabs* and other foods. It can be bought at any oriental food store

CHAPTER 13

Soups

The soups in Indian cooking are very distinctive with their special touch of fresh herbs, and delicate spices like cumin and black pepper. Their distinctive aroma has a special appeal in the western world. Soups were not an integral part of a regular Indian meal till recent times, and therefore, earlier Indian cookbooks did not even mention them. Soups in India were never served as first course like in the western countries but were served with a slice of bread as a light meal. It is amazing how fast they have gained an appropriate place in Indian cuisine and are now served for lunch with a salad and bread and are also served as the first course of a meal in restaurants too. Soups and salads are a delightful addition to Indian cuisine and have enhanced its beauty and charm tremendously.

There are several kinds of soups in Indian cooking. Some are creamy and smooth like Cauliflower Soup, Bottle Gourd Soup and Cream of Corn Soup. Then there are tangy sweet and sour soups like *Rasam*, Mulligatawny Soup and Tomato Soup. Some wholesome ones are Chicken Vegetable Soup, Mixed Vegetable Soup, Lentil Soup and Spinach Soup.

Hope you will like the soups offered to you in the following pages. Use seasonings at the end of each preparation according to your taste. When preparing a soup as a starter for a meal, select a soup that would complement your dinner and balance it.

Tomato Soup
Tamatar ka Shorba

A hearty and delicious soup. It can be served as an appetizing first course for a dinner or at a lunch with a hearty sandwich.

SERVES 6 – 8

Ingredients

Tomatoes (medium) peeled and chopped	6–8
Vegetable oil	3 Tbs
Onions medium chopped	1
Ginger chopped	1 tsp
Garlic chopped	1 tsp
Green chilies chopped (very mild)	1 tsp
Coriander grounded	1 Tbs
Cumin grounded	1 tsp
Red pepper	½ tsp
Turmeric powder	½ tsp
Black pepper	½ tsp
Salt	1 tsp
Water	6 cups
Heavy cream	½ cup
Garam masala	1 tsp
Green coriander chopped	1 Tbs
Sugar	2 Tbs
Heavy cream to garnish	2 Tbs

METHOD

1. Soak the tomatoes in warm water and peel them. Chop them finely and set them aside.

2. Heat the oil in a large saucepan and transfer onions, ginger, garlic, green chilies. Cook until light brown and then add the ground coriander, ground cumin, red pepper, turmeric powder, black pepper and salt. Mix well.

3. Add the tomatoes. Stir and add 6 cups of water. Cook over low heat until the tomatoes are completely soft and cooked.

4. Put the soup into a blender and blend thoroughly.

5. Strain it and add the heavy cream and 2 Tbs of sugar to the strained soup. Add more water, if needed.

6. Bring it slowly to a boil and serve it garnished with green coriander, a tablespoon of heavy cream and *garam masala*. Adjust the seasoning according to the taste.

Mixed Vegetable Soup
Sabzion ka Shorba

Vegetable soup with a refreshing aroma makes an elegant first course for a dinner or as an accompaniment at lunch.

METHOD

1. Cook the *toor dal* to a creamy consistency in 4 cups of water in a three-quart saucepan and set it aside.
2. Chop the vegetables and set them aside.
3. Heat the oil and add onion, ginger, garlic, green chilies and cook in a deep saucepan until the onions are light brown.
4. Add chopped tomatoes, cumin powder, turmeric powder, salt, coriander powder, black pepper and red pepper. Mix well and fry. Cook until the oil separates from the sauce. Add the vegetables and stir them well. Add the other 4 cups of water and cook on low heat until well blended and the vegetables are tender.
5. Transfer the cooked vegetables mixture into the saucepan with cooked *toor dal*. Simmer until the vegetables are well blended into the soup. If the soup is too thick add ½–1 cup of water.
6. When cool pour it into the blender and blend it smooth. Strain the blended soup through the soup strainer. Push the pulp through and discard residue, if there is any. Add 2 cups of boiled water to facilitate filtering.
7. Add the lemon juice. Serve topped with chopped green coriander and *garam masala* and a tsp of heavy cream.

SERVES 6 – 8

Ingredients

Toor dal	½ cup
Water	8 cups
Oil	2 Tbs
Onions chopped	2 Tbs
Ginger chopped	1 Tbs
Garlic chopped	1 Tbs
Green chilies chopped (mild)	1 Tbs
Tomatoes (large) chopped	2
Cumin powder	1 tsp
Turmeric powder	¾ tsp
Salt	2–3 tsp
Coriander powder	1 Tbs
Black pepper	1 tsp
Red pepper (to taste)	½ –1 tsp
Potatoes chopped medium	1
Cauliflower florets	1 cup
Carrots chopped	½ cup
Peas fresh or frozen	½ cup
Lemon juice	2 Tbs
Green coriander chopped	1 Tbs
Garam masala	½ tsp
Heavy cream	¼ cup
Boiling water	2 cups

Note: Different vegetables can be substituted for the ones used in this recipe.

The Exquisite World of Indian Cuisine

Cauliflower Soup
Gobhi ka Shorba

An elegant soup, that is almost a meal. A great first course for a dinner. Excellent to serve as a lunch accompaniment.

METHOD

1. Heat oil in a medium size saucepan and cook the onions, ginger, garlic and green chilies until light brown.
2. Add the potatoes and cauliflower. Add 1 tsp salt, cumin powder, coriander powder, turmeric and cayenne pepper and stir to mix. Add the chicken stock and bring to a boil. Cover and cook for about ½ hour until the vegetables are tender.
3. Put soup in a blender and blend until smooth.
4. Strain well to push all the pulp through.
5. Add the cream and gently boil once.
6. Serve garnished with a gentle sprinkle of *garam masala*, chopped green onions and coriander leaves and a dab of heavy cream.
7. Season to taste.

SERVES 4 – 6

Ingredients

Vegetable oil	1–2 Tbs
Onions chopped medium	1
Ginger chopped	1 Tbs
Garlic chopped	1 Tbs
Salt	to taste
Green chilies (mild) chopped	1 Tbs
Potatoes small peeled and chopped	2
Cauliflower florets or ¼ of a large head	2 cups
Cumin powder	1 tsp
Coriander powder	1 Tbs
Turmeric powder (optional)	1 tsp
Cayenne powder	½–1 tsp
Chicken stock or water	8 cups
Heavy cream	½ cup
Green onions chopped	1 Tbs
Coriander leaves finely chopped	1 Tbs
Garam masala to sprinkle	

Chicken Vegetable Soup
Murg aur Sabzion ka Shorba

A soup perfect for lunch. Chicken vegetable soup can also be served just with bread.

METHOD

1. Boil the *toor dal*, vegetables, chopped potatoes, cauliflower, carrots, celery and tomatoes with ½ tsp of salt in a three-quart saucepan with 6 cups of water until tender and set aside.
2. In a wok heat oil and cook onions, ginger and garlic till brown.
3. Add the cumin seeds and wait till they pop. Add the cooked *dal* and vegetables mixture. Cook for 5 minutes. Add salt, turmeric powder, red pepper, black pepper, coriander powder and stir to mix.
4. Pour the mixture into a blender and grind the vegetables. Strain them through a strainer and discard any residue.
5. Fry the chicken pieces in a frying pan until white. Drain the fat.
6. Add the cooked chicken to the soup mixture and add 2 more cups of water. Cook until the chicken is tender (about 20–25 minutes).
7. Serve sprinkled with green coriander leaves and a light sprinkle of *garam masala* and a dab of cream.

SERVES 6 – 8

Ingredients

Toor dal	½ cup
Water	8 cups
Onions chopped	2 Tbs
Ginger chopped	1 tsp
Garlic chopped	1 tsp
Cumin seeds	1 tsp
Chicken breast chopped into small cubes	1 cup
Salt	2 tsp
Turmeric powder	½ tsp
Red pepper	½ tsp
Black pepper	1 tsp
Coriander powder	1 tsp
Potato chopped (medium)	1
Carrots chopped	½ cup
Cauliflower chopped	½ cup
Celery chopped	½ cup
Tomatoes chopped	1 cup
Vegetable oil	2 Tbs
Green coriander leaves chopped	2 Tbs
Garam masala	½ tsp
Heavy cream	2 Tbs

Mulligatawny Soup

An internationally known Indian soup made with a base of coconut milk, tomatoes, onions, lemon, and curry spices. There may be few variations but it still is the best tasting soup I have ever had.

SERVES 8 – 10

Ingredients

Chicken raw, finely chopped	1 cup
Chicken broth	4 cups
Lemon juice	1½ Tbs
Water	3½ cup
Masoor dal	½ cup
Coconut milk	2½ cup
Onions	1 cup
Ginger chopped	2 Tbs
Garlic chopped	2 Tbs
Green chilies chopped (mild)	2 tsp
Tomatoes chopped	1½ cup
Cinnamon stick	1 inch
Cardamom	1–2
Cloves	½ tsp
Carrots peeled and chopped	½ cup
Celery chopped	½ cup
Potatoes peeled and chopped	1 cup
Turmeric powder	1 tsp
Cumin powder	1 tsp
Coriander powder	1½ tsp
Ground fennel seeds	1 tsp
Black pepper	1 tsp
Red pepper to taste or	1 tsp
Salt	2 tsp
Curry leaves	3–4
Mustard seeds	1 tsp
Vegetable oil	2 Tbs
Coriander leaves chopped	2 Tbs
Garam masala	½–1 tsp
Apple or zucchini peeled and chopped	½ cup

METHOD

1. Cook the chicken in a skillet until it turns white. Drain the fat and set it aside. Transfer washed *masoor dal* to a sauce pan and add 3½ cups of water. Cook the *dal* until tender. Set it aside.

2. Mix 4 cups chicken broth, 1½ cups of coconut milk, onions, ginger, garlic, green chilies, tomatoes, cinnamon stick, cardamoms, cloves, carrots, zucchini, celery, potatoes, turmeric powder, cumin powder, black pepper, coriander powder, ground fennel seeds, red pepper and salt in a deep three-quart saucepan or a Dutch oven. Cook until the vegetables are tender.

3. Strain the soup through a strainer, into a pan. Rub the vegetables through the strainer in to the soup.

4. Add the cooked chicken pieces and the cooked *dal* to the strained soup.

5. Add the other 1 cup of coconut milk and lemon juice. Let it simmer on low heat until the chicken is tender.

6. Heat the oil or the *ghee* in a small skillet and add the curry leaves and the mustard seeds. Wait till they start popping. Pour the seasoning over the soup and stir.

7. Serve topped with chopped coriander leaves, *garam masala* and 1 tsp of cream. Adjust the seasoning according to the taste.

Note: Potatoes, celery, and carrots are optional.

Mung Beans Soup
Mung Dal ka Shorba

This a very light soup made from washed *mung dal* rich in easily digestible lentil proteins. It is ideal for children and someone recovering from illness. When flavored with curry leaves, red pepper and tamarind, it is quite refreshing and delightful.

SERVES 6 – 8

Ingredients

Mung beans washed	½ cup
Water	7 cups
Ginger chopped	1 tsp
Garlic chopped	1 tsp
Green chilies chopped (mild)	1 tsp
Salt	1 tsp
Vegetable oil or *ghee*	1 Tbs
Cumin seeds	½ tsp
Curry leaves (small)	10
Turmeric powder	½ tsp
Coriander powder	1 tsp
Red pepper (optional)	½–1 tsp
Tomato sauce	½ cup
Tamarind pulp (optional)	½ tsp
Garam masala	½ tsp
Coriander leaves chopped	1 Tbs
Heavy cream	2 Tbs

METHOD

1. Boil the washed *mung* beans in 5 cups of water in a three-quart saucepan with ginger, garlic, green chilies and salt until they are completely dissolved and the *dal* is creamy and soup-like. Set it aside.
2. Heat the oil in a skillet and add the cumin seeds and wait until they start popping.
3. Add the curry leaves, wait till they start sizzling. Add the turmeric powder, red pepper, coriander powder and the tomato sauce. Add the dissolved tamarind pulp and two more cups of water. Boil it. Transfer the cooked *mung* beans into this spice mixture.
4. Cook for 5 more minutes and add the *garam masala* and chopped coriander leaves and 2 Tbs of cream. Stir to mix well.
5. Let it come to a boil. Remove from heat and serve. Adjust seasonings according to taste.

Note: Reduce the spices and herbs to half if you want milder soup. Use heavy cream to your taste.

Indian Hot and Sour Soup
Rasam

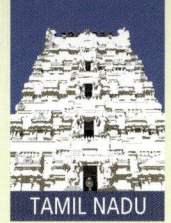
TAMIL NADU

A creamy hot and sour soup made of *toor dal* is a great specialty of southern India. Tamarind and coconut give it that unique texture and taste. You can make it hot as it is usually served but you can also make it mild by reducing the use of red pepper.

METHOD

1. Cook *toor dal* in deep saucepan with 2 cups of water until creamy. Set it aside.
2. Heat oil in a non-stick three-quart saucepan and add the mustard seeds, fenugreek seeds, cumin seeds and the curry leaves. When the mustard seeds start popping add the asafoetida powder. Immediately add the ginger and green chilies.
3. Cook till the ginger and chilies are lightly brown. Add the turmeric powder, coriander powder, red pepper, salt, black pepper, coconut powder, cumin powder, and the chopped garlic. Cook for two more minutes or until the coconut is slightly brown. Add the tomatoes, stir for a minute. Cook on low heat till the oil separates.
4. Add the tomatoes mixture to the cooked *toor dal* and add 6 cups of the remaining water.
5. Cook until the tomatoes are completely mashed.
6. Add the tamarind paste dissolved in 1 cup of water or the lemon juice. Let it cook till the mixture is smooth.
7. Remove from heat and serve it topped with cilantro leaves as an accompaniment to the lunch or dinner or as a soup prior to a meal.

SERVES 8 – 10

Ingredients

Toor dal	½ cup
Water	8 cups
Oil	2 Tbs
Mustard seeds	1 tsp
Fenugreek seeds	1 tsp
Cumin seeds	1 tsp
Turmeric powder	1 tsp
Curry leaves	20
Vegetable oil	2 Tbs
Asafoetida	¼ tsp
Red chilies whole	2
Green chilies (mild)	1 tsp
Coriander powder	1 Tbs
Red pepper	1 tsp
Black pepper	1 tsp
Cumin powder	1 tsp
Salt	2–3 tsp
Cilantro leaves chopped	2 tsp
Garlic chopped	1 tsp
Tomatoes chopped	4 cups
Ginger chopped	1 tsp
Unsweetened coconut powder (from your local Indian grocer)	1 Tbs
Tamarind pulp dissolved in 1 cup of water	1 Tbs
Or	
Lemon juice stirred in 1 cup of water	2 Tbs

Note: Use less tamarind if you like less tarty soup.

Illuminated arena of the stately Rashtrapati Bhawan (President's House) *and the North and South Blocks in New Delhi*

©Ishtihaar/Rajinder Arora

Bottle Gourd Soup
Ghia ka Shorba

Ghia or *tinda* soup is a creamy and delicate soup. It is quite light and makes an excellent first course to a sumptuous dinner.

METHOD

1. Cook the onions in one Tbs of oil in a deep saucepan until light brown.
2. Add the mustard seeds and wait till they start to pop.
3. Add the chopped gourd, salt and pepper and stir well.
4. Add 3 cups of water and let it cook and simmer on medium heat until the gourd is quite transparent and tender.
5. Remove from heat and strain the liquid. Purée the pulp and mix it with soup.
6. Transfer it back to the stove and put on medium heat. Add the milk and gently bring to a boil. Remove from heat and serve garnished with slivered almonds, a pinch of *garam masala*, coriander leaves and cream.

SERVES 2 – 4

Ingredients

Bottle gourd washed peeled and chopped	2 cups
Oil	1 Tbs
Mustard seeds	1 tsp
Onions chopped	½ cup
Water	3 cups
Almonds slivered	1 tsp
Salt	1 tsp
Black pepper	1 tsp
Milk	1 cup
Green coriander finely chopped	1 tsp
Garam masala	a pinch
Heavy cream	2 Tbs

The Exquisite World of Indian Cuisine

Potato Soup
Aalu ka Shorba

Potato soup is made by mixing mashed potatoes, cream and garnishing it with green onions, cumin, mustard seeds and green coriander leaves. It is really delicious and makes an excellent first course soup.

SERVES 4 – 6

Ingredients

Water	6 cups
Potatoes peeled and chopped	2 cups
Green onions chopped	2 Tbs
Ginger finely chopped	1 tsp
Green chilies	1 tsp
Garlic	1 tsp
Salt	to taste
Curry leaves	3–4
Red pepper	½–1 tsp
Heavy cream	2 Tbs
Vegetable oil	2 Tbs
Lemon juice	1 Tbs
Cumin seeds	1 tsp
Mustard seeds	½ tsp
Red pepper dry whole broken (optional)	1
Garam masala	1 tsp
Green coriander leaves finely chopped	1 Tbs

METHOD

1. Boil the potatoes in 3 cups of water with onions, ginger, garlic, green chilies, salt, curry leaves and red pepper in a saucepan until they are soft and purée the mixture into soup in a blender. Transfer it to a cooking pan and add 3 more cups of water and boil till it is smooth.
2. Add the cream and lemon juice and set it aside.
3. Heat the oil in a skillet and add the cumin and mustard seeds, and wait till they start popping. Add the whole red pepper, and when it starts sizzling, transfer the seasoning into the soup, holding the whole peppers back with the spoon. Stir well.
4. Before serving garnish very sparingly with *garam masala* and coriander leaves, if desired. Season according to taste.

Spinach Soup
Palak ka Shorba

This creamy soup is healthy as well as very delicious. Serve it as a first course or an accompaniment at lunch. It is very appetizing and nutritious.

METHOD

1. Mix the spinach with water, onions, garlic, ginger, green chilies, salt, turmeric powder, coriander powder, red pepper, potatoes and tomatoes in a two-quart saucepan or a Dutch oven and boil until the potatoes are soft and tender. Cool and blend the soup in a blender until smooth

2. Add the cream and stir. Bring to a boil and turn the heat off.

3. Heat the *ghee* in a skillet and add the cumin seeds, curry leaves, and wait till the seeds start popping. Pour the seasoning over into the soup holding the curry leaves behind in the skillet with a spatula and mix.

4. Heat the soup and serve topped with a sprinkle of *garam masala*, chopped coriander leaves, sprigs of mint and lemon slices on the side. Makes a great presentation. Season to your liking.

SERVES 8 – 10

Ingredients

Frozen spinach 15 oz pkg	1
Water	4 cups
Onions chopped	¼ cup
Ginger chopped	1 Tbs
Garlic chopped	1 Tbs
Green chilies chopped (mild)	1 Tbs
Salt to taste or	1 tsp
Turmeric powder	1 tsp
Coriander powder	1 tsp
Red pepper	1 tsp
Potatoes chopped	1 cup
Tomatoes chopped	1 cup
Cream	2 Tbs
Vegetable oil or *ghee*	2 Tbs
Cumin seeds	1 tsp
Curry leaves	2–3
Garam masala	½ tsp
Coriander leaves chopped	1 Tbs
Couple of sprigs of mint leaves and lemon slices (optional)	

Note: Increase the herbs and spices to make soup spicy. Use cream to garnish the soup at the end or add it to the soup as you wish.

The Exquisite World of Indian Cuisine

Cream of Pumpkin Soup
Kaddu ka Shorba

This is a colorful creamy soup. All you have to do is to flavor it with onions, lemon and some spices and you have one of a kind soup.

METHOD

1. Cook the onions in 2 Tbs of oil in a thick bottom large saucepan until light brown. Add the ginger, garlic and green chilies, and cook another 2 minutes.
2. Add the mustard seeds and when they start to pop add the pumpkin and stir-fry them with the onion mixture. Lower the heat.
3. Add the turmeric powder, salt, coriander powder, red pepper, and coat the pumpkin pieces well with all the spices.
4. Add the water and let it cook on medium-low heat until the pumpkin is soft (about 30–40 minutes) or longer.
5. Take the pan off the heat, cool it, and pour the pumpkin mixture into the blender to blend it smooth.
6. Transfer the soup back into the saucepan and add the milk and the sugar. Cook on medium heat for 3–5 minutes. Add the *garam masala* and lemon juice, and stir the soup well. Add more water, if needed.
7. Remove from heat and serve each helping topped with a tsp of cream, shredded almonds or pistachio and green chopped coriander.

SERVES 6 – 8

Ingredients

Onions chopped	½ cup
Vegetable oil or *ghee*	2 Tbs
Ginger chopped	1 Tbs
Garlic chopped	1 Tbs
Green chilies chopped	1 Tbs
Mustard seeds	1 tsp
Pumpkin peeled and chopped	4 cups
Turmeric powder	½ tsp
Salt	to taste
Coriander powder	1 tsp
Water	6 cups
Milk	2 cups
Garam masala	½ tsp
Red pepper	to taste
Pistachio or almonds thinly sliced	2 tsp
Cream	¼ cup
Sugar	2 Tbs
Coriander leaves chopped	1 Tbs
Lemon juice	2 Tbs

Note: Seasoning of *garam masala* or red pepper can be done according to taste. If you like your soup to be a little more sweet and sour, add more sugar.

Cream of Corn Soup
Makki ka Shorba

Corn and potatoes soup flavored with fresh ginger, garlic, cilantro and red pepper is different, but delicious. Serve it with crackers and some French bread and it is a complete meal.

METHOD

1. Boil 2 cups of corn with potatoes, onions, ginger, garlic, water and chicken stock in deep, medium size saucepan and add salt and black pepper. Boil till the potatoes are tender and soft.
2. Cool a little and pour the contents into a blender and purée them.
3. In the saucepan transfer the puréed soup and add the milk and remaining corn and gently bring it to boil.
4. In small skillet heat the sesame oil and add the mustard seeds till they pop. Pour the oil in a small bowl and set it aside.
5. Serve the soup garnished with a sprinkle of chopped green onions, chopped green cilantro and the flavored oil.
6. Serve this soup with any bread of your choice to make a light lunch or a first course of a dinner.

SERVES 4 – 6

Ingredients

Corn frozen or freshly husked	2½ cups
Onions white or yellow, chopped	½ cup
White potatoes peeled and chopped	1 cup
Fresh ginger and garlic peeled and chopped	1 tsp
Black pepper	½ tsp
Salt	1 tsp
Chicken stock or water	2 cups
Water	2 cups
Milk	1½ cups
Green onions chopped and cilantro	1 Tbs
Sesame oil	1 Tbs
Mustard seeds	½ tsp

The Exquisite World of Indian Cuisine

Coconut Milk Soup
Nariyal ka Shorba

Light and fragrant this soup is creamy and delicious with crushed peanuts, freshly chopped tomatoes and cucumbers.

METHOD

1. Mix the gram flour in coconut milk and set it aside.
2. Heat the oil in a two-quart thick-bottom pan on medium-low heat and add the cumin seeds. When they start popping add the chopped green chilli. Lower the heat.
3. Add the coconut milk, gram flour mixture, water, salt and black pepper to it and stir, keeping the heat very low.
4. When it starts to boil, add the chopped cucumber, crushed peanuts and tomatoes. Mix them in. Simmer and let it come to a boil. Cook for 2–5 minutes or until the soup is of smooth consistency.
5. Remove from heat garnish with chopped coriander and serve hot.
6. Garnish with seasonings as you wish.

SERVES 4

Ingredients

Coconut milk 16 ozs can	1
Tomatoes fresh, finely chopped	2 Tbs
Cucumbers fresh, finely chopped	2 Tbs
Green chilies finely chopped	½ tsp
Gram flour	2 Tbs
Cumin seeds	½ tsp
Olive oil or *ghee*	1 Tbs
Salt	to taste
Garam masala	a sprinkle
Black pepper	½ tsp
Roasted peanuts finely crushed	1 Tbs
Water	1 cup
Coriander leaves fresh finely chopped	1 tsp

CHAPTER 14

Drinks

India, being a tropical country, is one of the largest consumers of soft drinks. Day-to-day common drinks are not a luxury but a necessity. With hot and dry weather in its central states and hot and humid all along the coastal regions, quite a few nourishing and very highly delicious drinks have originated here over time. They replenish the lost electrolytes of the body and are refreshing. Some special Indian drinks are mango coolers like *Aam Panna*, *Zeera Paani* (*Jalzeera*), *Kanji*, *Nariyal Paani*, *Sattu*, *Nimbu Paani* and Kokum Water. These are seasonal drinks and depend on the availability of the fruit. They are inexpensive and a large number of people in India make them at home.

Then, there are nutritious Indian drinks like *Thandaai*, Mango *Lassi* and fruit *Sherbets* and squashes. *Sherbets* are age-old drinks of India but these days they are not as popular. These are made by bottling the extracts of fruit juices, herbs, petals of flowers, barks of trees, nuts with sugar syrup. Essence for flavor and preservatives are added later. For an Indian household these are not just drinks but also remedies for some common ailments. Squashes came to India a few hundred years ago with the British. These are made from extract of fruits like Lemon, Orange, *Phalsa*, Mango, Lichi and Pineapple. At the time of serving, squashes are diluted with water and ice.

Thandaai is an ancient drink made by mixing milk with the paste of ground almonds or cashew nuts, spices and sugar. It is then served cold with ice. It is still very popular in the summers of India. Plain *Lassi* and Mango *Lassi* are very popular drinks and liked all over the world. Most of the Indian restaurants serve this drink. Mango *Lassi* is made by gently stirring mango pulp in fresh yogurt, sugar and ice.

Spiced tea, *Kahva* and south-Indian coffee are very well loved hot drinks of India. Spiced tea called *Masala Chai* is becoming very popular in the US too. South India has coffee plantations all over and it is the most popular hot drink here. In these parts coffee is made by boiling coffee powder with milk, sugar and water which is foamed by pouring it from one glass to another. *Kahva* is Kashmiri green tea that is milder in flavor than the regular Indian tea. It is prepared by simmering the *kahva* leaves in boiling water and flavoring it with nuts and honey and is served without milk.

It is pertinent to mention here that some semi-alcoholic drinks are brewed in villages and mountain valleys across India by the country folk. Some of these are *Chhang* from the mountain regions, *Feni* from Goa, *Mahua* from Orissa, Bihar, Kerala and Gujarat.

Chhang is made by fermenting rice or barley and it tastes like beer. *Feni* is made by fermenting cashew nuts or coconut extract for a couple of days and then distilling it yields the crude extract, which through redistillation yields *Feni* which makes a good base for cocktails and is a popular drink of Goa. *Mahua* is made from the edible flowers of the *Mahua* tree. These flowers are also used to make syrup for medicinal purposes. *Mahua* drink is an essential item in the daily life of the tribals of Bastar, the Santhals and among certain tribes in Maharashtra. Then there is *Bhang*, which is marijuana. It is ground together with nuts, spices and milk and is consumed on the festival of *Shivratri*. It is believed that to please Lord Shiva, one should forget the world by intoxicating oneself with *Bhang* and dancing and chanting his name.

Yogurt Shake
Dahi ki Lassi

PUNJAB

Lassi is a very popular drink in north India. It is made with plain yogurt, sugar, pieces of ice, cardamom powder blended with some water in a blender. It is a very appealing and invigorating drink in the hot summer months. To make it more delicious, mango pulp is added, which is available abundantly in the summers. Canned mango pulp can be bought at a local Indian grocery store.

SERVES 4

Ingredients

Yogurt	4 cups
Sugar	4 Tbs
Water	2–3 cups
Crushed cardamom powder	¼ tsp
Saffron	½ tsp
Mint leaves	a few
Ground nuts	1 tsp
Salt & pepper	to taste
Mango pulp	1 cup
Ice as needed	

METHOD

1. Pour plain yogurt, water, sugar, cardamom powder into the blender except the ice and blend until well blended.
2. Serve in glasses with ice, couple of mint leaves and a sprinkle of saffron.
3. Plain salty *Lassi* (shake) is also very popular and it can be prepared by blending the plain yogurt with salt, pepper and ice. Serve with mint leaves.
4. For making mango *lassi*, blend together yogurt, mango pulp, cardamom powder and water, blend it until smooth. Pour it into a glass and serve sprinkled with saffron, mint leaves and fine grated nuts.

Mango, the **national fruit of India**.

South Indian Coffee

TAMIL NADU

Coffee in south India is as popular, a drink as *chai* in the north. It is made by adding well-roasted instant coffee to the boiling water and milk. Add sugar to taste before serving it.

METHOD

1. Boil the water and the milk and remove from heat before it boils over.
2. Mix coffee and sugar in a coffee pot or teapot and add the boiled mixture of water and milk and stir vigorously with a tablespoon until the coffee is a little frothy.
3. Serve hot.

SERVES 4

Ingredients

Instant coffee	2 Tbs
Water	2 cups
Milk or as needed	2 cups
Sugar	to taste

The Exquisite World of Indian Cuisine

One of the four exquisitely painted and carved gates (Gopuram) *of Meenakshi Temple, Madurai, Tamil Nadu*

Cumin Flavored Drink
Zeera Paani

A very ancient tangy, sweet and sour drink made by mixing roasted ground cumin powder, ground fresh mint leaves, black salt (sulphur salt) and other herbs into strained tamarind water. It has digestive properties and it can be served before or with meals at any occasion. This is a drink that is served with *golgappas*. (See Appetizers section). It is extremely delicious and refreshing during the hot, sweaty, summer months of tropical India.

SERVES 8 – 10

Ingredients

Tamarind pulp	2 Tbs
Or	
Amchoor	½ cup
Fresh mint ground	1 Tbs
Cumin ground roasted	1 Tbs
*Black salt	2 tsp
Ginger fresh, ground	1 Tbs
Lemon juice	¼ cup
Water	8 cups
Sugar	2–3 Tbs
Garam masala	½ tsp
Red pepper	1 tsp
Lemon slices	3–4
Sprigs of mint	3–4
Ice to chill	

METHOD

1. Mix the tamarind pulp well into 8 cups of water.
2. Grind the mint, ginger in a blender with help of lemon juice and add the roasted ground cumin powder, red pepper, *garam masala* and black salt to the ground paste. Pour this mixture into the tamarind water and mix the water well with a hand whisk or a large spoon.
3. Now, add the sugar and taste the tartness.
4. It should be sweet and sour.
5. Adjust the sugar and salt to your taste.
6. Filter it through a fine sieve and chill it with ice to serve immediately or refrigerate with the sprigs of mint and lemon slices.
7. It can be served as a punch (dilute it further) and is served always with the *golgappas* (hollow and translucent puffs of flour).

Note: Black salt (*Kala namak*) is actually a sulphur compound and has great digestive properties. It is used mainly as a sprinkle for *chaats* and is an ingredient of *chaat masala*. To me this salt brings back vivid memories of childhood. It is an integral part of a mix called *churan*. I used to buy this delicious concoction from a vendor outside our school. To make *churan*, black salt is mixed with ground dates, raisins and spices. I can still remember its delicious taste to this day. *Zeera paani* is somewhat similar to the *kokum* water of Maharashtra. It is made from *kokum* flower (a souring agent used in the cooking of this state).

Fermented Carrot Drink
Kanji

PUNJAB

This sour tangy drink is very popular in north India. It is made by fermenting carrots in water with ground mustard and salt for 48 hours and flavoring it with red pepper and *garam masala* before serving. It is very refreshing in the hot summer months and delightfully tasty.

SERVES 4

Ingredients

Carrots washed peeled and cut into 2 inch pieces lengthwise	2 lbs
Water	4 cups

METHOD

1. Boil one quart of water and add the chopped carrots to it. Set it aside and let it cool.
2. Transfer the cooled water with the carrots to a large size pitcher and add the ground mustard, black salt, salt and water to it and let it ferment for 48 hours in a warm place.
3. Taste it for tanginess and add the red pepper, *garam masala* and refrigerate.
4. Serve chilled with couple of mint leaves and carrot pieces.
5. It is great drink to have with meals or for a lazy summer afternoon drink.

Ground mustard	2 Tbs
Salt	2 tsp
Red pepper	1 tsp
Black salt	1 tsp
Garam masala	1 tsp
Mint leaves	1 Tbs
Small strips of fresh carrots	

Kokum Water

Konkani cuisine has a splendid appetizing drink prepared with Kokum and coconut milk. Dissolve 5-6 Kokum dry flowers into a cup of warm water for half an hour. When the water turns pink transfer it into a large glass. Add 1 cup of coconut milk to it. Also add ½ tsp each of green chilli and roasted ground cumin seeds . Stir to mix. Add salt and brown sugar to taste. Mix it well. Its sweet and sour taste will get you hooked on to this amazing drink.

Lemonade
Shikanjvi

Lemonade is one of the most popular cold drinks of India. It is enjoyed and prepared in many different ways. Basically it is made by mixing water, fresh Lemon (preferably lime) juice and sugar and is always served chilled. It is delicious and welcome drink in the dry hot months of Indian summer because it is not only refreshing but also replenishes the lost electrolytes of the body due to perspiration. It is a great energy booster for children who also love its sweet and sour taste.

METHOD

1. Mix together 2 cups of water and sugar. Stir until dissolved.
2. Add the lemon juice and mix well. Adjust the lemon juice and sugar according to your taste. Dissolve the saffron in ginger juice and add it to the *shikanjvi* and stir again.
3. Mix the remaining 2 cups of water. Add few ice cubes and serve. Flavor it with a pinch of salt, black salt and mint leaves if you wish.

Lemonade can be prepared in several different ways as follows:

To make pink lemonade:
Mix together 4 cups of water with 1½ cups of sugar. Add 1 cup of cranberry juice and 1 cup of lemon juice. Mix well and chill. Serve with ice cubes in 8 Oz glasses.

To make Strawberry lemonade
Puree in a blender ½ pint of washed and chopped strawberries with 2 cups of water and set it aside. Cook for 5 minutes in a saucepan on low heat until well dissolved. Set them aside.

Strain the cooked pureed strawberries into a saucepan and add 1¼ cups of sugar and cook till the sugar is dissolved. Cool and add 2 cups of lemon juice and 4 cups of water and chill in the refrigerator. Add more lemon juice if you want it more lemony. Season with salt and black salt if you wish and serve.

To make Raspberry and Watermelon lemonade
Blend together 3 cups of watermelon cubes without any seeds with ¼ cup of raspberries and half cup of water in a blender until smooth. Strain the juice and add ½ cup of lemon juice and ½ cup of sugar. Stir well. Adjust sugar and lemon juice. Chill and serve with ice

To make sparkling lemonade
Mix together 2 cups of water with 1½ cups of lemon juice and 1 cup of sugar and Stir well. Add a pint of sparkling water or club soda. Stir well. Chill and serve.

SERVES 2

Ingredients

Water	4 cups
Lemon juice	½ cup
Ginger juice (optional)	1 Tbs
Sugar	1 cup
Saffron	1 tsp

HINT:
Garnish or flavor each glass with ½ tsp of salt a pinch of black salt and mint leaves if you wish.

The Exquisite World of Indian Cuisine

Mango Drink
Panna

GUJARAT

The state of Gujarat is famous for its mangoes and some of the best varieties grow there. This appetizing sweet and tangy drink is made by boiling the pulp of slightly unripe mangoes in water and flavoring it with ground roasted cumin, black salt, brown sugar, lemon juice (if the mangoes are too sweet) black pepper and fresh mint. It is very refreshing when served with ice.

METHOD

1. Peel and chop the mangoes in small pieces and transfer them to a large saucepan along with the pit of the mango. Add the chopped green chilies and water and boil the mixture until the mango pieces are soft and tender (about 20 minutes).
2. Discard the green chilies and the pit of the mango and pour the chopped mangoes and water into a blender. Add brown sugar, lemon juice, a pinch of black salt, cinnamon powder, ground roasted cumin powder, black pepper and blend it smooth. Dilute further according to taste before serving, because this is a concentrate of the drink. Strain the *panna* and save it in a bottle.
3. Pour a couple of teaspoons of *panna* into glasses and add the water and the ice. Stir to mix and serve topped with couple of mint leaves.

SERVES 4 – 6

Ingredients

Mangoes slightly unripe and firm	2 large
Brown sugar or *gur* (jaggery)	1 cup
Water	6–8 cups
Cumin powder ground, roasted	1 tsp
Black salt	sprinkle
Lemon juice	¼ cup
Black pepper	a dash
Green chilies cut in half (mild)	2
Cinnamon powder	sprinkle
Mint leaves	a few

Note: Add green chilies, if you want a mildly hot drink.

The Exquisite World of Indian Cuisine

Spiced Tea
Masala Chai

GUJARAT

METHOD

1. Bring the water, cardamoms, cinnamon, and cloves to a full boil.
2. Add the tea leaves or the tea bags.
3. Lower the heat, let it simmer for two minutes.
4. Add the milk and stir well and let it come to a full boil and stir.
5. Using the tea strainer. Strain boiling hot tea in mugs or pour it into a teapot.
6. Keep the teapot hot by using a hot plate or teacozy. A stainless steel teapot can be used that can be heated on the stove to keep warm.
7. Prepared *chai* should be served within half an hour because it loses its full flavor if it is reheated and served again.

SERVES 5 – 6

Ingredients

Water	5 cups
Milk	1 cup
Tea leaves (3 Tea bags)	2 Tbs
Cardamoms	5
Cinnamon ½ inch by ¼ inch	1 stick
Cloves	5
Sugar	to taste

HINT

Omit the spices to make the plain *chai*, if desired. Indian or British blend teas can be purchased at the local Indian grocery stores. **Tea plants** grow wild in the cool and humid climate of the hills. The natives of hilly regions flavored their tea with ingredients such as saffron, honey, yak butter, *ghee*, herbs and salt. During the British rule rich people started having tea in the manner of the British aristocrats in the luxury of their lawns or estates with cream and sugar which started the large scale cultivation of tea in hill states of Sri Lanka and India.

Kashmiri Tea
Kashmiri Kahva

Kahva leaves are green tea leaves of Kashmir. It is sold as green tea of Darjeeling or Kashmir.

METHOD

1. Transfer 4 cups of water to a medium size saucepan and add cinnamon, cloves, cardamoms and fennel seeds. Heat the water and add the sugar or honey.
2. As soon as the water starts to boil add the *kahva* leaves. Let it simmer on low heat for 2 minutes.
3. Transfer and strain the tea into a heated teapot. Divide the nuts into 4 cups. Add a few sprigs of saffron to each cup and pour *kahva* into these cups and serve immediately. Makes an excellent hot drink in cold winters.

SERVES 4 – 6

Ingredients

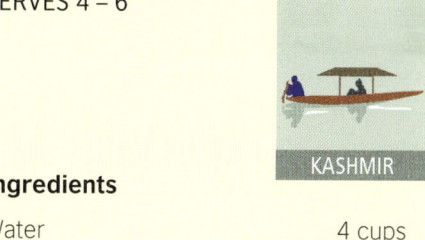
KASHMIR

Water	4 cups
Honey or sugar	2 Tbs
Fine crushed cashew and almonds	2 Tbs
Cinnamon sticks (small) one inch (crushed)	2
Cloves	½ tsp
Cardamoms brown broken	2
Kahva leaves	2 tsp
Fennel seeds	1 tsp
Saffron (optional)	a pinch

The most revered pilgrimage site for the Sikhs, Shri Harmander Sahib Gurudwara, Golden Temple at Amritsar, Punjab

Milk & Almond Drink
Thandai

PUNJAB

A nutritious and proteinaceous cold drink made with milk, nuts and spices is very popular in the state of Punjab during the summer months. Indians have used this drink for a very long time. Once you have the right ingredients it does not take too long to prepare it.

SERVES 4 – 6

Ingredients

Milk	4 cups
Cashew nuts	1 Tbs
Almonds	¼ cup
Poppy seeds	¼ cup
Watermelon and cantaloupe (*kharbuja*) seeds	¼ cup
Sugar	½ cup
Black pepper corns	½ tsp
Green cardamom seeds	½ tsp
Rose leaves (dry)	½ tsp
Saffron strings soaked in water (optional)	a pinch

METHOD

1. Mix together almonds, cashew nuts, poppy seeds, watermelon seeds (dehusked), black pepper, cardamoms and rose petals, and soak them in water overnight. Peel the almonds.

2. Grind the above ingredients with the peeled almonds in a blender to a fine paste with the help of half or one cup milk for few minutes. Add a little water to thin down the mixture and keep grinding if the mixture is still thick.

3. Transfer the mixture into a large bowl. Add the rest of the milk and sugar. Mix well. Strain the mixture through a muslin cloth or cheese cloth and squeeze well to get all the juice out from the mixture. Discard the residue.

4. Transfer the strained liquid to refrigerator or add ice to serve immediately.

5. Flavor the drink with the soaked saffron before serving in drinking glasses.

Note: Ready-to-make mixes of *thandai* are available at your local Indian grocery store. A drink called *bhang* is prepared mixing marijuana paste into *thandai*. This drink is traditionally enjoyed by devotees on *Shivaratri* fesitval.

paan

पान

A very old custom in India is to have some kind of condiment or digestive after the meals and there are many such digestives which are used. Among these the most prominent ones are Fennel seeds (*saunf* – sometimes sugar coated in different colors), shaved pieces of betel nuts, cardamom, cloves, roasted flax seeds, sesame seeds and *paan* (Betel leaf quid).

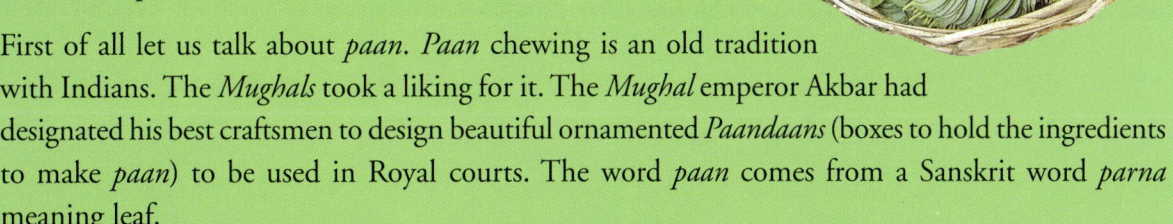

First of all let us talk about *paan*. *Paan* chewing is an old tradition with Indians. The *Mughals* took a liking for it. The *Mughal* emperor Akbar had designated his best craftsmen to design beautiful ornamented *Paandaans* (boxes to hold the ingredients to make *paan*) to be used in Royal courts. The word *paan* comes from a Sanskrit word *parna* meaning leaf.

The leaf of betel vine (*Piper betel*) is known for its medicinal properties. It is also a mild stimulant. They are served smeared with *choona* [wet lime powder paste of Ca (OH)$_2$] and *kattha*, the extract of the acacia plant which is red in color and acts as an astringent. It has been used in *Ayurvedic* medicine from ancient times. These leaves are then topped with crushed bits of betel nut, *gulukand* (tiny pieces of candied rose petals), sweetened coconut powder, cloves and some cardamom seeds. The leaf is then folded into a triangular shape and a clove is tucked into it to hold its shape. It is then offered to the guests after dinner. Offering of *paan* signifies a gesture of respect, honor and friendship for the guest. The gesture is similar to offering a special drink to a special guest in western culture. No gourmet dinner is complete without an offering of *paan* at the end of the meal. No religious function is complete without an offering of *paan* to the deities. It is auspicious and sacred to have *paan* leaves at religious or intimate functions.

Paan has unparallel digestive properties. Every community and neighborhood in India has its *paanwalla* (a *paan* vendor). Fennel seeds and green cardamoms (sometimes candied in different colors and coated with silver leaves) are also served as digestives in place of *paan*. Sesame seeds and flax seeds are also sometimes served as condiments to chew along with fennel seeds in small bowls separately. Fennel seeds and green cardamoms are primarily digestive in nature and you will find them at the exit point of good restaurants in India served for the departing guests. Roasted sesame seeds and flax seeds are very nutritive and rich in Omega 3 fatty acids which help in lowering cholesterol. Shaved betel nut pieces are also served as a digestive. They are usually softened by cooking and then colored and sugared. Betel nut is known to be a mild stimulant. It is for occasional use only since its regular use has shown to cause health problems.

Next time you happen to see a colorful condiment tray at an Indian function or at a restaurant you may want to try one of these digestives which will also enable you to complete your journey into fine Indian cuisine.

A plate of mouth-freshners usually circulated after meals.
The above plate has (clockwise from bottom left)
dry fennel seeds, cloves, cardamoms, sugar coated fennel seeds, flax seeds,
chocolates, fennel, and in the center ready-to-eat digestive *chooran* (sweet & sour) candies.

AN INDIAN WEDDING

SAMPLE MENUS

The famous writer Virginia Woolf once said: "one cannot think well, love well, sleep well and work well if one has not dined well".

Hope you will be able to dine well on the recipes you select. Please remove any whole spices from the main dishes before you serve them. When serving drinks, any light drink or soda goes very well with Indian food. Wine is also a very good alternative.

Given alongside are four sample menus of breakfast, lunch and dinner. These are easy for you to fix at home but if you are ordering at a restaurant they may be coming in different combinations.

BREAKFAST

Guava or Tangerine juice
Scrambled eggs with vegetables
(Frittata)
Poha with fruits
Chai

Plain lassi
Allu Parantha with Mint Raita
or Mango pickle
Fruit chat or fresh fruits
Chai

Mango or pineapple juice
Uppama (cream of wheat flavored with nuts and spices)
Vadas, with coconut chutney or Sambhar
South Indian Coffee

Mango Lassi
Lachedar Paranthas with potatoes stir-fry
Tropical fruits mix of Papaya, mangoes, chikus, pomegranates and raspberries
kahva

LUNCH

Pumpkin soup
Chicken Tikka
Nan with butter
Mint chutney
Kosambari salad
Chai or bottled water

Masala dosa
Sambhar
Channa dal chutney
Coffee

Mixed Vegetable Soup
Biryani
Cooked beans salad
Bottled water or chai

Rasam soup
Cauliflower Paranthas
Sweet and sour lemon pickle
Plain lassi

The Exquisite World of Indian Cuisine

FULL COURSE DINNER

Guidelines

Choose the dishes that complement each other. Choose the menu keeping in mind whether your guests are vegetarians or non-vegetarians.

For the **first course** choose one dish from soups and one appetizer.

Meat curry: Choose one dish from fish, chicken, lamb, beef or pork.

Vegetable curry: Any vegetable from the vegetables section in this book. In the event of a vegetarian dinner select two vegetables, a curry and a stir-fry.

Legumes: Any *dal*, *sambhar*, chick-peas or kidney beans.

Salads: Choose any two out of *raita*, *chutney*, pickle, salad and *papadums* depending on the type of main course dishes selected.

Rice: Plain rice, *biryani*, or vegetable fried rice, or any kind of *pulav*, making sure it complements the main meat and vegetable entree you are serving.

Last course: Any dessert of your liking and serve *paan* or *chai* or both depending how special the dinner is going to be.

Given below are five sets of menus.

Cauliflower soup
Samosas
Tamarind chutney
Palak paneer
Dal makhani
Rogan josh
Garlic nan
Onions Beetroots and tomato salad
Gulabjaman
Chai

Bottle gourd soup
Seekh kababs
Mint chutney
Chicken Tikka Masala
Pea pulav
Dal panchratan
Malai kofta curry
Puri
Mixed vegetable salad
Mango pie
Plain lassi

Chicken vegetable soup
Cocktail paneer
Mushroom fritters
Mint chutney
Lamb with spinach
Cauliflower & potatoes stir-fry
Chick pea curry
Plain rice, Mint nan
Boondi raita
Kulfi
Coffee

Rasam
Corn fritters
Peanut chutney
Masala dosa
Sambhar
Potatoes stir-fry
Coconut rice
Rice pudding or Kheer
Coffee

Bhelpuri
Cauliflower soup
Chicken Vindaloo
Vegetable fried rice
Whole stuffed okra
Whole mung dal
Plain paranthas
Carrots pickle
Jalebi
Kahva

Measurement Equivalents

Volume (Dry)

American Standard	Metric	American Standard	Metric
1/8 teaspoon	0.5 ml	¼ teaspoon	1 ml
½ teaspoon	2 ml	¾ teaspoon	4 ml
1 teaspoon	5 ml	1 tablespoon	15 ml
¼ cup	59 ml	1/3 cup	79 ml
½ cup	118 ml	2/3 cup	158 ml
¾ cup	177 ml	1 cup	225 ml
2 cups or 1 pint	450 ml	3 cups	675 ml
4 cups or 1 quart	1 liter	½ gallon	2 liters
1 gallon	4 liters		

Dry Measure Equivalents

3 teaspoons	1 tablespoon	½ ounce	14.3 grams
2 tablespoons	1/8 cup	1 fluid ounce	28.3 grams
4 tablespoons	¼ cup	2 fluid ounces	56.7 grams
5 1/3 tablespoons	1/3 cup	2.6 fluid ounces	75.6 grams
8 tablespoons	½ cup	4 ounces	113.4 grams
12 tablespoons	¾ cup	6 ounces	0.375 pound
32 tablespoons	2 cups	16 ounces	1 pound

Volume (Liquid)

American Standard (Cups & Quarts)	American Standard (Ounces)	Metric (Milliliters & Liters)
2 tbs	1 fl. oz.	30 ml
¼ cup	2 fl. oz.	60 ml
½ cup	4 fl. oz.	125 ml
1 cup	8 fl. oz.	250 ml
1 ½ cups	12 fl. oz.	375 ml
2 cups or 1 pint	16 fl. oz.	500 ml
4 cups or 1 quart	32 fl. oz.	1000 ml or 1 liter
1 gallon	128 fl. oz.	4 liters

Weight (Mass)

American Standard	Metric
½ ounce	15 grams
1 ounce	30 grams
3 ounces	85 grams
3.75 ounces	100 grams
4 ounces	115 grams
8 ounces	225 grams
12 ounces	340 grams
16 ounces or 1 lb.	450 grams

Temperature

American Standard	Metric
250° F	130° C
300° F	150° C
350° F	180° C
400° F	200° C
450° F	230° C

Glossary of English and Hindi names for cooking raw material

LEGUMES
Bean sprouts	*Ankur*
Black beans	*Urad dal*
Black grams	*Kala channa*
Chick peas	*Kabuli channa*
Red kidney beans	*Rajmah*
Split hulled black grams	*Channa dal*
Small pale yellow beans	*Toor dal*
Small red beans	*Masoor dal*
Black eye beans	*Lobia*
Whole green lentil	*Mung sabut*
Dried peas	*Matar dal*

GRAINS
Corn	*Makki*
Rice	*Chawal*
Millet	*Bajra*
Sorghum	*Jawar*
Wheat	*Gehun*

FLOURS
All purpose flour	*Maida*
Corn flour	*Makki ka aatta*
Cream of wheat	*Suji*
Gram flour	*Besan*
Millet flour	*Bajre Ka aatta*
Rice flour	*Chawal ka aatta*
Sorghum flour	*Jawar ka aatta*
Arrow-root flour	*Arraroot*

VEGETABLES
Ash gourd	*Dry petha*
Asparagus	*Shatwar*
Beans	*Sem ki phali*
Beetroot	*Chukandar*
Bell pepper	*Shimla mirch*
Bitter gourd	*Karela*
Bottle gourd	*Ghia*
Broccoli	*Sabz patta*
Cabbage	*Patta gobhi*
Carrots	*Gaajar*
Cauliflower	*Phool gobhi*
Coriander leaves	*Dhania patte*
Cucumber	*Kheera*
Dil	*Sooa*
Eggplant	*Baingan*
Fenugreek leaves	*Methi patte*
Jack Fruit	*Kathael*
Lemon	*Nimbu*
Lotus root	*Kamal kakadi*
Mushrooms	*Khumb*
Mustard greens	*Sarson*
Okra	*Bhindi*
Onions	*Pyaz*
Peas	*Matar*
Plantain	*Kachha kela*
Pointed Gourd	*Parwal*
Potatoes	*Aalu*

Pumpkin	*Kaddu*
Raadish	*Muli*
Round Gourd	*Tinda*
Soya	*Tofu*
Spinach	*Paalak*
Sweet corn	*Makki*
Sweet potato	*Shakarkandi*
Tomatoes	*Tamatar*
Turnip	*Shalgam*
Yam	*Arbi*
Zucchini	*Tori*

FRUITS

Apple	*Seb*
Apricot	*Khumani*
Banana	*Kela*
Phalsa berry	*Phalsa*
Cantaloupe	*Kharbooja*
Cran berry	*Karonda*
Grapes	*Angoor*
Guava	*Amrood*
Mango	*Aam*
Mulberry	*Shehtoot*
Papaya	*Papita*
Pear	*Nashpati*
Pineapple	*Annanaas*
Plum	*Aalu-bukhara*
Pomegranate	*Anaar*
Watermelon	*Tarbooj*

HERBS & SPICES

Asafoetida	*Heeng*
Basil	*Tulsi*
Bay leaves	*Tej patta*
Betel leaf	*Paan ka patta*
Black pepper	*Kali mirch*
Brown cardamom	*Badi illaichi*
Black cumin seeds	*Kala zeera*
Black mustard seeds	*Rai*
Black salt	*Kala namak*
Carom seed	*Ajwain*
Cayenne pepper	*Lal Mirch*
Cinnamon	*Dalchini*
Clove	*Laung*
Cobra's saffron	*Naagkeshar*
Coriander seeds	*Dhania*
Cumin seeds	*Zeera*
Curry leaves	*Karhi patta*
Dil seeds	*Sowa*
Dry mango powder	*Amchoor*
Dry raw pappaya	*Kachri*
Fennel seeds	*Saunf*
Fenugreek seeds / leaves	*Methi seeds / patta*
Garlic	*Lehsan*
Ginger	*Adrak*
Gooseberry	*Amla*
Green cardamom	*Chhoti illaichi*
Green chili	*Hari mirch*
Kokum	*Kokum*
Lemon	*Nimbu*
Mace	*Javitri*
Mint leaves	*Pudina*

The Exquisite World of Indian Cuisine

Neem	*Neem*
Nigella	*Kalonji*
Nutmeg	*Jaiphal*
Pomegranate seeds dry	*Anaardana*
Saffron	*Kesar*
Star Ainse	*Badal phool*
Stone flower	*Dagadh phool*
Sumac	*Sumac*
Tamarind	*Imli*
Turmeric	*Haldi*
Vinegar	*Sirka*

DRY FRUITS

Almonds	*Baadaam*
Cashew	*Kaju*
Dates	*Khajur*
Figs	*Anjeer*
Peanuts	*Mungphali*
Pistachio	*Pista*
Raisins	*Kishmish*
Walnut	*Akhrot*

DAIRY PRODUCTS

Clarified butter	*Ghee*
Curd / Yogurt	*Dahi*
Ricotta cheese	*Paneer*

MEAT & FISH

Beef	*Gai ka maas*
Chicken	*Murg*
Crab	*Kekra*
Fish	*Machhli*
Lamb Meat	*Gosht*
Lobster Prawn	*Samudri Jheenga*
Pork	*Suar ka maas*
Scallop	*Ghonga*
Shrimp	*Jheenga*
Squid	*Keet machhli*

MISCELLANEOUS ITEMS

Acacia paste	*Kattha*
Betel leaves	*Paan*
Lime paste	*Choona*
Candied rose buds	*Gulukand*
Coconut	*Nariyal*
Coconut milk	*Nariyal ka doodh*
Coconut powder	*Sukha nariyal*
Dried milk	*Khoa*
Egg	*Andaa*
Gold leaf	*Sone ka varq*
Henna	*Mehndi*
Honey	*Shehed*
Jaggery	*Gur*
Rice flakes	*Poha*
Rose water	*Gulab ka itar*
Screwpine	*Kewra*
Silver leaf	*Chandi ka varq*
Sugar	*Chhini*
Tapioca	*Saboodana*
Tofu	*Soya cubes*
Vermicelli	*Sevien*

Photos: © Chandni Arora

Alphabetical Index of Recipes by their English names

Almond Fudge	373	Coconut Rice	274	Gram Flour Balls Condiment	391
Andhra Dal	240	Cooked Beans Salad	426	Gram Flour Curry	256
Apple Dip	403	Cookies without Eggs	361	Gram Flour Fudge	382
Apple or Zucchini Pudding	362	Coriander Dip	402	Gram Flour Sweet Balls/Lentil Balls	357
Asparagus Stir–Fried	227	Corn Curry with Spinach	221	Gram Legume Dip	410
Assam Vegetable Curry	213	Corn Fritters	82	Green Chilies Pickle	416
Avakai Mango Pickle	420	Crab Croquettes Curry	154	Green Chilies, Onions and Ginger in Vinegar	415
Baby Vegetables Curry	222	Crab Stir–Fried	153	Green Mango Salsa	433
Baked Cauliflower	180	Cranberry Dip	404	Green Pepper Fritters	74
Baked Eggplant Condiment	393	Cream of Corn Soup	450	Griddle Flat Bread	283
Baked Spinach and Fenugreek Fritters	77	Cream of Pumpkin Soup	449	Griddle Fried Bread	292
Bananas & Raisins Condiment	387	Cream of Wheat Cakes	92	Griddle Fried Cheese and Legume Stuffed Bread	306
Bean Sprouts Stir–Fried	225	Cream of Wheat Crepes	303	Griddle Fried Corn Flour Bread	318
Beans and Potatoes Stir–Fried	209	Cream of Wheat Pudding	347	Griddle Fried Daikon Stuffed Bread	298
Beans with Coconut	194	Cream of Wheat with Vegetables	88	Griddle Fried Fenugreek Bread	296
Beef Curry with Nuts	323	Creamy Cheese Croquettes in Curry Sauce	186	Griddle Fried Gram Flour Pancakes	319
Beetroot Curry	230	Crisp Fried Pastries	309	Griddle Fried Rice Flour & Coconut Crepes	302
Bell Pepper, Potatoes and Tomatoes Stir–Fried	200	Crisp Potato Pastries	311	Griddle Fried Stuffed Cauliflower Bread	299
Biryani	270	Crisp Stuffed Pastry	381	Griddle Fried Stuffed Meat Bread	301
Bitter Gourd Stir Fried	195	Crunchy Lentil Sweet Rings	369	Griddle Fried Stuffed Potato Bread	294
Bitter Gourd Stuffed	196	Crunchy Lentils Wafers	99	Griddle Fried Tricolor Bread	300
Black Split Beans Curried	243	Crunchy Rice Puffs with Salad	97	Griddle Gram Flour Bread	316
Bombay Lamb Curry	325	Cucumber Condiment	390	Griddle Millet Flour Bread	312
Bottle Gourd Croquettes Curry	168	Cumin flavored Drink	458	Griddle Sorghum Flour Bread	313
Bottle Gourd Soup	446	Curried Kidney Beans	255	Grilled Chicken in Gravy	119
Bread Croquettes in Curry	191	Dal Vadodara	250	Grilled Chicken	55
Butter Chicken	125	Dal with Coconut Milk	259	Grilled Fried and Stuffed Onion Bread	293
Cabbage and Peas Stir–Fried	188	Dried Carrot Pudding or Fudge	350	Ground Meat Curried	326
Cardamom Chicken Curry	124	Dry Yam Curry	207	Ground Meat Kebabs	56
Carrots and Peas Stir–Fried	217	Egg Curry	162	Ground Rice Crepes	304
Carrots and Potatoes Stir–Fried	197	Eggplant Dip	401	Ground Rice Pudding	364
Carrots Pickle	413	Eggplant in Sweet & Sour Sauce	165	Hot Chicken Curry with Almonds	130
Cashew Fudge	370	Eggplant in Tamarind Sauce	164	Indian Cheese Cutlets	59
Cauliflower and Potatoes Stir–Fried	210	Eggplant Stir–Fried	160	Indian Hot and Sour Soup	443
Cauliflower Pulav	272	Eggplant, Potatoes and Tomatoes Stir–Fried	189	Indian Ice Cream	379
Cauliflower Soup	439	Fenugreek Leaves and Potatoes	182	Jackfruit Stir–Fried	233
Cauliflower with Figs	211	Fermented Carrot Drink	459	Kashmiri Beef Curry	327
Cheese and Mushroom Curry	178	Fermented Deep–Fried Bread	289	Kashmiri Tea	463
Cheese Balls in Sweet Syrup	352	Fish baked in Coconut Sauce	135	Kerala Beef Curry	331
Cheese Fudge	378	Fish Curry with Nuts	140	Kerala Vegetable Curry	183
Cheese Puffs	81	Fish Curry with Vegetables	137	Kokum Water	459
Chick–peas in Tamarind Sauce	238	Fish Curry with Yogurt	139	Kosambri Salad	431
Chick–peas Curry	237	Fish Curry	136	Lamb Cooked with Spinach	332
Chicken cooked with Lentils and Vegetables	111	Fish Flavor	412	Lamb Curry	335
Chicken Curry	112	Fish in Fenugreek Sauce	138	Lamb or Beef with Turnips	324
Chicken in Coconut Gravy	113	Fish in Mustard Sauce	145	Lamb Tikka Masala	334
Chicken in Creamy Sauce	115	Fish in Tamarind Sauce	144	Legume Stir–Fried	246
Chicken in Fenugreek Sauce	126	Flavored Zucchini	175	Lemon Pickle	418
Chicken Pickle Style	127	Flour Puffs with Tamarind Water	96	Lemon Rice Noodles	102
Chicken Stew	116	Fresh Vegetable Condiment	392	Lemon Rice	276
Chicken Vegetable Soup	440	Fried Cheese Cubes	68	Lemonade	460
Chicken with Cashew Nuts	120	Fried Chicken	128	Lentil Fritters	79
Classic Sweet & Sour Pickle	421	Fried Fish	141	Lentil Patties	78
Clay Oven Bread	285	Fried Potato Curry	181	Lentils and Vegetables in Tamarind Sauce	241
Clay Oven Grilled Chicken	118	Fried Shrimp	149	Lobster Delight	146
Clay Oven Grilled Fish	142	Fried Spiral Sweet Rings	368	Lotus Root and Mushroom Curry	226
Cocktail Cashew Nuts	65	Fruity Yogurt Poha	105	Lotus Root Cutlets	62
Cocktail Shrimp	69	Goa Beef Stir–Fried	330	Madras Chicken Curry	131
Coconut Dip	396	Goan Chicken Curry	114		
Coconut Fudge	376	Golden Cream Cheese Balls in Syrup	351		
Coconut Milk Soup	451	Gram Dal	252		

The Exquisite World of Indian Cuisine

Recipe	Page
Madras Fish Curry	143
Mango Condiment	394
Mango Drink	462
Mango Mousse	367
Mango Pickle	419
Mango Pie	366
Mango Salad	427
Marinated Leg of Lamb	336
Matar Dal with Meat	253
Meat Croquettes Curry	337
Meat Cutlets	57
Meat Pastries	63
Meatballs in Tamarind Sauce	64
Mediterranean Pork & Peas	339
Milk & Almond Drink	465
Milk Fudge	371
Milk Kneaded Griddle Bread	284
Mint Condiment	388
Mint Dip	395
Mint Bread	286
Mixed Vegetable Croquettes Curry	192
Mixed Vegetable Curry Baked	190
Mixed Vegetable Curry	166
Mixed Vegetable Salad	425
Mixed Vegetable Soup	438
Mughlai Lamb Curry	333
Mulligatawny Soup	441
Multicolored Pulav	268
Mung Beans Soup	442
Mushroom Pulav	267
Mushroom Fritters	76
Mushrooms in Spinach Sauce	232
Mustard Greens Curried	171
Okra and Peanuts	199
Okra Curry	231
Okra Stir-Fried	174
Onion & Coconut Dip with Onion Bread	287
Onion Chicken	121
Onion, Beetroot and Tomato Salad	432
Oriya Dal	251
Paneer & Potatoes in Coconut Sauce	184
Papaya and Mango Pickle	417
Peanut Dip	408
Peas & Cheese Curry	179
Peas and Cheese Pulav	264
Peas Pulav	266
Persian Bread	317
Pineapple Dip	409
Pistachio Fudge	372
Plain Cumin Rice	263
Plantain Fritters	73
Plantain Curry	208
Pointed Gourd Curry	219
Pork Curry in Vinegar Sauce	342
Pork Curry	338
Pork Stir-Fried	340
Pork with Potatoes & Peppers	343
Potato Croquettes	80
Potato Curry	170
Potato Cutlets	60
Potato Soup	447
Potatoes and Onions Stir-Fried	167
Pumpkin Stir-Fried	212
Radish Pickle	414
Radish Salad	430
Red Pepper Dip	406
Rice & Lentils with Vegetables	279
Rice and Lentils Crepes	308
Rice Flake Cutlets	90
Rice Noodles Stir-Fried	101
Rice Pudding	348
Ripe Mango Dip	405
Roasted Eggplant Curried	161
Rolled and Stuffed Wafers	100
Round Gourd Stuffed	218
Royal Mix Legume	248
Royal Pulav	265
Salmon Cutlets	58
Scallops & Squid Curry	152
Scrambled Eggs with Vegetables/ Italian Frittata	163
Shrimp Curry	147
Shrimp in Mango Sauce	155
Shrimp Masala Rice	278
Shrimp Stir-Fried	148
Sinhalese Vegetable Curry	214
South Indian Coffee	456
Soyabean and Carrots Curry	220
Spiced Rice Flakes	89
Spiced Sweet Potatoes	104
Spiced Tea	463
Spicy Fruit Salad	103
Spicy Saltine Sticks	107
Spinach and Potatoes Stir-Fried	224
Spinach Condiment	389
Spinach Dal	254
Spinach Fritters	71
Spinach Soup	448
Spinach with Fried Cheese	185
Steamed Ground-Rice Cakes	307
Steamed Lentil Cake	91
Steamed Lentil Rolls	93
Stuffed Bell Peppers	201
Stuffed Eggplants	203
Stuffed Mushrooms in Pomegranate Sauce	159
Stuffed Mushrooms	85
Stuffed Whole Tomatoes	202
Sugar Coated Doughnuts	360
Sweet & Sour Lemon Pickle	415
Sweet Balls of Cream of Wheat	358
Sweet Cheese Balls	355
Sweet Cheese Cakes	354
Sweet Cheese Patties in Cream	353
Sweet Corn and Beans	216
Sweet Mango Dip	411
Sweet Pancakes	383
Sweet pieces of Cheese	356
Sweet Potato and Spinach Curry	215
Sweet Rice	365
Sweet Vermicelli Pudding	363
Tamarind Dip	399
Tamarind Rice	275
Tapioca Potato Puffs	83
Tapioca Stir-Fried	106
Tofu Curry	176
Tomato Dip	398
Tomato Soup	437
Tortilla chips with Tamarind Sauce	95
Turnip Stir-Fried	177
Twice Cooked Chicken	129
Unfermented Deep-Fried Bread	288
Vegetable Fritters	70
Vegetable Masala Rice	277
Whole Black Beans with Cream	242
Whole Mung Dal	258
Whole Stuffed Okra	198
Whole Wheat Fried Puffs	290
Yam Curry	206
Yams in Peanut Sauce	84
Yogurt dipped Lentil Fritters	98
Yogurt Rice	273
Yogurt Shake	455
Zucchini Dip	407

Dear Reader

You can check which recipe comes under which Chapter by locating its respective page number in the following order.

Chapter	pages
Appetizers and Snacks	52 to 107
Chicken	108 to 131
Sea Food and Fish	132 to 155
Exotic Vegetables	156 to 233
Legumes	234 to 259
Rice and Pulav	260 to 279
Breads	280 to 319
Lamb, Beef and Pork	320 to 343
Desserts	344 to 383
Condiments, Pickles & Dips	384 to 421
Salads	422 to 433
Soups	434 to 451
Drinks	452 to 465

Colourful ceramic pots and jars... a speciality from Khurja in Uttar Pradesh